Republic to Reich

THE MAKING OF THE

NAZI REVOLUTION

Republic to Reich

✠ ✠ ✠

THE MAKING OF THE
NAZI REVOLUTION

TEN ESSAYS

Edited and with an Introduction

by Hajo Holborn

Translated from the German by Ralph Manheim

PANTHEON BOOKS
A DIVISION OF RANDOM HOUSE, NEW YORK

ISBN: 0-394-47122-9

Library of Congress Catalog Card Number: 79-79801

Manufactured in the United States of America

by American Book-Stratford Press

2 4 6 8 9 7 5 3

FIRST EDITION

Editorial Note

Before his untimely death, Professor Holborn had completed his selection of the essays included in this volume, written his Introduction, and read the translation. For further amplification of the text, editorial notes and background material were provided for the publisher by Susan Gyarmati.

ACKNOWLEDGMENTS

The essays in this book were all published in *Vierteljahrshefte für Zeitgeschichte,* the quarterly journal of the Institut für Zeitgeschichte in Munich. The German titles of the essays and the issues of the journal in which they appeared are as follows:

Theodor Eschenburg, "Die Rolle der Persönlichkeit in der Krise der Weimarer Republik: Hindenburg, Brüning, Groener, Schleicher," Vol. 9, No. 1 (January 1961), pp. 1–29.

Erich Matthias, "Der Untergang der alten Sozialdemokratie 1933," Vol. 4, No. 3 (July 1956), pp. 179–226.

Karl Dietrich Bracher, "Stufen totalitärer Gleichsaltung: Die Befestigung der nationalsozialistischen Herrschaft 1933/34," Vol. 4, No. 1 (January 1956), pp. 30–42.

Hans Mommsen, "Der Reichstagsbrand und seine politischen Folgen," Vol. 12, No. 4 (October 1964), pp. 351–413.

Hermann Mau, "Die 'Zweite Revolution'—der 30. Juni 1934," Vol. 1, No. 2 (April 1953), pp. 119–37.

Hans Buchheim, "Die SS in der Verfassung des Dritten Reiches," Vol. 3, No. 2 (April 1955), pp. 127–57.

Günter Moltmann, "Goebbels' Rede zum totalen Kreig am 18. Februar 1943," Vol. 12, No. 1 (January 1964), pp. 13–43.

Paul Kluke, "Nationalsozialistische Europaideologie," Vol. 3, No. 3 (July 1955), pp. 240–75.

Hildegard Brenner, "Die Kunst im politischen Machtkampf der Jahre 1933/34," Vol. 10, No. 1 (January 1962), pp. 17–42.

Hans-Günter Zmarzlik, "Der Sozialdarwinismus in Deutschland als geschichtliches Problem," Vol. 11, No. 3 (July 1963), pp. 246–73.

Contents

The Totalitarian State: Police, Propaganda,
National Expansionism, Culture

The Origins of Inhumanity

Abbreviations

AA	Auswärtiges Amt (Foreign Office)
ADGB	Allgemeiner Deutscher Gewerkschaftsbund (General Federation of German Trade Unions)
AFA-Bund	Allgemeiner Freier Angestelltenbund (General Federation of White-Collar Workers)
AfRGB	*Archiv für Rassen- und Gesellschaftsbiologie*
BA Koblenz	Bundesarchiv Koblenz (Federal Archives, Koblenz)
BDC	Berlin Documentation Center
CDJC	Centre de Documentation Juive Contemporaine (Paris)
DAZ	*Deutsche Allgemeine Zeitung*
DBFP	Documents on British Foreign Policy
DNVP	Deutsche-nazionale Volkspartei (German National People's Party)
HA	Hauptamt (Central or Head Office)
IfZ	Institut für Zeitgeschichte (Institute for Contemporary History, Munich)
IMT	*Der Prozess gegen die Hauptkriegsverbrecher vor dem Internationalen Militargerichtshof Nürnberg* (Trial of the Major War Criminals before the International Military Tribunal, Nuremberg)
KfDK	Kampfbund für Deutsche Kultur (Combat League for German Culture)

KPD	Kommunistische Partei Deutschlands (German Communist Party)
L&SI	Labor and Socialist International
NSBO	Nationalsozialistische Betriebszellenorganisation (National Socialist Factory Cell Organization)
NSDAP	Nationalsozialistische Deutsche Arbeiterpartei (National Socialist German Workers Party)
RGBl	*Reichsgesetzblatt* (Federal Legal Register)
RGO	Rote Gewerkschaftsopposition (Red Trade-Union Opposition)
RK	Reichskabinett
RKF	Reichskommissar für die Festigung deutschen Volkstums (Reich Commissar for the Reinforcement of German Nationality)
RMBl	*Reichsmitteilungsblatt*
RMVAP	Reichsministerium für Volksaufklarung und Propaganda (Reich Ministry for Popular Enlightenment and Propaganda)
SA	Sturmabteilung (Storm Battalions)
SAJ	Sozialistische Arbeiter-Jugend (Young Socialist Workers)
SAP	Sozialistische Arbeiterpartei (Socialist Workers Party)
SD	Sicherheitsdienst (Security Service)
SPD	Sozialdemokratische Partei Deutschlands (German Social Democratic Party)
SS	Schutzstaffel
TU	Telegraphen-Union (Telegraphic Union)
VB	*Völkischer Beobachter*
VDA	Verein für das Deutschtum im Ausland (Association for Germanism in Foreign Countries)

VJHfZ   *Vierteljahrshefte für Zeitgeschichte* (Quarterly of Contemporary History)

WTB   Wolffs Telegraphisches Büro (Wolff Telegraphic Bureau)

Introduction

The articles contained in this volume represent modern German scholarship on the history of Hitler's empire. All of them appeared in the *Quarterly of Contemporary History (Vierteljahrshefte für Zeitgeschichte)*, the journal of the Institute for Contemporary History (Institut für Zeitgeschichte), which has become the most important center of the study of National Socialism in Germany. The institute was established in Munich by the West German government together with the Bavarian and other *Land* governments in order to promote extensive research into the history of the Nazi period and to reveal to the Germans the truth about the events in which most of them had been willing though not always knowing participants. The German youth in particular was supposed to get a clear picture of the Third Empire and thus be prepared to build and defend democratic institutions.

The Munich institute, already founded on paper in 1949, began its work in 1952. Since that time it has built up a good special library and a valuable archive, which not only German but also foreign scholars like to visit. But the real contribution the institute has made rests in the publication of many solid monographs and studies on Nazi rule. In producing them it could rely increasingly on the younger generation in Germany, which has brought forth an unusually large number of able historians. These young scholars, who by now have taken over most history chairs in the German universities, benefited greatly from the teachers who had survived the years of Nazi domination without making concessions to Nazi ideas and practices. In most cases this had meant leaving Germany or at least their positions at German universities. The relatively small number of these men who resumed lecturing after World War II and thereby formed a bridge between the Weimar Republic and post-Hitlerian Germany have had considerable influence, especially on the study of contemporary history. They were largely responsible for the restoration of internationally valid standards of interpretation, and as mature witnesses and critical observers of the recent past they have added genuine color and life to its historical reconstruction.

The two foremost editors of the *Quarterly,* Theodor Eschenburg and Hans Rothfels, are among these elders. It seems fitting that Theodor Eschenburg's description of the major personal forces in the final stages of the Weimar Republic should open our volume. As a young historian Eschenburg had gained access to Gustav Stresemann, the German foreign minister, who acquainted him not only with much of his own political thinking but also with the workings of German politics. Personal memories and the full mastery of the historical resources which have become available since 1945 have been well blended in his article. The authors of the subsequent articles started their academic careers, in fact most of them their academic studies, after World War II. Erich Matthias, who has made himself one of the outstanding historians of the German socialist movement, gives us a reasoned appraisal of the causes and circumstances of the defeat of the Social Democratic Party, the biggest German political party in 1912–1932 and the greatest force for democracy in Germany.

Karl Dietrich Bracher is probably the internationally best-known German political scientist on account of his

profound and detailed studies of the origins and the establishment of the Third Empire. No serious student of
German history will turn to the years 1919–1945 without
first having familiarized himself with Professor Bracher's
writings. In our volume Bracher outlines the decisive
steps the Nazi leaders took in order to win total control.
The abolition of individual rights and the destruction of
Land governments, parliamentarism, political parties,
and labor unions were the chief means of accomplishing
this aim, and these were achieved not simply by legislative
acts but by massive political action of the party. Thus, for
example, the seizure of the *Land* governments was everywhere preceded by tumultuous demonstrations by the
Nazi storm troopers. Historians have been inclined to
assume that the first radical assault on liberalism, the
abrogation of individual rights, was prepared by the party
through setting the Reichstag building afire. Bracher
states well the case for this belief. But the case cannot be
defended any more. Following extensive investigations
by Fritz Tobias, a historical free-lance, Hans Mommsen
has subjected the old and new evidence to a close examination. He proves that the young Dutch Communist van
der Lubbe was the sole arsonist, acting on his own and
not as a stooge of the Nazis. Naturally, this calls for an
altered interpretation of the origins of the emergency decree that enabled the Nazis to disregard the rights of citizens guaranteed by the constitution.

While the picture that most of us had held of the events
surrounding the Reichstag fire has undergone some
changes, another fateful turn, the mass killing of Roehm
and the SA leaders on June 30, 1934, has been correctly
elucidated by Hermann Mau (the first director of the
institute, who tragically lost his life in a car accident).
His article brings out all the essential aspects of the actions of June 30: Hitler's desire to retain absolute control of the Nazi Party and extend his power over the state

as successor to the dying Hindenburg, the role of the army behind the scene, the power struggle between Roehm, Göring, Goebbels, and Himmler.

The blood bath of 1934 made the SS the strongest force in Germany. Hans Buchheim introduces the reader to the organization of the sprawling institution that grew in power almost to the last days of the Hitler regime. Usually the SS is understood to have been the exponent of the Nazi Party's will in the government and administration of the state, but Hans Buchheim shows that the SS was not subordinated to the party but only to Hitler as a third and superior power beyond party and state.

Günter Moltmann deals with the opening of the last stage of the Third Empire. The analysis of Goebbels' speech after the defeat at Stalingrad, in which he attempted to rally the German people in a total war effort, also illustrates the art of demagogic propaganda which contributed so much to the victory of National Socialism in Germany. The fighting of the men around the throne for Hitler's favor and for the building of personal feudal realms appears in this chapter, as in the two preceding ones. The author's observation that the Casablanca declaration on German unconditional surrender was not used by Goebbels deserves special notice in view of the assertion often heard on both sides of the Atlantic that the demand for unconditional surrender gave the Nazis a weapon with which to stir up fighting spirit among the Germans.

Hitler's conquest of Europe is occasionally seen as having been an attempt to achieve the desirable unification of Europe. Even in Nazi propaganda such a concept was given a place only very briefly. Actually, as Paul Kluke explains in his article, the Nazis had no concept of a united Europe, but thought only in terms of a Germanic empire ruling an enslaved Europe.

The arts were regarded by the Nazis as being expressions of philosophies of life and at the same time stimuli of the spread of such philosophies. Both arts and philosophies were, according to the Nazi creed, conditioned by race, and consequently only "Nordic" art could be promoted by National Socialism. These principles could lead in practice only to completely arbitrary rulings. Hildegard Brenner reports on the internal party feuds which developed in 1933–1934 and ended in the canonization of philistine art.

The last article in this volume is concerned with the rise of Social Darwinism and its impact on German thought. This impact was not uniform, as Hans-Günter Zmarzlik indicates. Hitler's racialist explanation of world history and his anti-Semitism constituted one of the more vulgar types of Social Darwinism, but the fact that even more refined schools of thought had become infected with Social Darwinism undermined the resistance to Nazi propaganda. The Third Empire was not, of course, caused by ideas alone, but these played an important part in solidifying the Nazi movement, justifying some of its political methods, and defining some of its aims beyond the mere acquisition of power, and as a weapon of polemics. The origins of the ideas used by the Nazis were complex, yet Social Darwinism was undoubtedly of crucial significance.

The articles in this volume demonstrate the variety of interests and approaches displayed by German historians in the study of National Socialism. What they have in common is their endeavor to get at the unvarnished realities of the German past and to place them in an objective light. This aim is not a distinguishing mark of German historians, and there is at present no point in speaking about a special school of German historiography. Moreover, quite a few of the younger German historians spent some years of study at American and English universities after World War II and have since visited them again as guest lecturers. This selection of their articles, which has been exceedingly well translated by Mr. Ralph Manheim, deserves many readers. Each article makes a contribution to our knowledge and understanding of major aspects of the Third Empire.

The Weimar Republic in Eclipse

✠ ✠ ✠

I

The Role of the Personality
in the Crisis of the Weimar Republic:
Hindenburg, Brüning, Groener,
Schleicher

THEODOR ESCHENBURG

In Weimar Germany the fall of the government was neither an infrequent nor a surprising occurrence. With no single party or combination of like-minded parties commanding a majority in or out of parliament, the republic was governed by a politically heterogeneous and unstable alliance. The prorepublican Social Democratic, Catholic Center, and liberal German Democratic parties, which alone among the numerous parties in the Reichstag proved capable of a modicum of compromise and cooperation, made up this partnership, the so-called "Weimar Coalition," which on two occasions was reluctantly joined by the more right-wing German People's Party under the prodding of its leader, Gustav Stresemann, and was then known as the "Great Coalition." To stave off the disintegration of their alliance and assure the continued existence of a functioning government, the coalition parties would with some regularity reconstitute the government under the same or a new chancellor, reshuffle cabinet posts, or shift to a policy of "toleration," that is, go into opposition but not bring down the government on a vote of confidence. General elections reduced or increased the votes of some parties but never fundamentally changed the balance of power in the Reichstag. Then on March 27, 1930, the "Great Coalition" cabinet, presided over by the Social Democratic Chancellor Hermann Müller, resigned.

In retrospect the demise of the Müller government, by consummating the collapse of parliamentary rule, proved of greater significance than first appearances would have suggested. The Great Depression was intensifying social conflict everywhere and not least between the labor wing and the economic conservatives and industrialists of the Weimar Coalition. The new Chancellor, Heinrich Brüning of the Center Party, failed to rally a parliamentary majority and resorted instead to the emergency-decree power vested in the President to carry out his program. Although the opposition in the Reichstag was in turn strong enough with Social Democratic support to override the President's decrees, it did so at the cost of a new general election which, on September 14, 1930, catapulted the formerly minor National Socialist Party into second position in popular votes and mandates. From this point on, the former coalition partners, even if they had wanted to or had been able to regroup, no longer commanded a Reichstag majority. Nor did Brüning's aspirations for putting together a majority of the right materialize, and the Social Democrats felt once again obliged to tolerate the decree government in the vain hope that the popular tide, which was shifting power decisively to the extreme right, could be stemmed before they risked a new verdict at the polls.

The presidential prerogative, based on a single article in the constitution, already had a history of liberal appli-

cation during periods of unrest. In the critical years of the Weimar Republic, continuous resort to this mechanism enhanced the power of the presidency far beyond constitutional intent, enfeebling the government's independence, and allowed a small group of people with access to President Hindenburg to decide the course of political events. In the beginning this group included Chancellor Brüning and Reichswehr (Defense) Minister Groener. In due course Brüning and Groener, however, fell victim to the pressure exerted by the extreme right and were ousted, the politically ambitious General Kurt von Schleicher helping to engineer their fall from grace. Brüning was succeeded in the Chancellery by Papen, Papen by Schleicher, and Schleicher finally by Hitler.

General Paul von Hindenburg was sixty-seven years old when he was recalled from retirement in 1914 to command the German Eighth Army on the Eastern Front. His victory against the Russians at Tannenberg in East Prussia made him the war's hero. Field Marshal Hindenburg was a venerable seventy-eight years old in 1925 when he successfully stood for election as the conservative candidate for President. Seven years later, during Brüning's second administration, he would stand for re-election and win against Hitler—supported by the Weimar Coalition and opposed by his former supporters.

Heinrich Brüning was a Center member of the Reichstag from 1924 to 1933, chairman of his parliamentary delegations, and Chancellor from March 30, 1930, to May 30, 1932.

General Wilhelm Groener, former head of the military railway system, succeeded Ludendorff in 1918 as First Quartermaster General of the Army, that is, Hindenburg's Chief of Staff. He was not the republic's most enthusiastic supporter, but he served it as Minister of Trans-

portation from 1920 to 1923, Reichswehr Minister from 1928 to 1932, and Minister of the Interior from 1931 to 1932.

General Kurt von Schleicher was Groener's protégé and the political spokesman for the army in the Reichswehr Ministry. He had a reputation for political intrigue, occupied the Chancellery from December 1932 to January 1933, and was murdered by the Nazis during the Roehm affair.

In the publications devoted in recent years to the crisis and collapse of the Weimar Republic the main emphasis has been on political ideologies and social forces, so much so that little interest has been taken in the leading figures of the day and their part in shaping events. Yet the question, To what degree are the events of 1933 attributable to the leading political figures, their characters and decisions? is and remains a matter of historical interest.

A striking example of how political developments can be determined by individuals is provided by the political conflict of the 1860's in Prussia. The development of Prussia and Germany might have taken a very different course if at the crucial moment King William I and Bismarck, or only one of them, had withdrawn from the political scene. Those two men were the key figures. Of course the development cannot be explained by them alone, but neither can it be explained without them.

Here we shall not go into the relative advantages of the social and personalistic approaches, and certainly not argue in favor of a one-sided personalistic approach. I am far from underestimating the value of such works as, in particular, Bracher's *Die Auflösung der Weimarer Republik*. I wish merely to draw more attention to the personal factor, the principal actors with their individual personalities and personal relationships. I shall confine myself to Hindenburg, Brüning, Groener, and Schleicher.

During the Brüning era, from March 1930 to May 1932, it was these four men who for all practical purposes guided the destinies of the Reich. Schleicher was at first Groener's aide, formally his subordinate; it was only in the course of time that he became one of the protagonists.

Perhaps I shall be accused of bias because I was personally acquainted with more than one of the political figures I shall here attempt to sketch, and even more so with their immediate circles. But it was precisely my memory of these experiences that led me to write a critical account of them.

Of course there is an interaction between personal and social forces. Yet, though fully aware of the drawbacks inherent in such an isolated view, I shall confine myself to the personal factor.

*   *

Stresemann* died in October 1929, six months before Brüning became Chancellor. He had been the architect of every government coalition since August 1923. It was largely Stresemann's personal accomplishment that, despite frequent cabinet crises, reshufflings, and new appointments, the government had maintained its continuity, especially in the field of foreign policy. The resignation of the Hermann Müller cabinet in 1930 is surely attributable to structural causes, particularly the well-nigh irreconcilable social antagonisms between the government parties; but an additional cause was the absence of Stresemann, who had handled the parliamentary mechanism with virtuosity and imagination. His death created a break in the political development of the Weimar Republic.

After the elections of autumn 1930, Brüning governed

---

* Gustav Stresemann, former National Liberal parliamentary leader, founder of the right-liberal German People's Party, Chancellor from August to November 1923. As Foreign Minister (1924–1929), he pursued a policy of reconciliation with Germany's former enemies.

chiefly with the help of the President's emergency decrees,
which were tolerated by a heterogeneous majority consisting of the middle-of-the-road parties and the SPD [So-
zialdemokratische Partei Deutschlands—German Social
Democratic Party]. This manner of governing, dictated
by the new constellation of the parties, suggests the methods of constitutional monarchy, but there was an essential
difference. In a constitutional monarchy the government
could count on the backing of parliament in its dealings
with the monarch. Parliament was the government's support. In Brüning's government, this support was lacking.
The Social Democrats were without enthusiasm for Brüning's emergency decrees but tolerated them in order to
avoid a dictatorship of the right. The National Socialists
under Hitler and the German Nationalists under Hugenberg* attacked the emergency decrees because they
wished to create the conditions for dictatorship. Consequently the existence of the Brüning government depended solely on the decision of the President. In this
respect the Brüning government was far closer to the cabinets under Frederick William III and Frederick William
IV. Either the cabinet was able, thanks to strong leadership and sometimes to inner unity, to assert itself against
the monarch, as Hardenberg† tried to do, often successfully, or else the cabinet merely served to elaborate and
carry out the royal decisions. The third possibility was
that monarch and cabinet were able to arrive only at temporary understandings, a state of affairs which sometimes
led to cabinet reshufflings or new cabinets. Hindenburg
showed a certain resemblance to Frederick William III:
on the one hand neither willing nor able to exercise true

* Alfred Hugenberg, right-wing publishing tycoon who captured the
leadership of the German National People's Party in 1928, was cofounder
of the ultra-right paramilitary Harzburg Front on October 11, 1931, with
Hitler and the veterans' organization Stahlhelm, and became Hitler's
first Economics Minister.
† Karl August Prince von Hardenberg (1750–1822), Prussian statesman
and reformer during the reign of King Frederick William III.

political leadership but on the other hand refusing to be led by the nose.

* *

For his contemporaries, at least up to the time of Brüning's dismissal, Hindenburg was not the legendary figure that he has now become in the eyes of the general public. But even in those years I was often struck by the sincere respect with which people in general spoke of Hindenburg, even when they were exchanging indiscretions in discreet conversation, and this was true even of persons who looked upon his political tendencies with extreme distrust. In those days there was no lack of ironical or even slanderous anecdotes about political figures, but about Hindenburg such anecdotes were avoided except by National Socialists and radical left-wing intellectuals.

I knew Stresemann well and saw him often. He told me a number of times that preparing himself for interviews with Hindenburg had been one of his most difficult and time-consuming tasks. Before the conclusion of the Locarno Pact and before Germany's entry into the League of Nations Stresemann had had bitter struggles with Hindenburg. Hindenburg, as Stresemann told me, was quick to grasp situations and paid close attention. He asked critical questions and listened carefully to the answers. But problems had to be explained to him slowly and clearly, in plain, simple words; only then was he able to grasp their substance. If he failed to understand a matter that was set before him, he could grow very angry. He was said to have had an astonishing memory. If in an oral or written report anyone contradicted his own previous statements or arguments without a convincing explanation, Hindenburg was capable of asking very embarrassing questions.

Walter Zechlin, who for many years as chief of the press section of the Reich government submitted to Hindenburg daily reviews of the press and had innumerable conversations with him, tells very much the same story as Stresemann. I know of a number of persons who, though not at all shy or easily embarrassed, lost their self-assurance and were overcome with stage fright when they faced Hindenburg. It was not only the authority of his office and still less that of his military rank; he must also have emanated a personal aura which very few men could withstand. Hindenburg knew the secret of the effect he produced. Unlike an actor, he did not deliberately adapt his gestures, tone, and expression to the role and situation, but he knew that he had to be in form, in full control of himself, in order to exert this Olympian effect, or at least in order to exert it most forcefully. Little is known of his behavior in his intimate family circle, but when he met outsiders he was always in form, conscious of his dignity, controlled even in his joviality. "Being in form" was for him a duty, which he took very seriously. What he said may often have been elementary, but he said it with dignity. This dignity often prevented others from expressing disagreement and spared him arguments which at heart he dreaded. Had it not been for his personal substance his presence would not have had the powerful effect on persons of very different origins and ideas; that has often been attested.

True, Hindenburg knew little about politics, but he had held high positions of leadership during the war, or at least since 1916 when he was made commander in chief and then again from 1925 when he became President of the Reich. In any case he had ample experience in formal leadership. In the First World War Ludendorff[*] and

---

[*] Erich Ludendorff was Hindenburg's chief of staff from 1914 to 1919 and is credited with most of Hindenburg's accomplishments and decisions during that period. The real power behind the throne during the second half of the First World War owing to the Kaiser's weakness and the military's wartime powers, he was largely responsible for concealing from the country the true military situation, for abruptly demanding both a change in government and peace negotiations in 1918, and for willfully distorting the record to lay the blame for the lost war and its

Groener, the chiefs of the General Staff, were formally his subordinates, but they were more creative and had more ideas than he. Their proposals, however, acquired their weight only through Hindenburg's confirmation. He lent authority, as it were, to his aides' advice by making it into his decision. This was not a mere formal act. Hindenburg was intelligent enough to understand and judge the plans and proposals submitted to him, although he did not always fully foresee their effects. He was neither an instrument in the hands of his aides, nor their mentor. His relation to Brüning later on was similar, although juridically Brüning's position was far more independent than that of the chiefs of staff. Hindenburg's special gift was the authority which his aides lacked or did not possess in sufficient degree. He was conscious of this authority and cultivated it.

His aides shunned the outward luster of power. In a sense he caught the light of his aides and reflected it with a new intensity. When Hindenburg had to proceed without the light of other men's ideas, he failed, as he did when Papen* and Schleicher were his advisers.

In general, Hindenburg did not seek out his aides; they were forced on him or proposed to him. When in 1914 he was appointed commanding general of the Eighth Army, he was given Ludendorff as chief of staff without being consulted. In 1918 Groener was proposed to him as Ludendorff's successor. Hindenburg knew him and decided in his favor after General von Kuhl, who had at first been chosen, rejected the post. Before appointing him Chancellor, Hindenburg had met Brüning once or twice and then

---

attendant hardships on the republic and its leaders. In 1923 he joined Hitler in the unsuccessful Munich putsch.

* Franz von Papen, who nominally belonged to the Center Party, was by all counts a reactionary with political acumen. He briefly became Chancellor in 1932 and later served as Hitler's Vice Chancellor and ambassador to Vienna and Ankara. At Nuremberg he was found not guilty. During World War I he had been expelled from his post of German military attaché in Washington on a charge of sabotage.

only briefly. He had only a passing acquaintance with Papen before appointing him Chancellor. Schleicher was an exception. They had worked together in the army for years and had also maintained personal relations.

Hindenburg put great trust in his aides as long as they did not become centers of attack, but he did not give them a blank check. They were obliged to keep him informed and to convince him time and time again. In general he left them a free hand but he liked to renew their powers all the time. Those of his immediate subordinates who were dependent on his final decision had to struggle with him, to keep winning him over to their points of view and warding off hostile influences. Though desperately busy, Stresemann sought out occasions for speaking with Hindenburg. He wished, as he told me, to guard him against other influences. Stresemann and Gessler* both told me that Hindenburg was reliable, that he stood by his decisions, but that in order to secure his support for future decisions it was necessary to prepare the ground. It would not do to go to see him only when one wanted something of him.

Brüning was too shy to maintain close contact with Hindenburg. His notions of etiquette were still those of the monarchy: a minister did not call on the chief of state unless he was summoned or unless there was some urgent reason. As Reichswehr Minister and Chancellor, Schleicher neglected his contact with the President, relying entirely on Hindenburg's son† and on Meissner‡ as intermediaries. To Papen it came natural to maintain close and constant contact with the President.

Hindenburg backed up his aides with his authority, but

* Otto Gessler, Democratic Party politician and Groener's predecessor in the Reichswehr Ministry from March 1920 to January 1928.
† Colonel Oskar von Hindenburg, who was acting as his father's personal adjutant.
‡ Otto Meissner, State Secretary in the Office of the President under Ebert, Hindenburg, and Hitler, in charge of presidential relations with the government.

was often unable to defend their plans and arguments against others. If their attitude and performance were persistently questioned, not to say condemned, by persons close to Hindenburg, he was usually incapable of putting up a critical argument; in the event of serious conflict he withdrew from his aides the authority he had lent them. Ludendorff, it is true, was responsible for his own resignation, which was indispensable and actually came too late, but once he had tendered his resignation Hindenburg dropped him immediately. He forced Groener and Brüning to resign when he no longer felt able to defend them against others. When Schleicher fell a victim to his own tactics, Hindenburg let him go. Papen was the only one of his aides whose attitudes and policies were seldom questioned by Hindenburg's entourage.

Hindenburg had strict but also very formal ideas of trustworthiness, of "loyalty" as he called it. He stood by his decisions. He backed up those who had proposed them, but he was cautious about taking on new obligations or confirming old ones. He took advantage of changes in the situation to break ties. He dropped Groener not for prohibiting the SA and SS [Sturmabteilungen and Schutzstaffeln, the storm-troop formations of the Nazi Party], but because of his parliamentary defeat.* After his re-election to the presidency, Hindenburg gave Brüning no assurance that he would remain Chancellor. But he demanded trustworthiness in others. Restricted in his movements by his age and position, he was not always able to obtain information; consequently he was distrustful, and with the help of his excellent memory kept close watch over the truthfulness of information and arguments. He did not forget lapses. Hindenburg reacted very sensitively to doubts concerning his leadership, especially

---

* A reference to Groener's ineffective defense in the Reichstag of the government's prohibition of the Nazi storm-troop formations which was drowned out in the tumult created by the Nazi members of the House.

if they emanated from persons whose esteem he valued; most of these were high army officers and fellow Junkers. For all his outward modesty, his positively sovereign modesty—highly placed persons find it relatively easy to be modest—he secretly, but with great vigilance and scrupulous care, cultivated his prestige and fame. He attached great importance to the esteem of those of his own social class.

In his attitude toward constitutional government Hindenburg was as correct as necessary. His ponderous build and solemn, well-controlled manner concealed an inner timidity. He did not wish to risk his fame and the honors of his rank, even though he was far more generous in his conceptions of class and tradition than many of his comrades and fellow Junkers, especially those of his generation. He felt out of joint with the republican form of government, but he sidestepped all inner conflict between his traditional ideas and his loyalty to the republic, because he did not feel up to it. He took his oath very seriously, but he understood the republican constitution only in a formal sense. Undoubtedly he studied his duties carefully, but only as a sergeant studies the drill regulations. And like the sergeant with his regulations, Hindenburg observed the constitution with formal correctness. Stresemann told of having had great difficulty in persuading Hindenburg to wear the Order of the Black Eagle; at first he had objected strenuously on constitutional grounds. Hindenburg never understood the constitution. In his patriarchal, authoritarian mind there was no place for the political dynamics of the democratic order, for the play of political forces—although he did have a certain feeling for relations of power. If he had been more of a democrat and more of a politician, he would have risked a *coup d'état* to save the constitutional order and would not by formal observance of the constitution have surrendered the democratic republic to its adversaries.

Hindenburg's aide in his first great government crisis

was Groener. It was largely thanks to Groener's shrewd, level-headed advice that Hindenburg was able to maintain his position amid the turmoil of revolution. The second crisis occurred when he abandoned Groener and Brüning. Hindenburg's tragedy was that at the height of this second crisis he was counseled by Franz von Papen, who more than any other of his aides corresponded to his political and class conceptions and was perhaps closest to him in a human sense, but for whom he had so much sympathy that he failed to discern Papen's functional inadequacy. Perhaps Hindenburg was by then too old to perceive Papen's political impotence. Hindenburg succumbed to Papen's charm. Papen knew better than anyone else how to handle him; but Hindenburg had hoped that through a constitutionally correct "reparation," by restoring the monarchy, Papen would release him from the sense of guilt toward the monarch and the monarchy that he had carried with him since the November days of 1918.

Hindenburg had no great understanding of human nature, but he did have a certain eye for a man's personal qualities and fitness for a position. This was the opinion of Stresemann, who discussed the filling of ambassadorships with him and sometimes had great difficulty in imposing his views. Hindenburg esteemed the great diplomatic gifts of Brockdorff-Rantzau* as opposed to other diplomats. He disliked Stresemann personally but respected his achievement. Hermann Müller's ideas were diametrically opposed to those of Hindenburg, but Hindenburg felt a strong sympathy for him. Oldenburg-Januschau† was the owner of the estate next to Hinden-

---

* Ulrich Count von Brockdorff-Rantzau was Foreign Minister and head of the German delegation to Versailles and, being opposed to the signing of the Treaty of Versailles, resigned. Later he became ambassador to Moscow (1922–1928) and a supporter of the policy of reconciliation with the Soviet Union.

† Elard von Oldenburg-Januschau, a Junker representing reactionary agrarian interests as a deputy of the Conservative Party in the prewar

burg's, and Hindenburg liked him personally. But he distrusted his violence.

It is none too surprising that Hindenburg should have stuck to Papen as long as he was Chancellor. That he wished to keep him when it was no longer possible and secretly retained him as an aide after Schleicher had been appointed and allowed him to intrigue against Schleicher —all this is no doubt explained by Hindenburg's advanced state of senility and by his profound penchant for Papen's idea of a restoration, the real dangers of which he was no longer able to perceive. Hindenburg was not a courtier, but he prized courtly forms. Papen was the only one of his aides who had learned them as a page at the imperial court. To Hindenburg he was a representative of the great old times, and that is why he so esteemed and trusted him.

* *

Groener was a very different man from Papen. Despite the enormous difference in their origins, outlook, and manner, Hindenburg, the old Prussian officer, and Groener, the Swabian *petit bourgeois,* seem to have worked well together and to have maintained close personal relations. Groener need not have become Gessler's successor in 1928. It might have been held against him that not only the retired superior officers but also a part of the active officers' corps disapproved of his alleged attitude toward the Emperor in the critical November days of 1918 and of his participation from 1920 to 1923 in several left-oriented cabinets. At the time of his resignation Gessler, as he personally told me, had warned Hindenburg against Groener and according to his oral account suggested General von Winterfeldt in far more emphatic terms than transpires from his memoirs. Political considerations had

Reichstag and of the German Nationalists from 1930 to 1932. He is known to have exercised considerable influence over Hindenburg on behalf of his East Elbian landowning compatriots.

little to do with Gessler's warning; he believed, rather, that the taciturn Groener, with his stiff, awkward manner and his aloofness, would not be able to acquire real authority in the Reichswehr or to exert a lasting influence on the government and parliament in favor of the Reichswehr. True, Gessler went on, the moderate and left-wing parties had political confidence in Groener, but he would probably be unable to exploit this confidence in the interest of the Reichswehr; Groener was a cultivated, highly intelligent man, but his grasp of political situations was purely intellectual; he lacked political instinct. Hindenburg must have had great confidence in him to appoint him Reichswehr Minister nevertheless.

Groener always spoke of Hindenburg with great personal respect; this respect was far from being merely conventional, and one had the impression that it was perfectly sincere. Groener was capable of withholding information, but he did not readily dissimulate. Although he was a shrewd and keenly critical thinker, well aware of Hindenburg's weaknesses, he needed Hindenburg's confidence to bolster up his self-assurance and invoked it time and time again, precisely because he suffered keenly from his isolation, especially in the old officers' corps. Groener was a soldier through and through, but he lacked the strict traditional sense of caste which the North German officers possessed and many of the South Germans had learned from them. Conscientious in the extreme, he thought things through with great care and re-examined ideas, plans, and situations over and over again. He was a great organizer, an organizational strategist, who worked with scientific meticulousness and an innate sense of order.

Groener was not an enthusiastic democrat, but his insight gave him a sincere respect for the constitutional order. If he enjoyed the confidence of the democratic parties, it was less because of his political attitude than because of his South German civilian manner and his absolute trustworthiness. Because of his origins, but even more so because he had formerly been in command of the military railway system, he was far more interested in improving the armament and training of the Reichswehr than in preserving its military and political tradition. He too wished to maintain the autonomy of the armed forces, but unlike Seeckt* he wished it to become the army of a democratic state.

Groener wrote well, but his speech was diffident and awkward. In conversation, and in his more or less impromptu speeches as well, his vocabulary was very limited and his sentence structure rudimentary. At the Reichstag celebration of the tenth anniversary of the constitution, he was obliged, as the senior minister present in Berlin, to deliver the concluding address to the President. Most of those present found his speech positively embarrassing. A sergeant could hardly have done worse on the occasion of the Emperor's birthday.

Accordingly Groener dreaded conferences and avoided cabinet meetings. He was clumsy in political tactics. Despite his unimpressive manner, he was extremely firm in his statements. The flexibility of his thinking was matched by the inflexibility of his outward attitude. In discussions he tried as far as possible to take account of his interlocutors' ideas and plans, but he knew very well exactly how far he was prepared to go in his concessions, and he sometimes showed real obstinacy in adhering to the limit he had set himself. He was a type not uncommon among Swabians, whose intelligence and determination are scarcely discernible at first sight, but become all the more impressive in the course of a conversation. Though Groener was a wholehearted supporter of Ger-

---

* General Hans von Seeckt, Chief of the Army Command from 1920 to 1926, was the chief theorist of Reichswehr political independence, a position which has been variously described as suprapartisanship and advocating the creation of "a state within a state." In any event, Seeckt found democratic government and its potential control of the army inimical.

man rearmament, he regarded it not as an end in itself but as part of an over-all policy. Stresemann told me on several occasions that Groener showed much more understanding for his foreign policy than Gessler, who was basically intimidated by the officers' corps.

Groener impressed people by the quality of his arguments. It seems probable that Hindenburg valued him for his reliability and for his monosyllabic but precise and clearly thought-out advice.

* *

Groener's aide was Schleicher, whom he took over from Gessler but had known for a long time. When at the outbreak of the First World War Groener was commander of the military railway system, he detached Schleicher, "one of his best young officers," as he himself said, to the office of the Chief of Staff. "Thanks to his great talent and his skill as a negotiator," writes Groener in his memoirs, "Schleicher soon exerted an important influence on the Chief of Staff." Schleicher is thought to have been one of the few officers, if not the only one, who was made a general although he had not commanded a battalion or regiment, as was normally required. Schleicher had last commanded troops before the war (except for a very brief combat command). Since then, apart from the time spent in General Staff school, he had worked exclusively at staff headquarters and then at the Reichswehr Ministry. Thus when he became Groener's aide at the Reichswehr Ministry, he had not seen military duty in the strict sense for fifteen years.

A man who knew his way about the world of political forces, who was an extraordinarily skillful tactician and negotiator capable of dealing with the bureaucracy and with parliament, was a rare phenomenon in the Prussian officers' corps. His special distinction was that he had mastered the technique of democratic, parliamentary operations without seeming to have lost the specific mentality of the officer caste. This combination was the basis of his almost monopolistic position.

Schleicher was a gifted agent and lobbyist. In carrying out his instructions he exhausted all the tactical possibilities. Overflowing with ingenious ideas, he could be extremely useful to his superior. He thought and acted politically for the benefit of the army. Despite his unusual versatility, all his ideas and plans hinged on the interests of the armed forces. In his scale of values they were the essential, to which he subordinated everything else. At about nine o'clock one night—early in 1929, as I recall—Stresemann emerged from a cabinet meeting thoroughly exhausted. He told me that Schleicher had spent two solid hours trying to persuade the cabinet (although there had been other, extremely urgent matters to discuss) that Stresemann should appeal directly to [French Foreign Minister Aristide] Briand to obtain permission for the Reichswehr officers to wear uniforms at the international riding meet at Aachen. (Aachen was then in the demilitarized zone.) Stresemann disapproved of the pettiness of the French military in this matter, but was infuriated by Schleicher's "gall" at holding up the cabinet for over two hours over a "trifle." He said he would speak to Groener, but the effect would be short-lived because, though Groener kept an eye on Schleicher in important questions, he was always giving him a free hand in minor matters.

As long as Schleicher was only head of the Ministerial Bureau,* this one-sidedness, this lack of programmatic scope did little harm. But for a chancellor or minister of a modern state, Schleicher's horizon was too narrow. Groener had a keener eye for political essentials and a broader view than Schleicher. Groener had far less knowledge of political detail than Schleicher but he had a broader perspective. Above all, Groener had patience and Schleicher did not. As long as he was Groener's aide, Groener was able to check the impetuousness of his pragmatic opera-

* Political office of the Reichswehr Ministry created by Groener.

tions. On the other hand, Schleicher possessed in high degree the tactical dexterity that Groener lacked. He was able to deal with all kinds of people, he had the psychological gift of adapting himself to the sensibilities of very different types of men. Even in fields that were strange to him he was quick to understand, though his understanding did not go very deep. He was full of tactical ideas and a brilliant improviser. For all his joviality, he was basically a sensitive man. In his own domain he was a realist, but impressions, especially emanating from fields that were strange to him, could affect him strongly and influence his ideas. Ideas came to him so quickly and abundantly that he had no time to think them through and test them. His social-romantic conceptions, which he advocated most particularly during his chancellorship, may have had their source in these impressions and in his unclear thinking, but also in his one-sided emphasis on tactics. He was never at a loss for an argument or a solution and had no scruples about correcting one mistake with another. He tended to express himself with imprecision, partly for tactical reasons but sometimes because he had not given, or did not wish to give, sufficient thought to the matter of which he was speaking. His expositions and arguments were often inconsistent. Councilor Planck of the Reich Chancellery, who was very close to Schleicher and was the chief of the Chancellery under Papen and Schleicher, complained to me when Schleicher was still head of the Ministerial Bureau that Schleicher was careless about his reports to Hindenburg and that Hindenburg had several times detected "slight inaccuracies" in his exposition and argumentation. Hindenburg had said nothing or had merely made a facetious remark, but, as Planck told me, the old man did not forget such things. Planck feared that with these bad habits Schleicher would never acquire Hindenburg's full confidence.

Groener often said, "Schleicher does my political work." By this he meant essentially that Schleicher converted Groener's strategic plans into tactical operations. Groener called Schleicher his *"Cardinal in politicis."* These words expressed the limits of Schleicher's function. In conversation with me Groener often praised Schleicher very highly for his ingenuity, his intelligence, and his absolute reliability as well, but also intimated that he did not take certain of his "tactical tricks" very seriously. He never characterized Schleicher as a great political thinker, but only as an officer uncommonly versed in politics. Occasionally, Groener told me, Schleicher got out of hand, but he always managed to rein him in.

From 1929 on Schleicher was officially head of the Ministerial Bureau, the political office of the Reichswehr Ministry. The Ministerial Bureau handled questions concerning both the army and the navy, and enjoyed equal rank with the High Commands of the army and navy. The head of the Ministerial Bureau held the rank of an undersecretary, but he was not the minister's deputy vis-à-vis the commanders of the army and navy.

In practice Schleicher was confidential political adviser to Groener, who depended on him in most political questions. Groener was not only the head of the Ministry but was at the same time a counselor in the cabinet; thus at cabinet meetings he had to participate in discussing and deciding on questions that went beyond his department or did not concern it at all. Groener once told me that though he discussed with Schleicher all departmental questions that were to be taken up at the cabinet, he himself examined them very thoroughly and made the final decisions. In all questions subject to the jurisdiction of the Food Supply Ministry, about which Schleicher knew nothing, Groener went to the President for instructions (an institutionally incorrect procedure). In all other matters, he usually let Schleicher work out and draft the department's decisions, because Schleicher knew more about these things than he did and could be trusted implicitly both from the political and from the human point of view. But they discussed everything together at least once a day; Schleicher always kept him informed in every detail. What interested Groener they discussed together, the rest he left to Schleicher. But much as he relied on Schleicher's adroitness and tactical virtuosity, Groener himself seems to have laid down the political guidelines, to which Schleicher seems at first to have conformed. The strategist and the tactician complemented one another as long as the division of labor was strictly observed by the more active of the two, that is, Schleicher. The close collaboration between them was made possible by a strong personal bond and frequent meetings.

Groener, who was otherwise so aloof, had unlimited confidence in Schleicher. He called him his "elective" or "adoptive" son. Seldom has a relationship between superior and subordinate been as close as that between Groener and Schleicher.

* *

Unlike Hindenburg, Groener, and Schleicher, Brüning was not a career officer, but he was not a total stranger to military affairs. He had volunteered at the time of the war. At first rejected because of his frail constitution, he had reapplied later and been accepted. At the end of the war, he was a reserve lieutenant. For Brüning military duty had been a real test of character. In spite of his poor health he had withstood the hardships of combat duty with great fortitude. Along with rational considerations and his general political orientation, this experience probably had a good deal to do with his favorable attitude toward the Reichswehr.

Apart from Stresemann, Brüning was the only chancellor of the Weimar Republic who really directed his cabinet. He acquired this position of leadership very quickly. He fully mastered the work of government. No minister and no parliamentarian belonging to any of the parties that supported or tolerated Brüning's government policy was willing or able to contest his leadership. He possessed a realistic over-all conception of political affairs, to which no one within the government or the parties supporting it could have offered an alternative. He was not a skilled negotiator; he lacked the agility, the cunning, but also the unscrupulousness and the diabolical touch of a Stresemann. His weapons were his intellectual superiority and his unquestioned sincerity. Thus he was essentially an administrator with high ethical standards, not a politician. It was only in that particular constellation that a man of his stamp could have effectively directed the government. The parties loyal to the constitution regarded him as irreplaceable, and for the time being he was also trusted in two all-important quarters that were, to say the least, skeptical of the constitutional order, namely Hindenburg and the High Command.

Brüning was the kind of man who is perpetually debating with himself. His decisions cost him days or weeks of struggle. He did not sidestep decisions, but he needed a long time to arrive at them. Perhaps he believed with an excess of scruple that by carefully weighing all the arguments in his mind he could make up for the virtual cessation of debate in parliament and in the parliamentary commissions. But once he had arrived at a fundamental decision, he clung firmly to it and consequently had little if any margin for bargaining. His hesitation, his slowness to make up his mind, the consequences of his thoroughness, often drove his friends and supporters to despair. The responsibility of his office weighed heavily on him. In a speech titled "The Statesman" delivered in 1947 to the students of the University of Chicago he declared:

> . . . a man with a sensitive imagination, possessing thorough knowledge of the outstanding personalities on the world stage and of the social and economic problems of the day, may be able to predict the .actions of individuals and the development of society correctly for years to come. But if the same man is confronted by re-

sponsible decisions, he may be just as perplexed to find the right solution as anyone else. During my term in office I myself experienced such perplexity and unfortunately [acquired] such exact foresight [only] in exile.

At first Hindenburg respected Brüning both personally and for his work, although Brüning did not know how to deal with him. Often Hindenburg had difficulty in following Brüning's ideas, which he couched in obscure technical terminology. For Hindenburg each one of the Chancellor's visits was a great strain, because Brüning's reports presupposed too much knowledge. He tried to convince the aged President with objective arguments when it would have been much better to win him over personally. But that was not in Brüning's character. As different as Ludendorff, Groener, and Brüning were, there was a certain similarity in their uncompromising characters. Hindenburg trusted them as long as he believed, or as others permitted him to believe, in their programs. The supple Schleicher was a very different type.

As long as Brüning dealt with matters of financial, economic, or social policy, which were outside Hindenburg's sphere of interest, Hindenburg was not greatly disturbed by the Chancellor's methods. Thanks to his own penchant for scrupulous thoroughness, Groener felt sympathy for Brüning's elaborate procedures, Schleicher with his leaning toward quick improvisation less so.

* *

Thus for a time the function of the Reich government depended in high degree on the ability of these four men to work hand in hand and complement each other, on their ties of personal friendship and trust, and at the same time on the fact that they held related though by no means identical ideas about the situation and the essential political tasks of the day. The leading mind was Brüning, but he was dependent on Hindenburg's authority and the support of the Reichswehr. At first Groener was in a sense

Brüning's advocate with Hindenburg. When necessary Brüning was able to curb Schleicher's activities through Groener's intercession.

The close relations among the four were favored by the fact that Hindenburg and Groener were widowers, while Brüning and Schleicher were unmarried. They were all free from family ties that might have interfered with their meetings. None of them was intimate with any outsider who might for personal motives have influenced their relations with each other. We know how hard Queen Augusta tried, even if she was unsuccessful, to alienate William I and Bismarck from each other.

In the autumn of 1930 Groener, then sixty-two, remarried. Of the four men it was no doubt he and Schleicher who had been the most intimate. It is not unusual for the relationship between bachelor friends to change when one of them marries. Frau Groener came between the two men and an estrangement set in. Who was responsible for this estrangement is uncertain but also immaterial; the essential is that they moved apart. They began to see each other less frequently. Their exchange of ideas grew less intense and their mutual confidence suffered as well. As their friendship cooled they ceased to complement each other in their work. Schleicher was forced into a position of independence, deprived of the wise instructor and friendly but strict supervisor. Groener felt the lack of the adroit adviser and helper.

Groener's marriage also led to an estrangement between him and Hindenburg. Frau Groener gave birth to a child conspicuously ahead of time. With his strict old-Prussian ideas of duty and morality, Hindenburg could not forgive the Reichswehr Minister for this irregularity. At that time Reichswehr regulations provided that officers must obtain permission to marry. To Hindenburg's mind, Groener had set the officers under him a bad example. The attacks on Groener for his attitude in November 1918, which had subsided over the years, now revived with new force. In the eyes of the old-Prussian conservatives, republic and democracy were symbols of decadence; they brought with them a breakdown of political and hence also of moral values. The conservatives held that in succumbing to the immoral spirit of the times Groener had shown that he was not a true officer. His marriage also dealt a blow to Groener's authority in the officers' corps. Hindenburg became more receptive not only to the old attacks on Groener but also to current accusations and suspicions. There was no open break, but their personal relationship was so shaken that from this time on it seemed likely that any political difference that might arise between the two would culminate in a serious conflict.

Groener was probably far more affected by the estrangement from Hindenburg and Schleicher than they were. They were more robust by nature. Groener lost his self-assurance. He suffered from loneliness and suffered at being less able to count on Schleicher's ingenious political advice and Hindenburg's protective authority. The relations between Brüning and Groener remained unchanged, but the question arose, Would Schleicher take over Groener's role as Brüning's advocate with Hindenburg?

Schleicher rushed into the vacuum that had arisen in Hindenburg's immediate political entourage, but he was also drawn into it. Conferring more and more frequently with Hindenburg, sometimes without previously consulting Groener, Schleicher gradually ceased to be an aide and became an acknowledged member of the group of leading statesmen of the Reich. It was frequently asserted at the time that perhaps to curry favor with Hindenburg, or perhaps merely because sarcasm was second nature to him, Schleicher fanned Hindenburg's resentment against Groener by making remarks about Groener's marriage.

A year later, in July 1931, Schleicher married a woman

who had recently divorced a general on his account. It seems likely that this too displeased Hindenburg, but it did not affect him as strongly as Groener's marriage.

The change in personal relations was soon followed by an institutional change: in the autumn of 1931 Groener took over the Ministry of the Interior in addition to the Reichswehr Ministry. In practice this was a further step in the rise of Schleicher, and increased his independence. The idea of joining the two ministries by a personal union is thought to have originated with Schleicher or with Planck. The two men discussed everything together and at that time had the same aim in view. Now the cumulation of offices, especially at the head of government departments, often has institutional consequences. Either one office becomes subordinate to the other or a shift in effective leadership occurs insofar as the official head of both departments confines himself to directing one of them, while the other is actually directed by someone else, often the minister's deputy in that department. It is hard to determine with certainty why Schleicher suggested this uniting of offices. Did he think it advisable that the Reichswehr Ministry should be subordinated to the Ministry of the Interior, or did he wish to involve his superior in new functions so as to be able to direct the Reichswehr Ministry himself with as little interference as possible or even eventually to take it over one day? Because the two ministries performed very different functions, his cumulation of offices created conflicts for Groener. The fact that the Ministry of the Interior was responsible for internal order and security made it, in the tense situation at that time, more open to attack than the Reichswehr Ministry. Moreover, there were acute antagonisms between the personnel of the Ministry of the Interior, largely taken over from the days of Severing and Wirth* and hence loyal to the republic, and the authori-

* Carl Severing and Joseph Wirth, respectively, Social Democratic Minister of the Interior from June 1928 to March 1930 and Center Minister

tarian officers of the Reichswehr Ministry with their professional interest in the paramilitary organizations of the right.

* *

In the winter of 1931 the political solidarity of the Reich leadership seems to have given way. Hindenburg and Schleicher began to doubt whether Brüning was really the right man for the chancellorship, whereas Groener remained firm in support of him. But for the present the preparations for the presidential elections scheduled for March 1932 prevented this conflict from coming to a head.

The results of the *Landtag* elections made it seem virtually certain that only a Hindenburg candidacy could prevent Hitler from being elected. Brüning had at first attempted to prevent an election from being held at the height of the crisis by putting through an amendment to the constitution that would extend the President's term in office, as Stresemann had done for Ebert's benefit in 1922. Schleicher had tried to win over the moderate right, especially the Stahlhelm,* for the re-election of Hindenburg. Both attempts had failed. The price demanded by Hitler, Hugenberg, and under Hugenberg's influence also Seldte, leader of the Stahlhelm, was the dismissal of Brüning. Hindenburg was not prepared to run at the cost of such a capitulation. Such a surrender to partisan demands was absolutely incompatible with his conception of personal prestige and of the dignity of his office. Thus the decision rested with the parties that had opposed Hindenburg in the elections of 1925, the Center, the Democrats, and the Socialists. They put forward no conditions. Their sole concern was to prevent a dictatorship of the

---

of the Interior from March 1930 to October 1931.
* First World War veterans' federation which opened its ranks in 1924 to nonveterans and became a militant, right-wing, paramilitary organization.

right. At the runoff election on April 10, Hindenburg won out. The figures showed that he owed his victory mainly to the center and the left.*

Hindenburg knew that he could not have declined this second candidacy. Despite his advanced age his sense of duty had retained its full force; no doubt he thought also of his place in history. His historic role would be questioned if he ceded without a struggle to the despised "Bohemian corporal." But because the right demanded the retirement of Brüning as the price for continuing Hindenburg in office either through re-election or through a constitutional amendment prolonging his term, Hindenburg was led to believe that Brüning was the main obstacle to his being maintained in office or re-elected without friction. Hindenburg believed that in accepting the candidacy he had made a sacrifice to Brüning and consequently had a right to his gratitude after his re-election.

Brüning, on the other hand, could claim to have made an important or perhaps even decisive contribution to Hindenburg's electoral victory. He had taken the lead in the election campaign and devoted every ounce of his energy to it. It is doubtful whether Hindenburg would have been elected without Brüning's efforts. He had saved Hindenburg from a plebiscitary defeat that the old man would probably not have outlived. Though objectively open to criticism, these subjective considerations on both sides are humanly understandable. Each of the two felt, if only unconsciously, that he had a claim on the other; and neither was really aware of the other's claim or prepared to recognize it.

Brüning was able to regard the elections as a popular confirmation of his own policy, a vote of confidence in him personally, and this view was widely expressed in the press. Before the elections certain of the government parties had shown distinct signs of a crisis over Brüning, most of all the German People's Party, which had turned

* His opponent, Hitler, obtained 13.4 million or 37 percent of the votes.

against him; but also in the State Party* there was considerable unrest. Even in the Center Party voices were raised against the Chancellor. For the present, in view of the impending presidential elections, these expressions of flagging confidence were without practical significance. Brüning must have felt that the election campaign had refuted them. Since it was he who had led the election campaign for Hindenburg, he was not unjustified in supposing that Hindenburg's victory must be regarded also as his victory.

But Hindenburg disliked to see his name coupled with Brüning's in this connection. During the election campaign the figure of the President had taken on well-nigh mythical dimensions in the public mind, and this must have made a certain impression even on this cool-headed man whom a superabundance of honors had rendered somewhat blasé. Hindenburg had been called a "leader of the German nation." Brüning himself had spoken of the "man sent by God." This may have heightened his consciousness of his sovereign position toward Brüning as toward everyone else. If he and Brüning were identified, did this not imply that he had been elected for Brüning's sake, a supposition disrespectful to his person and his office?

To his mind the position of a chancellor was not very different from that of a chief of staff, especially in an emergency-decree situation such as then prevailed. According to the constitution, the President appointed and dismissed the Chancellor and had the power to influence the policies of the Chancellor and the government by threatening to dismiss him or refusing to sign emergency decrees. In these ideas confirmed by the constitution he was encouraged by Brüning's enemies in his immediate and wider entourage. Many of these felt themselves to be above all institutional principles; not so long ago they had demanded an increase in the President's prerogatives;

* The former German Democratic Party, which had merged in 1930 with the nationalist Young German Order.

then they had made the re-election of Hindenburg con-
tingent on his abandonment of Brüning, in other words
demanded that Hindenburg bow to a party *Diktat;* now,
after the elections, they wished him to demonstrate his
sovereignty of decision by dismissing Brüning. Hindenburg, whose strength had waned in the last six months,
was too old to confront these advisers with their lack of
principles.

It was customary that the Chancellor should tender the
resignation of his cabinet to the newly elected, or in this
case re-elected, President. Would it not be a good idea for
Hindenburg to profit by the occasion and restore his
shaken authority either by compelling Brüning to change
his policy fundamentally or even by dismissing him? Just
as he had refused to capitulate to the right before the elections by dismissing Brüning, so now after the elections he
was under no obligation to maintain Brüning in office or
to tolerate a continuation of his present policy.

Brüning revered Hindenburg but his feeling for him
was rather that of a grandson for his grandfather, whose
dignity he sincerely respects but whose intelligence and
will he questions. Brüning did not, as has often been
claimed, feel himself to be a lieutenant or captain of the
marshal, owing him obedience. He held, rather, that his
position was equivalent to that of a prime minister in a
constitutional monarchy.

In 1862, on his appointment as Chancellor, Bismarck
had said to King William I in Babelsberg, and in 1863
had repeated in writing: "I do not envisage my position as
that of a constitutional minister in the usual sense of the
word, but rather as that of Your Majesty's servant. I obey
your supreme commands as the ultimate instance even if
they are not in agreement with my personal views." Brüning would never have uttered such words, for to his mind
the chancellorship signified the President's mandate to direct the government; Hindenburg as the ultimate instance preserved only the right to withdraw this mandate.

As long as there were no fundamental differences of opinion between them, this divergency in their conceptions of their positions did not appear on the surface. The situation changed, however, when the outcome of the elections gave rise to conflicting interpretations, which also became an issue between the various political tendencies. After the elections, accordingly, conflicting claims and conceptions brought a new tension into the relations between Hindenburg and Brüning.

Hindenburg was also unhappy about owing his reelection largely to his adversaries of 1925. He was concerned over his authority and his glory, but he also attached great importance to the esteem of the "right people." He did not wish to be regarded as a man of the Center or the left. He feared a taint at the end of his great career. He may well have held Brüning responsible for his Pyrrhic victory and blamed him for the failure of the "right people" to vote for him.

With his formal conception of justice Hindenburg had leaned slightly to the left in 1925 after his election by the right; for example, despite all the efforts of the German National [People's] Party and the Stahlhelm to influence him he had not appointed one of their number as his State Secretary, but had taken over Meissner, who had served in that capacity under his Social Democratic predecessor. Now that he had been elected largely by the left, he may have felt obliged to effect a visible turn to the right, which also fell in with his traditional views. Now more than ever he wished to appear independent of the parties, and he pondered on how he might lend visible expression to this independence. Brüning on the other hand believed for the time being that the crisis over his person and politics had been ended by the outcome of the elections; he was determined to continue his policy without interference.

* *

The prohibition of the SA and SS on April 13, 1932, three days after the elections, not only deprived Hindenburg of the possibility of a visible shift to the right, but made the impression of a concession to the left. The two paramilitary organizations of the NSDAP [National-sozialistische Deutsche Arbiterpartei—National Socialist German Workers Party] had offered ample cause for the prohibition. Undoubtedly it was justified by the facts, but its political expedience is questionable. The events leading up to it are extremely complicated. A certain historical reconstruction has been possible, but a good deal remains unclear.

The plan had originated with Groener as Minister of the Interior after certain of the *Länder,* particularly Prussia and Bavaria, had confronted Groener with the alternative: either the Reich must immediately issue the order or they would take measures of their own. The plan does not seem to have been discussed with Brüning, who had just returned from his election campaign. He regarded Groener's step as premature, but now that things had gone so far he was determined to back it up. Hindenburg gave his very reluctant consent after Brüning and Groener had threatened to resign. He had not been convinced, but had ceded to the pressure of Brüning and Groener. Hindenburg did not want a cabinet crisis for which he was unprepared. But since he was extremely touchy in those days after the elections, it seems likely that he was not quick to forgive Brüning and Groener for putting pressure on him.

Schleicher's attitude in this situation is largely enigmatic. He had had misgivings about the prohibition, but had not resolutely combatted it. He had not threatened to resign if the prohibition went through, as had Brüning and Groener in the event that Hindenburg withheld his signature. Oskar von Hindenburg, the President's aide-de-camp, was opposed to the prohibition, though not for political reasons but solely because he wished to spare his father. He felt that the old man should not be asked to sign such a decree since it would make him even more unpopular with the right. Oskar von Hindenburg and Schleicher were of the same age. They were old friends, having served in the same regiment. They met frequently, so that Schleicher was thoroughly informed of the President's state of mind.

Bypassing their minister, General von Hammerstein, the army chief of staff, and Lieutenant General von Bock, a divisional commander, informed Hindenburg of their misgivings about the prohibition of the SA and SS. This was an unusual proceeding. Oskar von Hindenburg had probably arranged their visit. But what is really astonishing is that Hindenburg, ordinarily so strict in his insistence on the need to "go through channels," should have permitted it. It is not likely that Hammerstein would have called on Hindenburg unless encouraged to do so by Schleicher, with whom he saw eye to eye in most military matters. This supposition is further supported by the fact that Schleicher had urged Admiral Raeder, the naval chief of staff, to intercede with the President against the prohibition. Raeder had declined to do so.

Furthermore, the Ministerial Bureau, allegedly on orders from Hindenburg, had compiled material that Hindenburg had used in a very unfriendly letter to Groener of the same day, demanding the prohibition of the Reichsbanner.* The letter was even published. It was clearly based on material emanating from the Reichswehr Ministry. This letter, which made public the cleavage in the Reich leadership and disavowed Groener in his capacity as Reichswehr Minister, cannot have been given to the press without Hindenburg's knowledge or against his will. Schleicher, who was in close contact with Oskar von

---

* The Reichsbanner Schwarz-Rot-Gold, an irregular but non-arms-carrying formation, was created in 1924 with the support of Social Democrats, Centrists, and Democrats for the defense of republican institutions. The Social Democrats from the beginning constituted a majority in the organization and with time became its almost exclusive constituent.

Hindenburg, seems to have passed on the publication of the letter. It seems hardly credible that Schleicher, who kept a firm grip on the machinery of the ministry, had, as he later claimed to Groener, known nothing of the compilation of material for Hindenburg's letter. As late as April 17, in a conversation with Groener, he insisted that he had had nothing to do with it. In the hope of putting an end to false rumors Groener ordered Schleicher to draft a circular to the district military commanders. Schleicher never executed the order.

There is little doubt that very shortly after the issuance of the prohibition Schleicher, without the knowledge of his minister or of the Chancellor, entered into contact with the NSDAP and its agents and informed them of his own attitude, and perhaps of Hindenburg's as well.

* *

The events leading up to and following the prohibition show that the solidarity of the Reich leadership was no longer intact. From the standpoint of administrative routine Groener had handled the prohibition with due care. This, however, was not an administrative but a political measure of the first importance. In his manner of putting it through, Groener showed a lack of political intuition. He suffered from the lack of Schleicher's tactical assistance. Brüning was taken by surprise, Hindenburg put under pressure.

Concerning Schleicher's evident change of camp many conjectures have been made. He must have felt very sure of himself, otherwise he would not have been likely to risk this triple affront to his immediate superior: communicating the material to Hindenburg behind Groener's back, asking Raeder to intercede with Hindenburg against Groener, and permitting the publication of Hindenburg's letter. Schleicher could not justify his behavior toward Groener by an order from Hindenburg, because he knew that even in military matters the President could not take action except through the Reichswehr Minister. When an official or officer of Schleicher's rank believes that he can no longer carry out the policy of his superior or of his government, he must tender his resignation. Unless this procedure is strictly observed, the functioning of the government is bound to be gravely impaired. It is contended that Schleicher thought of resigning. But once he decided to remain in office, he was under obligation to observe discipline. Instead, he proceeded to engage in political activities on his own. He acted as if the Reichswehr were a political party and he its leader. The whole incident throws a dismal light on Schleicher's character and bearing as an officer. Also the behavior of Hammerstein, who as late as April 9 had expressed approval of Groener's plan, shows by comparison with Raeder's that military ethics and discipline were no longer as intact in the army as in the navy. When Schleicher tried to persuade him to intervene with the President, Raeder had declined.

But was not Schleicher a subordinate only in a purely formal sense? Was he not in practice the Reichswehr Minister? His position was assuredly unique. Brüning and to an even greater extent Groener had contributed to putting him in that position or enabling him to carve it out for himself. Groener's dual position as Minister of the Interior and Armed Forces Minister had further increased Schleicher's independence. Brüning and Groener had commissioned Schleicher to carry on personal and political negotiations with the right, including the National Socialists. These missions offered him an opportunity to act as if he had been minister. Institutionally Schleicher's position had not changed; he was merely head of the Ministerial Bureau. But in fact his situation had changed drastically: his relations with Hindenburg had become far closer, and he had ceased to be on friendly terms with Brüning and Groener. Schleicher had become so much of a politician, through years of political activity, that he had lost the habit of strict military discipline to such a degree

that in all likelihood he himself did not always realize
how much he was overstepping the bounds of his official
functions. He lacked the firm hand of his superior, which
would have checked his activities.

Groener acted as if Schleicher had already replaced him
at the Reichswehr Ministry. Schleicher's affront and
breach of departmental discipline justified Groener in demanding his dismissal from Hindenburg. But after weighing his own and Schleicher's relative positions in the
given situation, Groener believed that he would not be
able to put through such a demand with the President.
He would have had to ask Hindenburg to decide between
him and Schleicher, which might have brought on a cabinet crisis. But if it was impossible to get rid of Schleicher,
he should at least have attempted to control his activities.
Groener, however, seems to have felt helpless to deal with
the schemer who had been his aide and had now become
his opponent. Groener did not even attempt to meet with
the generals and convince them of the necessity of his
measures, if only to restore his authority in the Reichswehr Ministry, which had been shaken by Schleicher's
conduct.

Brüning and Groener also did nothing to repair their
relations with Hindenburg and regain his confidence.
True, it was not easy to talk to Hindenburg, especially
after what had happened. They also had to reckon with
the fact that Schleicher would be informed in detail
through Oskar von Hindenburg of any interview they
had with the President. Groener and Brüning were both
reserved by nature, and this too may have played a part.
An attempt at a *rapprochement* with Hindenburg would
have cost them a great effort of will.

The prohibition of the SA and SS was not a mere administrative measure which once taken need be of no further concern to the government; on the contrary, there
was every reason to expect political consequences calling
for further discussion with Hindenburg to prepare him

for further measures. Though they knew something of his activities, Brüning and Groener left the field to Schleicher, partly because in their inertia they hoped that the unfortunate situation would soon mend itself, and partly for fear that an intervention with Hindenburg on their part would provoke a cabinet crisis. Perhaps also they, particularly Brüning, wished to gain time, in the expectation that the reparations conference postponed from the end of April to the middle of June would achieve a success in the field of foreign policy that would reinforce the position of the government. In any case, they did not show the initiative of leaders but waited for Hindenburg to decide the fate of the cabinet. A reversal of functions had occurred; Brüning and Groener acted like civil servants, Schleicher showed political acumen.

But even if Schleicher were the *de facto* minister, he crassly transgressed against the most elementary duties of a minister by dealing, behind the back of his *de jure* superior and of the Chancellor, with the leaders of forbidden organizations and their agents, by discussing with them ways and means of annulling the prohibition, and by passing official secrets on to them. Schleicher's conduct bordered on high treason. When in the following January Papen, following Schleicher's example, negotiated secretly with Hitler behind Schleicher's back, this was less reprehensible insofar as Papen at the time was neither a member of the administration nor a minister in office.

* *

In the course of time Schleicher, thanks to Groener's blind confidence, had built up a new system of personal connections, with the help of which he changed the relations of institutions to one another. Schleicher had been close to Oskar von Hindenburg for years. Though intellectually miles above him, Schleicher appreciated his strategic position. Colonel von Hindenburg, it is true, was no more than a high-class valet to his father; his abilities went no further—if not for his father he would have been pensioned as a captain. But he controlled the access to the President; no one was more familiar with the habits, moods, and interests of the aged Hindenburg; no one had greater power over his agenda, or greater possibilities of communicating information to him and of informing others of his views. He must have known that his father might die soon, and probably realized that his chances of making a career would then be ended. His first thought was therefore to secure a socially advantageous position for the future, and in this he counted on Schleicher's support. He was a pure opportunist, as became still more evident when early in 1933 he changed sides and began to intrigue with Papen against Schleicher.

Officially, State Secretary Meissner was in charge of the President's dealings with the government. But the older Hindenburg grew, the more Meissner's influence diminished and Colonel von Hindenburg's increased. It was necessary to shield the President from overwork and excitement, and this function fell principally on his son. Moreover, Brüning and Groener could no longer really count on Meissner's support, because he was the same variety of opportunist as Oskar von Hindenburg. Pressed by his wife, Meissner led an elaborate social life, and out of concern for his career after Hindenburg's death he did his best to put himself in the good books of those who might hold power in the future.

At the Reich Chancellery Councilor Planck was Schleicher's confidential agent. Years before as a cavalry captain he had been detached to the Chancellery to act as liaison officer with the Reichswehr Ministry. But he had soon retired from active military service and been appointed councilor. Planck was cultivated, intelligent, and extremely adroit. He was regarded as the best-informed official at the Chancellery. Although he dealt largely with matters of general policy and by no means exclusively with questions concerning the armed forces, although his advice had been sought by a number of chancellors including Brüning, he regarded himself as Schleicher's agent at the Chancellery. He received instructions from him directly and gave him information directly. Thus Schleicher was always abreast of the plans and decisions of the Chancellery, whereas Brüning knew only as much of Schleicher's activities as Schleicher wished him to know. It did not occur to Planck that his conduct might be incompatible with his official duties, in particular the duty of secrecy. And even if he had been aware of it, he would have justified himself by saying that the Reichswehr came first.

In this extremely critical situation the executive apparatus had broken down at central points because certain key officials had ceased to respect their duties. The functioning of the institutional order was severely impaired if not completely destroyed by a camarilla, a system of personal relations extending to several of the highest government organs. Through Oskar von Hindenburg, Schleicher attempted to exert a direct influence on the President, to keep an eye on his policies, and to isolate him from Brüning and Groener, while at the same time watching Brüning through Planck. He himself withdrew his ministry more and more from government control. This was the end of the Reich executive. These proceedings of Schleicher, amounting to a cold *coup d'état,* were made possible only by the passivity of Hindenburg, whose age prevented him from seeing what was going on around him and what was being done to him.

* *

The latent crisis that had been provoked largely by Schleicher entered an acute phase as a result of Groener's speech on the prohibition of the SA and SS, delivered in the Reichstag on May 10. When we now read the text of the speech, bearing in mind that Groener was known to be a poor speaker and that a good deal of what he said was drowned out by the uproar of the National Socialists, we are at a loss to understand the extent of the indignation it aroused. Because of this speech Schleicher, in the name of Hammerstein whom he had called back from a trip for the purpose, officially informed Groener that he must resign. In so doing he usurped the prerogatives of Hindenburg and Brüning. Hindenburg, who was at the latest informed of this step immediately after it took place (if he had not known of it before), raised no objection, which is very much to his discredit both as a man and as a statesman. Brüning wished to intercede with the President in Groener's behalf, but Groener deterred him, wishing to provide no cause for a cabinet crisis. For the same reason Groener resigned as Reichswehr Minister but remained Minister of the Interior.

Even if it was no longer possible to keep Groener as Reichswehr Minister, it was high time that something be done to end Schleicher's activities. But perhaps Schleicher had pressed Groener to resign precisely in order to provoke Brüning into resigning. And perhaps Brüning neglected to take action because he suspected Schleicher's motives.

At a meeting of the High Command eleven days later, on May 21, Hammerstein, undoubtedly drawing on information supplied him by Schleicher, explained Groener's resignation. He had argued like the spokesman of a special-interest group. With the support of the army High Command, he declared, Groener had taken over both ministries in order to transform the paramilitary organizations into suprapartisan athletic associations. Instead of discharging the suspect persons in the Ministry of the Interior, he had been "involved" by them. Consequently, the interests of the Reichswehr had not been furthered. The "unfortunate prohibition of the SA" showed that it had been a mistake to join the two ministries. Consequently it had been necessary to dissolve the union of the highly political and of the suprapolitical ministry.

*   *

On May 12 Hindenburg went to Neudeck, where he remained until May 28. Neither he nor Brüning had yet attempted to explain himself to the other. When Brüning expressed a desire to visit the President in Neudeck, Hindenburg discouraged him and Brüning offered no resistance. Meanwhile, Schleicher kept in touch with Neudeck —at least by telephone. Here we see that a valet can hold a very strategic position. When Brüning phoned, Meissner answered laconically, confining himself to the most urgent official business. Oskar von Hindenburg, however, was extremely receptive to the information given him by Schleicher, passed it on with alacrity, and kept Schleicher informed about the old gentleman's state of mind.

It is relatively unimportant what persons visited Hindenburg on his estate at that time. In view of Hindenburg's social connections, these persons must have been fellow Junkers and elderly high army officers. Apart from actual visits, Oskar von Hindenburg must have done his best to acquaint his father with the views of his immediate and less immediate neighbors. The right wished to eliminate Brüning. It had not succeeded in overthrowing him by an electoral capitulation on Hindenburg's part or by defeating him at the polls. Its last chance was to put pressure on Hindenburg to drop Brüning. This was certainly done with the bluntness peculiar to big landowners and old officers, and without regard for honesty or principled argument. Hindenburg wished to behave correctly toward the constitution, but not to be suspected of being a "democrat." He was afraid of being boycotted by the right, especially by his fellow Junkers and old comrades in arms. He knew how closely they could hold together thanks to their social tradition and class solidarity, and if one of their number flouted this solidarity they could isolate him socially and so destroy him. The fact that he had been elected by leftists and Catholics, which was constantly held up to him in private, struck him as a taint from which he wished to purge himself before his death, which might occur at any moment.

*   *

All that is known of Schleicher's actions at this juncture is that during Hindenburg's absence he met with Hitler and though Brüning was still in office elaborated a program for a new government—withdrawal of the decree prohibiting the SA and SS and dissolution of the Reichstag in return for temporary National Socialist tolerance of the new government—and that on May 26 he sent for Papen by telegram and conferred with him on May 28. Schleicher proceeded as if the President had charged him with forming a new government. Quite possibly Schleicher had heard from Neudeck that Hindenburg was inclined, or at least not unwilling, to drop Brüning; but it is very unlikely that he had received any direct instructions. Schleicher seems to have figured that Hindenburg would agree to dismiss Brüning only if a successor were in readiness. He was determined to find such a successor quickly for fear that Hindenburg, after having been carefully prepared in Neudeck for Brüning's fall, might on his return to Berlin be subjected to new impressions that would lead him to change his mind again. Besides it was necessary to take Brüning by surprise.

Schleicher's aim was a government broadened on the right but still including the Center. Accordingly his choice fell on a man belonging, if only in a formal sense, to the Center. He knew that Papen was in contact with Kaas, the president of the Center Party, whose role in this situation is still obscure, but he very much underestimated the political value of the connection. Another advantage of Papen was his unexceptionable antidemocratic attitude, which was close to that of the German Nationalists. Schleicher had known Papen since they had met as students at General Staff school, so that Papen fitted into Schleicher's system of personal connections. François-Poncet's* observation in his memoirs that Papen was taken seriously neither by his friends nor by his enemies faithfully reflects the opinion of Papen held by those who had heard of him before he became Chancellor. Whether Schleicher vastly overestimated Papen's qualifications for the job, or whether he was aware of his incompetence and proposed him precisely because he wanted a convenient straw man—in either case his choice was childish and irresponsible. Even Schleicher's close military associates, who were at great pains to defend him after 1945, could find no word of justification for his proposal of Papen.

In a technical sense Schleicher had again done excellent work—but only in a technical sense. Since a replacement for Brüning had to be produced and also quickly accepted, Schleicher exchanged the precious diamond ring that had ceased to suit him for an imitation made of glass and tin but which seemed to fit. The aged Hindenburg, who despite his holiday had entered on a period of particular apathy, was no match for Schleicher's conjuring tricks.

No less irresponsible was Schleicher's secret pact with Hitler, to whom he made important concessions: withdrawal of the prohibition of the SA and SS, and the immediate dissolution of the Reichstag. By provoking new elections, he gave the National Socialists an opportunity for dynamic action through electoral propaganda, in which they were superior to all other parties. Probably Schleicher regarded his agreement with Hitler, like his proposal of Papen, as a mere incidental. His central purpose was to create the conditions for Brüning's dismissal and to force this step on Hindenburg.

---

* André François-Poncet, French Ambassador to Berlin from 1932 to 1938, whose widely quoted memoirs, *The Fateful Years,* are a prime source on the period.

Schleicher wanted a strongly rightist government; but what he wished to gain by it is unknown. His technical arrangements for the formation of the new government were flawless, so that Papen had hardly to turn a finger. But at his two meetings with Papen on May 28 and 30, Schleicher scarcely mentioned a government program. He had no over-all conception. He was interested in the Reichswehr, he wanted to tame the NSDAP. At first he had the idea of removing the SA and SS from Hitler's control by combining them with other paramilitary formations (the Stahlhelm and the Reichsbanner) to form a politically neutral militia subordinated to the Reichswehr. But he gave no thought to the effect such a militia would have on the military structure as a whole. Later as Chancellor he tried to split the NSDAP by including Strasser* in his government, but took no account of the political content of such a government. A master of political tactics, Schleicher lacked political substance.

Schleicher's qualities were those of an assistant to the leadership. He had proved useful as an aide *"in politicis"* as long as he had obeyed orders and acted under strict supervision. He had isolated himself by his break with Brüning and Groener and proved a total failure when he began to engage in politics on his own. His tricks and intrigues, his disruptive anti-institutional behavior, his unscrupulous exploitation of the senile Hindenburg, did not serve an over-all conception. There was no carefully thought-out general plan that might have made his tactical capers pardonable.

Unsustained by ideas, Schleicher's ingenuity did not take him very far; Papen, who was tactically his equal and in dealing with Hindenburg his superior, used his own methods against him. In Schleicher's system of political connections Papen became a Trojan horse. At the end of his career Schleicher was isolated by his former accom-

* Gregor Strasser, leader of the revolutionary wing of the Nazi movement who was murdered during the Roehm affair.

plices Meissner and Oskar von Hindenburg, who had helped him to isolate Brüning and Groener.

When Schleicher became Chancellor and his negotiations to secure a new political base for the government had broken down, the only possibility open to him was a *coup d'état*. He was probably the only chancellor who, if Hindenburg had given him a free hand, could have prevented Hitler's seizure of power. But by his constant political manipulations he had lost all personal credit with Hindenburg, and with the Center and the Social Democrats as well. Those he had used to overthrow Brüning now overthrew him. He had corrected his mistakes with new mistakes until he himself fell a victim to them.

*   *

While Schleicher was doing skillful staff work and undermining the Brüning fortress until it was ready to be stormed, Brüning did nothing to defend himself. Brüning was later criticized for not having appealed to parliament. In all probability such an appeal was not constitutionally admissible, because Hindenburg had not formally dismissed him but had only forced him to resign by setting unacceptable conditions. After Hindenburg's re-election Brüning does not seem to have made any serious attempt to discuss the central political issues with him. He was convinced that his policy responded to the President's fundamental principles—cessation of reparations payments, Germany's equal right to armament—and expected that the President would tolerate, and as far as necessary approve, his carefully planned measures to attain these main aims. Brüning's policy had not changed since the elections, but Hindenburg's attitude had been modified by the impression the elections had made on him. Hindenburg expected his Chancellor to make political concessions. Brüning's only essential concern was success at the reparations conference scheduled for June 1932. He had made painstaking preparations for it and consequently wished to avoid any secondary measures, even if desired by the President, that seemed likely to interfere with his great plan.

Engrossed in his work, Brüning could think of nothing but his strategic plan; Hindenburg was consumed with worry over the prestige of his office and rank. Was Brüning unaware of this contradiction? In any event he did nothing to relieve it. He accepted the breach in silence and did not make the slightest attempt to avert it. While abroad he enjoyed prestige unequaled by any German statesman since Stresemann, at home he made things very easy for his enemies. When on May 29 Hindenburg confronted him with unacceptable conditions, deliberately so framed as to provoke his resignation, his sole response was to announce his resignation. On the following day he tendered the resignation of his cabinet in an audience lasting three and a half minutes.

On the morning of May 29, according to his own account, Brüning had received from the American ambassador in person some information concerning the disarmament negotiations. This information, he tells us, was favorable to the interests of the Reich and of the utmost importance (though today this allegation is subject to controversy). He wished to communicate it to the President and probably entertained certain hopes as to its effect. But knowing of this information, Hindenburg's entourage allegedly postponed Brüning's appointment, originally scheduled for 10:30 A.M. until shortly before 12:00 in order that Hindenburg should be pressed for time. Brüning accepted the unwelcome postponement and did not ask to have the meeting put off until the afternoon.

In the critical years 1862 and 1863 Bismarck struggled with William I to combat the hostile influences of the Queen and Crown Prince. In October 1862, after the King had seen his wife and the Grand Duke of Baden, also hostile to Bismarck, in Baden-Baden, Bismarck had gone to meet William on his return journey to Jüterbog and, finding him browbeaten and beset with fears of revolution, had revived his spirits. He had accompanied the King from the Frankfort Congress of Princes to Karlsbad and Gastein to prevent him from being exposed unseconded to the influence of Emperor Francis Joseph. After the war of 1866 he had struggled hard and passionately with William in Nikolsburg over the peace conditions. There were no such struggles between Hindenburg and Brüning. Of course they should not be compared to William I and Bismarck, much as Brüning liked to invoke a parallel between the two old German chiefs of state. In contrast to Bismarck, Brüning lacked the passion for power.

Brüning was not vain, he was not very ambitious, but he had a certain inward arrogance about his opinions, combined with old-maidish priggery. He expected Hindenburg to show confidence in his policy and a certain understanding of his plans that had cost him such an inner struggle. He himself was so morally and intellectually trustworthy that, since he revered Hindenburg, he counted on his trustworthiness as a constant. The same fatalistic attitude led him to accept Hindenburg's mistrust. Brüning was a distinctly ascetic type—his only indulgence was cigar smoking—who did nothing for himself and consequently made no effort to win support for his policies. He was not a psychologist. He had no understanding of the feelings of others; they did not enter into his calculations. He thought in terms of policy, not of human beings. Perhaps it was respect for Hindenburg that deterred him from speaking to him—even in substance— as he had spoken to parliament on May 12: "Above all let us not grow soft in the last five minutes—not lose, in our internal affairs, the calm that is the absolute essential in the last hundred yards before the goal." It was not in his nature to exploit the feebleness of Hindenburg's old age, but he also failed to defend Hindenburg or himself against those who did exploit it.

Regardless of what one may think of his political orientation and policy, Brüning was a political strategist both in thought and action, but he lacked on the one hand the psychological talent that might have enabled him to win over the chief of state and the people to his policies and on the other hand the tactical ability to secure his political position. He probably suspected Schleicher's intrigues, but did nothing to combat them. He let Hindenburg go to Neudeck without binding him to anything and after Hindenburg's rebuff he could not bring himself to visit him in Neudeck at the risk of being not received. Brüning took no pains to preserve his power base, without which he could accomplish nothing on the strategic level. He did not take daily soundings and plot his position on the political waters; he did nothing to rectify his position when it had changed to his disadvantage or to defend it when it was under attack. He was wholly preoccupied by the rightness of his cause. But in politics might is at least as important as right, and in Brüning the ability to think and act in terms of power was underdeveloped. He was a statesman but not a politician. Standing above the parties, groups, and trends, he thought only of solving the crisis in the right way. The tragic figure of Brüning shows that even a statesman of the highest intellectual gifts and strictest ethics cannot succeed unless he is also a politician.

2

The Downfall of the
Old Social Democratic Party in 1933

ERICH MATTHIAS

The Weimar Republic's Social Democrats have been widely praised for their democratic bearing and devotion to parliamentary government. They have been equally criticized for their failure to radically transform German society in 1919 and prevent the fascist takeover in 1933. The party's position during the Weimar years has hardly been less paradoxical than the criticism to which it has been subjected. When Social Democracy reached the pinnacle of popular acclaim—approximately 45 percent of the vote in 1919—it was organizationally divided against itself into the majority Social Democratic Party and the antiwar Independent Social Democratic Party. Though it was the largest political organization in the country (until July 1932 when the National Socialists displaced it), it could never attain a governing majority position. While its rhetoric always retained revolutionary overtones, its practice was wholly devoid of extraparliamentary ventures and its best-known and most influential leaders—party chairmen Otto Wels, Hans Vogel, and Artur Crispien, editor in chief of the party paper Vorwärts Friedrich Stampfer, Reichstag President Paul Löbe, Prussian party leader and Prime Minister Otto Braun, Prussian and former Reich Minister of the Interior Carl

Severing, economic theorist and former Finance Minister Rudolf Hilferding, secretary of the parliamentary delegation Paul Hertz, foreign affairs specialist, parliamentary leader, and former Prussian Minister of the Interior Rudolf Breitscheid, et al.—were dyed-in-the-wool parliamentarians. Finally, when a stalemated parliament failed to come to grips with the nation's crisis, the Social Democratic leadership stood by immobilized. The republic was yielded to its enemies in a dizzying succession of elections:

March 13, 1932, for President.

April 10, 1932, runoff for President.

April 24, 1932, for the Diets of Prussia (territorially two-thirds of the Reich), Bavaria, Wurttemberg, Oldenburg, and Anhalt. With this election the National Socialists captured the leading position in all German Länder except Bavaria, where they trailed the Bavarian People's Party by two seats.

July 31, 1932, for the Reichstag.

November 6, 1932, for the Reichstag.

March 5, 1933, for the Reichstag.

The permanent structural crisis of the Weimar Republic, the resignation of the democrats and their inability to take a realistic view of the danger or of the methods employed by their totalitarian adversaries, are among the principal factors that made possible the victory of National Socialism. Under the republic the Social Democrats were the only political party to persist in unequivocal and uncompromising opposition to the rising National Socialists. But they were no less responsible than the enemies of the Weimar Republic for the weakness that was made manifest by the breakdown of the Great Coalition. Even though the task that the German Social Democratic Party had set itself in 1918 was difficult or perhaps even impossible in view of the wretched economic situation and the equally wretched situation of Germany in relation to foreign powers, the Social Democrats' revolutionary passivity and lack of initiative did not result exclusively from outward factors. It can be shown that in a changed world the leaders of the Social Democratic Party continued to derive their guiding principles from the limited ideas and experience of prewar Social Democracy. In 1918–1919 the Social Democrats' possibilities for action were limited far more by their own petrified conceptions than by the much invoked "unfavorable circumstances," and unless this is recognized it is not possible to arrive at a sound judgment of Social Democratic policy. The same holds true for the period when the republic was disintegrating. Despite changes in matters of detail, Social Democracy was unable throughout the Weimar period to throw off its tradition-bound rigidity. The sense of responsibility and willingness to make sacrifices that led the SPD to tolerate the Brüning cabinet won it few new sympathies. But its passive resignation, which made possible the overthrow of the Hermann Müller government and manifested itself still more clearly in the party's attitude toward the Papen *coup d'état* in Prussia,* contributed materially to removing the obstacles to a National Socialist seizure of power. After January 30, 1933,† resistance on the part of the SPD alone seemed hopeless. But the months from then until the time when the party was officially outlawed‡ throw a bright light on the causes underlying the tragic failure of the strongest and most coherent force for parliamentary democracy in Germany. In this picture certain specific traits of Social Democratic behavior explainable only in terms of party history combine with features typifying the reaction of a liberal, democratic mass party to the assault of a totalitarian movement which, once it enters into the

---

* July 20, 1932, when Chancellor Franz von Papen removed the Prussian caretaker government headed by Otto Braun from office by means of an emergency decree.

† Hitler's accession to the chancellorship.

‡ June 22, 1933.

government, proceeds to subject the whole life of the nation to its control.[1] In calling attention to the notorious incapacity of the forces of the liberal, democratic era to combat their totalitarian adversaries, the present investigation deals with a problem that political science cannot disregard at a time and in a place of imperiled democracy.

The Will to Resist

It is difficult to estimate the strength of the will to resist among the Social Democrats in the period when the National Socialists were seizing power. The Social Democratic Party leadership remained passive and spontaneous actions were rare, but this is not the whole story. To gain a more accurate picture, we must consider the fluctuations of mood within the SPD after the elections of September 14, 1930.

It is true that the alarming increase in the National Socialist vote did not bring about any decisive change in Social Democratic policy; the immediate reaction, however, was a strengthening rather than a weakening of the will to resist. Even the statement issued by the Social Democratic Reichstag delegation after the September elections took account, if only vaguely, of the mood that had made itself felt, at least among the party's younger following. "For the first time," writes Julius Leber,* "an intense dissatisfaction with their leadership was discernible in the ranks of the Social Democrats." A feeling that the traditional parliamentary methods were inadequate became more and more widespread; and while the party continued to revolve "in the circle of its own indecision," [2] young activists poured into the streets to show the National Socialist

* Social Democratic Reichstag deputy and leader in Lübeck; one of the party's young activist-pragmatists; imprisoned 1933–1937, active in the resistance, arrested in connection with the 1944 generals' plot and executed.

soldiers of civil war that they were ready to defend the republic.

As early as February 1931 the "Defense Formations" (Schutzformationen), a militant elite troop of the officially suprapartisan and democratic Reichsbanner, were organized, and on November 16 of the same year delegates of the SPD, of the free trade unions,* and of the workers' sports organizations announced the formation of the "Iron Front," led by Karl Höltermann, president of the Reichsbannerbund, as a direct answer to the "Harzburg Front" of the antirepublican right.

There can be no doubt that new impulses were surging up from below. As Leber testifies, the Social Democratic Party leadership was not very enthusiastic about the "new invention"; but the idea of the Iron Front moved the "nameless masses of Bebel's old party . . . as a half-forgotten battle signal moves a body of men accustomed to fight and win." [3]

In his account of the Weimar period Stampfer also records the animation and encouragement produced by the Iron Front, but he speaks of it in the disabused tone of one who "knows" that in the event of civil war no amount of enthusiasm on the part of the mobilized masses can alter the fact that "everything hinges on the decision of the regular armed forces." [4] In Stampfer's view we undoubtedly find a fair share of the sober resignation and profit-and-loss accounting which were responsible for the decision of the Social Democratic Party leadership not to resist Papen's *coup d'état* of July 20, 1932.

Even if the republican "fortress" of Prussia could not have been held, this decision was disastrous. Karl Dietrich Bracher, to whom we owe a penetrating investigation of

---

* The German trade unions were grouped into the Free or Socialist unions, the liberal Hirsch-Dunker unions which supported the Democratic Party, and the Christian unions which had close ties to the Center. The Free Trade Unions were composed of three federations representing respectively manual workers, salaried white-collar employees, and civil servants.

the events surrounding July 20, comes to the conclusion
that apart from the psychological inhibitions of the republican leadership the objective considerations which
stood in the way of concrete resistance were serious but
not politically compelling or convincing. His political
analysis confirms Leber's statement of June 1933 to the
effect that July 20, 1932, "had laid bare the whole inner
weakness and indecision of the Weimar front" and prepared the way for January 30, 1933.[5]

The action against the Prussian government was not
unexpected. On July 16, at Severing's suggestion, the executive committee* of the SPD had taken up the question
of resistance and had decided unanimously "not to depart
from the juridical foundations of the Constitution regardless of what may happen." [6] It seems rather strange that
the same Otto Wels who along with Severing, Vogel,
Breitscheid, Crispien, Hilferding, and Stampfer had
signed his name to this decision felt that a "world had
collapsed" when a few days later the trade-union leadership voted against responding to the *coup d'état* with a
general strike; and yet this inconsistency is quite typical
of the Social Democratic leadership's divided state of
mind and incapacity for decision.

The optimism and reviving self-confidence of the Socialist membership, which had derived a deceptive sense
of strength from the imposing mass meetings and parades
of the Iron Front, led the party leadership to toy with the
idea of resistance; but at the decisive moment the misgivings of these responsible Social Democratic believers in
Realpolitik won out. Matured in a party hierarchy that
for decades had sidestepped all risks, imbued with a panic
fear of "experiments," "averse to bloodshed" by reason of
their humanitarian tradition, they postponed action and
instructed their supporters to wait until the impending
Reichstag elections. The possibility of appealing in the

* The *Parteivorstand,* elected by the party congress and consisting in
part of full-time, paid officers of the party.

old, accustomed way to the power of the ballot seemed to the party leadership the ideal solution to the dilemma. Accordingly, they called upon their supporters to do nothing that might interfere with the elections. And in the same spirit the trade-union leadership argued very questionably that a good general does not let the enemy impose the moment of action.

Wheeler-Bennett's contention that the Social Democrats were prepared "to call a general strike at once and meet force with force even at the risk of a civil war," and that they were only prevented from doing so by the trade-union leadership,[7] is a legend, though one can easily understand why such a legend should have arisen. For it is certain that on July 20, in a situation of general panic and confusion, every conceivable possibility was discussed theoretically among the party and trade-union leaderships, only to be rejected. This gave rise to an atmosphere that a seemingly well-informed observer describes as follows: "Everyone is in favor if the other fellow is in favor. Consequently everybody—and nobody—is in favor." [8] It is true that the unions were very reserved; but the inherently sound view that the situation was not comparable to that prevailing at the time of the Kapp putsch* became an obsession with the party leadership as well, and paralyzed all activity. And the party as well as the union leadership justified its passivity by pointing to the economic situation and mass unemployment which created the worst possible conditions for a general strike, to the attitude of the Reichswehr, and to the impossibility of joint action with the Communists. Whatever tensions there may have been between party and trade-union leaderships, they had no effect on the course of events and are therefore without relevance for historical judgment.

---

* Attempt on March 3, 1920, by the antirepublican right under the leadership of bureaucrat Wolfgang Kapp and General Walther von Lüttwitz to overthrow the government. The putsch was foiled by the calling of a successful general strike.

As is shown indirectly by the attempts at appeasement made by the party's leading organs and press, the masses of the Iron Front were extremely agitated. In all probability spontaneous actions were prevented only by the Social Democratic habit of discipline. As Severing tells us, Otto Wels, on questioning the leading functionaries of the unions, the party, and the Reichsbanner "immediately after July 20," found a general opposition to active resistance.[9] But this does not prove very much. To form an accurate opinion of the will to resist at that time it would have been necessary to determine to what extent the rank and file of the Iron Front were ready and willing to fight and make sacrifices.

To obtain a reliable picture of the preparedness and training of the Reichsbanner formations it would be necessary to question a large number of persons. Undoubtedly they, particularly the "Defense Formations," had been trained more or less intensively in "military sports." [10] The leadership of the Reichsbanner, however, had always refused to arm its members, holding it to be unnecessary, because "our police" was armed. Where members had obtained arms on their own initiative, chiefly pistols, they were supposed to serve for self-defense and for the protection of party and trade-union buildings.

At the urging of a few young members, including Fritz Heine and Alfred Nau, today [1956] members of the party's executive committee, the party leadership also made limited preparations for resistance. In the event that the *Vorwärts* building should be occupied, a radio network was set up between autumn 1931 and spring 1932. Covering all thirty-three district organizations of the party, it was designed to maintain communications between the leadership and the organizations throughout the country. At about the same time an armed self-defense organization was set up to defend the central headquarters of the party; as Heine recollects, it comprised some hundred members for whom rifles, machine guns, tommy guns, and pistols were obtained in the course of adventurous trips to Suhl. In case of an attack or attempted putsch, it was held, the organization was well enough armed to hold the building until the police arrived; here again the party reckoned as a matter of course with a functioning republican police. These defense troops were recruited partly from among the younger party employees and partly from the Berlin Reichsbanner. Particularly active were the two student companies of the Berlin universities who, harking back to Vienna, 1848, called themselves the "Academic Legion." In the winter of 1931–1932 they had undergone thorough training in jujitsu, street fighting, and pistol marksmanship under the direction of police officers.

When on the first day of the presidential elections a National Socialist march on Berlin was expected, some 150 armed men including Reichsbanner students stood ready to defend the *Vorwärts*. On July 20 the leaders of the Academic Legion, probably without orders from above, prepared their shock troops to storm the Prussian Ministry of the Interior and the Berlin radio building. Burning to attack, the students were only waiting for the general strike to be proclaimed. But nothing happened. At about 8:00 P.M. they left their positions and the action petered out.[11]

There can be no doubt that these young men were willing to give their lives for the republic. Nor does the argument that they were only a relatively few students with romantic ideas hold water. In the Magdeburg district, for example, the picture was very much the same as in Berlin. Here the regional party organization had begun on its own initiative to build up a defense organization in the spring of 1932; its effectiveness had been tested by practice alarms. At about 2:30 A.M. on July 21, when orders came from the executive committee in Berlin to abandon all resistance and to disalert the organizations, "men,

women, and young people who had taken their posts in
response to the summons . . . obeyed the order in tears
and with extreme indignation." [12]

So relatively high a degree of preparedness as in
Magdeburg, an old Social Democratic bastion, was assuredly the exception rather than the rule. But despite the
shortage or absence of arms and despite considerable local
and regional differences, the militant elite formations of
the Reichsbanner can quite legitimately be termed a nucleus of resistance. They really wanted to be something
more than "orderly squads" and in the decisive hours they
were present at their assembly points, waiting for a call
from the leadership.[13]

The possibility that in a situation of civil war the Iron
Front would have stood fast around its militant nucleus
cannot be dismissed out of hand. But there were two pre-
requisites: responding to the general indignation, the
party and trade-union leaderships would have had to
make a quick and unequivocal decision, and the Prussian
police, whose loyalty was never put to the test, would have
had to side with the Iron Front. Even more crucial than
the attitude of the leading functionaries was that of Braun
—who after the *Landtag* elections of April 24 had succumbed to utter resignation—and of Severing. These two
were generally looked upon as the strong men of the
party. The justification they offered after the event—that
neither the battle for the "reinstatement of a caretaker
ministry" [14] nor protest against a "decree issued by the
President" [15] was a cause such as to fire men with enthusiasm—would not have met with much understanding
amid the then prevailing excitement. Even the older Social Democrats looked up to them as the acknowledged
leaders in the struggle to defend the republic; no one suspected these tried Social Democratic statesmen of having
become "political bureaucrats." [16] However unfavorably
the party and union leaderships judged the prospects for
the success of a general strike, the voices of Braun and

Severing could not have failed to influence the prudent and disciplined Social Democratic factory workers.

All in all, it was possible to conceive of an impressive show of resistance that would have put the President and the Reichswehr with their dread of civil war in a different position. To proclaim a state of emergency as a precautionary measure is one thing, to take the responsibility for a massacre is another. Moreover, it was contrary to the policy of the Reichswehr leadership "to endanger the military preparedness of their instrument by political commitment." [17] This fundamental political line was largely responsible for Schleicher's attempts to arrive at a compromise with the NSDAP. It seems reasonable to suppose that in supporting the Prussian *coup d'état* he was motivated by the calculation that the left would probably be unwilling to assume full responsibility for a civil war and that consequently it would suffice to use the Reichswehr "as a threat and instrument of pressure" [18] without forcing it openly to abandon its (largely fictitious) "suprapartisanship." But in view of this attitude of the Reichswehr leadership an unexpectedly resolute demonstration of the left's readiness for civil war—a demonstration to which the cadres and not only the leadership of the Iron Front were not averse—might, despite the unquestionable military superiority of the Reichswehr, have played a decisive role in the political struggle. Moreover, open civil war might have compelled not only the Communists and the radical left-wing elements who were repelled by the passivity of the SPD, but also the governments of the South German *Länder* and the hesitant, passively waiting, or indifferent elements of the Center and of the bourgeois moderate parties to make a clear-cut decision.

Speculations of this kind ill become a historian but they are indispensable in judging a situation in which political imponderables were no less important than the force of arms. What eliminated the SPD as a political fac-

tor to be taken seriously was the resignation of its leadership and their patent demonstration on July 20, 1932,
that they lacked the will to resist. It is also characteristic
of the mentality of the Social Democratic leadership that
a secret fear of the consequences of an improbable victory
seems to have contributed to their indecision. In their
scheme of things a struggle for power outside the accustomed parliamentary channels held no legitimate place,
although the political possibilities of a bold decision to
resist would by no means have been exhausted by the alternative of victory or defeat.

Here we are dealing in hypotheses, but this much is
certain: on July 20 the last chance of extending the base
of republican resistance to the right and left was lost; and
a total failure could not have been more disastrous than
the political and psychological effects of inactivity.

July 20 struck the Iron Front at its most sensitive
point: it shook the naive trust of its members and so undermined its inner strength. At first the change of mood
was to some extent countered by the excitement of the
election campaign with its mass meetings, and "thanks to
discipline and tradition" [19] the Social Democratic vote remained relatively high from the July elections to March
1933. But large sections of the party were overcome by
fatalistic resignation, "mirror-image of the leadership's
passivity." [20]

More than ever before the SPD was isolated. It was able
to derive no benefit from the unquestionable (though not
yet fully understood) signs of disintegration* which became discernible in the National Socialist camp in the fall
of that year, although, if the Social Democrats had appraised the situation clearly, the possibilities of even exerting an effective influence in parliament were by no
means exhausted. The activities of the Iron Front served
mainly to reassure its own members; it was no longer

---

* The party's conflict with its revolutionary wing and the loss of two
million votes between the elections of July 1932 and November 1932.

possible to recruit new support on the strength of purely defensive slogans. True, the fact that the Social Democratic "organization," the strength of which had for many years been very much overestimated, still held together prevented panic from seizing upon the leadership or the members. A good many of the leaders failed to grasp the implications of the decision of July 20. Leipart,* the trade-union chairman, and Hans Vogel, the deputy chairman of the party, are quoted as remarking in the course of the ensuing period that they had only to press the button in order to set the mechanism of resistance in motion. Thus the last defenders of the written constitution and of the parliamentary system that had abdicated long since clung with seeming equanimity to their positions on the island of Social Democratic tradition. When they looked with resignation at the flood of events rushing by them and threatening to engulf their island, they found consolation in the thought that their companions were still at their posts and had no intention of deserting.

It must be attributed to the unquestioning loyalty of its members that despite the more or less open crisis of confidence provoked by July 20 the Iron Front's power to resist had not yet been sapped entirely. The elite formations of the Reichsbanner especially distinguished themselves to the end by a stubborn determination to resist, although many of their members had come to feel that they were fighting for a lost cause. Undoubtedly the relations between the Reichsbanner and the party leadership continued to be very strained; but the Reichsbanner was still unable to free itself from its inner dependence on the party's leadership.

Preparations for resistance were continued and probably intensified, but they remained inadequate and followed no plan. That much can be said despite the meager-

---

* Theodor Leipart, chairman of the workers' section of the Free Trade Unions, the General Federation of German Trade Unions (ADGB—Allgemeiner Deutscher Gewerkschaftsbund).

ness of our sources. Stampfer recalls that the members of the party's executive committee had arranged meeting places in the event that party headquarters should be occupied after July 20.[21] In the summer of 1932 the first arrangements for illegal party activity were made; we shall have more to say of this later on. Toward the turn of the year some of the younger members of the party headquarters staff organized two undercover emergency offices in Berlin.[22] Reichsbanner leader Höltermann tried, apparently without great success, to obtain arms. Some of the provincial Reichsbanner formations that attempted to stock weapons on their own hook met with firm opposition from the local party leadership, and the initiators of this illegal activity were threatened with expulsion from the party. It seems certain that in the period from July 20 to the National Socialist seizure of power the trade-union leadership drew up instructions to be followed in case of a general strike, but we have no reliable information about their nature and scope.

These few stones do not add up to a mosaic. But more important than the details, still largely unknown to us, of the fragmentary and unsystematic technical preparations for resistance is the psychological situation which on January 30 kindled what was left of the will to resist and fanned it to a blaze. Those activists of the Iron Front who had remained faithful had taken at their face value the rhetorical swashbuckling, in part based on honest self-delusion, of the leading functionaries who, while pursuing their strictly legal and attentist course, had time and time again brandished the ultimate weapons of a general strike and organized resistance. The institutionalist belief of the leaders that the Nazis' "undisciplined bands" would never be able to overpower the "solidly built organization of the historical German working-class party," [23] was interpreted not as a justification for inactivity but as a summons to activity. The Reichsbanner formations had little taste for sage predictions that everything would come out all right if the working-class organizations continued to stand at order arms, or for prudent calculations of the risks involved in extraparliamentary action. On July 20 they had submitted to discipline with murder in their hearts; now they were saturated with bitterness. To their way of thinking the leadership had been discussing and protesting far too long. When Hitler was appointed Chancellor, their tempers were at white heat. They clamored to do something at last, even if their action proved unsuccessful.

The clamor was so loud that the party and trade-union leaderships could not disregard it. On January 30 and 31 functionaries from all over Germany were in Berlin. On January 31 a meeting of the federal council of the General Federation of German Trade Unions [ADGB—Allgemeiner Deutscher Gewerkschaftsbund] was held, and the SPD's party council,* executive committee, and Reichstag delegation met with representatives of the Iron Front organizations. The official communiqués give only a fragmentary picture of these meetings. It seems certain, however, that many of the regional leaders returned to their districts with the unmistakable impression that the top functionaries were firmly resolved to give the signal for a concerted action and were only waiting for the propitious moment.[24]

Feverish preparations were made for this moment. Despite the inspections on the highways weapons were brought in from Suhl and Zella-Mehlis through February and even in the first days of March. Of course these shipments of arms were a drop in the bucket, insufficient to equip an effective army. But they proved that the will to resist was no laughing matter. There were men who kept their clothes on all night because they expected an uprising at any moment. Time and time again the cadres met and racked their brains trying to figure out why the

* The *Parteiausschuss*, an advisory body to the executive committee, composed of representatives of the regional and local party units.

leadership was still hesitating. The reports of the February demonstrations also bear witness to this last marshaling of the will to resist. There were many who still derived strength from their faith in the working-class organizations whose power seemed demonstrated by the huge crowds that gathered in response to the call of their leaders.

Especially in Prussia, where Goering was now Minister of the Interior, the National Socialists increasingly employed the instruments of state power in the service of terror and propaganda. In the first days of February the government had begun to suppress newspapers; in the second half of the month it became more and more difficult to hold meetings. All this was bound to affect the mood of the Social Democrats. A feeling of helplessness and disillusionment spread through the Iron Front and began to paralyze its will to resist; and, "as the National Socialist terror, under the protection and direction of the government, increased . . . the 'health of the membership' became the main preoccupation of more and more of the party's leaders and parliamentarians." [25] Nevertheless it is reported that only a few days before the Reichstag fire, Hans Vogel was still advocating an uprising of the Social Democratic masses;[26] and as late as February 27, Reichsbanner leader Höltermann, at a conference of the Iron Front in Munich, urged the necessity of procuring arms.[27]

A few hours later the Reichstag was burning and the psychological basis for mass action was destroyed for good. Civil rights were largely abrogated by the President's decree of February 28, "For the Defense of Nation and State"; and in the last days of the election campaign National Socialist terror raged unhindered. In the South German *Länder* the SPD retained a certain freedom of movement for a brief transitional period. But the will to resist, already gravely shaken at the end of February, now dwindled to next to nothing. With the National Socialist seizure of power in Bavaria, which completed the *Gleich-schaltung* ("integration") of the south, it vanished entirely.

Relations with the Communist Party

Nearly all Social Democratic writers on this period put the entire blame for the downfall of the German working-class movement on the KPD, [Kommunistiche Partei Deutschlands—Communist Party of Germany] which indeed, even after the National Socialist seizure of power, persisted in the belief that the "social fascist" Social Democracy was the main enemy. What is overlooked in this emotion-colored view is that the passivity of the Social Democratic leadership had a good deal to do with driving the desperate unemployed into the arms of the KPD, which almost doubled its membership between 1928 and 1932. In contrast, however, to the purely declamatory Communist appeals for a "united front," whose purpose was to disrupt the SPD, on the Social Democratic side serious efforts were made, beginning at the end of 1931, to improve relations with the Communists. These efforts, advocated in the executive committee of the SPD chiefly by Rudolf Breitscheid and Friedrich Stampfer, were summed up by Stampfer in *Neuer Vorwärts* at the end of 1933; he also speaks of them in his book on the Weimar period.

The first step was a speech delivered by Breitscheid in November 1931, to which Stampfer's *Vorwärts* lent enthusiastic support. Unwilling to sacrifice their democratic creed for the sake of the Communists, Stampfer and Breitscheid dismissed in advance the idea of a complete union between the two parties. But since to their minds the only way to prevent a victory of the National Socialists was to put an end to the cleavage in the German working-class movement, they pursued the limited aim of a defensive alliance, "a cooperation between equal parties for the defense of workers' rights," [28] which should replace the "suicidal tactic of struggle" [29] between the two parties. In the interest of this aim the *Vorwärts* abstained from all attacks on the Soviet Union and moderated its anti-Communist polemics. "Nor did it neglect to praise the Communist workers' idealism and spirit of sacrifice or on every possible occasion to point out the necessity of joint action against the common enemy." [30] The high point in this campaign was an impressive article by Stampfer in the *Vorwärts* for January 26, 1933, about a Communist demonstration on Bulöwplatz. A few days later, at a session of the party council on January 31, Breitscheid expressed the wish that the "new phase of struggle against fascism," inaugurated by Hitler's appointment as Chancellor, "might also usher in a new phase in the relations between the Social Democracy and the Communists." But this, he added, would be possible only if the Communists modified their attitude toward democracy and parliament.[31]

The speeches and articles of Breitscheid and Stampfer served to prepare the way for and support another initiative which deserves to be taken much more seriously and which, to my knowledge, was the only realistic move made toward a reconciliation between the Social Democrats and the Communists. Convinced that direct negotiations with the Moscow-dominated Communist Party leadership were pointless, Stampfer—with no mandate but with the knowledge of the executive committee—entered into contact with the Soviet embassy in Berlin. After introductory talks with Ambassador Leo Khinchuk he met several times in the course of the ensuing months with Vinogradov, first secretary of the Soviet legation.[32] Vinogradov, so it seemed to Stampfer, listened to his arguments politely and even with interest, but at their last meeting, a few days before the Reichstag fire, gave him plainly to understand that Moscow was reckoning with

German fascism as an inevitable transitional stage. The leaders of the KPD heard—how we do not know—that the talks had been broken off; and to Stampfer's surprise Doctor Neubauer* sent him word on February 27 that he and his friends wished to speak with him. A meeting with Neubauer and Torgler,† arranged for Tuesday, February 28, in the Reichstag building, was prevented by the Reichstag fire, which also ended all hope that the two large German working-class parties would reach a tactical agreement at the last minute.[33] In view of the Social Democrats' distrust and of the Communist leadership's lack of independence the prospects of such an agreement had been poor to begin with. Thus it is unlikely that the talks between Stampfer and the Soviet legation had the slightest effect on the attentist attitude of the Social Democratic leadership in February, although the Social Democratic and Communist workers were increasingly willing to cooperate. It is interesting to note that in mid-February even *Die Gewerkschaft* (The Trade Union), organ of the public employees' trade union, published an editorial headlined "The General Federation of German Trade Unions, the Social Democratic Party of Germany, and the Communist Party must join forces." [34]

The "Lie-Still" Policy

On January 30, 1933, the Social Democratic leaders faced a far more difficult decision than on July 20 of the preceding year. They could hardly hope that the National Socialist takeover of the government could be reversed by open resistance on the part of the isolated Social Demo-

---

* Theodore Neubauer, Communist Reichstag deputy; executed in February 1945 for resistance activity in Thuringia.
† Ernst Torgler, parliamentary chairman of the German Communist Party.

cratic masses. If they were reluctant to send their followers into a hopeless battle, their humanitarian motives are
deserving of respect.

Nevertheless it seems possible to hold that "the particularly demoralizing consequences of a collapse without a
fight" [35] might still have been averted. But in the discussions that took place at the time this consideration was not
taken into account. Nor did anyone ask whether a spontaneous action solely of the left immediately after January
30—a possibility for which the Reichswehr had made no
provision but which might under certain circumstances
have provoked a military state of emergency and so withdrawn command of the Prussian police from Goering
—might not have interfered with the National Socialists'
plans. Hitler was just at the beginning of his government
career. His appointment had produced a shock effect;
however, he had not become Chancellor through a *coup
d'état,* but "legally" on the strength of a constitution that
had lost its meaning, and the decisive steps toward his seizure of exclusive power were first made possible by the
Reichstag fire. The Social Democratic leadership did indeed envisage a protracted period of reaction, but was far
too much inclined to minimize this impending period as
an "episode" in the history of German democracy; for the
party they expected at the worst "a repetition of [Bis-
marck's] Anti-Socialist Law."

Yet there is no reason to doubt the subjective sincerity
of the will to resist evinced up to the last days of February
by some of the party's leading functionaries. Members of
the party leadership were faced with an inner conflict,
and it was only the Reichstag fire that ended a dilemma to
which they were unequal. Yet throughout these weeks of
indecision they deluded themselves in the thought that
they still held the initiative. As we analyze the situation
today, we find this "lie-still" policy foreshadowed in the
party's official statements of January 30 and 31.

The leading editorial of the evening edition of *Vor-*

wärts for January 30: "In its attitude toward this government with its threat of a *coup d'état*, the Social Democracy and the Iron Front stand firmly *on the ground of the constitution and of legality.* They will not take the first step away from it . . ."; and on the same day the Reichstag delegation decided, "as a matter of course," [36] to enter a motion of no confidence in the Hitler government. Breitscheid's report of January 31 to the party council also remained within the customary framework of parliamentary thinking; on the one hand it postponed active resistance to a time (difficult to determine in view of the abnormal conditions created by the emergency decree and in view of the tacit change of system preceding it) when there would be a clear-cut breach of the constitution, while on the other hand it expressed doubt as to whether such a postponement served any practical purpose.[37] Many of Breitscheid's agitated listeners interpreted Breitscheid's speech as an expression of the will to resist because at that moment of spontaneous indignation they were not receptive to doubt. But he now proceeded to discredit his will to resist even further: "We have now entered on a phase of class struggle from above in its purest form," Breitscheid declared and continued with apodictic certainty: "The reaction has played its last card, thrown the hordes of fascist mercenaries into the battle. If that card does not take, and it will not take, the hour will have come for the working class to speak the decisive word. It alone can save the people. Against *this* decisive hour we must gather all our forces, so as to commit them as a unified body." [38]

Breitscheid did not count on the spontaneous will to action that rose up to him from the membership, but on economically determined "developments" that would straighten everything out. The jubilation of Hitler's supporters might soon enough turn to disgust when they discovered that the price of Hitler's "victory" was total dependence on big capital and the Junkers.[39] Basically the task of the working-class organization reduced itself to maintaining its presence and keeping its nerves under control. Any attempt to intervene in the developments would be a mistake.

At a meeting of the federal council of the ADGB on the same day, Leipart spoke in very similar terms:

> The German working class knows, not only by its experience of the last few years, but by its whole history as well, that a period of social progress can sometimes be followed by a reverse and indeed by the passing success of deliberate reaction. This experience will not destroy the membership's faith in the power and future of the trade-union organization; this faith will return also to those whom today economic hardship has alienated from our organization.[40]

Breitscheid's report was published under the characteristic title: "Readiness Is What Counts!" The official proclamations took the same tone. Leipart coined the formula: "Organization—not demonstration—is the watchword of the hour. The unions have acted in this spirit for many years. . . ."[41] He was speaking not only as a good trade unionist but as a good Social Democrat.

Thus from the very start apparent determination concealed the doctrine of inactivity, which enabled the rigid, perplexed, and scrupulous Social Democratic Party leadership to treat the National Socialist seizure of power as a routine minor crisis. Although it became more obvious each day that behind the scenes of the Harzburg Front coalition cabinet, in which to a superficial observer the NSDAP seemed the weaker partner, the National Socialists were preparing single-mindedly to take full power, the Social Democratic strategy remained unchanged. Despite the increasing terror, "their resistance . . . in accordance with the traditions of a fully legal party, was limited to propaganda and election campaigning"; and "in accordance with their tradition, they put the main accent on references to the *potential energy* of a mass party." [42] Such were the limitations which the Social Democracy never succeeded in overcoming.

This cannot be concealed by the strong words that were spoken in the first weeks of the election campaign when it was still possible to hold meetings with relatively little interference. Yet it is not always easy to distinguish the high-sounding rhetorical diversions behind which the Social Democratic leaders concealed their impotence, and which served as lightning rods for the excitement of the masses, from expressions of a genuine desire to resist. It seems characteristic that an election proclamation issued by the SPD on February 2 demanded "the expropriation of the large estates and the distribution of the land among the peasants and farm workers," "the expropriation of heavy industry" and the "construction of a socialist planned economy based on the satisfaction of needs." [43] In the party this proclamation was not mistakenly felt to be a "return to the Erfurt program." [44] * Political sterility led to a flight into tradition. The "official radicalism" of pre-war Social Democracy, which gave this basically quietistic party lacking both in the will to power and in clear aims so grim a look, had resurrected.

The most that the Social Democratic leadership could hope from the elections was an "antifascist majority," and it required no prophetic gifts to foresee that such a heterogeneous majority "was not likely to be capable of coherent operations in the right direction." [45] Groaning under the weight of their responsibility, the confused leaders put their hope in outside help. Here again in the last analysis they merely carried on mechanically their passive policy of the crisis years. Eagerly the party leadership gave itself up to the wave of illusions that flooded the whole country after January 30. Hopes were set in the conflicts

* Really a reference only to the Marxist theoretical section of the statement adopted by the party at its Erfurt Congress in 1891. The second part of the program dealt with perfectly ordinary democratic demands such as universal suffrage, the secularization of education, and free social services.

within the cabinet, in insuperable economic difficulties, in conflicts of interest between the unequal coalition partners, in the rivalry between the SA and the Stahl- helm, in the corrosion and disintegration of the NSDAP, in the Reichswehr, in Herr von Papen, in President Hin- denburg, and in the South German *Länder*. Although one after another of these illusory hopes was disappointed, some of them were very long-lived. They survived the Reichstag fire and the Enabling Act, played a central role in the last session of the Reichstag delegation on June 10, 1933,[46] after the official dissolution of the party exerted a determining influence on the Prague *émigré* executive committee's appraisal of the situation, and gave courage to those members of the illegal party who were counting on the imminent collapse of the Hit- ler regime.[47] These forlorn hopes were accompanied by expressions of the fatalistic trust in "developments" which we have already encountered in the statements of Breitscheid and Leipart and which as late as the Paris Congress of the Labor and Socialist International in Au- gust 1933 inspired Otto Wels's comforting declaration that in spite of everything Germany "would probably be the first country in Europe to see a socialist revolution." [48]

Despite the profound shock of the Reichstag fire which enabled the government to outlaw the KPD immediately and to deprive the SPD of all freedom of movement, the basic attitude of the Social Democratic leadership under- went no change in the coming months, except that the "lie-still" policy which in February had been to some ex- tent masked by the election campaign became patent in March and April. Nevertheless, despite terror, despite the repressive measures against the Social Democratic press and an intense slander campaign, the Socialist voters had continued, to the satisfaction of the party leadership, to present an almost unbroken front. The March 5 message to the party proclaimed as a goal "reconquest of the work- ers' freedom of movement" and at the same time appealed to the Court of Election Review which would be called upon to decide whether the elections had been "free." In general the party's statements continued to consist largely of appeals to the law and constitution. "Those gentlemen now have a majority in the Reich and in Prussia," runs a commentary on the election returns; "they have been appointed by the President and confirmed by the people. They need only be a legal government and it goes without saying that we shall be a legal opposition." [49] The same idea recurs in Wels's courageous speech to the Reichstag on March 23.

It will forever remain a proud page in the history of German Social Democracy that on that day the SPD was the only party that dared to vote against Hitler's Enabling Act and professed its unrestricted loyalty to the principles of the defunct parliamentary democracy and the constitution of the Weimar Republic. "The bourgeois middle-of-the-road parties put extreme pressure on the Social Democratic Reichstag delegation either to remain absent from the session or to abstain from voting. The rumor was deliberately spread that if the Social Democrats dared to vote no, they would all be arrested and deferred to the 'tribunal of the revolution.' " When the Social Democrats stuck to their guns, Otto Wels was "stormed by bourgeois advisers" who counseled him "to let a younger, less known comrade read the Social Democratic statement, because as the delegation's official spokesman he was putting himself in the greatest danger." [50] At the last minute a leader of the Center pleaded with Wels to abandon the idea of making a statement against the Enabling Act. The National Socialist terror extended even to the Reichstag. The Social Democratic parliamentary group was already weakened by the flight of a few especially endangered members and by arrests. On their way to the Reichstag two members of the delegation were arrested. Politically speaking, to be sure, the vote of the 94 Social Democrats present (out of 120), was no more than an impressive demonstration. It shows, however, that Otto Wels and those who shared his responsibility for the passivity and defensive policy of the party had the personal courage to stand up for their convictions, although their freedom of decision was far more restricted than that of the secret opponents of the Enabling Act in the other parties.[51]

If the Social Democratic leaders were right in supposing that the illegal situation was only temporary and that constitutional guarantees at least would soon be restored by an intervention of the Reichswehr in league with the German Nationalists, then to be sure the essential, in March and April, was "to keep the party intact and to avoid its being forced into illegality." [52]

Wishing to give the government no pretext for measures against the party, the leaders sought to adapt their course to the modified conditions to the extent that this "seemed compatible with personal dignity and the time-honored principles of the party." [53]

From this policy they expected great benefits, even that the Social Democratic press would be allowed to reappear. Löbe conferred with Goering about the reauthorization of the *Vorwärts*. Since Goering held the German Social Democrats responsible for the reports about Germany in the foreign socialist press and made it clear that reauthorization was out of the question as long as the press of the Socialist International continued to agitate against Germany, a number of leading Social Democrats, among them Stampfer and Hertz, went abroad with Goering's encouragement to see what influence they could exert on the foreign socialist parties. It was true that the foreign press had published some "really absurd sensational reports," [54] based on rumors and exaggerations. Stampfer and Hertz concur in saying[55] that the purpose of their travels was to provide faithful information about what was going on in Germany and that it was never their intention to deter anyone from telling the unvarnished truth or from carrying on an energetic press campaign against the Hitler regime.

As early as March 20 Otto Wels had phoned Friedrich Adler, secretary of the Labor and Socialist International [L&SI] to protest against certain false reports that had been propagated by the International along with accurate information. On April 30, after he had failed to block the publication of the decisions taken by the executive of the International in the absence of its German members, he phoned in his resignation from the bureau of the L&SI on April 30. The united-front resolution of the L&SI struck him as particularly dangerous.[56]

The suspicion of illegal conspiratorial activities struck the party leadership as no less dangerous than the misinterpretation of the party's international ties. Thus at the beginning of April the party leadership joined the executive committee of the party's Berlin section in severe measures against the leadership of the Berlin SAJ [Sozialistische Arbeiter-Jugend—Young Socialist Workers] who had already been converted to illegal activity.[57] Such measures which, as Otto Wels admitted a few weeks later, "were not only bound to shock our comrades abroad but also to be incomprehensible to the masses of workers in Germany, to whom we could no longer speak through our press," [58] added to the demoralization of a party now vegetating in a state of semilegality. Other factors contributing to this effect were disillusionment over the absence of resistance, steadily mounting personal fear in view of the murders and tortures that had become known, the "flight" of Otto Braun,* which was "the most effective stroke of National Socialist election propaganda" [59] to date, and the attitude of the unions which began in March to dissociate themselves from the party.

Despite the large Social Democratic vote in the Reichstag elections, the SPD had been disintegrating both or-

---

* Braun, convinced of the futility of further parliamentary activity, had simply emigrated to Switzerland.

ganizationally and morally since the beginning of March. In Berlin, party life had begun to ebb in February in consequence "of terror and disillusionment," and in March "even the contact between Berlin party headquarters and the functionaries of the local groups" was severed.[60] A detailed study should be devoted to the intermediate period of semilegality, which in Prussia began early in February with Goering's terrorist measures and spread to the rest of the country in March and April. On the one hand a conspiratorial atmosphere prevailed in the back rooms where the Social Democratic functionaries met, while on the other hand every effort was made, and not only in the executive committee, to demonstrate that the party had no thought of conspiratorial activity. The National Socialists, while leaving the tip of the party pyramid relatively unscathed, redoubled their efforts to undermine the party base by terror, slander, and threats that those who remained loyal to the party would lose their jobs.

Because of regional and local differences in the degree of terror and in the inner stability of the Social Democratic organization, the process of disintegration was very uneven, as was shown by the debate on the state of the organization at the party congress on April 26.[61] But this did not alter the over-all situation, which forced the leadership to conclude that short of a miracle the organization would soon be "shattered by outside forces." Nevertheless the congress decided to adhere to the old course and to go on exploiting the "existing legal possibilities." Accordingly, when a new executive committee was elected, most of the former leaders who had remained in Germany were confirmed in office, including Otto Wels as chairman and Hans Vogel as deputy chairman. However, in order that all tendencies should be represented in the worst crisis that had ever struck the party, representatives of the left wing and of the younger generation were also elected.

Though in the first months after the National Socialist

seizure of power the policy pursued by the Social Democrats was based on illusory calculations and was continued even after the legal organization that this policy was designed to preserve had become a virtual fiction, nevertheless the behavior of the leading functionaries as a whole showed a high degree of integrity and loyalty to their beliefs. This was also attested by the party congress at which, despite all their differences in other matters, old and young were united in the determination to maintain "ideological resistance . . . even under the most difficult circumstances." A policy of adaptation, such as that adopted by the unions, was definitely rejected.

The Defection of the Unions

Even before the First World War the SPD had lost its uncontested leadership over the Free Trade Unions, but despite differences of opinion the party and the unions had always managed to work out a common policy. Even in the years of economic crisis this had not changed. But neither the party nor the trade-union leadership could make decisions in a vacuum. Despite their different functions both were dependent on the confidence of the Social Democratic workers who formed the core of their organizations. This common sociological base made it impossible to play off the two organizations against each other as long as they were relatively intact. Either they acted in the same direction or, when their differences made joint action impossible, paralyzed each other.

Under the Schleicher government the leadership of the officially nonpartisan Free Trade Unions may have been dissatisfied with this state of mutual dependency. But at that time, even if they had wished, they could not have thrown off their informal tie with the Social Democratic Party, any more than the party could have disregarded the unions which represented its members' interests. Nevertheless, the union leaders never tired of stressing their "total independence"; they did not recognize the party's claim to leadership, insisted on their right to make their own decisions, and tolerated no interference.

Commenting on the refusal of the trade-union leadership to continue its negotiations with Schleicher in January 1933, Bracher writes: "Leipart obeyed the executive committee of his party." [62] This is inaccurate. Leipart's "obedience" had nothing to do with subordination. Far more important to him was the fact that the factory workers and the lesser trade-union functionaries would not have approved trade-union support of the Schleicher government. Toleration of the Brüning government had been a very different matter. As long as they agreed among themselves the leaders of the party and of the unions were able to carry out an unpopular policy. In the new situation the policy contemplated by the trade-union leadership again presupposed the full confidence of the workers in the two leaderships. Without the support of the party leadership, the trade-union leadership would be unable to resist the pressure from below, from the common sociological base. How strong this pressure must have been is shown indirectly by the speech, larded with impassioned denials, with which Leipart opened the conference of shop stewards of the ADGB and AFA-Bund [Allgemeiner Freier Angestelltenbund—General Federation of Free White-Collar Workers] in Berlin on January 22.[63]

The reaction of the trade-union leadership to the sudden appointment of Hitler as Chancellor was the same as that of the party leadership, and throughout February the official statements show no difference in attitude. To be sure, [ADGB deputy chairman] Grassmann's remarks at the federal council meeting of January 31 included an unequivocal warning to "*any* party that should arrogate to itself the right to direct trade-union actions." [64] But this sentence would have taken on its full meaning only if there had been greater willingness among the SPD leadership than among the top trade-union officials to call for resistance and proclaim a general strike.

The first signs of the unions' defection became apparent after the March 5 elections. Commenting on the outcome, the *Gewerkschaftszeitung* (Trade-Union Journal) wrote that after this "far-reaching decision" the unions must rely more than ever "on their own strength alone." "Losses in the political sphere have cost the German workers a good part of their influence on social developments; they must regain this influence by strengthening the unions." [65] Since this article appeared in the official organ of the ADGB, it seems permissible to infer that immediately after the elections serious discussions must have been devoted to Papen's warning of March 4: "If the trade unions recognize the trend of the times and depoliticize themselves in high degree, they can today become a powerful support of a new social order." [66]

The trade unions were persecuted as much as the party, and this no doubt hastened their change of attitude. The decisive step was taken on March 20 when the federal executive of the ADGB drew up a statement that amounted to an assurance of loyalty. Leipart sent it to Hitler the following day. In this statement the trade-union leadership dissociated itself from the SPD; the unions, it declared, must perform their social function "regardless of the type of regime"; they were "an indispensable component of the social order" which "in the course of their history had for natural reasons merged more and more with the state." Abandoning the democratic, socialist principles which until a few weeks before they had never wearied of professing,[67] the trade-union leaders began to mouth empty abstractions that were supposed to bridge the ideological gap between the past and present.

On April 5 members of the ADGB executive committee, including Leipart and Leuschner,* met with leading officials of the NSBO [Nationalsozialistische Betriebszellenorganisation—National Socialist Factory Cell Organization]. Though the results were discouraging, the ADGB council decided at a meeting held the same day to continue on the new course. On April 19 they decided that the unions would participate in the regime's May Day celebrations and a call to that effect went out to the membership.

The ideological accompaniment to the decisions of the leadership was provided by a number of articles in the trade-union press. Franz Grosse attempted to prove to the new rulers that it was not in their interest to follow the fascist example of suppressing the unions. "Only by taking into consideration the forces that have grown up on our own national foundations" could "the national government not only equal . . . but also surpass the foreign model." [68] Speaking "from a trade-union standpoint" Franz Josef Furtwängler [Director of the Academy of Labor] lauded the "unity of the Reich after three hundred years";[69] and Walter Pahl saluted the First of May as a "day of victory"; the working class, he declared, expected the government to draft a plan for the nationalization of all German industry; this "socialist act" would convince even those who were still aloof and skeptical.[70]

Even if such effusions are taken as a mere surface manifestation of the unions' struggle for survival, they leave an unpleasant taste. Considered in conjunction with the statements of the trade-union leadership, they suggest the emergence of a "national trade unionism" apparently willing to accept the loss of democracy in return for the benefits conferred by one consolidated state, one consolidated union, and the nationalization of the economy.

The union leaders, like those of the party, were concerned primarily with preserving their organization.

* Wilhelm Leuschner, who later became a prominent member of the resistance movement and was executed in 1944.

There is no reason to suppose that they did not sincerely believe they were safeguarding the workers' interests. Only the SPD's total impotence led them to abandon the ship that was threatening to capsize because it had lost its old equilibrium. It seems probable that few if any of them intended to let themselves be engulfed by the National Socialist state. But in their policy of adaptation they overstepped the limits that the Social Democratic leadership, despite all its concessions, observed to the bitter end. Nevertheless the SA occupied the trade-union houses on May 2 and the top functionaries were arrested.

The Conflict Between Berlin and Prague

When on May 4, immediately after the suppression of the unions, the SPD executive committee decided unanimously to send some of its members abroad, it was still hoped that this would be only a temporary measure. There was no thought of transferring the executive committee, and the leaders selected to go abroad were reluctant to leave. Edinger's contention that there were already at this time two conflicting groups in the executive committee, one headed by Löbe, the other by Stampfer, is untenable.[71] It was the vote of the Social Democratic Reichstag delegation on May 17 that first provoked a conflict between those members who remained in Berlin and those who had gone abroad and established a foreign bureau in Prague.

By that time the majority of the executive committee had left German territory. On May 10 the regime had confiscated the party's funds, but for the present no further measures were taken against the SPD. The breathing spell which the international difficulties of the Hitler dictatorship procured the party, and which lasted until mid-June, encouraged illusions as to the benefits of loyalty and reinforced those leaders who had remained in Germany

in the decision to persevere in their policy of appeasement and passivity. Consequently the Reichstag delegation was unwilling to accept the proposal of the majority of
the executive committee, which had met in Saarbrücken,
that the Social Democratic members of the Reichstag
should boycott the session of May 17.

Somewhat more than half the Social Democratic Reichstag members attended the May 16 and 17 caucus. Stampfer and Vogel, who had returned to Berlin from
Saarbrücken to prevent the Social Democrats from
approving Hitler's "peace resolution," were unable to put
through the proposal of the executive committee. At the
most, "a small group . . . were prepared for tactical reasons to confine themselves if necessary to silent acceptance
of Hitler's speech on foreign policy." But if it became
impossible for the delegation to make an independent
statement, the overwhelming majority seemed decided to
boycott the session.[72] It was the blackmailing threats of
murder made by Frick* at the Council of Elders† on May
17 that turned the tide. Of the sixty-five members of the
delegation present at the session, forty-eight voted for un-
motivated approval.[73]

The attitude of the delegation majority and of the leaders who had remained in Berlin is not explained solely by
fear for their lives and security; they believed that their
compliance might prevent a new wave of terror and new
acts of vengeance against those already in the concentration camps. And the moderate tenor of Hitler's speech,
due solely to the dangerous diplomatic isolation of the
National Socialist regime, led a number of Social Democratic Reichstag members to delude themselves with the
fiction of a continuity in German foreign policy from

* Wilhelm Frick, Reich and Prussian Minister of the Interior.
† Committee of the Reichstag comprising the Reichstag President and
the heads of parliamentary delegations, which decided the calendar, committee assignments, etc.

Stresemann and Hermann Müller to Adolf Hitler. The decision of May 17 split the party. The extreme limit of legal, parliamentary resistance had been attained on March 23. Now, on May 17, many felt that the "party had dishonored itself and . . . capitulated." [74] Yet the advocates of the "Löbe policy," upheld by the Berlin members of the party executive committee and by the larger parliamentary group, had no intention whatever of submitting to *Gleichschaltung.* They merely clung convulsively to the old form of struggle and to their old organizational traditions; their main purpose was to rally the fragments of the shattered party and keep them together. They hoped that the Reichstag and the provincial parliaments would remain in existence. Although parliamentary immunity had in many cases been violated, many Social Democratic parliamentarians, and especially Reichstag members, continued to hold that it was their duty to defend the interests of the party under cover of their immunity. This notion was also largely responsible for the delegation's original plan of May 16 to read a statement of its own at the Reichstag session.

They seem to have reasoned more or less as follows: Social Democratic approval of Hitler's policy would appease the regime; a statement by the Social Democratic parliamentary group would maintain or restore contact with their disillusioned supporters. Roughly the same ideas animated the *Landtag* delegations which well into June rejected the enabling acts of the various *Länder,* but in hopes of fair weather accompanied their rejection with appeasing statements. The minutes of the last meeting of the Reichstag delegation, held on June 10, impress us with the sincerity of the proponents of the Löbe policy; but they also point up the extraordinary illusions by which they were motivated and the confusion prevailing in the party. It is interesting to note that the only member of the delegation who spoke realistically of the situation and indulged in no illusions about the intentions of the National Socialists or the prospects of the "literally atomized" SPD was Kurt Schumacher.[75] *

The Löbe policy, whose proponents at least for the time being thought they detected a tendency toward moderation or even "normalization" in the regime's diplomatic diversion, was seriously hampered after May 17 by the activity of the members of the executive committee who had left the country and who up until then had exercised restraint. Unlike the Berlin members of the executive committee, they realized after the confiscation of the party's funds that "the period in which we could hope to save something by avoiding actions that might serve as a pretext for violent measures . . . is past." [76] Though little hope remained, they wished at long last to take steps to check the far-advanced disintegration and demoralization of the party; and, since May 17 had proved that in the Reich there was no longer the slightest possibility even of a protest action and that any attempt to represent the party legally must inevitably lead to new misinterpretations both at home and abroad, they decided to transfer the executive committee officially to Prague.

Thus, beginning in the second half of May, a conflict arose between the rump executive committee in Berlin and the *émigré* executive committee in Prague. Both had the best of intentions; both had very much the same illusions about the inner erosion of the regime. What separated them was essentially a difference not of opinions but of perspective. Men who only a few weeks or days before had worked together in friendship and confidence suddenly ceased to understand each other because one group was breathing the air of freedom and the other was not. All attempts to convince one another were in vain and the conflict became more and more acute. The two bodies were

* Reichstag deputy since 1930, placed on the party's executive committee in September 1932, from 1933 to 1945 off and on in concentration camps, chairman of the SPD from 1946 until his death in 1952.

driven apart in spite of themselves, and suddenly found themselves involved in a sordid struggle for influence and posts. Each group claimed to be the sole representative of the party. And quite apart from their objections to the *émigré* policy, the feeling of those who had stayed home that they were doing their duty in standing by their defeated and shattered troops lent the conflict an intense emotional note.

The conflict came to a climax on June 19 with the election of a new executive committee in Berlin which issued a declaration to the effect that the party declined all responsibility for statements made by the *émigrés*.[77] But the National Socialist leaders failed to appreciate such legalistic subtleties. By June 22 all SPD activity had been prohibited and the Social Democratic parliamentary mandates annulled. A new wave of terror was in full swing. The regime was building up to the blow which within a few weeks was to sweep away the whole party system.

The Beginnings of Illegality

In the early days of the Papen government Otto Wels decided to take steps toward the building of an illegal organization side by side with the official party. His plan does not seem to have been discussed at the meetings of the executive committee. Apparently on his own initiative, Wels—perhaps after privately consulting a few fellow committee members—approached a number of trustworthy functionaries throughout the country in June and July 1932. In view of the lack of written sources an extensive investigation would be required to determine exactly where the plan was favorably received and what came of it in each particular case. The document of the Hanover "Socialist Front" speaks of a "few large cities . . . where as early as the summer of 1932 action was taken on the executive committee's suggestion that illegal groups be

formed, comprising the most reliable and active functionaries, to carry on the work of the party if the legal party
apparatus should be prevented from functioning." [78] This
was demonstrably the case in Leipzig, Hanover, and
Hamburg where Gustav Dahrendorf and his group took
charge of the preparations. Similar measures were taken
by the SAJ in Berlin.[79]

The Leipzig organization,[80] like those of Hanover and
of the Berlin SAJ, was based on groups of five, the principle also adopted by the Communists for their underground
activity; in Leipzig the groups were called "pioneer
chains." As opposed to Hanover where the organization
was confined to the city proper, the Leipzig preparations took in the entire region, or party district. The organizational plan was similar to that of Hanover.[81] The
illegal apparatus comprised some eighteen subsections,
corresponding to those of the legal party, eight within the
city of Leipzig and about ten in the territory of the party
district. The subsections communicated with the central
leadership through liaison men. By the late fall of 1932 a
network of some 250 to 270 groups of five had been set
up. This ambitious structure was a source of great danger.
Nevertheless the organization, which after January 30,
1933, simply went on with its activity, remained unim-
paired until June 1934, when it was broken up by police
action. Some parts of the network held out longer.

These limited preparations for illegality had little
effect on the party as a whole. In the spring of 1933 the
party leadership did nothing to encourage conversion to
illegal work and even tried to repress existing initiatives
on the ground that they endangered the "lie-still"
policy.[82] Otto Wels virtually disavowed the measures that
he himself had promoted in the summer of 1932.

The party's younger activists and left oppositionists had
no understanding whatsoever of the leaders' illusions as to
the benefits of legality. The conflict between the party executive committee and the leadership of the Berlin sec-

tion on the one hand and the leaders of the Berlin youth organization on the other is typical of the situation throughout the party in March and April 1933. In May all party offices and meeting places were confiscated and legal activity came virtually to a standstill. From then on illegal work assumed considerable proportions. Until the party was officially outlawed, three organizations existed side by side: the vestiges of the old party, the beginnings of the *émigré* organizations, and the illegal groups. Despite occasional contact between them they were essentially distinct.

The Socialist illegality that began in May and continued through the following months presents a complex picture. As we have seen, a few organizations had begun in 1932 to prepare for illegality. The party districts of Saxony and Thuringia, which were dominated by the left opposition and took a critical attitude toward the Berlin leadership, now tried to shift whole regional units to an illegal footing and, taking advantage of the period of semi-illegality, to build up a solid illegal organization. The work done in the Chemnitz district is of particular interest.[83] At the party congress of June 19, 1933, the question of illegal activity was debated, but Paul Löbe's influential group in the executive committee was still opposed to it. That same afternoon the supporters of the illegal course met in special session in a private home in Charlottenburg and attempted to improvise a centrally directed illegal Social Democratic organization covering the entire country.[84] This last-minute attempt was doomed from the start and achieved little. Truly characteristic of the first period of illegality were the thousands of small groups that shot up like mushrooms independently of each other.[85]

A number of Social Democratic groups—of the party, the youth organization, the Reichsbanner, etc.—were unwilling to disband and decided to remain in existence illegally. Utterly inexperienced, they tried under the most transparent disguises to adapt themselves to the new conditions and carry on their activity.

> In the weeks and months of their first groping efforts the members of the illegal SPD sang in newly founded male quartets, played skat, bowled, hiked, and met in groups at camp sites. . . . Even at a distance any experienced observer would say to himself: "That is certainly not a choral society, a skat or bowling club, but a political group," and often enough it was not hard to tell the political coloration of a particular group.[86]

Though the young were the most eager, there were also many older Social Democrats, including ranking functionaries, who simply could not accept the idea that suddenly everything was over. Characteristic is the example of Franz Klüh, former associate editor of the *Vorwärts,* who tried to engage in illegal activity and, suspect in advance, fell an easy prey to the Gestapo.

The main activity of these first illegal groups was propaganda. They distributed homemade leaflets but were also provided with material by the *émigrés.* They were endangered not only by their own inexperience, but also by the usually unintentional folly of the *émigré* bureaus which, for example, tended to ship their literature by mail.[87] By and large the members of the first illegal groups had no idea of the risks they were incurring. Like the *émigrés,* they did not expect the dictatorship to last long. Nearly all the groups were very short-lived; after the first police raids they took a more realistic view of the situation. Many began to doubt the possibility or efficacy of further illegal action, though in not a few places former party members and functionaries maintained a loose organization. Those who were determined to go on working in spite of everything and who managed to evade arrest were obliged to adapt their methods more and more to totalitarian conditions.

The illegal formations of the Socialist splinter groups such as the Internationaler Sozialistischer Kampfbund

[International Socialist Combat League] and Sozialistische Arbeiterpartei [SAP—Socialist Workers' Party] and
the Communist Party opposition had relatively better
chances of survival than those of the SPD or the KPD.
Their leaders and members were not so well known to the
police and moreover proved remarkably trustworthy,
while the Communist groups, which at first were able to
operate with striking intrepidity, suffered greatly from
the infiltration of stool pigeons.

The first phase of Social Democratic illegality—which
is difficult to date with precision but which in the main
was liquidated in 1934—derives its characteristic accent
from the remnants of the old party organization[88] and not
from independent groups built up on a new basis. Both in
its organization and in its ideas it was characterized by the
old forms of Social Democratic organization and thinking,
though it already showed signs of the new development
sparked off by the total catastrophe of 1933.

Among the groups that arose in deliberate opposition
to the spirit of the old party, Neu Beginnen [New Begin-
ning] was the most outstanding. It was first formed in
1929 when a number of small discussion groups of critical
Social Democrats and Communists sprang up in Berlin. It
gained new organizational cohesion in 1931 when it succeeded in preventing the Berlin section of the Social
Democratic Youth Organization, which leaned toward the
SAP, from splitting off from the party. Benefitting by the
illegal network established by the Berlin SAJ and by
the intellectual maturity acquired in the discussion circles,
New Beginning built up an illegal organization. Though
its center of gravity remained in Berlin, it soon branched
out to the whole of Germany.

Unlike the many illegal Social Democratic groups that
had sprung up in spontaneous reaction to the crushing of
the working-class movement, New Beginning, which for
years had discussed the problems of the Italian development and of the centralistic one-party state, had a relatively

realistic conception of "what distinguished a dictatorship, in which one party holds a monopoly on organization and propaganda, from any system of repression that continues to tolerate vestiges of democratic institutions." Thus New Beginning was able to develop highly effective methods of conspiratorial activity; after holding for a brief period that "complete fascism" would not develop in Germany, it soon adjusted itself to a "long-term perspective." [89]

The development of this group, which unfortunately has not yet been investigated in detail, shows certain parallels to that of the Socialist Front in Hanover, although there was no contact between the two. It is particularly worth noting that both groups decided in the summer of 1935 to broaden their narrow cadre organizations. Concerned for the security of the central organization, the original leadership of New Beginning had developed a strategy "which threatened to lead to the most radical isolation and sectarianism." But the great majority of its functionaries now took the position that

> though the rigidly organized groups must indeed be very small until such time as the regime is shaken by grave political crises, there will for a long time to come be many functionaries of the old movement with a strong need to hold together, rooted in the old tradition but continually replenished by the pressure of the dictatorship. A genuine political organization with definite aims must show itself capable of keeping constant contact with such circles, of helping them to solve the technical problems of illegality, of providing them with reliable information, and of furthering the development of their political thinking.

After hard inner struggles and a change of leadership in 1935 this point of view won out.[90] The Socialist Front was led by similar considerations to build up around their cadre organization "a group organization with a distinct tendency to become a mass organization." This group organization was to assume considerable proportions.[91]

Though relatively large at the start, the Social Democratic underground, even in the first months, comprised only a small fraction of the Social Democratic community, which despite the organizational and moral disintegration of the party and in sharp contrast to the Communist community proved exceedingly stable even after the March elections. An indication of this is provided by the partial results of the works councils elections of April 1935, which were so shattering for the NSBO that the elections were annulled. Only in the mining regions where the Communist "Red Trade-Union Opposition" [RGO— Rote Gewerkschaftsopposition] had held a dominant position did the NSBO achieve a noteworthy success (thanks to the rapid falling off of the RGO). The *Vertrauensrat* [councils of confidence]* elections, held later in 1935, were again so unwelcome to the regime that it did not dare to publish them unfalsified.[92] Since many of the former party and trade-union members still felt the need to keep contact with those of like mind, it is very difficult in many cases to establish the dividing line between active resistance and passive loyalty to socialist opinions. Even the subjective estimates of those concerned are highly divergent.

A thorough investigation of the Social Democratic resistance would have to consider many different groups of varying cohesiveness, from habitual meetings of friends in bars and restaurants to the close-knit cadre organization of New Beginning or the Socialist Front. It would have to examine the cooperation between Social Democrats and Communists, the connections between the different organizations, the contacts with the *émigré* organization, and the attempts made to influence unorganized but like-minded persons. It would have to distinguish between organizations of local and regional character and those with

* The Nazi successor organization to the works councils. Employees were entitled to accept or reject a slate chosen jointly by the employer and the leader of the NSBO cell.

bureaus and ramifications throughout the territory of the Reich. But most of all it would have to show how, with the increasing pressure of the dictatorship and the perfected methods of the Gestapo, but also under the influence of the inner—especially social and economic—development of the Third Reich and its success in the international sphere, the structure of the active Socialist resistance, whose forces became smaller and smaller, underwent a gradual change. Investigation of these matters, rendered extremely difficult by the almost total absence of written source material, has thus far been neglected. It is made all the more urgent by the fact that despite many valuable findings the investigation of the German resistance movement has concentrated more and more on the events surrounding the July 20, 1944, plot and has largely lost itself in a biographical blind alley. An investigation of the structures of the resistance movement could make it very much easier for us to arrive at a sound judgment of conditions under present totalitarian regimes, including the Soviet zone of Germany.

The Spirit of the old Social Democracy and the Progressive Change of Attitude

The illusions of the Social Democrats during the early period of National Socialist rule may seem incomprehensible to a present-day critic. Yet none of the anti-National Socialist or non-National Socialist political groups showed more foresight and courage than the last isolated defenders of the Weimar order who voted against the Enabling Act. Still, this general failure cannot blind us to the fact that the behavior of the Social Democrats after the Prussian *coup d'état* of July 20, 1932, and after January 30, 1933, shows specific traits stemming from the ossified thought structure of Social Democracy. The salient factors in this thought structure may be summed up as follows:

1. *Institutionalist thinking* shaped by the traditional party apparatus and its old familiar methods. The Social Democratic organizations had largely ceased to be means to an end and become an end in themselves, self-enclosed social organisms with laws of their own. This life confined to the organization made for a deep-seated conservatism and led them to overestimate their own strength; it blinded them to real dangers and paralyzed all political initiative by making them feel that the essential was to preserve the organization which political struggle was bound to endanger.

2. *Parliamentarianism*—another aspect of institutionalist thinking. Parliamentary democracy was felt to be the only conceivable order except perhaps for a relapse into the authoritarianism of the prewar period. Even at the last meeting of the parliamentary group, held in June 1933, many of those present showed that they were still living in a parliamentary, constitutional utopia. At first even the Karlsbad *Neue Vorwärts,* in viewing the German scene, took an attitude that "differed little from that of an active parliamentary opposition under democratic conditions." [93]

3. *Hierarchical thinking*—still another aspect of institutionalist thinking. A party like the SPD, which had grown powerful as a legal, parliamentary mass party but still clung officially to its revolutionary, socialist pretensions, required enormous inner discipline. Discipline alone made it possible to demonstrate the power of the masses effectively but at the same time to exclude any undesirable spontaneous move that would interfere with parliamentary action. From the party apparatus the "rigid party hierarchy," [94] against which many rebelled but to which in practice all submitted, was transposed to party delegations and to Socialist-dominated governmental bodies. As a general rule it did not create a cleav-

age between the top functionaries and the base but was rather a factor of cohesion; what conflicts arose resulted more from a difference of position within the hierarchy than from any basic difference in outlook. The party—and this was characteristic of its whole spirit—was directed by functionaries. The dilemma of July 20, 1932, and January 30, 1933, was that the thought-structure of the leadership rendered it incapable of initiative, while the activist sections of the workers' organizations, for all their seething militancy, looked confidently to the party leaders because party discipline forbade them to act spontaneously.

4. *Evolutionism.* Even in the catastrophe of the working-class movement evolutionist thinking performed its traditional function: it justified passivity and inspired new confidence by holding out the promise that the victorious reactionary and totalitarian power would disintegrate of its own accord. Evolutionism was at once an ideology and a feeling. As a feeling it was based mainly on the experience of the irresistible rise of the workers' organizations in the years preceding the First World War and on the resultant myth that despite passing setbacks and repressions they were indestructible. As ideology, it blends pre-Marxist humanitarian faith in progress with a pseudo-scientific Social Darwinism and superficially assimilated elements of Marxist doctrine and vocabulary. This pseudo-revolutionary ideology, misleadingly termed "Marxism" by supporters as well as adversaries of the party, leaves it to "conditions" to usher in socialism. It was inherited from the inwardly disunited Social Democracy of the imperial age.

5. *Humanitarian thinking.* By humanitarian thinking I mean the general pacifist attitude that came down to the Social Democratic movement from the prewar period. It is a precondition and component of evolutionism. Rooted in the Enlightenment, this humanitarianism is a holdover from the eighteenth century. Unrealistically confident in

reason and with no understanding of the irrational motivations of political drives, its proponents were helpless to
resist a dynamic mass movement like National Socialism.
Even in the midst of the catastrophe they continued to
brandish the weapon of "spiritual superiority." [95]

6. *Thinking in historical analogies.* Social Democratic
thinking, to which impulsive decisions and spontaneous
action are alien, is always on the search for historical analogies, benchmarks in the past. Hypnotic obsession with
the terrifying Russian example played an important part
in the development of 1918–1919. On July 20, 1932, the
party and trade-union leaderships comforted themselves
with the thought that all this was entirely different from
the Kapp putsch. After January 30, 1933, the Anti-Socialist Law provided the dominant analogy; but an analogy
was also drawn with the Fascist revolution from which it
was generally inferred that an Italian development was
unlikely because conditions were different in Germany.
Here it has been possible only to hint at the importance
of this analogical thinking, which also served to justify the
attentist attitude of the party; it has not yet been systematically investigated.

Taken together, the mutually conditioned factors just
described form a thought-structure typical of a group.
This thought-structure, in which being and consciousness,
mentality and ideology,[96] are inextricably intertwined,
may vary in intensity and coloration according to individual makeup and position within the party; but by and
large it characterized all Social Democrats, even its most
keen-sighted critics within the party, who time and time
again subordinated their insight and their independent
political initiative to "party loyalty."

This tenacious manner of thinking survived the catastrophe. Even the theoretical inner-party debates of the
émigrés were in the main reflections of the old party
mentality. The renascence of "radicalism" and the rejection of "reformism" were nothing new, but merely

showed the continuity of the left-wing opposition within the party, which in the defeat found confirmation of its traditional criticism of the dominant Social Democratic tendency.[97] The same is true of the left-wing radicalism which fell in with the spontaneous mood of the Socialist underground. Like the opposition groups of the emigration, the illegal groups in Germany took a radically negative attitude toward the Prague executive committee, which struck them as an embodiment of the reformist policy that had hitherto been in force. Compromised by the party's defeat without a struggle and their own policy of adaptation, the old leaders enjoyed little authority with the emigration or the illegal groups.

Yet despite the unmistakable conflict between the *émigré* executive committee and the underground, and despite the acute inner-party tensions among the *émigrés,* all those sections of the decimated and fragmented German Social Democracy that continued to work in an organized fashion began to undergo a profound change of outlook. The shock of 1933, the dissolution of the old party apparatus, and a drastically new experience shook the ossified Social Democratic thought-structure, and even the most conservative elements of the emigration—that is, the executive committee as well as the radical groups— could not for long escape this process. Even when it was in contact with the various trends of the emigration or identified itself with one of them, the underground was largely independent in its change of attitude. In general the illegal groups rejected the theoretical hair-splitting typical of the emigration and preferred, as the documents at our disposal show, a strongly subjective practical mode of thought and clear, simple aims.[98]

At an early date the most active groups showed a desire to make a fresh start and to break with the old party tradition. This desire was reflected in the names they took: Red Shock Troop, New Beginning, Socialist Front, etc. Both wings of the working-class movement had failed; the "new party" could only be a united workers' party for which there was no model. These people failed to understand why the Social Democratic and Communist *émigrés* persisted in their old squabbles. The Social Democratic underground was willing to work and carry on discussions with the Communists as far as security seemed to permit; "they refused to take a self-seeking, partisan" [99] attitude toward the KPD.

Another idea that took hold of the illegal groups in the years after 1933 was that the future socialist state could not be conducted by more than one party, that a strong authoritarian leadership was indispensable.

Both these perspectives, a united party and a dictatorial state, can easily be explained as a reaction to the defeat and failure of the pluri-party state. On a more theoretical basis, the left-radical *émigré* groups arrived at similar conclusions. This reaction to defeat was indeed still a far cry from a fundamental change of attitude, but as the copious literature of the Social Democratic *émigrés* shows, the tendency toward regeneration was so powerful despite the stubborn survival of the old ideas that one is justified in speaking of an advance in the Social Democratic consciousness. And the recently unearthed documents from the underground reveal the same interacting tendencies toward regeneration: a social revolutionary, a libertarian socialist, and a populist socialist tendency.[100]

It seems reasonable to infer that the emigration and the underground, despite all conflicts, misunderstandings, and differences in working conditions and rate of development, were acquiring a common ideological base, even though subjectively the two groups continued to attach vital importance to the differences between them.

I know of no record of the emigration that offers so palpable and direct an expression of this process of thought-revision as the document of the illegal Socialist Front. Its critique of the old Social Democracy coincides almost point for point with the mordant, undogmatic judgment expressed by Julius Leber in the summer of 1933. The author of the documents also holds it self-evident that a party which aspires to state power must take an unequivocal national stand.[101] He too despises the dreary "scientific" verbiage that serves as a mask for passivity and impotence, stresses the subjective will to power and the irrational motivations of the political will, sharply attacks those who operate with the concept of "class" as with a mythical symbol, and the "schematic classification of human individuals" prevalent in the old Social Democratic thinking. Both in Leber[102] and in the "thinking workers" of the Socialist Front[103] this Social Democratic self-criticism centers around a conscious rejection of the traditional rationalistic view of man. A new attitude toward man was in the making.[104]

Though in retrospect many of the political conceptions of the document seem illusory, it reveals the basic traits of a new realism far superior to the old Social Democratic *Realpolitik*.[105] The document rejects the traditional liberal "political democracy" but recognizes democracy as the fundamental "principle" of political life.[106] Despite its open plea for a dictatorial form of government, it marks a stage in the development toward a new concept of democracy in keeping with the new Social Democratic image of itself and of man. The essential is no longer the form of democracy but its meaning and content.[107]

Yet though the tendencies toward renewal seem—as the document of the Socialist Front points out—to justify the view generally held by the Social Democratic underground in 1936, "that a long and important chapter in the history of the German labor movement came to its end in 1933"[108] and that a new epoch began with the downfall of the old legal party, nevertheless there can be no doubt that the political consciousness of a great many members of the old Social Democratic mass army remained on the level of 1933. Many who, in total isolation or confined to small circles cut off from the outside world, remained "passively loyal" [109] to their old party and continued to derive moral strength from their tradition were virtually untouched by the ideological transformation that went on in the active resistance groups, in discussion groups within the concentration camps, and in the emigration. In the hour of rebirth these faithful Social Democrats, rank-and-filers and functionaries of every level, returned to the fold; but for them the newly arisen party was the old one. They had returned home from inner exile. Thus from the first the spirit of tradition and restoration made itself felt in the new party; those imbued with this spirit continued to regard the events of 1933 as a natural catastrophe to which the old Social Democracy had succumbed through no fault of its own.

NOTES

1. This aspect of my study has certain points of contact with Lewis J. Edinger's paper "German Social Democracy and Hitler's 'National Revolution of 1933': A Study in Democratic Leadership," in *World Politics*, April 1953, pp. 330–367, which was made available to me in the course of my preparatory research and with which I agree on essential points.

2. Julius Leber, "Gedanken zum Verbot der deutschen Sozialdemokratie," in *Ein Mann geht seinen Weg: Schriften, Reden und Briefe von Julius Leber, herausgegeben von seinen Freunden,* Berlin/Frankfurt a.M., 1952, pp. 187–247; quotations, p. 238.

3. *Ibid.,* pp. 239 f.

4. Friedrich Stampfer, *Die vierzehn Jahre der ersten deutschen Republik,* 3rd. ed., Hamburg, 1953, pp. 607 f.

5. Karl Dietrich Bracher, *Die Auflösung der Weimarer Republik,* Stuttgart/Düsseldorf, 1955, pp. 582 ff.; Leber, *op. cit.,* p. 243.

6. Carl Severing, *Mein Lebensweg,* Cologne, 1950, Vol. II, p. 347.

7. John W. Wheeler-Bennett, *Die Nemesis der Macht,* Düsseldorf, 1954, p. 276. (English title: *The Nemesis of Power.*)

8. Lothar Frey, *Deutschland wohin?* Zürich, 1934, p. 14.

9. Severing, *op. cit.,* p. 355.

10. *Das Reichsbanner,* April 23, 1932, sets the membership of the Defense Formations at almost 400,000. According to Bracher, *op. cit.,* p. 489 f. there were at that time roughly 400,000 SA men.

11. According to oral information received from Fritz Heine

(about the preparations for resistance at party headquarters) and from Georg Eckert (about the activity of the Reichsbanner students).

12. Ernst Schumacher, then SPD district undersecretary for the circumscriptions of Wandsleben and Oschersleben, written statement of January 1956, with oral additions.

13. Walter Hammer, ed., *Theodor Haubach zum Gedächtnis,* Frankfurt a.M., 1955, pp. 32 f., 35 f.; Frey, *op. cit.,* pp. 14 ff.; Franz Josef Furwängler, *OTV, Die Geschichte einer Gewerkschaft,* Stuttgart, 1955, p. 556; Evelyn Anderson, *Hammer oder Amboss,* Nuremberg, 1948, p. 206; letter of Wolfgang Abendroth to the author, dated October 22, 1955.

14. Severing, *op. cit.,* p. 356.

15. Otto Braun, *Von Weimar zu Hitler,* 2nd ed., New York, 1940, pp. 409 f.

16. Leber, *op. cit.,* p. 242; Bracher, *op. cit.,* pp. 434, 585, note 137.

17. Bracher, *op. cit.,* p. 662, note 39.

18. *Ibid.*

19. Leber, *op. cit.,* p. 242.

20. *Ibid.,* p. 243.

21. Oral statement.

22. Oral statement by Fritz Heine.

23. Stampfer at Bernstein's funeral, December 1932, according to Gustav Meyer, *Erinnerungen,* Zürich, 1949; Munich, n.d., p. 362.

24. Document 5, p. 203, in Erich Matthias, "Dokumentation: Der Untergang der Sozialdemokratie 1933," *Vierteljahrshefte für Zeitgeschichte,* No. 2, pp. 179–226. All "Document" citations in succeeding notes refer to this article.

25. *Die deutsche Sozialdemokratie im Jahr der faschistischen Machtergreifung* (see note 1 to Document 3, p. 196), p. 5. The words are attributed to Franz Künstler, SPD chairman for Greater Berlin.

26. Wenzel Jaksch, *Hans Vogel,* Offenbach, 1946, p. 23.

27. Wilhelm Keil, *Erlebnisse eines Sozialdemokraten,* Stuttgart,. 1948, Vol. II, pp. 490 f.

28. Stampfer, *Die 14 Jahre,* p. 608.

29. Stampfer in *Neuer Vorwärts,* Karlsbad, November 5, 1933.

30. *Ibid.*

31. Breitscheid, *Bereit sein ist alles.* Speech before the SPD party council on January 31, 1933, Berlin, n.d.; in this version distributed as a pamphlet certain passages are toned down as compared with the parts quoted in the press.

32. Oral information received from Stampfer.

33. Quoted from *Neuer Vorwärts, loc. cit.*

34. Furtwängler, *op. cit.,* pp. 577 f.

35. Leber, *op. cit.,* p. 276 ("Epilog von seinen Freunden").

36. Breitscheid, *op. cit.; Vorwärts,* January 31, 1933 (morning ed.).

37. Breitscheid, *op. cit.*

38. Quoted from *Internationale Information,* 1933/I, p. 53.

39. *Ibid.*

40. *Gewerkschaftszeitung,* February 4, 1933.

41. *Ibid.*

42. Max Klinger (pseudonym for Curt Geyer), *Volk in Ketten,* Karlsbad, 1934, pp. 18 f.

43. *Vorwärts,* February 2, 1933 (evening ed.).

44. *Die deutsche Sozialdemokratie im Jahr der faschistischen Machtergreifung,* p. 3.

45. *Vorwärts,* February 25, 1933 (morning ed.).

46. Document 1, pp. 181 ff.

47. Document 3, p. 199; Document 5, p. 208; see also below, pages 87–94.

48. Erich Matthias, *Sozialdemokratie und Nation,* Stuttgart, 1952, pp. 72 ff., 191.

49. *Internationale Information,* 1933/I, pp. 112 ff.

50. Stampfer (anonymous) in *Internationale Information,* 1933/I, pp. 143 f.

51. See the documentation on the attitude of the Center delegation in *Vierteljahrshefte für Zeitgeschichte,* No. 3, 1956.

52. *Die deutsche Sozialdemokratie im Jahr der faschistischen Machtergreifung,* p. 7.

53. Keil, *op. cit.,* p. 613.

54. Oral statement by Stampfer on Edinger's above-quoted article.

55. Oral statement.

56. *Internationale Information,* 1933/I, pp. 148 ff., 152 ff. In a letter to the bureau of the L&SI, dated May 17, 1933, Wels withdrew his resignation, which in any case was not binding on the party organization; see *Internationale Information,* 1933/I, pp. 281 f.

57. Document 3, pp. 196 ff.; see also below, pages 87–94.

58. Letter to Friedrich Adler of May 17, 1933, *loc. cit.*

59. Keil, *op. cit.,* p. 492.

60. *Die deutsche Sozialdemokratie . . . ,* p. 6.

61. *Internationale Information,* 1933/I, pp. 195 ff. The party congress met on April 26 (and not as stated on the 27th) in the rooms of the Social Democratic delegation in the Reichstag building.

62. Bracher, *op. cit.,* p. 700; to the contrary, Furtwängler, *op. cit.,* pp. 572 f.; Stampfer in *Vorwärts,* March 23, 1956, p. 24, who stresses Schleicher's unreliability.

63. *Gewerkschaftszeitung,* January 28, 1933, pp. 52 ff.

64. *Ibid.,* February 4, 1933, p. 67.

65. *Ibid.,* March 11, 1933, p. 146; characteristic is the reference to the wage contracts which had just been concluded and which Furtwängler, *op. cit.,* pp. 582 ff., still regards as an important argument.

66. *Papens Appell an das deutsche Gewissen,* Oldenburg i.O., 1933, p. 91.

67. *Gewerkschaftszeitung,* March 25, 1933, p. 177.

68. *Ibid.,* April 15, 1933, pp. 225 ff.

69. *Ibid.,* April 22, 1933, pp. 242 ff.

70. *Ibid.,* April 29, 1933, pp. 259 ff.

71. Edinger, *op. cit.,* pp. 355 f.; to the contrary, Document 1, pp. 183 ff., 190.

72. Stampfer in *Internationale Information,* 1933/I, pp. 246 ff., 282 f.

73. *Internationale Information,* 1933/I, p. 244.

74. *Ibid.*

75. Document 1, p. 190.

76. Wels, letter of May 17, 1933, *loc. cit.,* p. 282.

77. *Frankfurter Zeitung,* June 20, 1933.

78. Document 5, p. 205.

79. Information provided by Georg Eckert and Document 3, p. 196, which to be sure shows no indication of having been inspired by Wels or anyone in the executive committee. The question whether Social Democratic organizations on their own initiative made preparations for illegal activity in the summer of 1933 remains open.

80. Oral statement by Rudolf Rothe, who was responsible for building up the Leipzig organization.

81. Document 5, p. 218. The connecting line between A and C 3 in the diagram is a mistake and should be deleted.

82. See pages 69–79 above and Document 3, pp. 196 ff.; Document 5, p. 205.

83. Document 3, p. 199; see also Jaksch in *Ruhm und Tragik der sudetendeutschen Sozialdemokratie,* published by Treuegemeinschaft sudetendeutscher Sozialdemokraten for Jaksch's fiftieth birthday, Malmö, 1946, p. 109.

84. According to a manuscript prepared for the author in January 1956 by Ernst Schumacher, then district secretary in Düsseldorf.

85. Günther Weisenborn, *Der lautlose Aufstand,* 2nd ed., Hamburg, 1954, p. 145.

86. W. Schirrmacher, "Sozialistischer Widerstand in Köln," in *Mitteilungsblatt des Kreisverbandes Köln der SPD,* special issue, May 1955.

87. Document 2, p. 195; Document 4, p. 200.

88. Document 4, pp. 200 f.; Document 5, pp. 215 f.

89. *Neu Beginnen, Was es will, was es ist und wie es wurde,* hrsg. vom *Auslandbüro Neu-Beginnen,* mimeographed, London, 1940, quotation, p. 13; Document 3, pp. 196, 198 f.

90. *Neu Beginnen* . . . , pp. 27 ff.

91. Document 5, pp. 222 ff.

92. See the documentation of T.E. (Theodor Eschenburg) in *Vierteljahrshefte für Zeitgeschichte,* No. 3, 1955, pp. 311 ff.

93. *Die deutsche Sozialdemokratie* . . . , p. 33, with numerous examples.

94. Leber, *op. cit.,* p. 222.

95. Karl Kautsky in *Internationale Information*, 1933/I, pp. 116 ff.

96. Matthias, *op. cit.*, pp. 83, 303 f.

97. *Ibid.*, pp. 25 ff.

98. Document 4, pp. 200 f.; Document 5, pp. 201 ff.; the same tendency is to be found in the "Abschrift eines Programmentwurfs, wie es eine Berliner aktivistische und terroristische Gruppe unter der Führung des früheren Polizeimajors und Reichsbanner-Führers Heinrich verbreitet" of October 11, 1934, published under this title in *Internationales Institut für Sozialgeschichte*, Amsterdam.

99. Document 4, p. 201; Document 5, pp. 206 f., 213, 214 f.

100. Matthias, *op. cit.*, pp. 216–234. Document 4, pp. 200 f., and Document 5, pp. 201 ff., can be regarded as predominantly social revolutionary in this sense, whereas in the Heinrich document (see note 98 above) the populist character is predominant. Here too. however, there is an unmistakable libertarian and social revolutionary tinge. Document 5 clearly shows the influence of libertarian tendencies and, in the unpublished portion, of populist tendencies.

101. Document 5, unpublished part.

102. Leber, *op. cit.*, p. 216.

103. Document 5, pp. 208 ff.

104. Matthias, *op. cit.*, pp. 62 f., 250 ff.

105. *Ibid.*, pp. 61 ff.

106. Document 5, unpublished part.

107. Matthias, *op. cit.*, pp. 241–256.

108. Document 5, p. 209.

109. *Ibid.*, pp. 209, 215 ff.

The Third Reich:

✠ ✠ ✠

The Period of Consolidation

3

Stages of Totalitarian "Integration" (*Gleichschaltung*): The Consolidation of National Socialist Rule in 1933 and 1934

KARL DIETRICH BRACHER

The breakdown of the Weimar Republic and the consolidation of National Socialist rule offer a significant topic of study in two respects. From the standpoint of modern history the revolutionary events of these few years constitute a historic turning point. They abruptly conclude Germany's first democratic experiment and at the same time set the seal on a system that gave the ensuing decade its salient features, though the prewar and war years were to accentuate and intensify them very significantly. And from the standpoint of political science the first two years of National Socialist rule offer an instructive example of the political methods, the internal and external mechanisms employed in the totalitarian "integration" of economically, socially, and politically advanced society, and illustrate the stages in this integration process. The double perspective represents an interdisciplinary approach which brings out both substantive and methodological problems. Indeed, the seemingly smooth transition from parliamentary democracy to total dictatorship obliges us to re-examine the concepts of legality and revolution, for it has been contended with equal claims to certainty that the events of 1933–1934 were revolutionary and that they were not.

* *

Hitler was appointed Chancellor in a political situation that offers a classical example of the disintegration of a Western parliamentary democracy. The genesis and early development of the Weimar Republic had been marked by a number of makeshift solutions and compromises which were dubious both from an institutional and a psychological point of view and were accepted by a large section of the population only reluctantly and under the pressure of circumstances. These compromise solutions were used for their own interests by political leaders and groups who felt no genuine bond with the republic and its democratic institutions; they were systematically combatted and obstructed by their victims on the left and right. The Weimar state had to contend with a structure of consciousness which, long accustomed to the freedom from responsibility conferred by an authoritarian administration, was no more able to cope with the novel tasks and problems of the parliamentary republic than with the increased burdens brought on by the world economic crisis of 1929. The reasons for the disintegration that set in in these years have been discussed over and over again. Interest in them is not only scientific but also hinges on the concrete political concerns of the postwar era—a fact that does not always make for clear, objective discussion.

The political history of those years centers on an encounter between an unstable structure of consciousness and a no less unstable institutional power structure. The essential factors in this negative encounter were: on the one side, the structural and tactical weakness of the democratic and semidemocratic parties which prevented them from maintaining a viable coalition, and the resulting emasculation of the parliamentary order and drift toward an authoritarian presidential system; on the other side, the rise of the totalitarian mass movements and the militarization of politics, in other words the development of extraparliamentary action fostered by the susceptibility of the public, especially of the hard-pressed middle classes, to demagogy and propaganda. Other important factors were the ambiguous neutralism of a bureaucracy that was largely distrustful of the republic but wished to be the backbone of the executive; the exacerbated antagonism of powerful organizations representing economic and social interests and the obscure activity of certain pressure groups; and finally the self-willed, autonomistic policy of a Reichswehr that the civilian authorities maintained in an atmosphere of distrust, aloofness, and uncompromising uncooperativeness.

When this complex dynamic, directed almost exclusively against the scapegoat of parliamentary democracy, reached the point of crisis, the outward framework of the republic began to crumble and to cave in piece by piece. This occurred ten years after the adoption of the Weimar constitution. When at the end of 1929 and the beginning of 1930 the last majority government of the Weimar Republic entered into a crisis that was to have the gravest consequences, the first phase of the transition from parliamentary democracy to a totalitarian, one-party state had begun.

This first phase, characterized by loss of power, extends to the fall of Brüning at the end of May 1932. It began with the disintegration of the Great Coalition. The fall of the Müller government had two causes. One was the mounting antagonism over matters of social and economic policy which finally led to a break between the two key parties of the coalition: the SPD, supported by the Socialist trade unions, and the German People's Party, supported by important business groups. The second cause was the plan, pushed by the High Command and Hindenburg's conservative advisers, to reform democracy by introducing a supposedly more efficient authoritarian presidential system which though "suprapartisan" would of course be markedly rightist in orientation. The outcome was the Brüning government, which remained in office for two years, becoming more and more authoritarian and ruling by means of presidential emergency decrees invoking the well-known Article 48. The government was weakened by the more and more drastic exclusion of the parliamentary, democratic organs and by the narrowly bureaucratic character of the presidential system, which went its own way, relying on the support of the President and the Reichswehr and, despite the mounting social and economic crisis, ignoring public opinion and the political mood of the governed masses. The direct consequence was the increased activity of a frankly antirepublican "National Opposition" climaxing in the Harzburg Congress and above all the virtually unopposed explosion of the NSDAP into a mass movement. In the light of the events that followed, it is evident that the re-election of the eighty-four-year-old Hindenburg was only an apparent victory for the democrats and moderate reformers. When now after long delay a blow was finally struck at the NSDAP (the prohibition of the SA), the extent of the government's impotence became suddenly manifest. In large part through the intriguing of agrarian and military pressure groups around Hindenburg and in utter disregard of the Reichstag and the political parties, first Groener as the initiator of the measure prohibiting the SA and then Brüning were dismissed. The democratic version of the presidential system was at an end.

After May 1932, it is no longer possible to speak of parliamentary democracy. A transitional phase ensued, the Schleicher-Papen period, in which the power groups held each other stalemated; the result was a power vacuum. Neither the outmaneuvered democratic forces nor the uncompromising totalitarian efforts of the National Socialists or Communists, nor the authoritarian regime of an infinitesimal minority was able to gain effective control. The Prussian putsch of July 20, 1932, Papen's more ambitious plans for a *coup d'état,* the conversations between Hindenburg and Hitler, stormy votes of no confidence in the Reichstag, a series of dissolutions of parliament followed by elections—all this made no change in the state of general paralysis. Then when it was least expected, early in 1933 after the NSDAP had incurred its first electoral losses and was assailed by a serious crisis, the breakthrough occurred: the seizure of power began. The rest of this paper will be concerned with its successive stages.

In view of the constitutional as well as the practical and psychological developments of the preceding years, this decisive move presupposed the intervention of Hindenburg, and Hindenburg could only have been set in motion by persons belonging to the inner circle of the presidential palace, who had manipulated the constellation of the power vacuum. After the adroit General von Schleicher had taken over the Chancellery and worn out his prestige attempting an intermediate solution of his own, based on the illusory hope of a split in the NSDAP, this circle comprised Oskar von Hindenburg, the President's son and aide-de-camp, State Secretary Meissner, and above all former Chancellor Papen, who did not wish his former friend and patron Schleicher to achieve a success at his expense and was eager, for reasons of political ambition, to get back into the game. Here lies the historical significance of the negotiations between Hindenburg and Hitler which Papen, first with the support of heavy industry and then with the help of Ribbentrop* and Oskar von Hindenburg, fostered for almost four weeks beginning with the famous meeting in Cologne on January 4, 1933.† In view of the crushing weight of proof pro-

---

* Joachim von Ribbentrop, who became Hitler's Foreign Minister as of February 4, 1938, and was executed subsequent to the Nuremberg Trials.
† Secret Papen-Hitler meeting at the home of banker Kurt Baron von

vided by sources that have become available and by Ribbentrop's notebooks, Papen's vehement apologetics in his
memoirs can be taken no more seriously on this point
than on any other. The truth of the matter is that an
NSDAP paralyzed by the dilemma of the power vacuum
and undergoing a grave crisis as a result of internal conflicts, financial problems, and a loss of votes was suddenly
—and to its own surprise—taken into the political game
at the highest level and so saved from the threat of
Schleicher's countermeasures.

*   *

Contrary to general opinion, however, January 30 was
rather a beginning than an end. The National Socialist
seizure of power in the sense of conquest and integration
of the state was a process requiring a year and a half. It
was complete only when the army had definitely submitted and Hitler had succeeded in becoming Hindenburg's successor. The Weimar Republic was not fully
dead until the Wehrmacht* took the oath to Hitler in
person† and until the plebiscite of August 1934 gave
pseudo-legitimacy to the merger of the chancellorship
with the presidency after the blood bath of June 30,
1934,‡ had demonstrated that the constitutional state had
been replaced by a leadership state.

The first stage of this process covers the activity of the
Hitler coalition cabinet, the so-called government of national concentration. It is marked by the displacement,

---

Schröder to negotiate an agreement for the formation of a new government.

* Under the Weimar Republic the official name for the German army
and naval forces was Reichswehr. Wehrmacht is the equivalent of "armed
forces" and became the official name for the combined army, naval, and
air forces on March 16, 1935, and for the duration of the National Socialist regime.

† On August 2, 1934.

‡ The Roehm purge, discussed by Hermann Mau in "The Second Revolution," pages 223–48.

conquest, and consolidation of power, the political and legislative exclusion of all parties and power groups other than the NSDAP, the thrusting aside of the previous elite, and the founding of the one-party state in July 1933. This stage centers round the problem of a National Socialist revolution, which was to break out once again a year later in connection with the liquidation of the "Roehm revolt" and then to be solved by a ruthless consolidation of power. To be sure, this seizure and consolidation of power were accomplished by violent actions, but these actions were taken only step by step and often provided with a juridical cloak after the fact. Even today considerable space is given in the apologetic literature to the thesis that Hitler came to power "legally," so that resistance on a constitutional basis was difficult or impossible. In reality this purely formalistic view of the pseudo-legal tactics of the NSDAP—a prime example of the subversion of a democracy—paralyzed the will to resist of the leading republicans and led on January 30 to the fiction that Hitler as a regularly appointed chancellor was not dangerous since there were only three National Socialists in the cabinet as against eight conservatives, and Papen, Hindenburg's confidential adviser, was vice chancellor. The German Nationalists deluded themselves into thinking that they could tame Hitler's mass movement and use it for their own plans of reform—an illusion that found its expression in Papen's self-reliant answer to those who expressed doubt and alarm: "You are mistaken, we have tied him to us."

The true character of this government is revealed only by an analysis of the actual relations of power. The National Socialists held the Chancellery, the Reich Ministry of the Interior, the Prussian Ministry of the Interior, and—through the complaisant Blomberg,* the Reichs-

---

* General Werner von Blomberg became head of the Wehrmacht in 1935 and Reichswehr Minister in the Hitler-Papen cabinet, posts he held until he was forced to resign in 1938.

wehr Ministry. This meant control over all the key positions needed for total "integration." In the existing
situation the ministries of the economy, of labor, and of
foreign affairs, which in a functioning democratic government are important positions of power, were without
significance by comparison. Moreover, in connection with
Hitler, who had repeatedly stated his dictatorial aims, the
fiction of legality becomes an absurdity. It is characteristic
that later National Socialist jurists made no attempt to
conceal the profoundly illegal character of these actions.
In his *Verfassungsrecht des Grossdeutschen Reiches*, published in 1939, Ernst Rudolf Huber states plainly that legality concerns "only the outward regularity of actions"
but does not call "their truly revolutionary character into
question." The appointment of Hitler, this National Socialist authority on constitutional law points out, "was
obviously 'legal' in the sense of outward fidelity to the letter of the law, but no one will claim that it was in keeping
with the inner meaning of the Weimar constitution for its
sworn enemy to be placed at the head of the Reich."

Here the purely formalistic conception of a "legal"
seizure of power, which has animated not only the apolo-
gies of such central participants as Papen and Meissner
but also the juridical interpretations down to our own
day, is exposed with cynical frankness. The persons who
opened the road to power to Hitler were utterly irresponsible exponents of political and economic aims and
illusions, utterly unconcerned with constitutionality. The
responsible constitutional authorities, in particular the
parties, the Reichstag, and the President, allowed themselves to be excluded from, or misled by, these
activities.

Thus it becomes clear that the problem of legality cannot be an object of juridical interpretation alone, but
must be analyzed and judged from different points of
view if an over-all picture free from perspective distor-
tions is to be obtained. In other words, the juridical view

must be complemented by and checked against sociological, economic, psychological, ideological, and historical investigations if it is not to remain on the surface and misinterpret in important points the change of regime by pseudo-legal methods that we know as the "National Socialist revolution." For it is characteristic especially of this first stage that in eliminating civil rights, in carrying out mass arrests and mass dismissal from employment, the new rulers employed every means of deception to create a semblance of legality. It still seemed expedient to put the accent on order and legality. Knowing that a sudden break with the law and open use of force would not have met with support or approval of the majority, Hitler took a detour. He tried, by means of apparently democratic decisions, obtained by unscrupulously provoking and exploiting government crises, to put the law—a law in fetters, to be sure—on his side. Far more important than the theoretical study of an accumulation of laws and decrees is the political question of how, under what concrete circumstances, and with what concrete purposes those laws, that legality, came into being or was manipulated. An indication of this is provided by the often misleading discussions of the Wehrmacht oath in connection with the resistance movement and July 20, 1944: the formalistic invocation of the oath of August 1934 veils and falsifies the true political context, the fact that the oath was obtained by deceit and coercion.

It is essential to stress such methodological considerations so strongly because the process of totalitarian "integration," the consolidation of National Socialist rule, was to a great extent made possible by the selfsame legalistic camouflage that a good many writers on the subject, whether out of literal-mindedness or because it suits their purposes, are only too willing to take at face value. The political life of Germany was dominated by an unbroken authoritarian tradition, a distrust—based on ample experience—of open revolution and a need for order and security even at the price of freedom. After the unsuccessful putsch of 1923 the National Socialist insurrectionary movement was also obliged to take this course of pseudo-legal semirevolution. Here much more than in the Marxist, sociological thesis of the reactionary character of National Socialism lies the explanation for the markedly legal façade behind which the National Socialists carried on their policy of "integration." For though the authoritarian state of the Third Reich showed a certain psychological affinity with the absolute or semiabsolute prerepublican monarchy, its basic totalitarian structure had little in common with the monarchy. In their methods of manipulation and actual power structures the Communist and National Socialist systems are far from being as fundamentally different as Marxists even of the Western variety, with their distinction between "revolutionary" and "reactionary" dictatorship, contend.

*   *

In the first stage of the seizure of power the problems surrounding the so-called Enabling Act are particularly characteristic of the situation here outlined. Crucial importance is often attributed to the passage of this "Law to Eliminate the Peril to Nation and Reich," hence to the failure of the democratic parties to live up to their responsibility. In reality the much discussed Reichstag decision of March 23, 1933, had no more than a formal significance and merely supplied the legalistic façade for the abrogation of the constitution which Hitler had already achieved three weeks earlier with the two crucial decrees of February 28 ("For the Defense of Nation and State" and "To Combat Treason Against the German Nation and Treasonable Activities").

For practical purposes these so-called Reichstag-fire decrees replaced constitutional government by a permanent state of emergency and provided a political and legislative framework for "integration" and permanent terror. Formally they can be said to follow directly from the emergency-decree tradition of the Weimar Republic. The fact that the democratic constitution was set aside by stretching a single article of this same constitution demonstrates the absurdity of the entire preceding emergency-decree legislation. These decrees—and especially their political aspects—offer a lesson that might well be taken to heart by all those who are now considering emergency legislation. Their lasting importance for the National Socialist system may be seen from the fact that down to 1945 they were invoked in many of the death sentences administered to members of the resistance. Thus to its very end the National Socialist state was based on a law of exception that had been put through by a political manipulation in the grand style.

This political aspect is also of crucial importance in judging the Reichstag fire itself. Though it is still doubted in many quarters that the fire was deliberately staged by the National Socialists, various chains of evidence enable us to assign it a definite place in the over-all development. These include the circumstances under which the fire alarm was sent out, the first investigations, the questionable way in which the trial was conducted, and particularly the sudden wave of arrests and prohibitions immediately before the Reichstag elections of March 5. To the known evidence we might add the fact that Walter Gempp, head of the Fire Department of Greater Berlin, a specialist of international renown, who shortly before had received the highest praise from Hindenburg himself and as a member of the German People's Party can hardly be accused of leftist bias, declared on the strength of conclusive investigations at the scene of the fire that a Communist act of incendiarism was an impossibility and that van der Lubbe could not have acted alone. In a conference with the inspectors and fire chiefs, he expressed disagreement on crucial points with the official communiqué. In particular he pointed out that the fire alarm had been delayed, that oddly enough a number of SA men had already arrived on the scene, that Goering had at first expressly forbidden him to send out a top-level alarm or to employ all the firemen at his disposal, and finally that a whole truckload of inflammables had been found in the still intact rooms of the hermetically sealed-off Reichstag building—all of which argued against Communist authorship of the fire.* The upshot was that his affidavits were vigorously suppressed and he himself immediately discharged. After the trial, at which Gempp had stood by his well-founded statements, he was arrested and imprisoned; on May 2, 1939, shortly before he was to be tried, he was found strangled in his cell.† Thus a troublesome witness against the official justification of the state of emergency was put out of the way.

The immediate exploitation of the Reichstag fire constellation made it clear how welcome the fire was to the National Socialist authorities. However one may judge the controversial details of the fire, there can be no doubt that the facts concerning it were manipulated and that it was used as a political instrument. The matter is deserving of closer attention—and not only because of its enormous importance for the legalistic gilding of the totalitarian policies carried on until 1945; it is also of general and not least of methodological interest for a political science concerned with the unmasking of totalitarian forms of manipulation. For here more readily than elsewhere analysis can help us go beyond the mere events and despite the elimination of all dangerous witnesses to penetrate the hermetically sealed reality of totalitarian legality.

In this paper, however, we must confine ourselves to those factors of development that concern our central

---

* But see Mommsen, page 137 below, for a different point of view.

† For the foregoing the author has drawn largely on information provided by Fire Chief Gempp's son. Cf. *Das Gewissen steht auf, 64 Lebensbilder aus dem deutschen Widerstand 1933–1945, gesammelt von Annedore Leber, herausgegeben in Zusammenarbeit mit W. Brandt und K. D. Bracher,* Frankfurt, 1954, pp. 106 f.

problem. It remains to be shown that after the preparations for "integration" made in February 1933, the transformation of the "national uprising" into a system of National Socialist domination was based essentially on the two emergency decrees of February 1933. The state of emergency was permanently legalized, civil liberties were subjected to the whim of a state authority free from all controls, the federalist structure of the Reich was eliminated when the central government (modeling its policy on Papen's Prussian putsch) arrogated to itself the virtually unlimited right to interfere in the affairs of the *Länder,* so preparing the way for the step that immediately followed, the reduction of the *Länder* to Reich commissariats and later *Statthaltereien* [provincial governorships]. The intensive pressure on the population, which in the already heavily manipulated elections of March 5 still turned out a majority for non-National Socialist parties, was increased with the establishment of Goebbels' Propaganda Ministry on March 11. While the arrests of political opponents continued and the purging of the civil service began, the National Socialist state, with the opening of the Reichstag in Potsdam on March 21, gave itself the solemn mythical aura of a national resurgence in the tradition of Frederick the Great and Hindenburg; and once the Reichstag, under threats of terror and lured by vague promises, had passed the Enabling Act depriving parliament of all power, the National Socialists took their measures against the Stahlhelm, still supposedly their ally, and disavowed their German Nationalist coalition partner, whom they no longer needed, so revealing their true face.

The "integration of the *Länder,*" as the National Socialists officially termed the often violent and tumultuous elimination of the old regional governments, was also legalized as early as March and April 1933 by a new wave of decrees that deprived all monarchist as well as democratic projects of resistance of their juridical foundation. After

Hitler, addressing the Reichstag on March 23, had spoken openly of "integration," the "integration" of the government administration as a whole took its first great step forward with the basic law of April 7, 1933, which in cynical misrepresentation of its purpose was termed the "Law for the Restoration of the Civil Service." This law was designed to provide "legal" justification—in many cases after the fact, one more instance of *justificatio post eventum*—for the arbitrary dismissal not only of non-Aryan civil servants but of all those who "in view of their previous political activity cannot be relied upon to support the national state at all times without reservation." This offered a legal façade for every conceivable manipulation of civil service personnel.

* *

Revolutionary "integration" and pseudo-legalization continued to determine the rhythm of the consolidation of National Socialist power. The first stage came to an end in July 1933 with the dissolution of all parties other than the NSDAP, partly under coercion, partly of their own accord. In a sense this step, too, was legalized after the fact by a law prohibiting the founding of new parties and setting the seal on the one-party state. Meanwhile the Stahlhelm had been placed under Hitler's orders, the unions had been smashed, professional and economic organizations had been partly integrated. With this the political spontaneity of all extraparliamentary groups was quashed. The second stage of "integration" was devoted to the consolidation of acquired positions. Here the party's aim was to take over or strictly curtail all those institutions on the fringes of political life, which had not been directly affected by the "first revolution" and which, though perhaps compatible with a brief dictatorship, could not in the long run be tolerated by a totalitarian order.

This meant primarily an intensification and institutionalization of state control over social, economic, and cultural organizations and the churches. Already in his Reichstag address of March 23 Hitler had explicitly demanded a unified organization of cultural and national life. First the economic organizations of industry, handicraft, agriculture, and of the working class had been integrated and then, with the appointment of the Propaganda Minister, the large organs of public opinion; now, with the extension of the state-controlled Chambers of Culture (Kulturkammern) the party reached out its arm to those writers who had not been affected by the first book burnings and deprivations of German citizenship. Most important of all, it became increasingly clear that the virtual truce which the NSDAP had maintained in the first months of power with the Catholic Church, reassured by a concordat that was soon to be punctured, and with the still largely German Nationalist-oriented Protestant Church was giving way to increasing activity aimed at institutional and ideological control over these large and still independent organizations.

This first stage of the party's struggle with the Church is exceedingly complex. Still, the picture has become sufficiently clear to disclose the general character of the "integration" process in this second stage—and its limits as well: for the steady loss of prestige of the initially powerful "German Christians" * and the failure of attempts to install a National Socialist Bishop of the Reich marked the first setback of the "integration" policy. This was the beginning of the first discernible resistance of major importance. From this the significant inference must be drawn that the new antitotalitarian movements were far more successful than those vestiges of the old democratic groups that continued to resist after their organizations had capitulated and dissolved themselves in order to evade a totalitarian "integration" carried on with all the

---

* Protestants who subscribed to ultra-nationalist and racist positions and formed the German Christian Faith Movement in 1932 under the aegis of the National Socialists.

methods of modern state control. This was true not only
of the churches; it later became true of the army, which in
view of its tradition and political role could hardly be regarded as a pillar of democracy.

For the present, to be sure, the trend in the army was in
the opposite direction. For in connection with the process
here under consideration it is of crucial importance to
note that with the replacement of Hammerstein by
Fritsch as chief of the army command early in 1934 and
with Blomberg's subservience to Hitler the Wehrmacht
was even more willing to collaborate with Hitler than
after the dismissal of Schleicher. The interests at work are
here particularly clear. The old aim of enlarging the army
fell in with the National Socialist plans for rearmament.
After state and party had entered into an apparently in-
dissoluble union in the one-party state (specifically legalized by the Law "To Secure the Unity of Party and State"
of December 1, 1933) Hitler increased his efforts to integrate the Wehrmacht. He opposed the claim to leadership
of the SA and with great psychological acumen declared
the army, that last non-National Socialist power bloc, to
be "the nation's only bearer of weapons."

*   *

The third phase of the consolidation of power began
early in 1934. It involved internal conflicts among the rulers themselves and can, in line with a penetrating article
by Hermann Mau and Helmut Krausnick ("Hitler und
der Nationalsozialismus 1933–1945," in *Deutsche Geschichte im Überblick*, Peter Rassow, ed., Stuttgart,
Metzler, 1953), be termed the "second revolution." Its
background is that the revolution of 1933—if we wish to
use this term for the dual process of "integration" and legalization—had brought with it the conquest and first
consolidation of political power, but also considerable
tensions in the still incomplete new power structure. The
definitive consolidation of the totalitarian leadership state

required the cessation of the revolutionary impetus which had often made it difficult for the National Socialist leadership to control its own forces and was now replaced by the pseudo-legal, though no less brutal, domination of the central government.

This was the purge or housecleaning stage characteristic of every revolution. The purge was directed against the party's dissatisfied revolutionaries, first of all the SA leadership, who for reasons of competition disapproved in particular of Hitler's compromise tactics toward the Wehrmacht. The blow against them also provided an opportunity on the one hand to subjugate or liquidate the party's former allies, who had meanwhile seen the error of their optimistic view that the NSDAP would "run itself into the ground" or allow itself to be tamed, and on the other hand to oppose the intention of certain suspect party members to create a split in the NSDAP. The dramatic events leading up to June 30 offer an excellent and far from fully exploited object lesson in the technique of power consolidation, that is, the strategy of playing rival groups off against each other and, as supreme arbiter, gaining absolute control over them both. The way in which Hitler by pseudo-legal and opportunistic methods manipulated the opposing groups and enhanced his personal power by alternately using and rebuffing the Wehrmacht, the SA, and the SS was to be of decisive importance for the subsequent internal policy of the Third Reich. It was thanks to this strategy culminating in the blood bath of June 30 that the solemnly proclaimed liquidation of the revolution provided a basis for the definitive legalization of the total leadership state.

* *

This fourth stage, the institutionalization of National Socialist rule, began in earnest with the meeting of the integrated Reichstag on July 13, 1934, when Hitler's justification of the alleged seventy-seven murders (actually several hundred) was accepted without opposition. The massacre was now legalized after the fact and celebrated by Carl Schmitt, the well-known political jurist, in an article entitled "The Führer Safeguards the Reich." Here Hitler is represented as the sole source of law. Thus despite its formal legalization the National Socialist state had no juridical foundation except the Führer's will after August 2 when Hindenburg—by a coincidence of far-reaching consequences—died. The conservative planners of the "national revolution" had hoped that the President, then aged eighty-six, would limit their experiment and offer a safeguard against the totalitarian aims of the National Socialists. But he had long since retired in failing health to his East Prussian estate, where he was cut off from the scene of action and surrounded by advisers subservient to Hitler. Having become the mythical embodiment of the nation, he survived only in the publicity of the Third Reich, which used him as a "national" justification of the half-concealed terror.

Through this tactic of institutionalized terror Hitler—and this was its most important consequence—now gained control not only over a decimated SA but also over a seemingly victorious Wehrmacht. On the one hand the SS, on July 20, 1934, was declared to be an independent organization, that is, freed from its ties with the SA, a step that enabled it in the course of time to become a politically significant competitor of the Wehrmacht. On the other hand the Wehrmacht itself underwent a *de facto* integration when on the day of Hindenburg's death the High Command consented to a soldier's oath addressed not only to the National Socialist state but also to Hitler in person. This oath went further than any oath formula in history. The members of the Wehrmacht swore "by God" to give not only obedience but "unconditional obedience," while Hitler, the recipient of the oath, did not—though this is the very essence of a personal oath—recognize any obligation to protect the swearers of the oath or any duty to a constitution representing them, let alone to God. The fact that with the introduction of compulsory military service and of severe penalties for evading it the voluntary nature of this oath became illusory merely accentuates its questionable character and hence also the absurdity of invoking it, as the adversaries of the military resistance movement continued to do. Though also cloaked in legality, this oath was profoundly unconstitutional because, as can easily be proved, it was decided on *before* Hindenburg's death and in disregard of all constitutional provisions for the presidential succession— which according to the constitution fell to the President of the Reich Court and not to the Chancellor—and sworn *before* the manipulated "people's election" of Hitler as Hindenburg's successor on August 19. It was merely an expression of the actual relation of forces that after this election the Wehrmacht participated in the Nuremberg party congress of September 1934.

Climaxing in the Wehrmacht oath and the union of the chancellorship with the presidency, this stage of institutionalization extended from the dramatic final acts of the revolution to the permanent consolidation of the total leadership state. Its tool was the silently administered concentration camps which in the first months after the seizure of power seemed designed only for temporary elimination of inconvenient adversaries but later, with the rise of the Gestapo, became an indispensable, steadily expanding institution. Up to 1938 when the dynamic of National Socialist rule exploded automatically into foreign adventures the only serious difficulty encountered by the regime was the increasing resistance of the churches. A characteristic feature of this policy of consolidation, this technique of domination over every sphere of the state and of society, was the interlocking of a centralist rule and chain of command on the one hand, and on the other hand of a system of delegated responsibilities that masked this same centralism. The antagonism between rival agencies was resolved solely in the omnipotent key position of the Führer. But precisely therein and not in the functioning of the state as such lay the profound purpose of an "integration" that was by no means complete. For the key position of the dictator derived precisely from the complex coexistence and oppositions of the power groups and from conflicting personal ties. The increasing effectiveness of the organs of control and coercion in the total police state also had its root in these power conflicts.

In this system of domination there remained one permanent problem and element of danger: the latent dualism of state and party, which in part was deliberately promoted and institutionalized as a means of domination, but in part had to be accepted as inevitable.

In conclusion let it suffice to observe that what essentially distinguishes the totalitarian state from the seemingly far more unwieldy but in reality organically equilibrated compromise-order of constitutional democracy is not—as is commonly supposed here in Germany despite recent fascist and Communist experience—greater efficiency of government, but an artificial, coercive, and in practice infinitely wasteful order in which the rulers are subject to no legal control by the ruled. And another point I wish to stress is that a totalitarian movement—as the rapid consolidation of National Socialist rule proves —must be combatted before it gains a foothold in the state and not after it has been admitted to participation in power, under circumstances that are supposed to offer guarantees. But this prescience cannot rely on political feeling and instinct alone; to provide it with a scientific foundation is among the essential tasks of political history. The historian of contemporary affairs must strive to remove the experience of the recent past from the area of resentment, accusation, or convenient forgetfulness and raise it to the light of consciousness. Once clearly understood, this experience will make for a sense of civic responsibility in the present and future.

4

The Reichstag Fire
and Its Political Consequences

HANS MOMMSEN

*On February 27, 1933, one month after Hitler had become
Chancellor, the Reichstag, or more accurately, the main
hall of the German Parliament, went up in flames. A
young Dutch radical, Marinus van der Lubbe, was apprehended in the burning building and willingly confessed to setting the fire. He further claimed sole responsibility and inspiration for his action, which he explained
as an attempt to rouse the German working class to spontaneous resistance against Nazism. However, the event
and van der Lubbe's part in it were almost universally
seen in another light. The National Socialists and many
others on the right assumed that an organized Communist
conspiracy was behind the fire, while the Communists and
many anti-Nazis felt certain that the National Socialists
themselves had planned and set the fire in order to destroy
constitutional guarantees and reap a victory in the coming elections. The latter view was strongly supported by
the fact that Land and Reich governments, the SS, and
the SA began an immediate roundup of Communists and
political opponents, and by the proclamation on February 28—only one day after the fire—of the so-called
Reichstag fire decrees which abrogated the bill of rights*

and states'-rights provisions of the constitution. The case against the Communists culminated in the Reichstag Fire Trial. When it opened on September 21, 1933, the defendants before the German High Court in Leipzig were Marinus van der Lubbe, Ernst Torgler, the parliamentary chairman of the German Communist Party, and three Bulgarian Communists then living in Germany: Georgi Dimitrov, Simon Popov, and Vassili Tanev. Dimitrov was later identified as the Communist International's West European chief. The case against the Nazis took concrete shape under the direction of Willi Münzenberg, the expert German propagandist who had organized and managed a far-flung Communist publishing and film empire and masterminded the famous international front organizations. Münzenberg got to work on the publication of the Brown Books and on a London countertrial which proved so effective that even the leading National Socialists began to suspect each other of complicity in the fire. In the judgment read on December 23, 1933, Torgler, Dimitrov, Popov, and Tanev were acquitted for lack of evidence but the court continued to hold that van der Lubbe had had accomplices. Van der Lubbe was found guilty of high treason, insurrectionary arson, and attempted common arson, was sentenced to death on the basis of a retroactive decree issued on March 29, 1933, and was hanged on January 10, 1934. In 1962, Fritz Tobias, who is by profession a civil servant, published a study he had made of the Reichstag fire affair in order to satisfy his own questions about it. His book, Der Reichstagbrand *(The Reichstag Fire, published in an abridged edition by G. P. Putnam's Sons in 1964), reopened the controversy.*

In attempting to throw light on the origin of the fire that broke out in the Reichstag building on February 27, 1933, and to analyze its political consequences, a historian finds himself in a peculiar situation. Here is an event which remained a mystery to all but a few contemporaries, and now, thirty-five years later, he is trying to unravel the mystery. In the face of the countless rumors and conjectures to which, quite understandably, an event of this sort gives rise, he must ask the sober question: What can be empirically established? He will avail himself of hypotheses only where they are necessary to point up the connection between the established facts, but he will remain open to the possibility of reinterpreting historical situations. On the other hand, he will not pursue speculations, even of contemporary origin, unless they can to some extent be verified.

The confusion that surrounded and still surrounds the Reichstag fire is primarily the consequence of such contradictory speculations, whose bearing on reality was not increased by the fact that the National Socialists or their adversaries used them for propaganda purposes or merely believed them. It is not surprising that the fire which broke out in the Reichstag building a few days before the March elections, at a time of intense political tension and general nervousness, should have brought forth conjectures and rumors. One need only recall the assassination of President Kennedy, which under far more "normal" conditions gave rise to the most far-fetched conjectures, to realize that the legends which began to crop up immediately after the Reichstag fire offer us very little help in determining what really happened. If the numerous versions attributing the fire to the National Socialists were so long-lived, it was partly because of Willi Münzenberg's successful propaganda campaign, and partly because of the National Socialists' reputation for cynical ruthlessness, but also because the trial of van der Lubbe before the Reich Court offered no serious explanation of the crime.

The inner mechanism of the crime remained a mystery to contemporaries, regardless of whether they put the blame on the Communists or on the National Socialists. Those who were officially concerned with the matter were equally in the dark. On the night of the fire Rudolf Diels* thought it likely that van der Lubbe had acted alone; then for a time he held that Communists must have pulled the strings, and only three weeks after the fire he envisaged the possibility of National Socialist complicity. Since 1945 he has been questioned by persons representing every conceivable shade of opinion, who held that as the then head of the Political Police, he was bound to possess reliable information. But Diels was not even able to provide fruitful hints; in the end he himself suggested a scientific investigation, though he did not believe that a solution to the Reichstag fire mystery was still possible.[1] Martin Sommerfeldt, who as Goering's press secretary studied the first reports on the night of the fire, had grave doubts at the time about the official version drawn up by Goering, but his subsequent investigations yielded only vague rumors which finally led him to suspect that Goebbels had masterminded the fire. After 1945 he too came to believe that the mysterious affair could never be cleared up.[2] On the night of the fire Goering was apparently convinced that the Communists were behind it; later he began to suspect that van der Lubbe might after all have acted alone, but once he began to claim that he had saved Germany from Communism, these suspicions were quelled.[3] Later he was not so sure. In Nuremberg he admitted the possibility that an undisciplined SA commando might have set the fire without his knowledge.[4] These contradictions have been interpreted as an indication of guilt; but almost everyone who can be regarded as a direct or indirect witness in the affair has contradicted himself. Nearly all have modified their original opinions, either under the influence of the general psychosis resulting from the fire or after the collapse of the Third Reich.

---

* Chief of the Political Police in the Prussian Ministry of the Interior and first chief of the Secret State Police (Gestapo) until 1934.

After 1945, Inspector Scranowitz (in charge of Reichstag security) withdrew his original opinion that van der Lubbe must have had accomplices. The report drawn up later by the Berlin Fire Department was diametrically opposed to the sworn and seemingly unimpeachable statements of the same officials before the Reich Court.[5] We might easily extend this list, so showing the questionable character of late testimony in a case that has become a center of impassioned public discussion; hardly one of the surviving witnesses has remained unaffected by the mass of rumors and truisms that grew up around the incident.[6]

We owe a debt of gratitude to Fritz Tobias for having subjected the legends concerning the Reichstag fire to critical investigation. These legends owe a good deal to Münzenberg's effective misrepresentations. But even without Münzenberg the immediately emerging rumor that the National Socialists were involved was bound to gain a considerable hearing. Moreover, certain National Socialists accused their own movement,[7] but their statements prove nothing. They are historically relevant because they show that the National Socialists thought themselves quite capable of committing such a crime and that they tended to attribute the fire, in their opinion a welcome event, to a consummate plot. Opponents of the regime simply took National Socialist complicity for granted, which explains why, despite the arguments to the contrary, such self-accusations have found their way into historiography.[8]

In view of the hopeless confusion prevailing among contemporaries of the Reichstag fire, it was generally assumed, up to the appearance of the *Spiegel* series,* that the mystery could no longer be cleared up. There are certain truths which in a given historical situation may per-

---

* " 'Stehen Sie Auf, Van der Lubbe!' Der Reichstagbrand 1933. Geschichte einer Legende. Nach einem Manuscript von Fritz Tobias," *Der Spiegel*, 1959, Nos. 43–52; 1960, No. 1.

haps be uttered, but are immediately rejected. Such a truth is the prosaic fact that no one outside of the Dutchman van der Lubbe set the fire, and that he was instigated by no political group. Yet this is clearly attested by the concordant statements of Police Inspectors Heisig and Schnitzler. A historical inquiry must start by examining all the different versions for their soundness and demonstrability, critically sifting all available information, and discarding unfounded conjectures. Accordingly, we cannot leave the question of the crime's authorship to the experts, but must subject their activities and methods to critical analysis, and bear in mind most particularly that political or other bias sometimes detracts from the credibility of their statements. Such an inquiry cannot disregard the "criminal case" to concentrate on the "political affair." [9] Because from the very start the "criminal case" derived a political coloration from political attitudes and political prejudices. By this I mean not that the findings of the police were politically manipulated, but that the police work itself was from the start hampered by the preconceived idea that the fire had been a "political signal." The "myth" of the Reichstag fire, the interpretation of the fire considered as a political symbol, impeded the solution of the crime.

Up to the appearance of the *Spiegel* series specialized students of the case continued to assume that the National Socialists were responsible for the fire; since then they have been slow to discard this assumption and have done so only with extreme reservations. Surely this cannot be accounted for by political bias alone; it also stemmed from a certain methodological narrowness: students of the early phase of the Third Reich tended to restrict their inquiry to factors indicative of systematic totalitarian manipulation. The Reichstag fire struck them as a prize example of the terrorist methods employed by the National Socialists to take their opponents unawares and to impose their dictatorship. Implicitly the Emergency Decree for the Defense of Nation and State appeared to be a well-calculated step in the gradual process of cementing totalitarian power.[10] After the publication of the *Spiegel* series, Martin Broszat declared that it was of little historical significance to determine whether the National Socialists were "virtuosi at exploiting situations" or whether they themselves had set the fire.[11] He failed to take account of the crucial questions that must necessarily arise if the National Socialists were not the incendiaries: Did the National Socialist leadership really show virtuosity in exploiting an event that they surely did not expect in this form? Were Hitler and his closest henchmen really such outstanding manipulators? Did they owe the electoral success occasioned by the Reichstag fire and its effects on the public to political shrewdness or to political stupidity? An investigation of the complex of events surrounding the Reichstag fire must be concerned not with justifying the National Socialist leadership in one point or another,[12] but with showing that everything which helped them to cement their rule was not the result of a systematic, carefully drawn-up plan. In their own statements—especially in Goebbels' propaganda—there is a deepseated tendency to interpret every unpremeditated reaction provoked by bewilderment, surprise, and insufficient planning or foresight as a masterpiece of statesmanly improvisation. Of course a historian must not overlook the artful duplicity of National Socialist tactics, but neither must he forget that National Socialism, unlike Bolshevism, possessed no purposeful, systematic revolutionary strategy, but owed much of its success to unpremeditated, spur-of-the-moment decisions and to the extreme flexibility of its general aims. The self-accusations of the National Socialists in connection with the Reichstag fire are also a consequence of this rationalization, for propaganda purposes, of their own actions after the fact. The "uneasiness" with which, as Martin Broszat remarks, the general public received Tobias' findings—and the same can be said of the undue skepticism of the specialists[13]—stems from the fact that these findings ran counter to the widespread tendency of anti-Nazis to overrate the manipulative character of National Socialism, especially in connection with a question that has taken on a "symbolic" significance.

Moreover, by taking over the "facts" of the criminal investigation without verification and accepting, though in reverse, the analysis of the Reich Court, the specialists actually barred the way to clarification of the problem. This approach left them open to the direct and indirect influence of Münzenberg's masterly Brown Book forgeries, which left their mark on numerous works that appeared at the time to be above suspicion. An important secondary achievement of Fritz Tobias is to have shown the profound influence, reaching down to our own time, of the Communist forgeries.[14] The views of the Reichstag fire set forth in the literature on the subject were drawn largely from these sources. Richard Wolff's unfortunate investigation[15] also failed for want of the most rudimentary source criticism. Fritz Tobias' unquestionable merit in having broken the sound barrier of Communist-influenced testimony has been generally overlooked by his opponents, who in this connection were much too quick to accuse him of "legend-making." [16] In view of the bitter attacks leveled against Tobias' work, I should like to state here that, controversial as his interpretation may be, his book must be set down not as a collection of "sensational revelations" but as a serious inquiry. It is based on a vast amount of carefully collated material that cannot be dismissed.[17] If the specialists had been as scrupulous and had remembered that even the prosecution in Nuremberg did not list the Reichstag fire among the crimes of the National Socialists,[18] an outsider would not have been able to convict them of neglecting the principles of source criticism.

While Tobias' study is meeting with increasing acclaim

in the West, it is quite naturally encountering bitter criticism among the historians of the German Democratic Republic, who, in trying to revive the old Brown Book theses, have become the last victims of Münzenberg's gift for forgery.[19] Of course there is no need to refute the grotesque imputation that Tobias, and with him the historians of West Germany, are trying to exculpate the National Socialists by warming up the old anti-Communist version of the fire.[20] In general the East German historians, who wish no doubt to mask the failure of the Communist Party of Germany in those decisive weeks when the National Socialists were consolidating their power, seem to have formed a united front with a number of Western publicists who continue, with almost incredible obstinacy and no understanding whatever of the available source material, to take conjecture for secure knowledge.[21] For a clear understanding of what would seem after all these years of discussion, not all of it very competent, to be established facts, we must first examine the question whether van der Lubbe acted alone and then proceed to the central historical problem: the political consequences of the Reichstag fire.[22]

Origin of the Theory That There Was More Than One Incendiary

The assertion that van der Lubbe can have set fire to the main hall of the Reichstag only with the help of others is a hypothesis. There is no definitely established indication that he had accomplices. No clues, no tools, no traces of combustible materials that might have justified this assumption were ever found. All the persons suspected at any time presented airtight alibis,[23] or had no connection with the fire whatsoever. It was only thanks to this unparalleled anonymity of the "accomplices" that the examining magistrate was able to solve the equation by substituting the names of Dimitrov, Popov, and Tanev for an unknown number of unknowns, while the Brown Book and Gisevius* did the same with National Socialist names. During the preliminary investigation these unknowns were transformed, in accordance with the "proofs" available at the moment or the dominant conjectures, into accomplices, higher-ups, or persons who merely had cognizance of the plot; in the countermyth they wore brown uniforms and were executed at the latest on June 30, 1934.

For this reason even the prosecution said little of the number of accomplices and based their arguments on the conclusions of the fire experts. After the meticulous search for clues had failed, the court in its verdict narrowed down the original assumptions to the contention that van der Lubbe had been aided by at least *one* and possibly several persons.[24] This one accomplice existed only on the strength of mutually contradictory and inherently questionable testimony.[25] It has repeatedly been asserted that the search for clues was conducted in a deliberately one-sided manner and hence offers no proof of the nonexistence of National Socialist accomplices. But the police investigation was not obstructed or steered. The statements of Albrecht, the National Socialist Reichstag member who entered and left the Reichstag during the fire, were checked in a perfectly regular way by the police.[26] The argument that subjective bias led the police to look only for evidence incriminating the Communists is not applicable to the first investigation. Investigation showed that the tunnel housing the water pipes, which was thought to have served as an escape route, could not have accounted for the disappearance of the accomplices.[27] Otherwise there were only vague conjectures without any real foundation.[28]

* Hans Bernd Gisevius, a police and Gestapo officer who had early contacts with the resistance and appeared as a witness for the prosecution at the Nuremberg trials.

How under these conditions could it come about that the vast majority of those who participated in the preliminary investigation as well as the trial excluded the possibility that van der Lubbe may have acted alone? The notion of a group of incendiaries fastened itself on their minds quite independently of the evidence. After the main hall had in a few minutes been transformed into a sea of flame, none of the eyewitnesses could help thinking that the crime had been carefully planned. The persons present at the scene of the fire were not yet aware that the great height of the main hall and its extraordinary ventilating system made it a virtual chimney in which a fire could spread with lightning-like speed. Building Inspector Scranowitz, who was understandably excited but also liked to dramatize, declared that six to eight men must have been involved and confirmed this statement when questioned on March 2.[29] From then on this first impression reigned supreme, unshaken by the findings of the investigations.

In view of the widespread anti-Communist psychosis the rumor that the fire had been a Communist action was already in vigorous circulation even before van der Lubbe was questioned and a Communist leaflet found on his person. Assistant Secretary Grauert declared at once that Torgler and Koenen* had been last to leave the building,[30] and this remark was transformed into a direct accusation by the suspicions of Reichstag officials Hornemann and Kohl. Goering's spontaneous idea of having the tunnel, which had already attracted attention in connection with an alleged Communist assassination plot, investigated, reinforced those present in the conviction that the fire must have been a well-planned act of Communist terrorism, so that Goering greeted the party leaders who arrived on the scene with the definite assurance that the fire had been the work of the Communists.[31]

* Wilhelm Koenen, Reichstag deputy and Communist Party Central Committee member.

While such rumors were spreading in the burning building, the arrested incendiary was questioned by Police Inspectors Heisig and Zirpins. Their judgment had not been swayed by the sight of the blaze. They gathered from van der Lubbe's statements that he had set the fire alone. The final police report of March 3, based on the hearings of van der Lubbe, the investigations at the scene of the crime, and general detective work, declared: "The question whether van der Lubbe acted alone can be answered without scruple in the affirmative." This view, still according to the report, was supported by "the objective facts" as well as the "exact indications given by the incendiary himself," whereas a number of new clues had not stood up under investigation.[32] Thus there could be no question of a "group of incendiaries." When at Goering's behest his press secretary, Sommerfeldt, applied for official information about the fire, he was informed along these lines and drew up a report—based on statements by members of the Fire Department, police officers, and Assessor Schnitzler—which spoke of *one* incendiary and left the question open as to whether there were others behind him.[33]

However, by late in the night of February 27 these observations had lost all chance of asserting themselves against the rumors of a well-planned action carried out by a group of incendiaries. These rumors directed against the Communists became the historical foundation of all the suspicions later directed against the National Socialists. The idea that the fire could have been the work of one man struck the frenzied imaginations of all those who had witnessed it as absurd. Rudolf Diels tried in vain to combat this impression. With the first hearings of van der Lubbe still fresh in his mind, he was summoned by Goering to give a report before a group of party leaders assembled at the scene of the fire. When he tried to explain that van der Lubbe was "a lunatic," Hitler interrupted him excitedly and declared that the fire had been "a subtle plot, prepared long in advance." [34] Diels left the gathering and remarked to Schnitzler that the place was a "madhouse."

The next to fail was Sommerfeldt. When at about 1:00 A.M. he came to Goering with his provisional report for the Official Prussian Press Service, Goering shouted wildly at him, changed the amount of inflammable material and the number of incendiaries, and reacted to Sommerfeldt's objections with the outburst: "Nothing is impossible! One man? It wasn't one man, it was ten or twenty men! Do you refuse to understand? It was the Communists! It's a signal for the Communist uprising! A flare! This is it!" [35] We shall explain below how he arrived at this interpretation. In any case Goering was irritated because Sommerfeldt's communiqué looked feeble beside the information which Goebbels had meanwhile sent the Official News Bureau. He rejected it and, apparently on the basis of material stemming from Goebbels, wrote a new report based not on the investigation but on the conjectures uttered at the scene of the fire. [36]

With this the idea that van der Lubbe had acted alone was finished. The number of alleged accomplices oscillated and finally came to rest at seven. [37] To account for this development there is no need to insist on propagandist purposes. The idea of a group was in keeping with the superficial observations made at the scene of the fire. For example, thirty separate original fires were reported. [38] Moreover, there is no reason to doubt that Hitler and Goering were personally convinced of the version implicating Torgler and Koenen, especially after learning that National Socialist Reichstag members Karwahne and Frey, as well as the Austrian National Socialist Kroyer, claimed that Torgler had met with the incendiary. Later it turned out that these three busybodies had come to this conclusion on the basis of an unfounded radio report to the effect that Torgler and Koenen had left the Reichstag building "in mad haste" [39] at about ten o'clock. [40] For propaganda purposes it would have sufficed to speak of Communists acting behind the scenes; there was no need of Communist accomplices. The former assertion would have spared the Public Prosecutor [Oberreichsanwalt] his frantic efforts to prove that Torgler had taken an active part. But deliberations of this sort were hardly to be expected in the hectic atmosphere prevailing on the night of the fire.

Things already looked different on the day after the fire. The arrests of numerous Communist functionaries had still supplied no information pointing to possible accomplices. Torgler had given himself up. No new grounds for suspicion had materialized. The police worked feverishly, because the government hoped they might turn up some information that would help to combat the campaign against Goering in the foreign press. The final police report encouraged the general anti-Communist psychosis by assuming that van der Lubbe had set the fire on orders from the Communist Party.[41] But this was pure hypothesis. Van der Lubbe's statement of March 2 showed clearly that he had no connection with the Communist Party and felt rather hostile to it.[42] Consequently the report spoke of Communists behind van der Lubbe—not accomplices—but declared that van der Lubbe had thought he was acting alone. The allegedly "unmistakable indications" on which this assumption was based were supplied chiefly by the unverified misstatements of Karwahne, Frey, and Kroyer. There is no need to suppose that pressure was put on the police investigators.[43] The theory of an organized action had dug itself into their minds.

Even before the final report was delivered, the Reich cabinet discussed preparations for the trial. Goering was opposed to entrusting examining magistrate Doctor Braune with the preliminary investigation because he had formerly shown severity in the prosecution of party members. His remarks on the subject are not free from internal contradiction:

> Even though it must be assumed that he (Braune) would not let himself be influenced in his work, his personality is hardly suited to the handing of this case. It is possible that he would confine the investigation to the one defendant, although in the opinion of the experts at least six or seven persons must have been involved. He might possibly release Reichstag member Torgler prematurely.[44]

Hitler seconded this view; like Goering he did not stress the political objections to Braune but doubted whether he possessed sufficient stature.[45] These statements make it seem likely that Goering, on the strength of the information at his disposal, was already thinking of having van der Lubbe, Torgler, and other Communist accomplices tried "regularly" for high treason; in other words, a special court would not be set up and no direct political influence would be exerted on the court. And indeed, apart from the replacement of the examining magistrate, no direct political influence was brought to bear.[46]

This procedure could not have been envisaged unless the party leadership was convinced that several persons had participated in the crime and that the Communists were implicated. They were well aware that world opinion was looking on. "A botch," said. Goering, "could have intolerable consequences." Hitler regarded the "agitation against the German government in the world press as extremely dangerous." A firm believer in short shrift, he reproached himself for not having had the incendiary hanged immediately. In the present case his hostility to legal methods was intensified by the feeling that the party leaders had maneuvered themselves into an embarrassing situation. There was no concrete evidence with which to counter the opinion widely expressed in the foreign press that the accusation of the Communists was a farce. On the night of the fire Hitler had demanded that all Communist members of the Reichstag should be hanged immediately.[47] That, of course, was out of the question. Frick, the Minister of the Interior, suggested an attenuated version of this idea: Why not hang van der Lubbe publicly on Königsplatz? The energy that Hitler and Frick expanded on these chimeras was characteristic of the atmosphere of frantic hatred prevailing on the night of the fire. The "Lex van der Lubbe" decreed on March 29—oddly enough solely with a view to van der Lubbe— was not merely a propaganda maneuver but a symptom of obstinate vengefulness. All this suggests that the fire had thrown Hitler into a state of uncontrolled nervous agitation, and that he thought he could compensate by such atavistic acts for the anti-National Socialist campaign in the foreign press.[48] Such behavior does not indicate that the National Socialists had any inside knowledge concerning the authorship of the fire; if they had, one would have expected them to proceed more calmly and coherently.

Goering was not exactly reassured by Hitler's reaction. After all, it was he who had put forward the thesis of a Communist uprising and nothing of the sort had taken place. He was responsible for misinforming the public about the origin of the fire. When the final report was submitted to him on March 3, he should have admitted to himself that his tactics had been at fault. Diels and Detective Superintendent [Kriminalrat] Heller in charge of Communist questions informed him that they regarded Torgler's complicity as excluded and believed van der Lubbe had acted alone. But Goering was incapable by character of taking a step backward. He directly contradicted Diels and Heller. In a lucid moment he said to Police Inspector [Kriminalkommissar] Braschwitz, in charge of the preliminary investigation, that the population did not believe van der Lubbe had acted alone and that he himself was not able to convince them that he had.[49] It was characteristic that he thought only of the momentary reactions of the public and not of the consequences of the trial.

It would be a mistake to suppose that from this time on Goering merely made a display of putting the blame on the Communists. Typical of the man was the primitivism with which he stifled the slightest stirring of self-criticism and persisted with almost childlike obstinacy in believing that the police were incapable of ascertaining the true facts. The arrest of the three Bulgarians relieved him of any last fear that the trial for high treason might prove a farce. He rejected Diels's repeated warnings against prosecuting Torgler and the Bulgarians, although Diels predicted that the Communists would be acquitted. Whereupon he forbade Diels to take any part in the preliminary investigation. Incapable of disavowing himself in his role—in part deliberately assumed, but in part sincere—as the defender of Germany against Communist revolution, he took a blind gamble and was rewarded by the unwelcome acquittal of the Communists.

In the new examining magistrate, Reich Judge Paul Vogt, Goering found a helper who was no more capable than himself of checking his wishful thinking against reality. Vogt, who to this day is convinced of the guilt of the acquitted Communists, had no need of suasion to follow the preestablished line. He was convinced from the start of Torgler's complicity. Yet he was not a National Socialist and was later one of those judges who dared to oppose the all-powerful party.[50] He was typical of a generation of German jurists who thought it his duty to employ ruthless severity in defending the abstract order of the state against Communist revolution, and tended to apply a double standard in political cases.[51] Tobias has convincingly shown the disastrous bias with which Vogt conducted the preliminary investigation. His characteristic cliché-ridden mentality is revealed by his statement on the witness stand: "I believe I have had a certain experience in conducting preliminary investigations and also in the handling of Communists." [52] It cannot be doubted that his way of conducting an investigation was more than questionable, and there is no need to invoke the embarrassing scenes in which he tried vainly before the Reich Court to justify the illegal shackling of the accused and was forced to admit that he had tried to trap van der Lubbe by telling him that Torgler had already confessed.[53] By changing examining magistrates the government had leaped from the frying pan into the fire; if the trial was a complete fiasco, Vogt was largely to blame.

Although the records of the preliminary investigation are not available,[54] it is possible to form a reliable picture of the way in which it was conducted. Vogt's bias, increased by misleading testimony, led him to give credence to the most untrustworthy witnesses as long as their evidence fitted into his picture of a Communist conspiracy. With grotesque obstinacy he clung to the idea that the Bulgarians arrested on March 9 had participated in the crime, although this was asserted by only one witness, whose testimony was inherently questionable.[55] Even before Dimitrov, Popov, and Tanev were identified, the examining magistrate informed Schlegelberger* that they were the sought-for accomplices. Thus Schlegelberger was able to report at the cabinet meeting of March 15 that the investigation had given rise to the suspicion "that van der Lubbe had not acted alone." He also informed the cabinet members "that, among others, a Swiss, a Bulgarian, and another Dutchman had been arrested." [56] Most embarrassing of all, Vogt announced publicly that Georgi Dimitrov was identical with the Dimitrov who had set off a bomb in the cathedral of Sofia, although the dates alone made this an impossibility.[57]

From the very start Vogt declared that van der Lubbe was lying when he said he had acted alone, and it was this attitude on the part of the examining magistrate that

* Franz Schlegelberger, Undersecretary in the Reich Ministry of Justice.

created the worst confusion. He was convinced that in claiming to have acted alone van der Lubbe was carrying out the orders of his Communist superiors. He disbelieved Torgler equally.[58] As a rule he neglected to confront the defendant with the accusations that he had painstakingly constructed from dubious testimony. The consequence was that the prosecution's artfully constructed edifice collapsed like a house of cards at the trial. It was also largely the fault of Vogt that van der Lubbe responded more and more to the questions asked by the examiners and later by the president of the Senate, which struck him as absurd, with silence or with the typical "I couldn't say." He had answered Police Inspectors Heisig and Zirpins freely. Vogt explained this by saying that they had not tried to deny van der Lubbe the glory of having acted alone.[59] Vogt was troubled by van der Lubbe's strange laugh, which, as Police Inspector Marowsky related,[60] had first made its appearance when he was questioned about his contacts in Neukölln.* Vogt accounted for it by the formula: "He laughed when he was lying," but later decided that van der Lubbe was lying only when he laughed softly, not when he laughed loudly. Even Vogt admitted, however, that the accused laughed especially "when he is asked questions which in his opinion are superfluous and absurd, because he regards the answers as obvious." [61]

Then as now, people racked their brains to account for van der Lubbe's behavior at the trial. It was believed, and some persons still believe, that he was concealing information about the National Socialists who had given him orders. The theory that he took drugs and other such groundless speculations were refuted by the affidavits of the psychiatrists.[62] In response to the flood of psychological speculations Tobias hit for the first time on a simple and

---

* A working-class, therefore "red," district of Berlin. Van der Lubbe apparently spent some time there trying to talk people into offering resistance and finally set fire to the Welfare Bureau.

obvious explanation which accounts for all the established facts: after six months of imprisonment in shackles,
after innumerable interrogations that must have struck
him as absurd, van der Lubbe finally despaired of being
believed. Not only Vogt but the court as well regarded
him as a faker, who above all wished to shield his accomplices.[63] On the witness stand Vogt declared: "In all other
points, whenever the question arose of whether others
were implicated, he lied deliberately." [64] Van der Lubbe's
silence, he went on, had begun when, in connection with
the alleged "liaison in Neukölln," Vogt had brought up
his relations with the Communist Party and "the party
leadership itself." "He denied everything—and that is the
strange part of it—which might have provided a link with
the Central Committee." [65] Thus van der Lubbe's silence
did not set in when the question of a possible National
Socialist complicity was raised, but in response to objectively absurd questions; for the idea that van der Lubbe
could have had connections with the Central Committee
of the Communist Party was an absurdity, characteristic of
the odd beliefs then current about the conspiratorial character of the Communist Party. Faced with an almost end-
less flow of unintelligible accusations, van der Lubbe fell
silent and, as Tobias has convincingly proved, he had good
reason to do so. This is shown most impressively by the
decisive episode of the nonflammable piece of curtain
from the western lobby encircling the main hall. Vogt
called the affidavits of the fire specialists to van der
Lubbe's attention. Van der Lubbe answered simply:
"The experts can say what they please, but in my opinion
it does burn." Vogt continued to maintain that the curtain was nonflammable. Van der Lubbe had this repeated
to him and then inferred that perhaps he had not been
there. When thereupon Vogt pointed out to him that the
curtain actually had burned, van der Lubbe replied that
in that case he must have tried to light it. Vogt believed

that by this maneuver he had led van der Lubbe to confess that others had helped him.[66] Although Vogt did not
read this alleged remark of van der Lubbe into the record,
he testified before the Reich Court that van der Lubbe, in
answer to a remonstrance, had once said: "Well, then the
others will have to tell what they did" (in other words, he
should be shown his accomplices), but that the sentence
had unfortunately been omitted from the record because
of its vagueness.[67]

Tobias speaks aptly of "artificially induced" contradictions,[68] which indeed so confused the Reich Court that in
the verdict we find the untenable assertion that van der
Lubbe had not been in the main hall at all.[69] Tobias does
not deny that van der Lubbe occasionally gave false testimony—for example, that he had arrived at the Reichstag
only about 4:00 P.M. and not, as the testimony proves,
about 2:00 P.M.; that he was not in the vestibule of Portal
2; and finally that he was unacquainted with certain persons with whom he was supposed to have had the ominous
"fire conversation" in Neukölln.[70] In the main his statements were true, and it was chiefly the methods of the
examining magistrate that made him sometimes take refuge in lies. If he had been a hireling of the National Socialists, why should he have covered the Communists with
whom he had allegedly conversed? Indeed, the examining
magistrate's procedure almost entangled Torgler too in a
net of unfounded, utterly fantastic accusations; at times
Diels feared the worst for him.[71]

By and large—as the first police officers to question van
der Lubbe also believed—his statements are almost entirely worthy of belief. Statements made in the awareness
that the death penalty might well await him—those of the
famous forty-second session, for example—cannot be
swept away on the strength of unconfirmed conjectures
and rumors. Why should van der Lubbe have been wrong
when on that November 23 he replied to Bünger, the pres-

ident of the Senate:* "I can only admit that I lighted the
fire alone, but I am not satisfied with the development of
the trial. I now demand that I be given punishment; what
is being done here is a betrayal of persons, of the police, of
the Communist and the National Socialist Party. I demand that the sentence be pronounced, that I be pun-
ished by imprisonment or death." [72]

The view prevailing until recently was that van der
Lubbe had accomplices or superiors in the National Socialist camp, but naturally refrained from mentioning
them. The police officers on the investigating commission
did everything possible to determine van der Lubbe's
itinerary and his contacts with third parties. Of course
certain gaps remained; in particular, van der Lubbe's
statements about the afternoon hours of February 27
could not be verified. The repeatedly made assertion that
the search was conducted in the wrong direction has a
core of fact, namely, that the investigating officers were
unable to find the slightest indication to serve as a basis
for a search in the other direction. The sworn statements
of Police Inspectors Zirpins and Braschwitz, and the declarations of Heisig as well, all denying that the investigation was one-sidedly "steered," cannot be thrust aside
when there is no reason for doing so.[73]

Consequently, the supporters of the "Reichstag fire
myth" have backtracked more and more, finally confining
themselves to the hypothesis that the fire was an undisciplined act of the SA, an assumption which, according to a
report by Sir Horace Rumbold, made its appearance immediately after the fire.[74] The later reports of Gisevius
have proved to be myths, influenced no doubt by the
Brown Books.[75] Most recently, Wolfgang Schwarz has
taken the position that the official agencies had known
nothing of the fire plot, and that van der Lubbe was left
in the dark as to the "identity and motives" of his help-

* Wilhelm Bünger, President of the Fourth Criminal Senate of the High
Court, i.e., the chief justice of the Reichstag fire trial.

ers.[76] This conjecture is based solely on the fact that the fire experts and the Reich Court thought it impossible that van der Lubbe could have acted alone. Fraenkel cites the Mimi Storbeck incident* in support of this interpretation; but the incident itself is quite incredible and has in part been disproved; moreover, even if it had occurred it would offer no proof whatever of the alleged National Socialist exploitation of van der Lubbe.[77] For countless internal and external reasons it is impossible that such a meeting, or an attempt to influence van der Lubbe, should have taken place in the castle, the city hall, or the welfare bureau before the fire; and in Henningsdorf† there was neither time nor opportunity;[78] on the day of the fire van der Lubbe decided independently to go to Berlin and set fire to the Reichstag and purchased unaided the coal lighters that he used for the purpose. The alleged exploitation would have had to be prepared during the few afternoon hours in which van der Lubbe, after deciding to set fire to the Reichstag and observing the building from outside, had bummed around Berlin, warmed himself in the post office, and read a few leaflets he had picked up.[79] It takes a good deal of imagination to suppose that on that afternoon contact had been established between van der Lubbe and some SA men without van der Lubbe learning anything about the identity of his helpers, that during this time the necessary inflammables were procured, that a decision was arrived at as to the best time for the accomplices to enter the building and how they were to escape undiscovered, and so on.[80]

All these combinations were based on the belief that more than one person had been involved. This belief had

---

* Mimi Storbeck, a public-health nurse in Neukölln, alleged that she had encountered van der Lubbe in the course of official duty in the company of a man whom she recognized as a member of the SA.

† A small town on the outskirts of Berlin through which van der Lubbe had passed and where he had received shelter for the night at the police station. According to Dimitrov's theory it was there that van der Lubbe had made contact with his Nazi accomplices.

no foundation in sober reasoning. But as Tobias has shown, it asserted itself long before any empirical facts were known, and became so deeply ingrained in all participants and in the public as well that except for Heisig and Schnitzler even those who at first believed that van der Lubbe had acted alone were misled by it. It was the affidavits of the experts that converted the "several incendiaries" theory into an inviolable dogma. They decisively influenced the outcome of the trial, and to this day they have been the cardinal point of all discussion on the Reichstag fire.[81]

The Affidavits of the Experts

Unwilling to accept the allegedly objective findings of the experts, Fritz Tobias subjected them to historical criticism. Indeed, the apodictic certainty with which Doctor Schatz, the chemical expert, as well as Professor Josse and Fire Chief Wagner excluded the possibility of van der Lubbe having acted alone was hardly justified by their meager empirical findings. Moreover, the examining magistrate took no account of the experts appointed by the police, whose findings backed up van der Lubbe's testimony.

As we know, the Fire Department experts maintained that the main hall had been carefully prepared with the help of inflammable liquids. This had been spontaneously conjectured on the night of the fire. In particular, Fire Chief Gempp, who directed the work of extinguishing the fire, came to this conclusion on the strength of the so-called "pouring trace" on the carpet of Bismarck Hall. A press report dated February 27 ran: "The incendiary set fire to a door and by pouring fuel on the carpet made a track to the next door. . . ."[82] Professor Brüning tested this assertion at the behest of the police and found that the pouring trace had not been produced by the use of liquid inflammables.[83] This seemed for the present to dispose of the inflammable liquids theory. The Wolff Telegraphic Agency* announced on February 28 that tar derivatives and torches had been used to kindle the fire. The former were van der Lubbe's coal lighters and the latter were a mistake: Scranowitz had mistaken a piece of burned rolled-up cloth from one of the curtains for a torch.[84] This fitted in with the information Sommerfeldt had received.[85]

Still, no one believed that van der Lubbe could have lighted the fire with miserable coal lighters. Building Inspector Scranowitz conjectured that the incendiaries had put gasoline-soaked rags inside the Reichstag members' desks.[86] Gempp seems to have envisaged a similar possibility; in any case he later testified that he had smelled gasoline or benzol, but withdrew this statement when Schatz asked him to define the odor more closely.[87] In any case his statement was doubtful; the other witnesses to the fire had noticed no unusual smell and no suggestion of the smoke clouds that such fuels often produce. WTB reported accurately that the experts presumed gasoline had been used in addition to the coal lighters, but not benzol, kerosene, or alcohol because no smell had been noticed.[88] The indictment also stated that no traces or vestiges of containers had been found suggesting such volatile liquids as kerosene, gasoline, benzol, or ether, and that accordingly the experts were reduced "largely to conjecture." [89] This did not prevent the experts from insisting that gasoline had been introduced into the main hall, for they could not discard the idea that the fire had been prepared systematically. As provided by German penal law, all three experts did not, in forming their opinions, confine themselves to those of the investigators' findings that were relevant to the fire, but also took all the material unearthed in the preliminary investigation into consider-

* WTB, one of the two major news services. The other was the Telegraphic Union (TU).

ation. They were in no position to see through the many false statements suggesting that the fire had been well organized. Thus they were subjected to a certain psychological pressure; it was as if they had been called upon merely to provide technical details with which to bolster up an already completed demonstration.[90]

Apart from the bias of Josse and Schatz in the question of whether van der Lubbe had acted alone, it was inevitable that the experts should be grossly misled by a piece of testimony to which the preliminary investigation attributed the utmost importance. This was the testimony of a star witness, Building Inspector Scranowitz, who not only later but apparently also at the scene of the fire showed a tendency to develop theories of his own.[91] At about 9:23 P.M. he had looked into the main hall for the "fraction of a second" and allegedly seen a large number of separate fires in the first two rows of seats and on the platform. This directly contradicted the observations of the firemen and policemen who looked into the hall shortly before and shortly afterward. In particular, Sergeant Poeschel had looked into the hall over the shoulder of Scranowitz himself without noticing these "separate little fires." One member of the court called attention to the blatant contradiction between the two statements. Nevertheless the court followed Scranowitz, although Poeschel's testimony accorded with those of the other witnesses to the fire and also fitted in with the way in which the fire had developed.[92]

Scranowitz was a poor witness in other matters as well. Toward the end of the trial he was obliged to retract his sworn statement that he had seen the Bulgarians before the fire. His account of van der Lubbe's arrest also showed his tendency to dramatize.[93] His statement about the separate little fires can easily be explained without recourse to Tobias' questionable "reflection-in-the-mirror" theory. When imaginative, publicity-seeking witnesses—and Scranowitz displayed these qualities any number of times in the course of the trial—reflect on their observations—as Scranowitz demonstrably did; he had plenty of time, because he was questioned much too late—their testimony tends to be worthless. Failure to take a critical attitude toward this witness was a grave omission on the part of van der Lubbe's court-appointed lawyer.

Scranowitz' testimony fitted in only too well with the general opinion about the fire and even with the melodramatic ideas of those who looked upon it as a political signal. If a critical comparison of this testimony with those of the other witnesses was avoided in the preliminary investigation, it was because of the examining magistrate's general tendency to pass over contradictions in silence and to dispose of divergent testimony in brief summaries. Another factor was that the building inspector had a reputation for being reliable. In any event his isolated testimony, corroborated by no other findings, was decisive for the outcome of the trial. It reinforced the experts in their assumption that liquid fuel had been used by making it seem unthinkable that the fire had developed "naturally." According to Wagner's affidavit all other evidence indicated that the fire had developed normally.[94]

Scranowitz' alleged observations also presented the fire experts with riddles which they were unable to solve even hypothetically. The assertion, based on his evidence, that artificial fuels had been introduced into the building did not in itself solve the central problem of why the fire had developed in so amazingly short a time—Wagner calculated four minutes. The sudden flaring up of the whole main hall resulted from a blast which shattered the glass roof and windows, so giving the fire an enormous impetus. It was established that the ventilating system was not operating at the time of the fire; but thanks to numerous ventilation channels and the swinging doors, there was no appreciable lack of oxygen at any stage in the fire.[95]

The witnesses had first seen fires in the curtains on the

front wall of the hall. Then came Scranowitz' declaration. Fire Chief Klotz reported that before the sudden flare-up the hall had been dark and full of smoke (not vapor).[96] Scranowitz' little fires must meanwhile have gone out. First the experts busied themselves with the question of the gradual progress of the fire. Since at this time van der Lubbe had already been arrested, they presumed that the fire had been produced artificially, with the help either of strips of celluloid film or of the self-igniting fuels later suggested by Schatz. Josse and Wagner overlooked the fact that such fuels take effect within a few seconds, whereas demonstrably two and one-half minutes had elapsed between the first fires observed in the main hall and the last observation before the whole hall went up in flames. Without Scranowitz's observation the course of the fire would be much more intelligible; an intense blaze at the front of the hall and a brief smoldering period were followed by the blast that led to the general blaze.[97]

Later the chemist Schatz—contradicting his first affidavit—[98] put forward the theory that after preparing the main hall with rags soaked in hydrocarbon the incendiaries had used coal-lighter cubes soaked in a self-igniting solution of phosphorus in carbon disulphide. This use of phosphorus dissolved in carbon disulphide to light the fire and of coal lighters and oakum, paper, and rags soaked in hydrocarbon to spread it presupposes a highly complicated preparation of the hall that could not possibly have been effected by van der Lubbe alone. Josse and Wagner had not gone so far. Josse thought of a preparation with benzol or something of the sort to account for the blast. Wagner regarded the blast as normal, but started from the same assumption because he could not otherwise account for Scranowitz' observation. No attempt was made to explain why the fires seen by Scranowitz had gone out despite the adequate oxygen supply. Both these experts left it to the chemical expert to determine what fuel had been used. The first fires observed had burned with a clear flame; this made it necessary to assume that volatile fuels with a low flash point, such as gasoline, had been used. On the other hand, the fire had spread rather slowly at first, although the burning curtains had thrown off considerable heat, which ought to have ignited such highly inflammable fuels.

The experts, to be sure, were convinced that the incendiaries could not simply have poured out a canister of gasoline or some similar fuel, because this would have produced an immediate explosion. But even if rags had been soaked in these explosive fuels, gases would have formed which would have exploded when larger fires developed.[99] Less inflammable fuels such as benzol or kerosene would have produced a different kind of flame. Soot deposits found in the stenographers' room and especially in the ventilation channels suggested this, but Wagner took the view that the heat was such that these fuels would also have produced inflammable and explosive gases which would have resulted in a much larger explosion than that indicated by the blast effect.[100] Schatz referred to the "fume-producing liquids" that had created the observed effect as a petroleum derivative, probably heavy motor oil. No one noticed that in this statement Schatz had contradicted himself twice. In the first place, though Klotz had used the word "vapor," he had meant common smoke; in the second place, "vapor" had led Schatz to infer a self-igniting liquid which according to his statement gave off white fumes.[101] But such fuels had been expressly excluded because no smell of any kind had been noticed.

Thus the problem of how the fire had been lighted remained unsolved. No agreement was reached concerning the nature or quantity of fuel employed. Josse estimated that twenty to forty kilograms of fuel had been brought into the building. Schatz spoke of a maximum of from four to five liters.[102] The only argument in favor of this estimate was that a five-liter tin would have fitted into

Torgler's suspect briefcase. According to Schatz the curtains had also been sprinkled with it, which would have
left very little for Scranowitz' separate fires. But the utterly arbitrary estimates of these experts are explained by
a detail which any layman can understand. Schatz believed that 300 cubic centimeters of self-igniting fuel were
enough for forty coal lighters. He made no statement
about the quantity actually used; it was generally supposed to be about two to three liters, plus five liters of
heavy motor oil. In opposition to Josse, Schatz maintained that the glass roof might have caved in because of
low pressure, "resulting from contraction brought about
by the combinations that formed between the anhydride
in the fuel and the water in the atmosphere." [103] But how,
considering that the hall had a volume of some 11,000
cubic meters, that this hall had swinging doors, that the
ventilating shafts were open, and that liquids were meanwhile turning into gas, could a chemically induced contraction of the atmosphere amounting at most to a few
liters have reduced the pressure sufficiently to shatter a
glass roof?

Even an expert preparing a sworn affidavit can make
mistakes; but Schatz's mistakes were blatant.[104] The Reich
Court took his word for it that in examining samples of
earth, mortar, and soot he had found substances produced
by the combustion of a petroleum-like liquid (gasoline), of
naphthalene (coal lighters!), and of phosphorus dissolved
in carbon disulphide. The igniting fluid conjectured by
him has an extremely penetrating odor; at first Schatz
stated as much but then denied it when Sack drew the
inference that Torgler, who was presumed to have distributed this fuel, must then have carried the smell about
with him.[105] Apart from his assistant, no one witnessed
Schatz's chemical analyses.[106] But there are a number of
other considerations, having nothing to do with chemistry, which argue that his hypotheses cannot be taken seriously.

In the first place Schatz was convinced of what he would find before he analyzed anything. "In view of observations I have made in the last few years," he declared to the court, "chemical analyses would, in my opinion, have been quite unnecessary; for I have so often observed fires that spread like these, particularly like the one in the main hall, and the soundness of my observations has been so repeatedly confirmed by confessions in the course of subsequent hearings, that even if my analyses had yielded no positive result I should feel certain that inflammable liquids were used." [107] Where could Schatz have seen a comparable fire when, as his colleagues demonstrated, the conditions prevailing in the main hall had been unique? When Schatz came to speak of van der Lubbe's overcoat, he stressed that he had "unfortunately" been unable to find any liquid fuel.[108] Thus Schatz came to the conclusion at variance with all the findings of the preliminary investigation, that van der Lubbe could not have entered the main hall.[109]

As the trial record shows,[110] Schatz came to this conclusion because otherwise van der Lubbe would have smelled of fuel when arrested. Nevertheless, he put forward the theory that van der Lubbe had not used his coat as a torch, but had been obliged to remove it because, having been sprinkled with the self-igniting liquid, it had begun to burn.[111] Finally, despite the previous negative findings, he discovered vestiges of the self-igniting liquid in the overcoat and in the "pouring trace" as well. When it was called to his attention that this threw doubt on his theory that the fires in the main hall and in the restaurant had developed in entirely different ways, he said that van der Lubbe had found a remnant of the self-igniting fuel or been given it by a third party.[112] From this self-contradictory theory the verdict drew untenable conclusions.[113]

The theory that while dashing through the building van der Lubbe could have found remnants of self-igniting fuel—in a container that must have been inflammable—is easily refuted. According to Schatz the time it took the self-igniting fluid to ignite was determined by the strength of the solution. On one occasion he said that half an hour, on another that from one to two hours had intervened between the distribution of the fuel and the time it ignited—depending on the momentary requirements of his demonstration. If an igniting time of roughly thirty minutes is presumed—the minimum if accomplices were at work—van der Lubbe's overcoat (even under varying conditions of evaporation) would have had to catch fire, because the liquid had run from the bottle into the pocket. Remnants of the igniting fluid would have had to take fire in the restaurant, in the presence of witnesses. On the other hand the development of the fire in the main hall becomes inexplicable if such fuels were employed. Though it is conceivable that rags soaked in benzol or some similar fluid would not have spontaneously taken fire from the heat radiation and the overheated air, this would be impossible in the case of an igniting fluid which derives its efficacy from the fact that even under normal conditions it evaporates quickly and in evaporating takes fire.[114]

The assumption that a self-igniting fuel had been used gave rise to a chain of contradictions and absurdities. What gave Schatz the idea? At first he had thought of fuses to explain the spread of the fire after van der Lubbe's arrest. The function of the self-igniting fuel was to make it seem probable that Torgler had played an active part in setting the fire. From this fiction it followed that van der Lubbe had nothing to do with setting the fire and was present in the Reichstag building only to take the sole blame on himself.[115] According to the verdict, van der Lubbe had not been in the main hall, "since in view of the self-igniting (liquid) employed that would have been entirely superfluous," and had acted in such a way as "to incur suspicion of being the author, and indeed the sole author, of the fire. This is borne out by the line of defense to which, faithful to the Communist instructions for courtroom defense . . . he adhered unswervingly throughout the trial. . . ." [116] A further argument put forward in the verdict was his "ostentatious behavior, quite unsuitable for one who wished to light a fire secretly!" But if van der Lubbe's function was to take the sole blame on himself, why would his accomplices have put a container of self-igniting fuel in his pocket, the existence of which would prove that he had not acted alone? Consequently Schatz departed from his original idea that inflammables had also been used in the restaurant, and declared that van der Lube could not have had much fuel on him. [117]

There is no indication that Schatz's "magic fluid" was used. Traces of phosphorus and sulphur can be found everywhere. Consequently this hypothesis can be excluded. There remains the question of whether the main hall had been "prepared." As stated above, Wagner inferred from Scranowitz' testimony that it had been. Josse had come to the same conclusion on technical grounds. His affidavit, however, was totally uncritical. Josse expressed surprise that the ventilating system was not operating, although it seems reasonable to suppose that "while making preparations for the fire—and especially when lighting it —the incendiaries would have made use of this means of fanning the blaze. In view of the *extremely expert* job done in the main hall, this could hardly have been overlooked." Instead of inferring that in this respect the job had not been "expert" at all, the expert maintained that "to keep the ventilation shafts open would not have been in keeping with the desired development of the fire." [118] He did not so much as consider the possibility that van der Lubbe had acted alone! Testifying before the Reich Court, he based his idea of an "expert job" first on the choice of fuel (nature unknown), second on the way it had been distributed throughout the hall (a matter on which no evidence was available), third on the blast (which Wagner regarded as natural), fourth on the rapid development of heat at the beginning of the fire (pure hypothesis), and fifth on van der Lubbe's expression of surprise after the fire that the dome of the Reichstag building had not been destroyed! [119] Josse admitted that no fuel container of any kind had been found. Otherwise he left all questions open, except for the calculation that the energy needed to create such heat in the hall could only have been created by inflammables brought in from outside and that the soot deposits precluded a naturally induced fire. It was Josse, to be sure, who thought up the diversion theory, according to which van der Lubbe had lighted the fire in the restaurant in order to keep the firemen away from the main scene of the fire, though if that had been his purpose it would certainly have been more reasonable to refrain from lighting a fire on the periphery of the building.[120]

These affidavits are not convincing. They are contradicted by the statements of Ritter and Brüning.[121] The detectives who questioned van der Lubbe had been informed by the firemen that it was quite possible van der Lubbe had set the fire alone.[122] Tobias has assembled the arguments and facts which refute the theory of the fire experts in other points. But perhaps it will be worth our while to deal briefly with one problem that in recent years has been heatedly discussed in the press. In the course of the trial, as we know, doubts arose as to whether van der Lubbe could, in the computed time, have completed the itinerary within the Reichstag building, described by him in the course of the hearings. Schatz was first to doubt this, but his arguments were self-contradictory. Recently it has been suggested that van der Lubbe's eye injury would have prevented him from moving so quickly in the dark Reichstag building.[123] As always in such cases, it is a matter of controversy how much time the incendiary had at his disposal; the calculations fluctuate between fifteen and twenty minutes.[124] The detectives who questioned van der Lubbe at the scene of the fire have been criticized for not allowing enough time for the setting of the different fires; by daylight van der Lubbe required fifteen minutes to cover the itinerary.[125] But there were plenty of witnesses present at the time who regarded van der Lubbe's record run as perfectly possible.[126] Moreover, the shots fired while he was lighting the fire spurred van der Lubbe to the greatest haste. The fact that a good many of the fires went out immediately shows that he was in too much of a hurry. The curtains, which it was easy to set afire while hurrying past, were solely responsible for the big fire in the main hall. To set fire to the main hall van der Lubbe required at the most two minutes.

The opinion has also been put forward that van der Lubbe completed only half of his alleged itinerary. And it has been inferred from certain contradictions that his whole statement was untrue. These contradictions can largely be explained by the above-described methods used in the preliminary investigation. Moreover, it seems hard to believe that van der Lubbe would have given such precise information about his complicated itinerary if he had wished to hide something; he could plausibly have said that he could not remember exactly, or he could have omitted to mention the stretches he had covered twice. There is no compelling reason to believe that van der Lubbe could not have lighted the fires in the main hall by himself, especially since—the verdict to the contrary notwithstanding—his presence in the main hall has been amply demonstrated, and since this was where a fire could have been lighted in the shortest time.[127]

Thus it can be stated beyond a shadow of doubt that all the arguments against van der Lubbe's claim to have lighted the fire by himself are based on hypotheses that cannot be proved objectively and that are in large part self-contradictory or untested. The theory that he acted alone is supported by van der Lubbe's unequivocal and

repeated confessions, by the findings of the police investigation, by the numerous contradictions which the experts
testifying before the court made no attempt to clear up
and the verdict merely compounded, and not least by the
fact that the general obsession with the theory of a well-
organized Communist plot made impossible an unbiased
approach to the evidence, thus, despite all efforts of the
court to avoid being influenced, preventing the defense
from being conducted properly. Consequently we can dispense with the fantasy of an "undisciplined" SA commando, not to mention the theory that Goering was in the
know or that van der Lubbe had somehow received instructions from National Socialist higher-ups.

The Political Consequences of the Reichstag Fire

Having refuted the theory that the fire was the work of
more than one person and shown that it was possible for
one person to set the main hall of the Reichstag building
on fire, we have no need of a detailed investigation to determine whether the reactions of Goering and Hitler immediately after the fire were genuine or feigned. Their
surprise was genuine. When Hanfstaengl phoned him the
news, Goebbels thought it was a bad joke.[128] Goering
seems to have been utterly thunderstruck; he went at
once to the burning building. His first thought was to
save the tapestries and the library.[129] He arrived at about
9:30 P.M., shortly after the main hall had gone up in
flames and the fire had reached ten-alarm proportions. It
cannot be inferred from Goering's behavior that he welcomed the fire.[130] He gave the necessary instructions,
spoke chiefly with Fire Chief Gempp, and inquired after
Councilor Galle, the President of the Reichstag. Assistant
Secretary Grauert, who was with him, inquired at once
into the origin of the fire, learned of the grounds for suspecting Torgler and Koenen, and was convinced from

that moment on that the Communists were behind the fire.[131]

Goering later said that the moment he heard the word "incendiary" the idea that the Communist Party was to blame had come to him spontaneously.[132] But it seems more likely that the idea was first suggested by the information he obtained from Grauert. A little later Rudolf Diels arrived, accompanied by Assessor Schnitzler, learned that van der Lubbe had been arrested, and took part in the first hearings.[133] At the same time Goering seems to have been told that the only one of the incendiaries to be apprehended was a Dutch Communist—it was assumed from the first that van der Lubbe was a Communist. Goering did not question the generally prevailing view that the fire had been organized on a large scale by a considerable number of incendiaries. He ordered a search of the pipe tunnel, which was carried out without results by his bodyguard, the SS man Walter Weber, and three policemen.[134]

Sommerfeldt tells how he was awakened at about 11:00 P.M. and taken to the Reichstag building in a car. This, however, must have occurred considerably earlier, at about 10:15, for he met Goering before Goering, as Goebbels reports,[135] "got all steamed up." According to Sommerfeldt, Goering was perfectly calm and gave the impression "of being somewhat affected by this incendiary act, but of not attaching too much importance to it." Goering had calmly instructed him to draw up the above-mentioned report.[136] Shortly after ten o'clock Goering, in his capacity as Prussian Minister of the Interior, must have ordered the first security measures. When Hitler arrived, Goering reported that he had mobilized the entire police force and placed all public buildings under police protection. The other security measures are reported in the WTB for February 28.[137]

In all probability Hilter, Goebbels, and their retinues did not arrive at the scene of the fire before 10:20 P.M.

Delmer informs us that Goebbels first sent Gauleiter Hanke to find out what was actually going on.[138] Goering received Hitler at the entrance to the lobby adjoining Portal 2. According to Delmer, Goering explained that it was undoubtedly the work of the Communists, that an incendiary had been arrested, and that several Communist Reichstag members had been in the building twenty minutes before the outbreak of the fire. Papen had arrived earlier; Goering had greeted him with the remark: "This can only be a plot against the new government!" [139] Papen expressed no doubts.

Thus it is clear that, on the basis of rumors that had come to his ears, Goering hit on the idea that the Reichstag fire was connected with a projected Communist uprising. This accounts for the elaborate security measures which he spontaneously ordered and which Sir Horace Rumbold termed a manifestation of "hysteria." [140] Delmer comments: "I am convinced that he took it seriously and was not play-acting." [141] After Goering's report the VIPs made a tour of the building while the firemen were trying to contain the terrible fire in the main hall. The main hall served to illustrate the danger that Goering had conjured. Delmer, the only journalist who succeeded in entering the building and in speaking to Hitler in the course of his tour, reported the following utterances: " 'I hope to God,' he said to me, 'that this is the work of the Communists. You are now witnessing the outbreak of a great epoch in Germany history.' " And Delmer quotes Hitler as saying a little later to Papen: "This is a signal sent by God, Herr Vice Chancellor. If, as I believe, the fire is the work of the Communists, then we must crush the murdering monster with an iron fist." From these utterances Delmer inferred that Hitler was not quite sure. That night, he writes, the Chancellor was "not yet fully convinced that this was a Communist plot." [142] But beyond a doubt Hitler soon became convinced. Did he believe in the plot, or was he putting on an act?

Rudolf Diels speaks of Hitler's reaction in his memoirs. He writes that he met Hitler and his entourage on a platform opening out on the main hall. Hitler had been extremely agitated when Goering came up to him and said, with the emotion of a man conscious of his historic mission: "This is the beginning of the Communist uprising. They are about to strike. There is not a moment to lose!" [143] The VIPs gathered in the room of the president of the Reichstag. Diels tried to tell Hitler about the hearings on van der Lubbe. Hitler was completely out of control, demanding that every Communist functionary should be shot on the spot and that the Communist members of the Reichstag should be hanged that same night; it was also high time, he said, to stop handling the Social Democrats and the Reichsbanner with kid gloves. Under these circumstances Diels's efforts to convince Hitler that van der Lubbe had set the fire by himself were hopeless.[144]

Diels's story is corroborated by Schnitzler's notes that were drawn up independently of Diels:[145]

> Diels characterized the National Socialist conference in the burning Reichstag, at which the first political measures were decided upon, or rather ordered on the spur of the moment without being clearly thought out, as "agitated" and "wild." After Hitler had recovered from a kind of cataleptic trance, he had, still according to Diels, flown into an interminable outburst of rage and vilified the Communist "subhumans." He no longer required any semblance of proof to be convinced that the Communists by "shamefully setting fire to a German palladium had wished to give the signal for their loudly heralded mass action." Hitler had seriously given the order to hang all Communist Reichstag members.[146]

Was Hitler's customary monomaniacal rage still rationally controlled at this point? Was this the feigned agitation which led Hitler, while speaking, to believe in the truth of his words? Undoubtedly the following entry in

Goebbels' diary is more than suspect: "The decisive moment has come. Not for one moment does the Führer lose his calm; it is admirable to see him giving his orders, the same man who only half an hour ago was still having a carefree chat with us at dinner." [147]

This conference in the Reichstag President's room lasted little more than half an hour. In addition to Goering, Hitler, and Goebbels, Minister of the Interior Frick, Police President von Levetzow, whom Goering had sent for, and probably Count Helldorf [148] * and Mayor Sahm were present, whereas Papen had left the building to notify President Hindenburg.[149] The conference was taken up mainly by Hitler's tirades; calm not to say lucid discussion was out of the question. Hitler seems to have confined himself mainly to ordering measures of terror and violence against the Communists. In all probability he was thinking chiefly of the elections. A later press report[150] contains the information:

> As previously noted, Adolf Hitler announced while still at the scene of the fire that, come what might, the elections would take place on March 5. He declared that the Reich government would take the measures necessary to crush and exterminate this dire threat not only to Germany but to Europe as well.

Nonetheless, it was not Hitler who issued orders, but Goering; Hitler's outpourings of hatred had given him the green light. This was Goering's great hour. Diels tells us that Goering subjected him to a flood of rather confused instructions, including "police on an emergency footing, shoot to kill, mass arrests of Communists and Social Democrats." [151] "During the conference," Schnitzler recalled,[152] "Diels noted the various points on a sheet of paper, and afterward worried whether he had carried out

---

* Wolf Heinrich Count von Helldorf, leader of the SA in Berlin-Brandenburg and Police President of Potsdam.

the orders given in their frenzy by the agitated members of the new government, untroubled by the slightest knowledge of the instrument of power and law which they claimed to be able to play." Without a doubt Goering had also demanded the arrest of all Social Democratic functionaries, and not only a two weeks' suspension of the Social Democratic press in Prussia. This can be inferred from the fact that the parallel action of Helldorf, who was either present at the conference or received orders from Goering a little later, included the Social Democrats. It was presumably with Diels's approval that Schnitzler issued instructions to all police radio stations to send out a call for the arrest of all Communist members of the Reichstag, of the provincial diets, and of the town councils as well as of all Communist functionaries, and for the suppression of all Communist newspapers.[153]

What chiefly struck Diels and Schnitzler in connection with this episode was that far-reaching political decisions were made by men who had lost all self-control and gave no thought to the political consequences. The National Socialist leaders were among themselves; hence there was no reason to engage in theatricals for propaganda purposes. These were not cynically calculating politicians putting on a show for the public. Thus the theory that they had a clear grasp of the situation and exploited it with virtuosity for their purposes is without foundation. Manifestly Hitler and Goering were in such a state that they could not listen to the real facts about the fire, and it would even be misleading to say that they did not wish to do so. They reacted on a subrational level, dominated by instinct and vanity. Hitler's outbursts of rage and hatred, culminating in the absurd demand that the Communist Reichstag members be hanged immediately, cannot be viewed in a rational light. Nor were Goering's reactions feigned; under normal circumstances he was capable of giving clear, intelligible orders. Undoubtedly the desire to

put himself, as Prussian Minister of Police, in the lime-
light had a good deal to do with it, especially in view of
the keen rivalry between himself and Goebbels.

Under these circumstances it is not irrelevant to ask
whether Goering's orders to Diels were motivated by the
situation or based on fantasy. Goering's belief in a Communist uprising was not merely an emanation of his overheated imagination. It was encouraged by reports from
police headquarters. Police Inspector Heisig questioned
the incendiary at police headquarters. On the witness
stand he stated once again that van der Lubbe had used
the words "signal" and "flare" [*Fanal*] and had said it was
time to "strike" to do away with a system that was hostile
to the working class.[154] At the time this was interpreted by
him and the observers present at the interview, including
Police President von Levetzow, as pointing to a Communist uprising. In the hectic, unreal atmosphere of that
night, these words sufficed to transform suspicion into certainty. Only a few remained free from this psychosis,
which developed spontaneously and which there was no
need to foster artificially. It is adequately accounted for
by the tense political situation. There is no reason to believe that the National Socialist leadership did not take
the specter of a Communist uprising seriously, especially
as they had been expecting something of the sort. On
January 31 Goebbels had written in his diary: "The attempt at Bolshevist revolution must first flare up. Then,
at the right moment, we will strike." [155] Concerning the
conference in the burning Reichstag building he noted:
"There is no doubt that the Communists are here making
a last attempt to create confusion by arson and terror, in
order to seize power amid the general panic." [156] What
danger if any the National Socialist leadership in their
calmer moments really feared from their Communist adversaries is a question that can be left open for the moment. All indications are that the orders for the arrest of
Communists were a spontaneous reaction to the key

words "Communist uprising" as they fell on the avid, overheated imaginations of the National Socialists.

* *

The inclusion of the Social Democrats in these measures was connected with van der Lubbe's statements under questioning, from which it was inferred that the SPD as well as the KPD was behind the supposed plot, though the examining magistrate was obliged to deny that this was so in a statement to the press of March 22.[157] This grotesque inference was made possible by the weird, unreal atmosphere, in which the most absurd rumors were believed, and by the propaganda and mentality of the National Socialists, who consciously and unconsciously lumped the Communists and Social Democrats together. Moreover, the threat of a general strike called by both parties was still taken seriously by the government, as Article 6 of the February 28 Decree to Combat Treason Against the German Nation bears witness.[158] It is hard to imagine what would have happened if Diels had taken seriously the order to arrest the Social Democrats, disband the Reichsbanner, etc. If there was any calculation behind this order, it was only the idea of making a clean sweep in a situation of civil war.

The conference in the office of the Reichstag President ended at about eleven o'clock and brought no further results. But the idea of proclaiming a state of emergency seems already to have been brought up at this time. According to a press report, the cabinet "was to meet again during the night in special session" to deliberate "on the political consequences of the Reichstag fire." [159]

At about 11:15 Hitler and Goering left the still smoldering Reichstag building and went to the Prussian Ministry of the Interior. There a conference was held which seems to have been what the above-mentioned press report refers to erroneously as a cabinet meeting. It was attended by Vice Chancellor von Papen, Police President von Levetzow, Assistant Secretary Grauert, State Secretary von Bismarck, and Councilor Diels. Frick, who had attended the previous meeting, was absent, perhaps merely because the competence of this body extended only to Prussia. The composition of the meeting indicates that it was called chiefly to discuss security measures and arrests. Concerning this meeting Goering had the following to say in his testimony before the Reich Court: "We again discussed the whole situation. It was decided at the very start that I should immediately cancel . . . my election rallies . . . scheduled for the next few days. Because in such an atmosphere I could obviously not leave Berlin." He went on to say that he had been authorized to take all necessary measures, and that a cabinet meeting had been called for the following day.[160] As can be gathered from the above-mentioned press report on Hitler's remarks at the scene of the fire, his chief concern was that the elections should be held "under any circumstances," and one wonders what led him to make this strange statement. According to the testimony of Detective Superintendent Heller, the arrest orders previously given in feverish haste were repeated and made official at this session, and a list of the persons to be arrested may have been drawn up.[161] The much discussed "Reichstag fire decree" was not at the center of the discussion. Probably with a view to the fact that nothing had been done to legalize the arrests, the German Nationalist Grauert suggested an "emergency decree against arson and terrorist acts." Thus Grauert, who was firmly convinced that the Communists were responsible for the fire, suggested what was to be a decisive step toward Hitler's unlimited dictatorship.[162]

The emergency decree proposed by Grauert was undoubtedly very different from the draft submitted to the Reichstag the following day. The original plan seems to have been a decree applicable only to Prussia, and it is possible that this accounts in part for Frick's reference to the Prussian decree of July 20. For otherwise we should be at a loss to explain Blomberg's remark at the March 1 meeting of the High Command:[163] "Thanks to Hitler's foresight, the new emergency decree was extended to the entire Reich." In this view, Hitler accepted Grauert's suggestion, but decided that it should be discussed at next day's cabinet meeting. This fits in with Grauert's statement that the matter had been taken out of the hands of the Prussian Ministry of the Interior.[164]

After the meeting at the Prussian Ministry of the Interior Hitler and Goebbels went to the offices of the *Völkischer Beobachter;* they stopped the presses and had a new front page written.[165] The South German edition had already appeared and contained not a word about the Reichstag fire. Goebbels launched a wild press campaign. That same night he wrote an inflammatory editorial, painting the horror of a successful Communist campaign of terror and stating that the Communists were planning to seize power in the midst of the "general panic." [166] In the dispatches of the Official Prussian Press Bureau, which the WTB published in the second edition of February 28, the Reichstag fire was characterized as a "signal for bloody revolution and civil war"; it was declared that "the first assault of the criminal forces has been beaten off," [167] a statement inspired by Goering's bluster, for at the time the report was sent out the police action had barely begun.[168] The police, the report went on, had been put on a top emergency footing and two thousand members of the SA auxiliary police had been called in to defend the capital. On March 1 the *Völkischer Beobachter* spoke of a projected "Saint Bartholomew" in Berlin, and disclosed Communist plans for insurrection which Goering had borrowed from obsolete directives for civil war.[169]

Despite all its efforts, as Tobias has shown, Goebbels' press bureau blundered, and not only in connection with the reporting of the fire and its causes. Amid the general confusion, even the *Völkischer Beobachter* reported that Torgler had given himself up voluntarily and was obliged to change its story the following day.[170] But it is understandable that on the night after the fire Goering should have termed Sommerfeldt's communiqué "crap," "a police report from Alexanderplatz" [police presidium] which he could have no use for at a time when he was preparing to strike a crushing counterblow against the Communists.[171] Sommerfeldt believed that Goebbels was behind this change of heart on Goering's part, but the truth was much simpler; even if Goering had believed that van der Lubbe had acted alone, it was too late to retract the "political signal" theory without making himself—and his police measures—look ridiculous.

That was the situation on the night of February 27. It raises a number of questions. As we have seen, the National Socialist leadership was taken by surprise and acted in a state of excitement. Were the National Socialist leaders really convinced that the Reichstag fire was an act of Communist terror? At first, as we have seen, Hitler was not quite sure; but this does not mean that he did not immediately swing over to Goering's view, especially as the results of the investigation, including the misstatements about Torgler, confirmed his suspicions and as a political exploitation of the fire was in the air in any case. Thus it may be presumed that the National Socialists were convinced that the Communists were behind the fire. A much more difficult question to answer is whether, and if so in what degree, they believed in a Communist uprising or a planned series of terrorist acts, and at what moment they recognized this to be a mistake. It is hard to answer this question because we possess virtually no statements on the subject that do not admit of, or indeed call for, a tactical interpretation, and because the essential character of National Socialist thinking, even in the consciousness of its proponents, was to substitute resentment for the experience of reality. Goebbels' expectation of a "Communist attempt at revolution" fits in with a good deal of indirect testimony[172] to the effect that the National Socialists did not believe the Communists would let them come to power without putting up a fight. Our present knowledge of the situation and policy of the KPD in the weeks after the seizure of power[173] permits us to infer that the National Socialists had overestimated their adversary. Undoubtedly Hitler's conviction that it was politically inexpedient to outlaw the KPD, as his German National partners wished, was not motivated solely by the tactical consideration that this would have added appreciably to the Social Democratic vote.[174] The history of his own movement taught him that there was very little to be gained by outlawing a political party.[175]

At the same time, however, the National Socialists derived an appealing campaign promise from their undertaking to combat Communism successfully, and there is no doubt that the bourgeoisie's fear of Communism, fanned by the propaganda of all the right-wing parties and also by the actual situation of civil war between the KPD and the NSDAP, contributed very considerably to the rise of National Socialism. Thus for tactical reasons it was to the advantage of the National Socialists not to eliminate this adversary until they themselves were firmly in the saddle. Nevertheless it seems probable that the National Socialist leadership were increasingly alarmed at the question of why, generally speaking, the KPD took the increasing provocations of the SA lying down and failed to strike the counterblow that would release Hitler from the shackles imposed on him by the German National cabinet members and the independent position of the Reichswehr. The extraordinary agitation into which Hitler worked himself on the night of the fire suggests that he really thought the great conflict was at hand, that he regarded a Communist putsch as imminent. This would account for the hasty reaction of the National Socialists, the immediate measures for the security of public buildings, museums, castles, bridges, and railroads. Because, if that were the case, it became essential to get the jump on the Communists.

In order to appraise this hypothesis we must first determine whether the situation gave the government cause to believe that the Communists were planning an armed uprising. True, the memory of Communist uprisings under the Weimar Republic was still fresh. The actual situation, however, was much more complicated. The tactics of the KPD in those weeks were vacillating and inconsistent. While in the Central Committee plans for an active struggle of the working class against Hitler were postponed indefinitely, the Communist organizations were provided with literature calling indirectly or often directly for armed resistance.[176] Large amounts of such material reached the news bureau of the Ministry of the Interior, and at the same time large stores of weapons were found.[177] The nature of the material found in the second search of the Karl-Liebknecht House, which Goering cited as the main justification of his measures, remains unknown.[178] These finds along with the rumors then circulating increased the general nervousness and fear of a Communist uprising. On February 27, the Berlin Criminal Investigation Department [Landeskriminalpolizeiamt] broadcast a report to the effect that the KPD was planning systematic armed attacks on police patrols and "national" organizations on the day of the Reichstag elections, or shortly before or after, and recommended that "suitable countermeasures be taken immediately and that Communist functionaries should perhaps be taken into protective custody." [179] This information was more than dubious, but should not be interpreted as a deliberate propagandist invention; rather, it indicates the general overestimation of Communist activity, and shows that the idea of Communist responsibility for the fire was in the air. A great mass of material has been assembled in connection with the Reichstag fire and the propagandist use to which it was put. This material confirms the fact that despite acts of individual terror the Communist Party leadership remained passive.

In the light of what we now know of Communist revolutionary strategy, the evidence that the Communists were planning an uprising was meager. But in the then prevailing atmosphere, propaganda pamphlets like Sommerfeldt's *Die Kommune* were taken at face value. Even the high police officials concerned with the case, who at that time had by no means been "Nazified" [*gleichgeschaltet*], tended to overemphasize the activity of the Communists. In a report of March 14 the view was expressed "that not only does the organization of an armed uprising for the overthrow of the government figure in the Communist program; they are determined to carry out their programmatic demands and principles in practice." [180] Before the Reich Court, Detective Superintendent Heller, testifying as an expert, submitted material to prove that the Communists were planning an uprising, but then denied that they were prepared for action.[181] Nevertheless, Heller continued to believe that his exposé justified the assertion that the Communists had been planning an uprising.

As for Goering, it seems certain that at least on the night of the fire he believed in the specter of a Communist uprising. Ever since he had become Prussian Minister of the Interior it had been his dream to crush such an uprising.[182] As he stressed at the cabinet meeting of March 2, he did not expect one before the elections. The cynical frankness and tactical ineptitude of Goering's testimony before the Reich Court make it seem likely that he was telling the truth, and it is no doubt for this reason that his remarks were sharply criticized by Goebbels. The Reichstag fire, Goering declared, had come as a surprise to him and had not fitted in with his plan of action. True, he had been resolved from the start to strike a counterblow against the Communists, but the police apparatus he had taken over was still deficient; in particular, it lacked the determination to strike with the necessary ruthlessness. Goering expressly claimed authorship of the "shoot-to-kill" order, as it came to be called. He had considered carrying on the fight with the SA and SS alone, but had deliberately discarded this idea:

> In the first place, there was the newly created state with its whole civil service corps which I wished to rebuild, to transform, and to imbue with the new spirit—I could not totally exclude it from this task which offered an opportunity to employ it for the first time as a state organ for the preservation of the new state. That would have shaken the confidence of the civil service corps in the new state from the very start.[183]

It is certain that at the time of the Reichstag fire, the Prussian police had not yet been transformed into a reliable instrument of National Socialism. The SA auxiliary police established by the decree of February 22 was still in process of organization; in Berlin it took no appreciable part in the campaign of arrest.[184] And the changes of personnel at the Berlin Police Presidium were only in their beginnings.

If the improvised campaign of arrests nevertheless brought appreciable results, it was primarily because the old Political Police apparatus was still intact; the old officials from Severing's day were still on the job. The arrests were carried out on the basis of lists that had been drawn up by the democratic government for the eventuality that the Communist Party would be suppressed; Goering had had these lists completed and brought up to date.[185] Despite the official statements that four thousand Communists were arrested in the weeks after the Reichstag fire, there can be no doubt that the action was improvised and premature, a stroke in the dark, which induced the KPD to build up its underground organization. Sir Horace Rumbold reported on March 2: "Though Communist leaders have been arrested, I am told on reliable authority that organization has gone to ground and is intact, but that no instructions for armed resistance have been issued to the party members." [186] Although the KPD was taken by surprise—at the time of the fire the Central Committee was in session and even party functionaries were unable to reach it[187]—numerous prominent Communists evaded arrest.

Thus the action was by no means the brilliant success that the National Socialist press claimed. Indirectly Goering admitted as much when he remarked that he had felt the Reichstag fire to have "interfered completely" with his "beautifully laid plans"; he had found it "inconvenient, extremely inconvenient"; he had been in the situation of "a general, who wants to carry out a great battle plan and is then compelled by an impulsive action of the enemy to proceed in an entirely different way, to move his troops in haste and take up battle positions." He had expected the Communist counteroffensive later, during the three or four weeks between the Reichstag fire and the meeting of the Reichstag, "that is, at a time when the Communist mandates had been annulled but of course no Communist leaders were yet under arrest." He had wanted the enemy to open hostilities, but not until he had completed his deployment. "The elections were to be the climax, if only because they would provide a rough idea of the strength of the Communist following. After the elections," Goering went on, "the Communist mandates were of course to be annulled." It was not likely, in his opinion, that the party would accept this measure without a struggle, for then it would have lost face in the eyes of its adherents. In either case the party could easily have been crushed, and a part of the leadership would not have been able to save themselves as they had after February 27.[188]

This statement made under the eyes of world opinion is typical of the cynical frankness with which the National Socialist leadership revealed the motives of their actions. It shows not only that the National Socialists wished to provoke a Communist uprising, but also that the government planned to annul the Communist mandates in case it should prove impossible to gain a two-thirds majority for the Enabling Act by quasi-legal methods.[189] It would not have been to the interest of the National Socialists, Goering explained, to outlaw the Communist Party, because then the Communist electorate would have voted for the SPD or the Center Party.[190] Goering now admitted that the first search of the Karl-Liebknecht House had been undertaken chiefly for propaganda reasons and had not brought very impressive results, and that only consideration for the prevailing mood of the people had led him to attack during the night of the fire.

Was this an admission that Goering had decided on arrests and the measures of violence against the KPD for electoral reasons, in consideration of "the prevailing mood of the people"? Goering's statement fits in with Hitler's remark at the cabinet meeting of February 28, to the effect that the "psychological moment" had come for dealing with the Communists.[191] A number of considerations argue against such an oversimplification. Goering's remarks were made at a time when the passivity of the KPD had rendered the idea of a large-scale revolutionary plan absurd. That, precisely, is what made the suspicion vented in the world press that Goering was the actual incendiary seem so plausible. Exactly like the police investigators, Goering tried to represent the Reichstag fire as a link in a chain of terrorist acts leading to revolution, since it was no longer possible to uphold the original contention that the fire was to be the immediate signal for an uprising. Goering clung tenaciously to his over-all suspicion and described the events as though the measures taken on the night of the fire had got the jump on the Communists. In response to Torgler's objections, he asked with none too convincing irony why the Communists had issued instructions for civil war if they had no intention of carrying them out.[192] It was the same Goe-

ring who had heedlessly, without regard for Diels's warnings, initiated the preparations for the monster trial for
high treason.

From all this it follows that the National Socialist leadership were indeed expecting a Communist counterac-
tion, but only at a later date. Our fragmentary sources
enable us to give only a partial answer to the questions of
how Hitler and his followers judged the political situation on the night of the fire and what political measures
they were considering. It is conceivable, however, that
Hitler became more and more obsessed with the idea,
noted in Goebbels' diary, that the Communists wished to
provoke a general panic. His first reactions, such as demanding that all the Communists be hanged, were absurd.
It was perfectly possible to quench Communist agitation effectively by suppressing their newspapers, meetings, and demonstrations, and this had largely been done.
Undoubtedly Hitler, with his keen instinct for the mood
of the population, thought of using the "Communist bug-
aboo" for purposes of electoral propaganda. This may
have been the motivation for the security measures which
Rumbold calls "hysterical," [193] and which were not suspended after the elections but remained in force for two
weeks. But the inclusion of the Social Democrats in these
arrests would largely have deprived them of their effect
and above all constituted a break with the tactical line
that Hitler followed in the weeks before the Enabling
Act, to wit, emphasis on the legal methods of the new government.

In this context the statement that the elections must
take place on March 5 "under any circumstances" takes
on a particular weight. The main topic discussed at the
conference at the Prussian Ministry of the Interior was
the continuation of the election campaign. The following
morning at the cabinet meeting Hitler took up the matter
again: "The attack on the Reichstag building must have
no effect on the date of the elections or the reconvening of

the Reichstag." At the same time he suggested the castle of Potsdam as a meeting place for the Reichstag.[194] From this it may be inferred that Hitler looked on the fire as a primitive attempt to prevent the Reichstag from meeting. It is not clear, on the other hand, why, even before the meeting at the Prussian Ministry of the Interior, Hitler should have come out against a change in the date of the elections. Had Papen suggested that under the circumstances it might be expedient to postpone them? This is unlikely, because in this case Hitler would not have bothered the cabinet with the question. What was the meaning of "under any circumstances"? It can only have meant that the elections must take place even in an exceptional situation, perhaps a state of emergency. Neither his spontaneous belief in a Communist putsch nor his insistence that the elections should not be postponed can have resulted from propagandist designs.

In view of the hysteria that had gripped the National Socialist members of the government in the burning Reichstag, one inclines to infer that in this "crime against the new government" Hitler saw an attempt to deprive him of the weapon of legality, to force the NSDAP into a civil war, and above all to prevent it from carrying through the elections. In this connection Hitler's introductory remarks at the cabinet meeting of February 28 are significant:

> The Chancellor declared that a ruthless confrontation with the KPD had now become indispensable, that the psychological moment for this confrontation had come, that there was no point in waiting any longer, that the action against [the KPD] must not be subordinated to juridical considerations. Since the Reichstag fire, he said, he no longer doubted that the government would obtain 51 percent at the elections.[195]

From this it follows, first of all, that the National Socialist leadership had decided that the showdown must take place sooner than they had expected. For this there were two reasons: as usual with Hitler, the propagandist necessity and the practical necessity of the confrontation went hand in hand. It is true that since the night of the fire, when Communist actions were felt to be imminent, the situation had grown calmer. No one could claim that a putsch was in the offing. Still, it can hardly have been a purely propagandist exaggeration when Hitler said that the KPD had decided to stop at nothing. It could still not be foreseen that the KPD would be crushed without a struggle. Hitler's remark that this action must not be "subordinated to juridical considerations" referred not so much to the methods of the SA auxiliary police as to the fact that the arrest of the Communist Reichstag members would transgress the principle of parliamentary immunity.[196] Hitler's saying that he no longer doubted that the government would obtain a majority implies that on February 27 the National Socialist leadership was not yet sure the elections would bring the desired results; the frequent statements that they would remain in power in any case point in the same direction. In the given context Hitler's remark was probably an argument against postponing the elections because of a potential or actual civil war situation.

Interestingly enough, the Chancellor attached relatively little importance to the emergency decree, the last point on the agenda of the conference, perhaps, for one thing, because he had little knowledge of it. In any case, he still spoke of it as a merely defensive measure, remarking for example on the necessity of "special measures to safeguard all the cultural documents of the German people." Grauert's proposal had been along these lines. But meanwhile Frick had taken the matter in hand and probably in the morning hours had prepared his draft which differed radically from all previous emergency decrees. Characteristically, it did not occur to the author of the new decree to modify the Decree to Combat Treason Against the German Nation[197] which had been voted by the cabinet on the morning of February 27 and submitted to the President for his signature on the following day, although it partly covered the situation created (in the National Socialist view) by the Communist act of incendiarism. This indicates the spontaneity with which the Reichstag fire decree came into being and is presumably also explained by the fact that the initiators of the first decree knew nothing about the drafting of the second.

The genesis of the Reichstag fire decree, which Helmut Krasnick calls the "Fundamental Law of the Third Reich" [198] and whose crucial importance for the stabilization of the National Socialist system has been demonstrated by Karl Dietrich Bracher,[199] is obscure. What we know for sure is that it came into being spontaneously and that there had been no plans in this direction before the Reichstag fire. At the cabinet meeting Frick observed "that he had originally intended, because of the fire in the Reichstag building, to modify the Decree for the Defense of the German Nation of February 4 of this year." [200] The February decree placed the first serious restrictions on the parties competing with the NSDAP in the elections. Frick may have thought of increasing and extending the penal provisions; in particular, he may have considered a new version of Article 22, so as to remove all limitations on the use of protective custody against the Communists.[201] A contributory factor may have been that in view of the urgency of the situation it seemed too complicated to modify the February decree, which was rather unclear to begin with; in any case Frick made it known that he then decided to use the Prussian decree of July 20 as a basis for the new decree.

With this the decree took on a fundamentally different character. The originally intended version was reflected only in the harsh penal provisions of Article 5 against high treason and a number of criminal acts imputed to the Communists. Some of these provisions go back to the modifications desired by Gürtner, which incidentally show that he was not present when the decree was drafted.[202] As for the genesis of the two decisive provisions of the decree, the suspension of constitutional rights and the infringement embodied in Article 2, on the sovereignty of the *Länder*, we can only resort to conjecture. Undoubtedly there is a direct connection between Article 2 and Goering's statement at the cabinet meeting of the previous day to the effect that by March 6 at the latest, that is, the day after the elections, he would request authorization to place the Hamburg police under the Reich Minister of the Interior.[203] A little later Goering spoke of Hamburg as a "rallying point for Communism," and even earlier pressure had been put on the Senate to replace the Socialist chief of the Hamburg police by a National Socialist.[204]

To strike a nation-wide "counterblow" at the Communists, it was necessary to simplify the complicated mechanism governing the cooperation of the police in the various *Länder* with the central government. In its struggle against the extremes of right and left the Weimar Republic had been seriously hampered by the absence of any central police authority: the Reich Public Prosecutor could take action only through the public prosecutors of the *Länder* and their subsidiary organs.[205] On March 1 Frick, invoking the decree, called on the governments of the *Länder* to suppress all Communist publications and meetings; formally, the ministers of the interior of the *Länder* decided in what degree to accept the measures demanded by Berlin.[206] Article 2 of the new decree went much further, however, and for that reason Papen objected to it at once. This article had been inspired by Frick's interests as Reich Minister of the Interior. Already on February 20 and 21, when Württemberg had complained that the Reich government was overstepping its prerogatives, Frick had responded by threatening to appoint a Reich commissioner in accordance with Article 48, Paragraph 2; on February 24, in a public speech, he addressed the same threat to Bavaria and Hamburg.[207] By February 27 it was rumored that Reich commissioners were about to be appointed in the *Länder*.[208] Beyond any doubt Frick intended to press the *Gleichschaltung* of the *Länder* with the help of Article 2. The changes in the decree obtained by Popitz* and Papen proved ineffectual.[209] At first, to be sure, Frick denied the intention attributed to him and on March 1 assured the Württemberg ambassador that the decree was aimed primarily at the Hanseatic cities, since the government did not wish the *Länder* governed by "Marxists" to obtain the powers conferred by Article 1.[210] This statement accurately reflects the original intention of the decree; but it is obvious that he was acting in the interest of his ministry.

But whose idea was it to abrogate the basic civil rights rather than curtail them as was usually done? This remains an open question. Possibly this idea also originated in the Reich Ministry of the Interior, though probably it did not occur to Frick at the time that this was the most effective way in which to legalize the ruthless persecution of the Communists.[211] As the *Frankfurter Zeitung* commented on March 1,[212] the new situation created by Article 1 came very close to a proclamation of martial law. This meant a considerable deviation from the political line followed since January 30. The emergency decree cannot be regarded as an organic preliminary phase of the Enabling Act which the National Socialist leadership had been striving for from the start; though formally it remained within the framework of the President's right to issue emergency decrees, it was actually a kind of *coup d'état*, anticipating the Enabling Act. This is also shown by a comparison of its style with that of earlier decrees. Whereas the earlier decrees, that of Febru-

---

* Johannes Popitz, Reich Minister without Portfolio and Reich Commissar in charge of the Prussian Finance Ministry in 1932; Prussian State and Finance Minister, 1933–1944.

ary 4 for example, formally retained certain legal guarantees—such as the principle that the acts of government agencies were subject to review by the courts; the right, in practice ineffectual to be sure, to register complaints with higher authorities; and an exact definition of the situations to which the decree was applicable—the Reichstag fire decree simply abrogated the principle of constitutional rights. It gave the government a blank check, subject only to a fictitious time limit.[213] The motivation cited in the preamble—"defense against Communist acts of violence"—did not in any way limit its sphere of application. It was no accident that Frick invoked the model of Papen's Prussian decree. The crucial difference between the Prussian decree and the present one was that not the President but the Reich government decided when Article 2 was to be applied. Consequently Papen suggested feebly in the afternoon session of February 28 that it would be better to let the President decide whether Reich commissioners should be appointed in the *Länder*.[214]

Up to now the Reichstag fire decree has been attributed largely to electoral motives. But why was it needed? True, it created a "better" legal basis for measures directed against the press and freedom of speech and assembly, for breaking up election meetings and demonstrations, confiscating leaflets and propaganda material, searching party offices, and arresting Socialist and Communist leaders. The February decree was invoked in justification of the arrests on the night of the fire. A large part of the opposition press had already been suppressed on the basis of existing decrees, and where the legal basis was insufficient, that did not greatly trouble the authorities. An analysis of the repressive practice in force before the Reichstag fire shows that the change occurring in the days after February 8 was not so much qualitative as purely quantitative. In the non-Prussian *Länder* the

Reich Minister of the Interior had been able even before the decree to put through far-reaching repressive measures against the Center press and other newspapers.[215]

The implementation order of the Prussian Minister of the Interior of March 3, 1933, points in the same direction. It states "that the Decree for the Defense of Nation and State of February 28, 1933 is to be invoked for measures which become necessary against members or institutions of other than Communist, Anarchist, or Social Democratic parties or organizations, only when these measures serve to combat Communist efforts in the broadest sense." In other cases the decree of February 4 was to be invoked.[216] Goering demanded frequent and detailed reports from the various government agencies, informing him how often and under what circumstances the Reichstag fire decree had been applied. These reports and the résumés drawn up at the ministry show clearly that the decree was seldom used against the bourgeois parties, that at first the overwhelming majority of the measures taken were directed against the KPD, and that the persecution of the SPD did not take on importance until April.[217] It seems likely that Goering's purpose in limiting the application of the decree was to counter the accusation that the decree had been issued solely to help the National Socialists in their election campaign.

If the emergency decree was created with a view to electoral considerations, it was a means of further terrorizing the voters. But the relative success of the NSDAP concealed the fact that such a measure cut both ways. The sharply critical attitude of the *Frankfurter Zeitung*, which pointed out that elections in Germany had never before been held in a state of emergency,[218] indicates that this obvious break with the constitutional order, for which *provocateurs* or undisciplined subordinates could no longer be blamed, alienated the sympathies of certain sections of the electorate. After the elections, moreover, the Enabling Act would have been passed in any case, and the full powers anticipated by the emergency decree would have fallen into the government's lap.

There are a number of indications that on the night of the fire and the following day the leading National Socialists, with their utter inability to distinguish between reality and imagination, were misled by Hitler's visions of Communist terror and revolution. After the conference at the Prussian Ministry of the Interior it was rumored that a state of emergency would be declared. All indications are that on the night of the fire such a measure, limited to Prussia, was considered, and that Ebert's decree of September 26, 1923, was taken as a model. According to press reports, it was decided at the cabinet meeting of February 28 not to proclaim martial law.[219] The idea did actually come up. At the High Command meeting recorded in Liebmann's notes, Blomberg discussed the emergency decree and the question of the relationship between the Reichswehr and the nationalist paramilitary organizations. In the present context the following note is significant: "Significant that Army has been left out (military support at first intended. But this would have meant martial law). Not likely that Army will be drawn in." [220]

As we have seen, it is difficult to draw a clear dividing line between the statements Hitler made for tactical reasons and his real estimate of the situation, and this in turn makes it difficult to interpret the negotiations between the party leadership and the Reichswehr that must have taken place after the Reichstag fire. The High Command meeting itself had been scheduled before the fire and took place on the morning of March 1.[221] The topics under discussion were the emergency decree and, in view of the projected actions against the KPD, the relations between the Reichswehr and the SA auxiliary police. The probability of serious clashes on election night between the nationalist organizations and the KPD was discussed. And the question of proclaiming a "state of revolution" was raised.[222] On March 3 Liebmann issued an order implementing Blomberg's instructions that all passes should be canceled on election night from 8:00 P.M. to 6:00 A.M., that all troops should be confined to their barracks and those living off post should stay at home during this period, that the telephone switchboards should be kept in operation, that the commanding officers and post commanders were to remain within reach, and that on the night of March 5 no military personnel of any description should appear on the street in uniform.[223]

These instructions permit of various interpretations. First of all, they fit in with Goering's statement at next day's cabinet meeting that the Communist leadership had originally intended to strike in the evening and night of election day.[224] This would lead us to presume that the National Socialist leadership were really counting on a Communist counterblow, and that since it had not occurred at the time of the Reichstag fire, they assumed it would take place at a later date. At the time when the emergency decree was framed, it was thought that the Communists would definitely strike on election night, but on March 2 Goering expressed the belief that they had postponed their action until March 15. From the High Command meeting it can be inferred that the National Socialist leadership had been impelled to revise their views concerning the nature of the Communist counterblow. The terse utterances of Goebbels, Goering, and Hitler give the impression that at first a regular uprising, an attempt at revolution, had been expected. For such an action the republic provided precedents. A general strike and military engagements would have led to an overt test of strength, in which the government could have obtained the support of the Reichswehr. A feverish study of the available material relating to Communist activity—it would seem that at the time of the fire the documents confiscated on March 26 at the Karl-Liebknecht House had scarcely been looked at—and the total absence of revolutionary action despite the provocative arrests showed these suppositions to be unfounded. Nevertheless it is conceivable that the National Socialists at first considered calling on the Reichswehr but immediately dropped the idea, because a declaration of martial law would have meant postponing the elections and would have strengthened the German National element in the government coalition.

It is certain that Hitler wished to avoid involving the Reichswehr in the political conflict. The correspondent of the *Frankfurter Zeitung* reported that the government did not intend to call on the Reichswehr.[225] Still, it is interesting to note that the idea did arise. Conservative circles may have suggested it on the night of the fire, which would explain why Hitler insisted on going through with the elections and why he insisted on February 28 that the government would gain an absolute majority. That the idea was in the air is confirmed by Dertinger* (a none too reliable witness, to be sure), who noted under March 7 that Blomberg had asked the President to declare martial law, arguing that this solution would make it possible "to maintain order in the contested capitals of certain *Länder*." On March 9 Dertinger notes: "To preserve the relation of forces in the cabinet, the idea was put forward of entrusting the executive power in the entire Reich to a Reich commissioner or of declaring martial law." [226] This reflects the conservatives' utopian hopes of checking the consolidation of Hitler's power at the last moment. But it permits the supposition that the application of martial law was demanded in connection

---

* Georg Dertinger, a former editor of the *Stahlhelm* and a German Nationalist who first became press officer, then general secretary of the Christian Democratic Union in the Soviet Zone, was Foreign Minister of the German Democratic Republic from 1949 to 1953. Arrested for espionage and treason in 1953 and sentenced to 15 years, he was amnestied in 1964.

with the Reichstag fire and the civil war situation invoked by Goebbels and Goering.

All this may have led Hitler to conclude that everything must be done to avoid a situation into which the Reichswehr would have to be drawn. This consideration would account for the marked haste of the National Socialist leadership and also for the change in their view (apparent from Blomberg's speech) of the Communists' aims. Now they spoke of the "new tactics" adopted by the KPD, which had realized that it could not overthrow the government by gaining control over the "larger centers of power" (that is, presumably, by seizing the big cities with the help of a general strike) and had consequently shifted over to guerrilla warfare that could be combatted by military means. Consequently the Reichswehr should remain neutral, "benevolently" so of course, while the fight was carried on by the "people," that is, by the SA shock troops. True, the emergency decree enabled the government to employ all organs of state power against the Communists, but the legal military power—the Reichswehr—would not be adequate.[227]

In the High Command meeting Blomberg had the greatest difficulty in overcoming the generals' attitude of skepticism toward the "national revolution" and the National Socialist army of civil war. He himself characterized the actions of the SA as "expeditions of vengeance," but excused them by saying that as in Italy they were unavoidable. Inconsistently he on the one hand demanded benevolent support, "in order that the SA should not be impeded in its struggle against the Communists," and on the other hand made it clear that a "soldier must stand apart and not involve himself in the 'acts of vengeance' of the SA and the police." The divided attitude of the Reichswehr is made evident by Blomberg's speech, in which he largely deferred to the wishes of the National Socialists. The Reichswehr Ministry, as Rumbold reported on March 2,[228] feared a National

Socialist coup on election night. In deciding to take the offensive against the Communists, Hitler may consequently have aimed not only to terrorize the parties of the left, but also to secure his power in case he were defeated at the polls.

The "Emergency Decree for the Defense of Nation and State," decided by the cabinet on February 28 and immediately submitted to Hindenburg for signature, substituted a civil state of emergency for the military state of emergency (martial law) desired by the conservatives. It entrusted the Reich cabinet with all the powers which in case of military dictatorship are normally conferred on the commander in chief; indeed, it fell short of military dictatorship only in one point, namely, that the appointment of Reich commissioners in the *Länder* was made subject to certain conditions (though, to be sure, these were fictitious). This explains its deviation in form from all comparable emergency decrees, including the Decree to Combat Treason Against the German Nation. There is good reason to believe that the President's agreement to sign it at once was obtained in part by the argument that this was a lesser evil than martial law—a parallel to the situation at the fall of Schleicher.

The decree was drawn up *ad hoc*. By setting aside constitutional guarantees it played an important psychological role in the elections. Hitler deliberately disregarded the plea to nullify the decree as soon as possible.[229] Nevertheless the National Socialists did not make use of the power conferred by the decree to "integrate" the *Länder* until after the elections. There is reason to believe that Hitler expected greater resistance. At the scene of the fire he obviously believed that it would be necessary to strike ruthlessly, to employ all legal and semi-legal means in order to put through the elections and to win them. This does not mean that Hitler was panic-stricken; his reaction was not, as Tobias supposes,[230] a "reaction of terror." Hitler was too much of a monomaniac for that; it was not fear but autosuggestive faith in his mission that made him a power-intoxicated dictator, and this was nothing new. On the other hand, the campaign of arrests and the actions that followed it were not the outcome of clear and purposive decisions. Nor was it "adroit" manipulation that led to the emergency decree of February 28, but a kind of "flight forward." This is especially true of Goering, who became so obsessed with the idea of a political signal on the part of the Communists that from the standpoint of propaganda he made considerable mistakes.

Goebbels' reaction to the absence of Communist action was characteristic. "Resistance nowhere in sight. The enemy camp *seem* to be so bewildered by our sudden intense action that they no longer dare to defend themselves." [231] Actually the fact that nothing happened to justify the excitement on the night of the fire does not indicate great astuteness on the part of the National Socialist leadership. The headquarters of the Communist conspiracy had not been discovered. Everyone could read in the papers that the police were working on pure conjecture. At the cabinet meeting of February 28 Goering raised the question of why the Communists had set fire to the Reichstag and answered it by saying—a typical blunder—that they had been unable to accept the confiscation of the secret material in the Karl-Liebknecht House, which allegedly incriminated them gravely.[232] In his much heralded radio speech of March 1 he admitted that the KPD had not yet completed its preparations for civil war. He documented his allegation that the Communists had planned a large-scale campaign of terrorism with obsolete material borrowed from the white elephants of anti-Communist propaganda. Commenting on the alleged flight of Torgler and Koenen from the burning Reichstag, reported over the radio on February 27, as proof of Communist guilt, he declared that "in one form or another there has been a plot which the Public Prosecutor's office and the police are doing their utmost to elucidate." [233] It was not until March 2 that he came into possession of concrete incriminating evidence, which was authentic as far as it went but not very significant.[234]

Most of the charges against the Communists were based on material which had been provided by the Political Police, but the significance of which was of course exaggerated. Only a few assertions, for example, that van der Lubbe had admitted his connection with the SPD or that large-scale looting expeditions had been scheduled for the afternoon of February 28 in Berlin, were pure invention. The absence of really damaging material does not diminish our impression that Hitler and Goering were convinced of the Communist determination to stage an uprising; conversely, if the National Socialists had invented such an accusation in order to make tactical use of it, it seems unthinkable that they would not have taken the trouble to obtain proofs, or forge them if necessary. Actually they had no serious material with which to counter the anti-National Socialist stories in the foreign press.[235] Finally, when the foreign press persisted in suspecting Goering,[236] the National Socialist leadership instructed the examining magistrate to compile material incriminating the Communists.

In order to understand why the National Socialists let themselves in for the Reichstag fire trial against van der Lubbe, Torgler, Dimitrov, and his two fellow Bulgarians, one must be familiar with the grotesque image of Communist activity which in the first days of March occupied the minds of responsible figures including Goering. This image was pieced together from uncritically interpreted Communist propaganda pamphlets, from the questionable statements of Communist renegades, some of them common-law criminals, and from the exaggerated, misleading reports of regional police authorities; it included notions about the technique of Communist conspiracy that strike us as utterly childish even if we take into account the contradictory tactics of the KPD at that time.[237] Up to the last moment the National Socialist leaders looked for further incriminating material.[238] The trial was brought about by fear and resentment of the Communists and was conducted accordingly from start to finish. The political naiveté of the Public Prosecutor, the judges, the experts, the witnesses, and a large part of the press correspondents is almost unbelievable; it shows, however, why National Socialist propaganda was able to meet with belief especially among the bourgeoisie, and why the voters did not give a negative answer to the emergency decree of February 28.

But from the standpoint of foreign propaganda the Reichstag fire affair was a disaster from the start and resulted in a serious loss of prestige which infuriated Hitler. Münzenberg's propaganda was enormously successful, thanks in part to the constant blunders of the government and of the Reich Court. As we have seen, the case for the prosecution collapsed at the outset; Hitler had wanted a quick trial; instead, the preliminary investigation dragged on until the end of June and the trial itself from September to December 23, 1933. Only when it was too late did Goebbels attempt, through his control over the National Socialist press, to cover up the bad impression.[239] In the end the *Völkischer Beobachter* protested vainly against the acquittal of the Communist defendants, which amounted to a conviction of the National Socialists. It is the fate of dictators to be taken in by their own propaganda, which blinds them to reality. That is exactly what happened to Hitler in connection with the Reichstag fire; it is characteristic that in later years he tolerated no mention of the topic.[240]

The acquittal of the Communist defendants was no particular act of heroism on the part of the court. In the face of foreign opinion, which followed the proceedings in every detail, the court could not have convicted them if it wished to preserve a vestige of credibility. The Public Prosecutor's final plea was lamentable; if he still included Torgler in the indictment, it was because he could not openly confess his mistake.[241] At times the trial proceedings were merely an attempt on the part of the National Socialist members of the government to vindicate themselves against the well-known Brown Books— with so little success that to this day historians find it necessary to prove that the National Socialists had nothing to do with the fire. In this point the government was so much on the defensive that they had no other recourse than to release Dimitrov, Popov, and Tanev.[242] The execution of van der Lubbe, which quite apart from the inadmissible retroactive introduction of the death penalty[243] seems at least questionable from the juridical point of view,[244] was carried out quietly. The plan for a public execution of the incendiaries, still demanded by Hitler in a government declaration of March 23, was dropped.[245] Marinus van der Lubbe, who had protested in vain against the systematic injustice of the new Germany, went to his death with composure.

Summary

Our investigation, which would have been impossible without the basic research of Fritz Tobias and largely confirms his findings, shows that even the political aspect of the affair precludes the possibility of National Socialist complicity in van der Lubbe's act of incendiarism. Not only the National Socialist leadership but their German National coalition partners as well were convinced of the Communist authorship of the fire. Precisely because they could not fully understand the political purpose which they felt obliged to impute to the KPD in connection with the fire,[246] they fell a victim to their own hallucinations, induced in part by their propaganda. They truly believed that an armed Communist uprising was imminent; it was more than propaganda when they undertook to save Germany from "Marxism," it was an integral part of their political creed. The fascist cult of the leader obliged them to regard Hitler's political activity after the Reichstag fire as the self-assured conduct of a man who fully mastered the situation and was clearly conscious of his aims. Goebbels' entries in his diary during these weeks show to what extent the habit of representing their actions as "heroic" and "historically significant" had affected the very thinking of the National Socialist leaders. When Goebbels spoke of the Reichstag fire as "the last mishap," [247] when Goering represented himself as the savior of state authority from the Communist threat, or Hitler felt himself to be the champion of Europe against the "Asiatic plague" of Bolshevism[248]—in every case they were the playthings of their wishful thinking.[249]

Incapacity for calculated tactical exploitation of the situation and blindness to reality induced by their own aims and resentments were the determining factors in the action of the National Socialists after the Reichstag fire. Their reactions were not guided solely by propagandist considerations but also by a false estimate of the political situation. Not only did they exploit the powerful emotional currents with which the political life of Germany was then charged, especially certain social groups' exaggerated fear of Communist and Marxist strivings for power; they were themselves driven by these currents. Under normal political circumstances, this lack of perspective would have been fatal to them—but not in the overheated, irrational atmosphere of Germany in the spring of 1933. The National Socialists were relatively successful in the elections of March 5, 1933, though less so than they had expected. But this success was largely a product of their spontaneous, unconsidered reactions and not of any shrewd, well-thought-out plan.

After having steered a seemingly moderate, pseudo-legal course, accompanied to be sure by increasing terrorist activity on the part of the SA and the SS, Hitler, on the night of the fire, suddenly entered into a phase of totalitarian experimentation. The emergency decree was a kind of *coup d'état,* anticipating the parliamentary Enabling Act at which the National Socialists had been aiming. It was not planned in advance, but resulted from the nervous impatience with which the National Socialist leadership reacted to the imaginary Communist counterblow. Hitler had no way of knowing that he would gain unlimited power without a struggle, at the very first try. In response to the supposed signal for total Communist resistance, he put down all his chips like a poor roulette player, and won. Obviously a civilian chancellor did not, as Fritz Tobias quite mistakenly puts it,[250] become a power-intoxicated dictator overnight, but it cannot be denied that the state of hysteria into which the fire drove him was an important factor in making Hitler overcome his last inhibitions and throw himself completely into into the battle for power.

In our account of the genesis of the Emergency Decree for the Defense of Nation and State and of the policy pursued by the National Socialist leadership in the interval between February 27 and March 5, we have striven, without losing sight of individual motivations, to analyze an abundance of data, some of which are in part mutually contradictory and some of which have never before been taken into account, including the statements of the National Socialist leaders, which cannot be fully understood if they are interpreted as pure propaganda. In view of the inadequacy of the source material, in particular the lack of official documents not intended for the public, we are reduced to hypotheses in certain matters, such as the question whether the National Socialist leadership actually thought for a time of calling in the Reichswehr or whether the idea was brought up solely in order to move the Reichswehr to tolerate National Socialist terrorism.

We do not know how much Hitler himself had to do with the emergency decree. In any case it responded to the needs of various government agencies, and quite possibly was not a deliberate step toward unrestricted dictatorship but only the simplest possible means of crushing an adversary whose strength had been overestimated—which does not mean that Hitler did not immediately perceive its value as a totalitarian instrument. The decree shows that the first "crisis"—and it seems likely that the Reichstag fire was at first regarded as a crisis—convinced the National Socialist leadership that the normal resources of an authoritarian state apparatus were no longer adequate. The centrifugal tendencies that became so pronounced later on—conflicts between government departments, lack of coordination between party and state, the far-reaching influence of personal rivalries among leaders—were already apparent at this stage. An example is the tendency of the SA and SS, beginning with the above-discussed campaign of arrests, to set up private concentration camps. But perhaps the measures made possible by the Reichstag fire—the seizure of absolute control over the state and the police through the emergency decree—also helped to enable Hitler to resist the radical National Socialists' demand for a revolutionary *coup d'état;* in any case the conferences between the National Socialist leadership and the heads of the Reichswehr make this a plausible hypothesis.

The Reichstag fire hastened the unrestricted dictatorship of National Socialism. Dictatorship, however, is never solely the work of those who strive for it, but is also a product of the circumstances. Germany fell a prey not to coldly planning practical politicians, but to brutal, unscrupulous, uncontrolled, and grossly cynical *condottieri,* who displayed their motives more openly than a good many people wished later to admit. The factors that enabled Hitler to take power were the opportunistic support of the conservative right and a lack of political clearheadedness or sense of justice in those German voters who were accessible to mass psychoses. The historical significance of the Reichstag fire is to be sought not least in the fact that it shows the enormous importance of political myths for the breakthrough of totalitarian forces.

NOTES

1. Cf. Rudolf Diels, *Lucifer ante portas,* Stuttgart, 1950, pp. 193 ff.; IfZ Zeugenschrifttum Reichstagbrand A-7, Diels's letter of June 6, 1955: "What interested me about the matter at an early date was the origin and development of the propaganda theme that the Nazis were the incendiaries—as a contribution to the 'doctrine' that rumor is a factor in the making of history. . . ." Cf. Fritz Tobias, *Der Reischstagbrand, Legende und Wirklichkeit,* Rastatt, 1962, pp. 528 f. In an article of September 23, 1955 (IfZ Zeugenschrifttum A-7), Martin Sommerfeldt writes that in the spring of 1934 Diels spoke of ten murdered SA men who had engineered the Reichstag fire under orders from Goebbels, but this late addition to his account is questionable (*Ich war dabei,* Darmstadt, 1949). R. Wolff, in "Der Reichstagbrand 1933," in *Aus Politik und Zeitgeschichte,* Supplement to *Parliament* for January 18, 1956, justifies his distrust of Diels by referring to the story of the ten SA men; Diels retorted sharply in an article in *Reichsruf,* February 25, 1956.

2. Sommerfeldt, *Ich war dabei,* pp. 29 ff.

3. Cf. Diels, *op. cit.,* pp. 202 f.; confirmed by the statement of Kriminalkommissar Rudolf Braschwitz (letter of August 17, 1961, to the Oberstaatsanwalt beim Landgericht Dortmund, Archiv Tobias).

4. IMT IX, pp. 481 ff.; extract in R. Wolff, *loc. cit.,* pp. 42 ff.; cf. Tobias, pp. 253 ff.

5. Cf. Tobias, p. 304; *Lübecker Nachrichten,* July 21, 1954: "Die Nacht im brennenden Reichstag." The "Feuerwehrbericht" (IfZ Zeugenschrifttum A-7, reprinted in Wolff) is based almost entirely on unverified rumors; cf. Tobias, pp. 4 f., and his annihilating criticism of Wolff's methodological incompetence, pp. 269 ff.

6. Attorney Stomps, who originally believed that van der Lubbe had acted alone and who was chosen by van der Lubbe's family to defend him (cf. Stenographischer Bericht der Reichsgerichtsverhandlung gegen van der Lubbe u.a., 2 Sitzungstag, pp. 92 f. [hereinafter referred to as ST]), now thinks it possible that National Socialists were behind van der Lubbe; hence Heinrich Fraenkel's complaint that Tobias had not made adequate use of the Dutch sources (in *Der Monat,* Vol. 14 [1962], p. 12); similarly Kriminalkommissar

Zirpins (article of December 26, 1951, Archiv Tobias): "I hastened to bring the hearing of van der Lubbe to a close because the political line could not be reconciled with the conclusion I arrived at in the course of my criminal investigation that van der Lubbe had acted alone"—whereas he had originally supposed that others were behind him, cf. "Abschlussbericht," in Tobias, App. 1, pp. 597 ff.

7. Alfred Rosenberg to Delmer during the fire: "I only hope our people have nothing to do with it. Some of them would be capable of just such stupidity" (from Sefton Delmer, *Die Deutschen und ich*, Hamburg, 1962, p. 188); characteristic are the statements of Hans Georg Gewehr: "After the Reichstag fire I was occasionally referred to with knowing smiles in party circles as the technical organizer of the Reichstag fire. I always responded energetically to these aspersions" ("Stellungnahme vom 27.3. 1960," Archiv Tobias); in the opposite direction the researches of Sommerfeldt, *op. cit.*, pp. 29 ff.; cf. Tobias, p. 237, and Wolff, p. 38. Heinrich Fraenkel reports (*loc. cit.*, p. 14) that Karl Ernst made remarks to Bertus Smit, the Dutch National Socialist, suggesting complicity on the part of the National Socialists. According to entries in Hassell's unpublished diary, Diels was suspected by the Gestapo of having organized the Reichstag fire (communicated by the Hassell family through Doctor Krausnick). The well-known testimonies of Halder and Rauschning (cf. *Der Spiegel*, No. 52 [1959], p. 47) prove nothing, as Tobias has demonstrated (*op. cit.*, pp. 239 ff.).

8. H. Mau and H. Krausnick, *Deutsche Geschichte der jüngsten Vergangenheit*, 1st ed., 1953, 2nd ed., 1960; Karl D. Erdmann, in Gebhardt, *Handbuch der deutschen Geschichte*, Stuttgart, 1954–60, Vol. IV, p. 189. Walther Hofer, *Der Nazionalsocialismus. Dokumente 1933–1945*, 1st ed., Frankfurt/Hamburg, 1957. Bracher in Bracher/-Sauer/Schultz, *Die nationalsozialistische Machtergreifung*, 2nd ed., Cologne/Opladen, 1962, still cites, though with reservations, the version of the Brown Books. The specialized literature has been influenced accordingly. William L. Shirer, *The Rise and Fall of the Third Reich*, New York, 1962, pp. 268 ff., is totally uncritical.

9. "M. Broszat, in his criticism of the *Spiegel* series (Zum Streit um den Reichstagbrand, *Der Spiegel* 8 [1960], p. 277), fails to note that this precisely is Tobias' productive idea."

10. Karl Dietrich Bracher, "Stufen der nazionalsozialistischen Machtergreifung," in *Vierteljahrshefte für Zeitgeschichte*, No. 4, 1956, pp. 36 ff., and Bracher/Sauer/Schulz, *op. cit.*, pp. 75, 81.

11. *Loc. cit.*, p. 277.

12. A passage in Broszat may be taken as such a falsification of Tobias' findings: "Here again it might be 'proved' by a striking example that the National Socialists were 'not really so bad' " (*loc. cit.*, p. 278). Similarly Bracher, when he links Tobias with the *Reichsruf* (*loc. cit.*, p. 81); Tobias, however, makes it very plain that there is no reason to whitewash Hitler (*op. cit.*, p. 591).

13. Broszat, *loc. cit.*, p. 277; Bracher, *loc. cit.*, p. 81, note 25;

Rudolf Pechel in *Deutsche Rundschau,* 1960. The crude review by A.C. (?) in the *Neue Zürcher Zeitung* for April 8, 1962, accuses Tobias of trying to mislead the reader by mentioning Ernst Lemmer; but we know that Tobias was misinformed by Lemmer, who neglected to call his attention to Caratsch. Cf. Seraphim's review in *Das Historisch-Politische Buch,* Vol. 10 (1962), p. 176, and the concordant reviews of the English edition of Tobias' book by Hugh Trevor-Roper in *The Sunday Times* for November 17, 1963, and by Alan Bullock in *The Spectator* of November 29, 1963, as well as A.J.P. Taylor's introduction to the English edition, London, 1963.

14. I fail to understand why Bracher, *loc. cit.,* p. 81, still sticks to his version of the Gempp story, when it has been clearly demonstrated that Gempp never contradicted the official line (cf. his statement before the Reich Court, 16th ST, as well as *Völkischer Beobachter,* March 3, and October 15–16, 1933, reprinted in Tobias, pp. 667 ff.).

15. Wolff's analysis, which was accepted by the specialists for a time, is a masterpiece of tendentious bias despite his otherwise honest efforts. It is impossible to see why he did not follow up Schnitzler's leads; cf. Tobias, pp. 269 ff.

16. H. Fraenkel, "Zu viel und zu wenig. Kritische Bemerkungen zu Der Reichstagsbrand von F. Tobias," in *Der Monat,* Vol. 14 (1962), pp. 19 ff.; Gisevius in *Die Zeit,* Vol. 15 (1962), pp. 10 ff.; Harry Schulze-Wilde, "Legenden um den Reichstagsbrand," in *Politische Studien,* Vol. 13 (1962), p. 295. Recently, K. O. Freiherr von Aretin, "Zeitgeschichtliche Aufklärung von Legendenbildungen um Ereignisse von 1933," in *Frankfurter Hefte,* Vol. 19 (1964), pp. 600–602, in which we find a characteristic reversal of the causes and political effects of the Reichstag fire.

17. I am indebted to F. Tobias for numerous papers from his archives, for an abundance of suggestions and advice, and in general for his unstinting helpfulness. The form of his work made it easy for critics to maintain that his methods were lacking in exactness. Such criticism has been made in particular by Hans Schneider (cf. the article by Wolfgang Schwarz in *Süddeutsche Zeitung,* December 21–22, 1963). While admitting the presence in Tobias' book of several trifling misquotations and mistranslations, I cannot concur in or even understand Schneider's view that Tobias was guilty of "objectively falsifying the facts." It remains to be seen whether Schneider publishes his refutation of Tobias, which I have seen in manuscript. I am indebted to him too for valuable suggestions.

18. Senate President Paul Vogt has declared ("Unterredung mit ORR Tobias und Reg.-Dir. Grossmann vom 26.1.1957," transcript in Archiv Tobias) that he was questioned about the Reichstag fire by Reich Court Judges Fröhlich and Wernecke and that he wrote a thirty-two-page memorandum (in which he adhered to his belief in Communist guilt). After the war the Russians confiscated the fifty-

two still extant volumes of trial records. Cf. the statements of Goering, IMT IX, pp. 481 ff.; of Halder, *ibid.,* p. 484, and II, p. 129,
and V, pp. 402 f. The prosecution was able to invoke only the by
then already questionable statement of Gisevius (IMT XII, pp.
277 ff.), which has meanwhile been refuted (cf. also the judgments
of the sixth *Zivilkammer* of the Düsseldorf Landgericht of February
2, 1962 (Az 60 160/60) and of the fourth *Zivilsenat* of the Düsseldorf
Oberlandgericht of August 6, 1963).

19. Ernstgert Kalbe, *Freiheit fur Dimitroff. Der internationale
Kampf gegen die provokatorische Reichstagsbrandstiftung und den
Leipziger Prozess,* Berlin, 1963; K.-H. Biernath, *Der Reichstag
brennt. Hintergründe und Auswirkungen der faschistischen Reich-
stagsbrandprovokation,* Berlin, 1960; O. Winzer, *Zwölf Jahre Kampf
gegen Faschismus und Krieg. Ein Beitrag zur Geschichte der Kom-
munistischen Partei Deutschlands 1933–1945,* Berlin, 1955; Alfred
Kurella, *Dimitroff contra Göring,* Berlin, 1964. The new material
available to Kalbe in microfilm in IfZ, Akten des AA, MA 194/1–3
contains only documents of secondary importance concerning diplomatic transactions connected with the Reichstag fire, and newspaper clippings showing how effective the accusation of the National
Socialists had been. Kalbe is utterly uncritical, makes use of the
London countertrial as a source (p. 45), characterizes Wolff's work
as reliable (p. 51), cites the Fire Department report (p. 55), believes
the Oberfohren memorandum to be authentic (p. 43), and finally,
after declaring (p. 15) that Kalbe's book had cleared up the problem
of the Reichstag fire "except for certain residual circumstances
(!)," declares: "It can no longer be determined with complete (!)
certainty what fascist leader hit on the idea of setting the Reichstag
on fire" (p. 51, note 51).

20. Cf. *ibid.,* p. 34: "Obviously it is only a short step from the
open rehabilitation of fascism to the incrimination of the Communists along the lines of Goebbels' propaganda." One is amused by
the allegation that West German specialists had failed to mention
the fifty-two volumes of records of the preliminary hearings (cf. note
18), from which we infer that they are not in the Soviet-occupied
zone either.

21. Along with Heinrich Fraenkel, Harry Schulze-Wilde, and von
Aretin, Hans Bernd Gisevius, 1st ed., *Bis zum bitteren Ende,* Hamburg, 1947, stuck to the version implicating the National Socialists.
His account may have been influenced indirectly by the Brown
Books (cf. Erich Wollenberg in *Echo der Woche,* August 12, 1949,
p. 9). The much discussed Rall story cannot have come to his
attention until much later, as is proved by the testimony of Grauert ("Aussage vor der Kriminalpolizei vom 12.10.62," Archiv
Tobias), who as Gisevius' immediate superior must have known
something about it. On the whole matter, cf. Tobias, pp. 352 ff.
Tobias, it might be mentioned, obtained an oral statement from

Rall's still living brother, which shows that Rall cannot possibly have been a member of the SA, a fact corroborated by Tobias' version.

22. The following inquiry is based on Tobias' detailed investigation, which was checked against the material available at the time and in whose findings I concur except for certain matters of detail.

23. Karl Ernst, Helldorf, Heines, and Schulz had unimpeachable alibis (cf. Tobias, pp. 249 ff.); despite their wealth of information, Münzenberg and his helpers brought forward no other concrete accusations.

24. "Urteil," p. 20: "At least *one,* and probably *several* accomplices of van der Lubbe participated in the preparation and setting of this fire in the main hall of the Reichstag."

25. Cf. Tobias, pp. 21 f., 19 ST, pp. 197 ff.; 20 ST, pp. 143 ff.; 43 ST, pp. 203 ff., 212.

26. Tobias, pp. 294 f., after "Handakten Sack."

27. On this particular point, Tobias, pp. 101 ff. "Aktenauszüge Sack," *Hauptakten,* Vol. G, "Gang," BA Koblenz. We shall not go into the tiresome affair at any length. This tunnel emerged near the permanently occupied gatekeeper's lodge in the palace of the Reichstag President; no doubt can be thrown on the sworn statement of the gatekeepers to the effect that the tunnel had not been used (cf. "Urteil," pp. 35 f., 18 ST, pp. 187 f.; 19 ST, p. 37.

28. (1) The mysterious skylight on the second floor, which so fired the imagination of witnesses Weberstedt and Scranowitz (26 ST, pp. 212 ff.). Here the police investigation brought no results (27 ST, pp. 61 ff., "Aussage Bunge"). Nevertheless, the verdict makes no bones about declaring that "one of the participants hid there, and on the night of the fire at the approach of the patrol that was searching the building . . . was led outside to safety." (2) The fire mark which Police Inspector Lissigkeit claimed to have found on the stairs leading to the second floor, first reported in an article in *Der Telegraph* (Berlin) for February 27, 1963, and which, for want of confirmation of any kind, can only be regarded as a late lapse of memory. (3) For the sake of completeness, some matches not belonging to van der Lubbe (communication of Schneider), to which, reasonably enough, the court lent no consideration.

29. Cf. Tobias, pp. 295 ff.; "Handakten Sack," Vol. I, pp. 27 ff.

30. "Aussage Grauert vom 3.10.1957," Archiv Tobias; cf. Tobias, p. 110.

31. Delmer, *op. cit.,* p. 190.

32. Reprinted in Tobias, App. 5, p. 609; on the theory that others had been behind van der Lubbe, cf. below, pages 140–42.

33. Sommerfeldt, *op. cit.,* pp. 25 ff.

34. Diels, *op. cit.,* p. 193.

35. Sommerfeldt, *op. cit.,* p. 27.

206   *Hans Mommsen*

36. This was Sommerfeldt's later, not improbable impression cf. p. 31; cf. WTB, 2nd early ed., "Bericht vom 28.2," reprinted in Tobias, App. 14.

37. Tobias, p. 123.

38. WTB, early ed., February 28, 1933; Tobias, App. 14, p. 631.

39. The National Socialist Reichstag member Doctor Albrecht had been mistaken for Torgler; cf. Tobias, p. 294.

40. Cf. "Aussagen," 24 and 25 ST, pp. 164 ff., 242 ff., or 11 ff. On the error of prematurely confronting the witnesses with van der Lubbe, cf. Tobias, p. 387. Characteristic of the examining magistrate's uncritical attitude toward these witnesses is the letter of the Public Prosecutor to the Foreign Office of September 6, 1933, containing the request that the Foreign Office support the Austrian citizen Kroyer's application for permission to leave Austria, "since Kroyer is an extremely important witness whose appearance at the trial is of the utmost importance" (AA/Rechtsabt., Microfilm IfZ MA 194/2, Bl. 125).

41. Cf. Tobias, p. 611: The report declared that van der Lubbe had been an "excellent tool" in the hands of the Communist Party; "he was manipulated but thought he was acting independently." W. Schwarz (*op. cit.*) says the same, although in the case of Zirpins this suspicion is quite unfounded.

42. Tobias, pp. 603 f.

43. Police Inspector Heisig attested this (as reliably reported by Franz von Papen in *Der Wahrheit eine Gasse*, Munich, 1952, p. 303), and it is further confirmed by Heinrich Schnitzler (referred to in Tobias and Diels at his request under the pseudonym Schneider) in his anonymous article, "Der Reichstagsbrand in anderer Sicht," in *Neue Politik, Organ für Freiheit und Recht*, Zürich, 1949, Vol. 10, No. 2 (quoted from photocopy in IfZ-Zeugenschrifttum A–7). Only later was Heisig disciplined because of an interview given in Holland, in which he contended that van der Lubbe had acted alone (cf. Tobias, pp. 87 ff.), which does not argue that he had been influenced by political bias in his investigation. "Aussage Braschwitz" (cf. note 3 above): "During my participation in the investigation I received from Nazi circles no indication concerning possible accomplices. . . ." Later suspicions, he goes on to say, were based on rumors "without any tanglible basis that would have justified investigation in this direction." Moreover one can hardly, with Bracher (*loc. cit.*, p. 81), speak of a conscious manipulation of witnesses, although National Socialist personalities were clearly given preferential treatment and Communists were treated rudely. It is true that the fellow witnesses Zachow and Bienge mentioned by Panknin, who were unable to corroborate his testimony, were taken in hand by the Gestapo after the trial, as Tobias learned in the course of a visit to Bienge.

44. "Reichskabinettsitzung vom 2.3.1933," in Tobias, App., p. 623.

45. A criticism which seems rather ironical in view of Vogt's poor

showing (cf. Tobias, App., pp. 623, 398 ff.; A. Sack, *Der Reichstags-brandprozess*, Berlin, 1934, p. 242).

46. To be sure, the party leadership thought of setting up a special court to speed up the proceedings; see Schulz in Bracher/-Sauer/Schulz, *op. cit.*, pp. 524 f., notes 34 and 38.

47. Diels, *op. cit.*, p. 194; "Reichskabinettsitzung vom 2.3" (Tobias, p. 624), vom 24.3 (*ibid.* pp. 628 ff); Henry Picker, *Hitlers Tischgespräche im Führerhauptquartier, 1941–1942*, ed. P. E. Schramm, Stuttgart, 1963, pp. 325 f.; on the whole subject, Tobias, pp. 94 ff.

48. Cf. Schulz, *op. cit.*, p. 523.

49. Cf. note 3 above; Braschwitz recalls the following incident: "About a week after the Reichstag fire I was summoned to the then Premier Goering, who at the time still had his office in the building of the former Prussian Ministry of the Interior on Unter den Linden. Present at my arrival was Ministerialrat Diels and Detective Superintendent Heller. They told me later that they had had a conference with G., in which G. had expressed his conviction that van der Lubbe could not have acted alone.

"Premier Goering also expressed this view to me. As he was speaking, a demonstration about something or other came marching down Unter den Linden; Goering stepped over to the window with me and said 'the people down there' certainly did not believe van der Lubbe had acted alone and he himself was unable to convince them that he had."

50. Cf. Vogt's testimony (note 18 above); *Deutsche Richter-zeitung*, October 1951; Tobias, pp. 338 f.

51. Cf. Gotthard Hasper, "Der Schutz der Republik," *Studien zur staatlichen Sicherung der Demokratie in der Weimarer Republik 1922–1930*, Tübingen, 1963, pp. 125 ff.

52. 6 ST, pp. 193 f., 201 f.; for Vogt's bias, accounted for in part by a personal mishap, cf. Tobias, p. 324.

53. *Ibid.*, pp. 136–140.

54. Only the extracts which Sack caused to be made are extant (BA, Ll. Erw. 396/1; extracts reprinted in Tobias, pp. 671 ff.); "Gutachten Josse" BA R 43/II, 294.

55. Cf. Sack, *op. cit.*, pp. 206 ff.; 56 ST (Plädoyers), pp. 72 f.

56. "Reichskabinettsitzung vom 15.5" (RK 43/II, 294); the incident shows that Schlegelberger did not follow the investigation very attentively, because on March 15 the identities of the Bulgarians had long been known.

57. *Völkischer Beobachter*, March 23, 1933; Tobias, pp. 334, 363.

58. Cf. Vogt's statement, 6 ST, pp. 142, 193.

59. *Ibid.*, pp. 51 ff., 102 ff., 154 ff.

60. *Ibid.*, pp. 141, 152.

61. *Ibid.*, p. 142.

62. Affidavit of the psychiatrists Bonhoeffer and Zutt, in Tobias, App. 27, pp. 675 ff. Cf. 2 ST, pp. 11 ff.

63. See the note of Professor Justus Heidemann (BA, Kl. Erw.), who after a conversation with Landgerichtsdirektor Rusch reports that Rusch was of the belief that van der Lubbe was "a total simulator" (p 117).

64. 6 ST, p. 155; cf. Marowsky's statement, *ibid.*, p. 122.

65. *Ibid.*, p. 170.

66. *Ibid.*, pp. 144–151; cf. Tobias, pp. 321 f.

67. *Ibid.*, pp. 156–160.

68. Tobias, p. 322; similar abuses occurred in the questioning of other defendants.

69. "Urteil," p. 34.

70. Tobias, pp. 314 f.; cf. "Handakten Sack," Vol. I, p. 381.

71. Diels, *op. cit.*, p. 200.

72. Excerpt reprinted in *Der Spiegel*, No. 52, 1959, pp. 45 ff.; cf. Tobias, pp. 492 ff.

73. Cf. note 42 above.

74. Rumbold's report of March 1, *Documents on British Foreign Policy*, Second Series, Vol. IV, No. 246: "I find there is a feeling shared by many level-headed people that the act of incendiarism may have been inspired by Nazi elements, but not by the leaders of the Nazi party."

75. Tobias' criticism (pp. 533 ff.) of Gisevius on this point is irrefutable.

76. Note 17 above; this view is essentially unfounded; at the most one might adduce the negative argument that if necessary van der Lubbe would have shielded his accomplices; cf. A. Weiland (*Der Monat*, No. 164), who writes that he heard van der Lubbe speak of alleged accomplices, but this must be a misunderstanding or lapse of memory on Weiland's part.

77. Fraenkel, *loc. cit.*, p. 11. One thing that makes this whole story incredible is that everything connected with Neukölln was thoroughly investigated. If a flying squad had been alerted, the police would have known about it. Moreover, in view of the constant flow of members between the NSDAP and the KPD the fact that van der Lubbe was accompanied by an SA man would have proved nothing.

78. Cf. "Anklageschrift," pp. 38 ff.; Tobias, pp. 55 ff. To be sure, Flöter later withdrew his statement to the effect that the unknown man who had alerted the Fire Department on the night of the fire had been named Neumann. This does not add credibility to Schulze-Wilde's Waschinsky theory.

79. Cf. van der Lubbe's later correct statement in "Handakten Sack," Vol. I, pp. 381 ff. Schneider assumes that van der Lubbe was influenced by the National Socialists during this time. The assumption that they organized the fire involves the greatest complications, because the preparations would have had to be made earlier. The numerous arguments that make this seem unlikely cannot be repeated here.

80. It should be noted in passing that the theory of the "best time to enter the building" taken over in the verdict is not tenable, especially as it was mere chance that prevented van der Lubbe from arriving at the same time as the postman who came earlier than usual (cf. Tobias, p. 469).

81. Cf. so early a work as Douglas Reed, *The Burning of the Reichstag*, London, 1934, pp. 266, 298 f., cf. "Urteil," p. 21, also Seuffert's statement in his plea: "And so the only evidence against van der Lubbe is the affidavit of the respected Doctor Schatz . . ." (quoted from Sack, *op. cit.*, p. 269).

82. WTB, 2nd early ed., February 28, 1933 (in Tobias, App. 14, p. 635).

83. "Handakten Sack," Vol. II, p. 17; Gempp's testimony at the session of October 14, 1933; cf. Tobias, pp. 432 f.

84. Interrogation of Scranowitz, March 13, after "Aktenauszüge Sack," reprinted in Tobias, App. 25, p. 673; "Urteil," p. 24; so interpreted by Schatz but then designated as a torch after all, cf. 22 ST, p. 222.

85. Cf. Sommerfeldt, *op. cit.*, pp. 26 ff.

86. Cf. 22 ST, pp. 48–50.

87. Cf. Tobias, p. 433.

88. *Ibid.*, p. 634; it was only later that Schatz, in disagreement with his previous affidavits, spoke of artificial fuel. Brüning in "Handakten Sack," Vol. II, pp. 131 f. This referred not only to the restaurant but also to the main hall. Also Ritter's affidavit (*Ibid.*, p. 48) and Bunge's report of March 13, 1933, concerning his discussion with Professor Brüning on the cause of the fire in the main hall. Cf. Tobias, pp. 447 ff.

89. "Anklageschrift," p. 120.

90. Cf. Tobias, pp. 421 f.; this also explains why no attention was paid to the affidavit which Brüning had drawn up for the police, although it was in the records and Brüning as director of the Prussian Institute for Foodstuffs, Pharmaceuticals, and Forensic Chemistry was more competent in the matter than an independent scientist like Schatz. One argument raised against Brüning is that he made no chemical examination. He probably regarded such an examination, for good reasons, as pointless.

91. Cf. the *sangajol* experiment he performed before the court (52 ST, pp. 181 f.).

92. Cf. 15 ST, pp. 55 ff., 58 ff., 184 ff., 190 ff. A detail which illustrates the unreliability of the witness: first he admits that he can say nothing about the color of the sheaves of flame (p. 182); then when asked again he answers: "reddish-yellow"; a little later he says with great assurance: "yellowish-red" (p. 185). For his way of reflecting on his observations, cf. *ibid.*, p. 181: "I was surprised that it was burning just at the places where there were no drawers." Question from Bünger: "Did you see that immediately?" Witness: "Yes, there were table drawers left only in the first row. . . ."

How did Scranowitz arrive at the false notion of prepared drawers? He could not possibly have made such an observation while looking in for the fraction of a second? This is a typical fixation after the fact. Cf. the statements of the firemen reprinted in Tobias, App. 24, and his account, pp. 195 ff.

93. 52 ST, pp. 191 ff.; cf. Tobias, pp. 301 f., and Douglas Reed, *op. cit.*, p. 133; Scranowitz was not an isolated case; one need only think of the many statements made by otherwise reliable persons who claimed to have seen the defendants before the fire, or of Gericke's testimony to the effect that van der Lubbe had been in the Reichstag before; also the assertion that van der Lubbe had been seen in the Prussian *Landtag* (*Völkischer Beobachter*, March 2, 1933).

94. "Anlage zu 22, ST," pp. 14 ff., p. 20.

95. Cf. "Gutachten Josse" (RK 43/II/294), pp. 10 ff.; "Gutachten Wagner," pp. 20 f.

96. "Handakten Sack," reprinted in Tobias, App. 24, pp. 671 ff.

97. Cf. the timetable in "Gutachten Josse," *op. cit.*, pp. 2 ff.

98. Excerpt in "Handakten Sack," Vol. I, p. 3.

99. "Gutachten Wagner," pp. 18 f.

100. 22 ST, p. 19; "Gutachten Wagner," p. 21.

101. "Anlage zu 22. ST," pp. 34, 42.

102. *Ibid.*, p. 34: ". . . in my opinion the quantities could have been very small; I don't want to commit myself about quantities, but just a few liters, four to five, would have been quite sufficient"; "Gutachten Josse," *ibid.*, pp. 35–40; Schatz, *ibid.*, p. 40.

103. "Anlage zu 22. ST," p. 36.

104. Cf. Schatz's incredible blunder in connection with Lateit's testimony. Lateit stated that the curtains had burned from the bottom up. Schatz questioned the witness again and then proceeded to reverse his statement and say that the fire had spread downward ("Anlage zu 22. ST," p. 47), an error which was taken over by the verdict. The list of such mistakes could easily be expanded (cf. Tobias, pp. 432 ff.).

105. "Anlage zu 22. ST," pp. 56 ff.

106. Even if founded, the suspicion that during the preliminary investigation persons unknown entered the room in the Reichstag building where Schatz's belongings were kept under lock and key would not begin to prove that there had been accomplices.

107. "Anlage zu 22. ST," p. 31.

108. *Ibid.*, p. 43: "In time . . . combustion products pass into different stages of oxydation. . . ." Nevertheless Schatz believed earlier that he had demonstrated their presence.

109. *Ibid.*, pp. 51 f., cf. pp. 54 ff. Refuted by Borchardt's statement that a piece of the curtain from the stenographers' room had been found with van der Lubbe's overcoat; also van der Lubbe's statement ("Abschlussbericht," *op. cit.*, p. 600), that he had then gone "into the big church" (i.e., the main hall).

110. *Ibid.,* p. 64. In answer to Seuffert's objection that van der Lubbe must then have had this smell on him when arrested: "That is correct. For that reason I am of the opinion that van der Lubbe had no reason for going there and did nothing in the main hall. That is my firm conviction." A short time before, however, Schatz had thought it possible that van der Lubbe had run through the hall. Later, in connection with the incrimination of Torgler, he denied that this fuel gave off a smell and put the fuel back into van der Lubbe's hands. Obviously this is a highly arbitrary construction which adjusts concrete facts to fit fantasies.

111. 23 ST, pp. 104 f.; contradicted by Torgler's simple and cogent arguments, pp. 439 f.

112. 23 ST, pp. 23 f.; after supposedly proving that the fuel in question gave off little smell Schatz expressed himself much more moderately. Then on the twenty-eighth day of the trial, when he envisaged the possibility of unburned remnants in the floor (in which case his cherished "stages of oxydation" would have lost their force of proof), he suddenly maintained that the proof was possible after all (p. 44) but that van der Lubbe had had nothing to do with lighting the fire in the circular corridor, whereas he had set fires in the curtains, in the restaurant, and in the Bismarcksaal (pp. 46–50).

113. "Urteil," pp. 31 f., according to which van der Lubbe worked chiefly with igniting fluid.

114. Tobias, p. 438.

115. "Urteil," pp. 33 f.

116. *Ibid.,* p. 34. Cf. p. 37: moreover such an activity in the main hall would "not have fallen within the task apparently assigned van der Lubbe in his collaboration with his accomplice or accomplices."

117. 28 ST, pp. 43 ff.

118. "Gutachten Josse," *op. cit.,* pp. 22, 47.

119. 22 ST, p. 45.

120. "Gutachten Josse," *op. cit.,* p. 46; here too the theory that the incendiaries had chosen the restaurant because of its special air evacuation system, but then Josse was obliged to conclude "that the program was modified because of an unforseen circumstance, namely, that the special air evacuation system was apparently not in operation."

121. Cf. "Gutachten Brüning," excerpt in Tobias, p. 447.

122. Cf. Braschwitz' statement of April 5, 1961, and his letter to the Public Prosecutor of April 17, 1961 (Archiv Tobias), to the effect that he had asked a Fire Department official (probably Oberbaurat Meusser) about the causes of the fire: "In response to my question about what had made it possible for the fire to spread as it did, this official explained to me that the walls of the hall were sheathed in oak which was about forty years old and thoroughly dried out, which accounted for the relatively rapid diffusion of the

fire—especially after additional oxygen had been introduced by the bursting of the glass roof. For this reason the official thought it perfectly possible that a single person could have set . . . a fire of this size." Fire Chief Gempp made a similar statement (cf. Tobias, p. 285), but did not draw the same conclusion. From the fact that the witnesses had not heard the crackling of burning wood the experts inferred that the wood sheathing had caught fire later; they also saw fit to conclude that the furniture was uncommonly fire-resistant, and supported this inference by experiments conducted under radically different conditions. Cf. Tobias, pp. 420 ff.

123. Fraenkel, *loc. cit.*, p. 13; but Heisig's testimony already indicated the contrary (22 ST, p. 46). Albada was of the opinion that in compensation for his eye ailment van der Lubbe had a particularly good sense of orientation. This seems likely to me.

124. 22 ST, pp. 50 f. Schatz expressed the opinion that when questioned at the scene of the fire van der Lubbe had not taken the combustion rate into consideration. Schatz calculated that he had only fourteen minutes at his disposal.

125. Cf. "Abschlussbericht," *op. cit.*, p. 605.

126. Cf. Tobias, pp. 65, 294. Even the indictment allowed the possibility that van der Lubbe had covered the itinerary (pp. 91 f.); Josse spoke of van der Lubbe's "nimbleness," cf. 22 ST, p. 91, 27 ST, pp. 55 ff., 81. Cf. also Zirpins's story in *Süddeutsche Zeitung*, December 13, 1953, in which he quotes van der Lubbe as having said when questioned at the scene of the fire: "If I had known the building as I know it now, I would have gone about it in an entirely different way. As it was, I used up all my lighters before I reached the main hall. What do you suppose would have happened if I had still had them?"

127. Schneider studied the matter with great precision and on the basis of variations in van der Lubbe's statements distinguishes several different versions of his itinerary through the Reichstag building. He points out that his removal of his garments was not considered in computing the time, etc. Schneider agrees that van der Lubbe must have been in the main hall, but questions whether he set the fires outside it. This notion is at variance with all other theories and in particular precludes Schneider's own suggestion that van der Lubbe was unaware of the identity and working methods of his accomplices.

128. Ernst Hanfstaengl, *Unheard Witness*, Philadelphia, 1957, pp. 210 f.; corroborated by Goebbels, *Vom Kaiserhof zur Reichskanzlei*, Munich, 1934, pp. 269 f.; cf. Fraenkel, *loc. cit.*, p. 14, who supports Hanfstaengl's version.

129. Goering's reaction was later attested by F. W. Jacoby, who was then his aide-de-camp (F. W. Jacoby, "Mitteilung vom 16.2.1961," Archiv Tobias): "On the day of the Reichstag fire, I, who was then his only aide-de-camp, reported the incident to Goering. I was then convinced and still am convinced that his surprise was authentic."

Similarly the statement of Undersecretary [Staatssekretär] Grauert of October 3, 1957 (Archiv Tobias): he was in conference with Goering when an official (Grauert had Daluege in mind, but it was Jacoby) rushed in and announced that the Reichstag was on fire. "Goering's reaction was so unmistakable and convincing that Grauert did not have the slightest doubt either then or later that Goering was truly surprised." Cf. Tobias, p. 108.

130. Sommerfeldt, *op. cit.*, p. 25; "Aussage Gempp," Tobias, p. 668. See also note 135 below.

131. "Aussage Grauert," corroborated by Goering's statement before the Reich Court, 31 ST, pp. 104 f.

132. *Ibid.*, p. 94: "When (after being stopped by the police guard) I heard the word 'arson' . . . it was as if the curtain had risen at one stroke and I saw the play clearly before me. The moment the word 'arson' fell, I knew that the Communist Party was guilty and had set the Reichstag on fire." If this was true, it provides one more indication that "Reichstag fire myths" beclouded men's minds from the start.

133. Diels, *op. cit.*, p. 192, who mistakenly places the hearing in the Reichstag building (guardroom at Brandenburg Gate) but charasteristically cites Lateit's impression that van der Lubbe was a madman (cf. Tobias, pp. 66 f.).

134. *Ibid.*, p. 111. In 1960 Weber expressly confirmed to Tobias the statement he then made.

135. Goebbels, *op. cit.*, p. 170.

136. Sommerfeldt, *op. cit.*, p. 25.

137. Tobias, App. 14, p. 635.

138. Delmer, *op. cit.*, p. 188.

139. Papen, *op. cit.*, p. 303.

140. DBFP, No. 245; Rumbold managed to enter the cordoned-off Reichstag on the night of the fire.

141. Delmer, *op. cit.*, pp. 191 f.; Letter to *Der Spiegel*, No. 52, 1959; earlier in *Daily Express*, July 21, 1939.

142. Delmer, *op. cit.*, p. 190.

143. Diels, *op. cit.*, p. 193.

144. Cf. above, pages 140–41.

145. We are aware that Diels's statements must be treated critically. However, in matters connected with the Reichstag fire, they are largely corroborated by Sommerfeldt and by the testimony of the witnesses. Above all, Schnitzler corroborates his crucial account of the events in the burning Reichstag building. Diels had no cognizance of Schnitzler's article until it was in proof (Diels, *op. cit.*, p. 200), and Diels's account, as a comparison of their texts shows, was not influenced by Schnitzler; from 1934 on, the relations between the two men were strained. Schnitzler checked his information chiefly by consulting Heisig, who had no reason for taking an apologetic attitude (cf. Schnitzler's letter to Heisig, Archiv Tobias, and correspondence with Tobias), and also questioned Zirpins.

Cf. also Schnitzler's letter in IfZ Zeugenschrifttum, which Wolff rather surprisingly failed to take into consideration. The parallel accounts of Diels and Schnitzler preclude our original supposition that the arrests were first decided upon in the session at the Prussian Ministry of the Interior (Goebbels speaks of a cabinet meeting).

146. Schnitzler, *loc. cit.,* p. 2.

147. Goebbels, *op. cit.,* p. 270.

148. Diels, *op. cit.,* p. 194; Schnitzler, *loc. cit.,* p. 2; before the Reiche Court Helldorf denied having been at Goering's on the night of the fire, whereas Goering—truthfully in all likelihood—declared expressly that Helldorf had come in response to his summons (31 ST, p. 105). One of these two witnesses was guilty of perjury. Sahm's presence is indirectly confirmed; [former German Nationalist Party leader Gottfried] Treviranus, who had been invited to Sahm's that evening, has stated verbally that Sahm came home at about 11:15. Cf. Tobias, p. 112.

149. Delmer, *op. cit.,* p. 192; Delmer's interpretation of the conversation reported to him between Hitler and Papen is dubious, particularly because Papen was present at the later conference at the Prussian Ministry of the Interior.

150. *Völkischer Beobachter,* March 1, 1933: "Der Fanal des Bolschewismus."

151. Diels, *op. cit.,* pp. 194 f. When one has read Diels's account of these events, it seems impossible to dispose of Hitler's speech as "play-acting," even if one takes account of Henderson's remark (in Alan Bullock, *Hitler. Ein Studie über Tyrannei,* Düsseldorf, 1961, p. 375) that Hitler's capacity for deluding himself was a part of his technique.

152. Schnitzler, *loc. cit.,* p. 11.

153. Even earlier, by order of the Prussian Ministry of the Interior, a police radio call (No. 171) had gone out to "all police headquarters and top police officers of the West sectors," invoking the Reichstag fire and "increased activity of the KPD" and ordering confiscation of all leaflets and periodicals of the KPD and SPD, alerting the local riot police, calling up the auxiliary police, and ordering "a thorough surprise search action at the homes of all Communist functionaries" (St. A. Oldenburg. Best. 205, Staatspolizei [Schutz-Ordnunspolizei, Aktenband Geheim und "Persönliches" vom 1.1.29.3.1933]; I owe this and other documents to the careful researches of State Archivist Doctor Schieckel).

154. 2 ST, pp. 71 ff.

155. Goebbels, *op. cit.,* p. 254.

156. *Ibid.,* p. 270.

157. WTB, 2nd early ed., February 28, 1933, in Tobias, App. 14, p. 633. When van der Lubbe was questioned by Heisig, it was not clear at first whether he was a Communist or a Social Democrat. Cf. "Aussage Heisig," 2 ST, p. 61. That night it was inferred from van der Lubbe's working-class contacts that he was connected with

the SPD, and it was mistakenly concluded that he had confessed to Social Democratic connections (cf. "Aussage Goering," 31 ST, p. 104). Denials in *Völkischer Beobachter*, March 23, 1933, and elsewhere. Cf. Tobias, p. 112. The suspicion cast on the SPD was immediately doubted by the non-National Socialist press. Cf. *Frankfurter Zeitung*, March 1, 1933, leading editorial: "It is only too understandable that in view of an election campaign which consists essentially in upholding the fiction of a common 'Marxist front,' which in the National Socialist formulation brands the Social Democrats and the Communists indiscriminately as 'Communist rabble,' defensive alliances may spring up spontaneously in the working class." But, the article concludes, it is absurd to accuse the Social Democrats of originating the fire.

158. RGBl I, 1933, p. 86. Cf. also Tobias, p. 113.

159. Cf. *Braunschweigische Landeszeitung*, February 28, telegram.

160. 31 ST, p. 106.

161. 46 ST, pp. 60 ff.; as the order for the arrest of Torgler (Archiv Tobias) indicates, the arrest orders were mimeographed in the first hours of February 28. They invoked Sec. 22 of the emergency decree of February 4.

162. "Aussage Grauert vom 3.10.51," Archiv Tobias. According to this statement, Hitler himself took no part in drafting the law.

163. IfZ-Zeugenschrifttum ED 1—Liebmann, p. 44. General Liebmann's manuscript notes.

164. There is no other evidence of Hitler's initiative. The records of the Reich Chancellery (BA Koblenz) contain none, those of the Reich Ministry of the Interior are lacking; hence it is not possible for the present to go beyond hypotheses in respect to the genesis of the Reichstag fire decree. Papen, who might have been expected to know what happened, obviously confuses this decree with the Decree to Combat Treason Against the German Nation, of February 28 (*Der Wahrheit eine Gasse*, p. 304).

165. Goebbels, *op. cit.*, pp. 270 f.; Picker, *Tischgespräche*, p. 325; the account of Wilfried von Oven (*Mit Goebbels bis zum Ende*, Buenos Aires, 1949–1950, pp. 115 ff.) is not credible.

166. Joseph Goebbels, *Wetterleuchten*, Berlin, 1943, pp. 373 ff.; cf. Diels, *op. cit.*, p. 195.

167. In Tobias, App. 14, p. 633.

168. Cf. *ibid.*, pp. 262 ff.

169 VB, March 1, 1933. The lists of persons to be assassinated were alleged to include names from every section of the bourgeoisie. On March 2 the paper reported that van der Lubbe had regularly attended meetings of the Communist action committee, which he had persuaded to enlist his services for the incendiary action. Most of the other news stories about the fire consisted of false reports issued by the police, for example, the rumor that the Communist leaders had given advance notice of the Reichstag fire (VB, March 4/5, 1933). Dertinger's report (Sammlung Brammer, BA Koblenz)

of March 2, 1933, speaks of a "news muddle." The countless conflicting rumors bear witness to the agitation of the public.

170. VB, March 1 and 2, 1933.

171. Sommerfeldt, *op. cit.*, p. 26.

172. Cf., for example, Delmer, *op. cit.*, p. 190.

173. Cf. Siegfried Bahne, "Die Kommunistische Partei Deutschlands," in *Das Ende der Parteien*, ed. E. Mattias and R. Morsey, Düsseldorf, 1960, pp. 685 ff., 710 ff. However, there is no reliable material on the basis of which to appraise Communist activity after the seizure of power (cf. Schulz, *op. cit.*, p. 527, note 48). In her memoirs Maria Reese (BA Koblenz, Kl. Erw. 379–4) criticizes the KPD severely for putting out irresponsible propaganda while remaining passive in practice. Some informative material, though for the most part confined to Communist propaganda, is to be found in the records of the Reichssicherheitshauptamt (R 58) in BA Koblenz. The latent civil war situation with numerous bloody clashes continued (cf. Diels, *op. cit.*, pp. 186 ff., 402 ff.); also the account of the atmosphere in Hamburg in Jan Valtin, *Tagebuch der Hölle*, German ed., Berlin, 1957.

174. Cf. the intention of the National Socialists, described by Bracher, to change the order of the agenda if necessary in order to obtain a majority for the Enabling Act (Bracher, *loc. cit.*, pp. 158 f.).

175. As late as the cabinet meeting of March 24, 1933, Hitler doubted the expediency of suppressing the Communist Party. Such a measure, he held, would serve a purpose only "if it were possible to deport the Communists"; there was no point in sending them to concentration camps. Tobias, p. 628.

176. Cf. the material presented at the trial (45 and 46 ST), and the memoirs of Maria Reese (note 173, above).

177. For example on January 24, 1933, the news bureau of the Reich Ministry of the Interior distributed to the news bureaus of the *Länder* an educational pamphlet (RFB-Schulungsmaterial) entitled "Der bewaffnete Aufstand in Reval" (R 58/1, 672). This material is used tendentiously in Martin H. Sommerfeldt, *Die Kommune*, Berlin, 1934.

178. Diels, *op. cit.*, pp. 189 f. Adolf Ehrt's propagandist work *Bewaffneter Aufstand*, Berlin/Leipzig, 1933, is based on this material. Goering took up most of the March 2 cabinet meeting with it.

179. St. A. Oldenburg, cf. note 153, above.

180. Sent out by the news bureau on April 19, 1933 (BA R 58/1–78).

181. 46 ST, p. 61, "Aussage Heller"; "The evidence presented leaves no room for doubt that the KPD intended very seriously . . . to stage a general strike, followed by an armed uprising." But on p. 64 he declared that the KPD had organized the Reichstag fire in order to put the blame on the National Socialists and so "create an unbridgeable gulf between them and the supporters of

the SPD, the members of the unions and the members of the Reichsbanner. This was the true and intended significance of the Reichstag fire. Thus it was intended less as a signal for action, as it was partly taken to be in the provinces, than as the central action that would draw the hesitant masses over to the Communists." To which Torgler replied: "I can only say with Herr Goebbels: that is completely absurd." Typical for the state of the evidence is a communication of April 7, 1933, from Nuremberg police headquarters to the effect that there had indeed been prospects of a violent seizure of power by the KPD, "but that positive evidence pointing to a direct connection between the Reichstag fire and such revolutionary intentions is not available" ("Handakten Sack," Vol. 1, pp. 343 ff.).

182. Cf. Diels, *op. cit.,* pp. 170 ff.

183. 31 ST, pp. 34–40, 43 ff., 52.

184. Cf. Schulz, *op. cit.,* pp. 430 f., 438 ff.; Sauer, pp. 866 ff.; also Schnitzler, *loc. cit.,* p. 5.

185. 31 ST, pp. 81 f.; IMT IX, pp. 481 f.; Diels, *op. cit.,* pp. 194 f.; and Grauert's statement of October 3, 1957 (Archiv Tobias).

186. DBFP Second Series, Vol. IV, No. 253, p. 438.

187. Cf. Bahne, *loc. cit.,* p. 692.

188. 31 XXX ST, pp. 86 ff.

189. Cf. Bracher, *loc. cit.,* pp. 158 ff. The change in the agenda seems to have been a mere stopgap, for in fact the mandates of the Communist Reichstag members were not annulled formally as originally intended, but rendered inoperative by their arrest.

190. 31 ST, p. 84.

191. Cf. above, page 167; on it is based the interpretation of M. Broszat (*loc. cit.,* pp. 176 f.) among others. Broszat says the National Socialists "quickly and shrewdly exploited a political revolution; they did not bring it about."

192. 31 ST, pp. 72 f.

193. DBFP Second Series, Vol. IV, No. 246, p. 431; cf. Tobias, p. 133.

194. Reprinted in Tobias, App. 11, p. 623; also numerous press reports to the effect that the elections would take place "in any case" (cf. *Generalanzeiger* [Wuppertal], February 28, 1933, *Braunschweiger Neueste Nachrichten,* March 2, 1933, *Nazionalzeitung* [Berlin], February 28, 1933, etc.).

195. Tobias, App. 11, p. 623.

196. In any case it was unclear whether Communist Reichstag members were to be included in the arrest action (cf. 47 ST, p. 94).

197. Drafted on February 28, proclaimed on March 1, 1933 (RGBl I, 1933, pp. 84 ff.); Bracher (*op. cit.,* p. 87) speaks somewhat misleadingly of "Reichstag fire decrees."

198. Helmut Krausnick, "Stationen der Gleichschaltung," in *Der Weg in die Diktatur 1918 bis 1933,* Munich, 1962, p. 183.

199. Bracher, *loc. cit.,* p. 83.

200. "Reichskabinettsitzung vom 28.2 vormittags," in Tobias, App. 8, p. 619.

201. RGBl I, 1933, pp. 35 ff.

202. Tobias, p. 617.

203. "Reichskabinettsitzung vom 27.2" (*ibid*, p. 617).

204. Cf. Schulz, *op. cit.*, p. 434.

205. Cf. Jasper, *op. cit.*, p. 162, the example of the suppression of the Red War Veterans' Association; Hans Buchheim, "Die organisatorische Entwicklung der Politischen Polizei in Deutschland in den Jahren 1933 und 1934," in *Gutachten des Instituts für Zeitgeschichte*, Munich, 1958, pp. 197 ff.

206. Cf. Telegr. pol. Funkdienst Leitstelle Braunschweig (Records of the Braunschweig Staatsministerium, copy in Archiv Tobias). In Hamburg the arrests seem to have begun only after the appointment of the police senator (testimony of Kriminalkommissar Will, 47 ST, pp. 94 ff.; testimony of Kriminalsekretär Staeglich, *ibid.*, pp. 110 ff.). Braunschweig, Oldenburg, and Mecklenburg applied the police measures immediately (cf. *Völkischer Beobachter*, March 3, 1933, and the Oldenburg State Police records mentioned in note 151 above). It would be worthwhile to investigate the behavior of the South German *Länder*. Neither Besson nor Schwend (cf. note 207 below) mentions a corresponding request on the part of the Reich Ministry of the Interior. With the exception of the Rhine Province and Westphalia, where according to the *Völkischer Beobachter* of March 3, 1933, respectively 1,200 and 850 persons had been arrested the previous day, the arrests were slow in getting under way in the Prussian provinces, as can be seen from the statements of the police officials before the Reich Court.

207. Cf. Waldemar Besson, *Württemberg und die deutsche Staatskrise 1928–1933*, Stuttgart, 1959, pp. 336 f.; Karl Schwend, *Bayern zwischen Monarchie und Diktatur*, Munich, 1954, p. 510.

208. Besson, *op. cit.*, p. 338.

209. They were concerned with the question of jurisdiction, which their authors claimed, was not with the Reich Ministry of the Interior but with the Reich government as a whole. They also introduced a substantive restriction by adding the words "insofar as." Cf. Schulz, *op. cit.*, p. 432, note 225. The commentary of Ministerialdirektor Kurt Häntzschel of the Reich Ministry of the Interior (*Die Politischen Notverordnungen* . . . , 4th ed., Berlin, 1933, Stilkes Rechtsbibliothek, No. 115) has the following to say on Article 2: "By Reich government is here meant the competent minister, i.e., the Reich Minister of the Interior!"

210. Besson, *op. cit.*, p. 538.

211. Unfortunately it has not been possible to establish who was entrusted with the drafting of the decree. Possibilities are Doctor Werner Hoche, Ministerialrat at the Reich Ministry of the Interior and author of the emergency decree of February 4 (cf. *Juristische Wochenschrift* 8 [1933], p. 506), Dammers, or Doctor Kaisenberg.

212. *Frankfurter Zeitung*, March 1, 1933, 1st ed., telegraphic dispatch of March 28.

213. Bracher, *loc. cit.*, p. 86; he rightly stresses that even before this time the police authorities had for all practical purposes been free to act as they saw fit.

214. "Reichskabinettsitzung vom 28.2 nachmittags" (Tobias, p. 619). Broszat correctly points out that the cabinet approved the decree in "all essential points" (*loc. cit.*, p. 276). Thus his contention that Goering, Hitler, and Frick had played "adroitly, each taking his allotted role" (p. 275) is groundless, especially as at this time Papen neither could nor wished to raise any further objection, and Gürtner obviously supported the decree.

215. Cf. *Völkischer Beobachter*, February 28, 1933: Report on the suppression of numerous publications (*Die Rote Fahne* until April 15) including newspapers of the Center Party in Bavaria.

216. Tobias, App. 10, p. 622.

217. DZA Potsdam, Rep. 77 (Microfilm IfZ MA 198/2).

218. *Frankfurter Zeitung*, March 1, 1933, 1st ed., leading editorial.

219. Cf. DAZ, February 28, 1933; *Niedersächsische Zeitung*, March 1, 1933; *Frankfurter Zeitung*, March 1, 1933; *Nazionalzeitung*, February 28, 1933.

220. IfZ Zeugenschrifttum ED 1—Liebmann, p. 40.

221. Letter from Liebmann, August 8, 1955 (*ibid*, pp. 361 f.), who dates the meeting of the High Command (which earlier writers assumed to have taken place before the Reichstag fire) on March 1. This is confirmed by the transparent allusion to the "emergency decree" in Liebmann's notes. Liebmann rejects Ott's contention (IfZ Zeugenschrifttum 279/I—Ott, p. 9) that not Blomberg but Reichenau presided over the conference. Blomberg was present at the Reich cabinet meeting on February 28. The content of his speech presupposes previous negotiations with the National Socialist leadership and shows that the Reichstag fire must have played a role of considerable importance in regularizing the relations between the Reichswehr and the National Socialist movement, chiefly by paralyzing the opposition within the Reichswehr.

222. Liebmann's notes on the questions raised by Blomberg's speech (*ibid.*, p. 43).

223. *Ibid.*, pp. 46 f.

224. Tobias, p. 623.

225. The Reichswehr should "not be involved in this question of domestic politics" (telegraphic report of February 28 in 1st ed. of March 1, 1933); cf. the remarks of Sauer, *op. cit.*, pp. 720 ff.

226. BA Koblenz, Sammlung Brammer, Zsg. 101/26, pp. 167, 175; Cf. the report of March 11, p. 181, which reiterates that Papen and Blomberg had demanded martial law, but that the President had urged a compromise with Hitler.

227. Liebmann-Notizen, *loc. cit.*, pp. 40 ff. The tactical arguments suggest Hitler's influence, although there is no proof that

he made any such statements, and these matters were not mentioned at the cabinet meeting of February 28; on Blomberg's attitude, cf. H. Krausnick, "Vorgeschichte und Beginn des militärischen Widerstandes gegen Hitler," in *Vollmacht des Gewissens,* Munich, 1956, pp. 210 f.; on the other hand the version of the High Command meeting now available shows that on March 1 Blomberg deviated from the suprapartisan attitude of the Reichswehr: "*One* party on the march. In such a situation 'suprapartisanship' loses its meaning and there remains only one answer: unreserved support."

228. DBFP Second Series, Vol. IV, No. 253, p. 438. Goering denied this in his radio speech and spoke of forged SA and Stahlhelm orders (in Tobias, p. 640).

229. DBFP Second Series, Vol. IV, No. 255, March 3, 1933, p. 439, according to which Neurath spoke up at the cabinet meeting in a conversation with Rumbold expressed the hope that the decree would be annulled immediately after the elections. "In his opinion it was not possible to maintain such a state of exception for any length of time."

230. Tobias, pp. 113, 115 f.

231. Goebbels, *op. cit.,* p. 271.

232. "Reichskabinettssitzung vom 28.2 vormittags," *op. cit.,* p. 618.

233. *Ibid.,* App. 17, pp. 641 f.

234. "Reichskabinettsitzung vom 2.3. 1933" in Tobias, p. 623. Cf. Schultz, *op. cit.,* p. 527: "No further proof is needed that the material with which Goering duped the Reich ministers on the day after the Reichstag fire existed only in his imagination." At the cabinet meetings Goering argued on the strength of material that had been put at his disposal by the Political Police. Later as well Goering made use of the thoroughly dubious conjectures brought forward in the preliminary investigation, which were not even very suitable for propaganda purposes. The questioning of the police inspectors before the Reich Court (45, 46, and 47 ST) throws light on the genesis of the material incriminating the KPD, yet the participants, including so outstanding an expert as Heller, held this material to be reliable. For example, the charge of "poisoning public kitchens" (cf. "Aussage Kriminalkommissars Will," 47 ST, pp. 24 f.) goes back to an episode in Düsseldorf when the police believed they had arrested a "Communist poisoning team." Experts calculated that the confiscated poison would have sufficed to poison 18,000 persons. Although the investigation had not even begun, the report was passed on to higher authority. This impelled Gürtner to introduce into the emergency decree a provision for increased penalties in cases of murder by poisoning. The assertion that van der Lubbe had had close ties with Moscow ("Kabinettssitzung vom 2.3," WTB, February 28) derived from van der Lubbe's statement that he had wished to visit the Soviet Union in 1932. It is characteristic of the uncritical mentality of all the participants that the German

Embassy in Moscow was subsequently asked to track down the alleged instigators of the Communist uprising in Germany. The embassy wired back on September 14, 1933: "It would be desirable that the State's Attorney's sources should provide more detailed information if we are to arrive even at indirect conclusions that may be of any use" (telegrams to ORA, AA/Rechtsabt.: "Korrespondenz und Zeitungs-Ausschnitte zum Reichstagsbrandprozess," Microfilm IfZ MA–194, 1, p. 125).

235. Cf. the telegrams of February 28 and March 3, 1933, to the foreign missions, reprinted in Tobias, App. 15, pp. 636 f.

236. Mentioned in Schulz, *op. cit.*, p. 527. This shows the utter helplessness of the government in the face of Münzenberg's offensive; cf. also BA Koblenz, R 58/718: "Denkschrift über die kommunistische Wühlarbeit im Winter 1932/33 betr. die Vorbereitung der gewaltsamen Verfassungsänderung durch die KPD vom 14.3. 1933."

237. This has never been investigated in detail. For the Political Police's dubious appraisal of Communist tactics, cf. confidential report of April 7, 1933 (Nachrichtensammlung, R 58/626): Up to March 5, it was believed, the Communists had considered themselves to be in the stage of preparation for an armed uprising, but Neumann's more radical view set forth in his book *Der bewaffnete Aufstand* was making headway.

238. Cf. Rudolf Hess's letter of September 16, 1933, to the Supreme SA Command, requesting it to send immediately all available material proving that the Communists were planning an uprising, and to find out "whether there are in the SA any former Communists who are able and willing to testify if necessary that arson etc. are among the methods forseen by the KPD within the framework of such actions" (BA Koblenz, Sammlung Schumacher, *Röhm, Röhmputsch und Reichstagsbrand,* p. 402).

239. Sammlung Brammer, BA ZSg. 101/26, Anweisungen Nos. 55, 62, 77, Mitteilung No. 107.

240. A. François-Poncet, *Als Botschafter in Berlin 1931–1938* Mainz, 1949², p. 94; but cf. *Hitlers Tischgespräche*, p. 325.

241. Cf. for example the report of the *Münchern Neueste Nachrichten*, December 14, 1933.

242. Cf. Diels, *op. cit.*, pp. 269 f.

243. Cf. Schultz, *op. cit.*, p. 523, "Urteil," p. 94 ff., also Schlegelberger's affidavits and opinions, BA Koblenz, RK 43/II/294.

244. Tobias (p. 470) correctly points out that the *in dubio pro re* principle was crassly transgressed in the verdict, which started from the assumption that van der Lubbe had acted "in conscious and deliberate collusion with unknown accomplices." Seuffert moved that van der Lubbe's action be qualified only as "an act of preparation for high treason," which would have avoided the death penalty (cf. 55 ST, pp. 133 ff. and Sack, *op. cit.*, pp. 269 ff.). The attempt to rehabilitate van der Lubbe in 1955 is irrelevant to

the present context (Aufh. 473/55, Gen. St. A., Berlin). On August 6, 1963, the Oberlandgericht in Düsseldorf took the position that there was no reason to presume "that the judgment of the Reich Court was a deliberate miscarriage of justice, or that the judges of the Reich Court stretched the law," but admitted that the verdict had been strongly influenced by National Socialist thinking.

245. Cf. Tobias, p. 628. The harsh criticism of the Leipzig verdict in the National Socialist press and the attitude of the Reich Ministry of Justice are dealt with in Schulz, *op. cit.*, p. 563, and in Hubert Schnorn, *Der Richter im Dritten Reich*, Frankfurt, 1959, pp. 67 ff.

246. The position taken by Bormann in a letter of March 2, 1933, to Elfriede Conti strikes me as characteristic: "It seems almost unbelievable that Communists should have been so exceptionally idiotic as to stage the fire in the Reichstag building a few days before the elections, because from a pure party standpoint nothing better could have happened to us" (Sammlung Schumacher, see note 238 above).

247. Goebbels, *op. cit.*, p. 271.

248. This expression is recorded by Delmer, *op. cit.*, p. 195.

249. Cf. the analysis of Rudolf Vierhaus, "Faschistisches Führertum. Ein Beitrag zur Phänomenologie des europaischen Faschismus," in HZ 189 (1964), p. 631: "The leadership cult prevented almost everyone from seeing to what extent the leaders were the playthings of their wishful thinking. . . ."

250. *Op. cit.*, p. 593. For all our criticism of this exaggerated interpretation, Tobias' guiding idea should not be overlooked, to wit, the fundamental importance "of the incorrigible blindness to reality [that prevails] in an authoritarian Führer-state." It is only with this in mind that we can gain a full historical understanding of the actions of the National Socialists.

5

The "Second Revolution" —June 30, 1934

HERMANN MAU

In its first phase the National Socialist revolution had appeared to be a "national uprising," in which all the bourgeois opponents of the Weimar Republic believed they could play a part. Hindenburg, almost more than Hitler, seemed to be its central figure. But in the President's emergency decree of February 28 and in the Enabling Act of March 23, the National Socialist Chancellor had already secured the means of obtaining undivided power for his party and in the last analysis for himself. Following through the "dynamic" of the National Socialist "revolution," of which he now spoke quite openly, he proceeded to eliminate the political parties without distinction between friend and foe—with the sole exception of his own party! Indeed, in the process of so-called integration (*Gleichschaltung*), he extended the organizational principles of the NSDAP, the core of which was the much invoked "leadership principle," to the entire political life of the German nation and also to the spheres of life that had hitherto been unpolitical. Every possibility of direct or indirect resistance was thus excluded in favor of a power apparatus controlled from above, every part of which, it was thought, would carry out the Führer's commands with perfect precision. It looked as if the "revolutionary" new "order"—a questionable term, as events were soon to show—would function according to program.

But in the course of the National Socialist revolution it soon became evident that Hitler was not master of the forces he had unleashed. In mid-July 1933 he made an attempt to halt the revolution. In speeches to the SA leaders on July 1 and to the provincial governors [*Reichstatthalter*] on July 6 he declared that the revolution was complete. A proclamation of Minister of the Interior Frick on July 11[1] summing up these statements, indicates what kind of revolutionary activity on the part of his own followers was becoming unwelcome to Hitler: disrespect for government authority and even attempts to undermine it, the usurping of government functions by "various organizations or party bureaus," the disorganization of the economy through the interference of unauthorized persons. The proclamation made it clear that this was a political, not a disciplinary question. Hitler demanded that "the stream of revolution" now be "guided into the secure river bed of evolution."[2] The difficulty was that, as Frick stated in his proclamation, certain people were speaking of a "continuation of the revolution" or of a "second revolution"; thus the transition to evolution was "seriously endangered."

Here the profound differences of opinion within the National Socialist leadership as to the aim and mission of the revolution came to light for the first time. In the second phase of the revolution they were to culminate in a bloody conflict. At first Hitler's pleas to conclude the revolution were seemingly successful. A certain appeasement followed, and at the end of 1933 it was widely believed that life in Germany would soon resume its accustomed course. But beneath the surface the flame was still smoldering. The revolution had not by any means died down. In the spring of 1934 there was again talk of a "second revolution" and the tensions *within* the National Socialist leadership assumed dangerous proportions. At length it became evident to all that the conflict cut straight across the leadership. On June 30, 1934, Hitler settled this conflict in his own way.

The history of that day is still shrouded in almost impenetrable darkness. There is hardly another episode of the National Socialist period whose traces have been effaced with such meticulous care. The persons who bore the main responsibility are no longer alive. The essential elements can be reconstructed. But for a number of details we are dependent on circumstantial evidence because documentary sources are almost totally lacking.

In order to understand the forces at work we must go back to the early history of National Socialism. The National Socialist movement sprang from two distinct roots: the party and the national defense leagues [*Wehrverbände*], two organizations with very different social backgrounds. On the one side there was the German Workers' Party [*Deutsche Arbeiterpartei*], the small group of political-minded civilians that Hitler had met in Munich in 1920 and in which he began his political career; on the other side there were the national defense leagues, radically nationalist formations consisting chiefly of war veterans organized along military lines for political purposes. Munich was a center of these formations characteristic of the postwar period in Germany. The man who had the strongest influence and the clearest political ideas within the Bavarian national defense leagues was Ernst Roehm, a native of Munich and captain in the Reichswehr.

When Hitler and Roehm, both radical nationalists, met in Munich, Hitler was in every way in a position of inferiority. Roehm was a man of power and real influence, in a position to speak for the thousands of members of the highly disciplined national defense leagues. Hitler was merely the exponent of a small civilian party, an eccentric whose remarkable gifts, it is true, were immediately apparent to Roehm. For a long time Hitler remained de-

pendent on Roehm. Hitler was then a shabby orator of
the working-class suburbs, plagued by feelings of social inferiority. Roehm was one of those who made him socially
acceptable and procured him the political contacts he
avidly desired. Under Roehm's influence Hitler, to whom
the military character embodied by Roehm was alien by
nature, acquired the exaggerated esteem for "soldierly"
bearing that ultimately led to his stylized "Führer" personality. Hitler's "soldierly" bearing was always something put on and among his intimates quickly thrown off.
But Roehm was above all the source of the idea, crucial
for the rise of National Socialism, of combining the national defense leagues with the party. Hitler adopted this
idea and the National Socialist German Workers' Party, as
Hitler had meanwhile renamed the reorganized German
Workers' Party, was amalgamated with the national defense leagues, which became the National Socialist "Sport
Sections" or "Storm Battalions" [Sport- or Sturmabtei-
lung, SA].

From the very start there was a misunderstanding between Hitler and Roehm, to which they no doubt closed
their eyes in the happy days of their relationship: they
had entirely different conceptions of the role of the SA in
the movement. Hitler regarded himself as exclusively a
political figure. His field of action was the political party.
In his eyes the SA could only be an auxiliary political
body. In this connection he took the word "soldier" in a
wholly figurative sense: the SA men were to be soldiers of
the National Socialist idea. Since this type of organization
had shown a great power of attraction, he wished to make
use of it side by side with the party to advance his political
aims.

Roehm had very different ideas. Unlike Hitler, he regarded himself exclusively as a soldier. To him the military organization was not a political instrument as it was
for Hitler, but a way of life and the symbol of an order
into which he wished to draw all Germany. He despised

civilian politicians; in the world as he saw it a political
party could have only a subordinate function. The last
edition of his *Memoirs,* published in 1934, contains the
sentence: "I demand the primacy of the soldier over the
politician." [3] Beyond the shadow of a doubt this also determined his attitude toward Hitler. Roehm's view of his
relationship with Hitler was made clear in 1925 when,
after Hitler's release from imprisonment in Landsberg,
the National Socialist movement was to be reorganized.
Roehm, who had been given a suspended sentence for his
part in the putsch of 1923, had meanwhile combined the
national defense leagues including the remnants of the SA
into the *Frontbann,* which to his mind would be the nucleus of the new organization. He suggested that Hitler
assume political leadership over the *Frontbann,* while he
himself would retain the military leadership. He looked
upon the political and military leaderships as equal in
rank, so that Hitler and himself would be on the same
plane. He further proposed that both of them, with the
Frontbann, should subordinate themselves to Ludendorff,
whom he passionately admired. Hitler rejected this proposal, in which Roehm had been true to his idea of the
"primacy of the soldier over the politician." This led to
the first falling-out between them. Disillusioned, Roehm,
who had been discharged from the Reichswehr in 1923,
retired to private life for several years.

But the conflict over the position of the SA went beyond Roehm's person. Even after its re-establishment by
Hitler in 1925 the SA remained conspicuously different
in social origin from the party. SA and party were still
two fully independent organizations, united only in the
person of Hitler as their supreme leader. This situation
remained unchanged up to the summer of 1934.

Thus Hitler found himself in a contradictory position
with regard to the SA. The civilian party organization
had always been closer to him, for there his leadership,
supported by associates on whose devotion he could rely,

was uncontested. For all his sentimental attachment to the soldierly virtues, he was not by nature suited to lead a military organization like the SA. Here he had to rely on others. This was particularly distasteful to him because the leadership of the SA was dominated by former officers, in his dealings with whom he could only in rare cases dispel a feeling of embarrassment resulting from his sense of social inferiority. On the other hand, it was largely to the SA that the National Socialist movement owed its rise to a position of power. Into every village it carried the image that attracted so many followers: the image of a world in which there were uniforms, in which men marched and obeyed, in which everyone knew the difference between top and bottom—of a world that seemed once more to be "in order." It was the SA and not the party that shaped the style of the National Socialist struggle for power. In view of this development Hitler accepted the risk to himself inherent in the SA's attitude of independence toward the party. He even decided to give greater political weight to the SA, which was so obviously the most effective instrument of his political struggle. This alone explains why late in 1930 Hitler dismissed former Reichswehr Captain von Pfeffer, who was then in command of the SA, and recalled Roehm, who had been serving as an instructor with the Bolivian army. Their old difference of opinion about the SA seemed to be forgotten. It is also possible that Hitler, impressed by his experience with the SA, had moved closer to Roehm's views and was now prepared to regard it as the center of gravity of his movement. It is certain in any case that he had meanwhile become so sure of himself and of his leading position that gratitude toward the man who had made possible his rise outweighed his fear of a possible rival. In two years Roehm developed the SA, which had fewer than 100,000 members in January 1931 when he took it in hand as "chief of staff" (Hitler was officially the "supreme leader"), into an army of 300,000 which was to be Hitler's irrefutable argument in his final struggle for power. It was largely to Roehm and the SA that Hitler owed his victory.

When Hitler came to power and the days of parades and torchlight processions were past, a question arose for which no one was fully prepared: What was to become of the SA? The SA regarded itself, not without justification, as the true victor. But the anticipated reward was not forthcoming. Hitler could think of no other use for the SA than as an auxiliary police force of a revolution which the SA claimed as its very own. Nor did Roehm obtain any post. This was probably not Hitler's intention; Roehm's homosexuality had long been notorious, and there is no reason to suppose that Hitler held it against him any more than he had ever done before. But the only office that really interested Roehm, that of Reichswehr Minister, was beyond the reach of the National Socialists. The police—though a number of SA men had become local police chiefs—was barred to him by Goering, who as Prussian Minister of the Interior wielded greater influence in this sphere.

In this situation the dissatisfaction and frustrated activism of the SA discharged themselves in the terrorist actions of local SA units. At first these were directed largely against adversaries, but they were far from stopping there. Hundreds of murders, thousands of beatings, and arbitrary arrests made the SA the scourge of the revolution. It was chiefly to stop this wave of terror that Hitler declared —in vain— that the revolution was over. The "supreme SA leader" had no control over the SA.

The problem could no longer be solved by pleas. The fact remained that the SA, which had meanwhile enrolled several hundred thousand more recruits, had no function and followed the development of the new regime with increasing dissatisfaction. The SA was still an independent organization side by side with the party. This was reflected in the official usage; the party and the SA were always mentioned separately in statements referring to the National Socialist movement as a whole. It is highly significant that the basic "Law to Safeguard the Unity of Party and State" of December 1, 1933, conferred the rank of minister on both the "Führer's Deputy" and the "Chief of Staff of the SA"—that is, on the heads of the movement's political organization (the party) and of its military organization (the SA). Significantly, this law was amended after June 30 to the effect that the Chief of Staff of the SA no longer became a minister ex officio.[4]

We do not know how the personal relations between Hitler and Roehm developed in the shadow of this inexorable problem. At the end of 1933 they cannot have been seriously impaired, for among Hitler's New Year messages to his closest collaborators, which were published by the German press, Hitler's message to Roehm is conspicuous for its cordiality and for its use of the familiar *Du* which occurs in none of the other messages. The acrimony between them can only have developed in the ensuing months.

Roehm—and the same is true *mutatis mutandis* of the entire group of higher SA leaders whom he wholly dominated—shared the dissatisfaction of his men. He was not prepared to content himself with the passive role that had fallen to him. He knew the power of the SA, which a word from him could mobilize, and he spared no effort to strengthen it still further by setting up new units and arming them systematically. He had no thought of disloyalty to Hitler. But he felt more and more that Hitler was going against their common aims. He was willing to concede that in view of the concrete political realities confronting him since he had come to power, Hitler could not do otherwise. But from this he inferred that where Hitler had failed to carry out their common aims, he, Roehm, must prepare the SA to do so by force. This was the substance of the call for a "second revolution" which made itself heard in the SA soon after the seizure of power, which was temporarily silenced, but resumed all the more insistently in the spring of 1934.

The crux of Roehm's criticism of the course the revolution had taken was the question of the future German army. Partly out of resentment at having been discharged in 1923, he despised the Reichswehr leadership. He regarded it as reactionary and knew that Hitler agreed with him. It struck him as a grave mistake that Hitler should collaborate with this leadership instead of dismissing it. The elimination of the top-ranking officers and the transfer of responsibility for the Reichswehr to the SA leadership struck him as a logical consequence of the seizure of power. That would have made it possible to merge Reichswehr and SA into a militia, a National Socialist people's army, which to Roehm's mind would have been the crowning of the National Socialist victory. This conception remained at the core of his political plans. He must have believed that Hitler could be won over to his views, for in the spring of 1934, without taking any discernible precautions, he discussed the question of a militia, which of course had serious diplomatic implications, with a number of foreign military attachés.[5]

Roehm must also have had other misgivings about Hitler's policies. He was interested in social problems and he took the socialism in the National Socialist program seriously; he can hardly have approved of the fact that this aspect of National Socialism had been totally neglected since the expulsion of Gregor Strasser. It is not known whether in the crucial weeks and months before June 30 Roehm maintained any significant contact with Strasser. Hitler later accused him—perhaps with some justification—of plotting with Strasser. Roehm's aide-de-camp, SS Gruppenführer Bergmann, who on June 30 miraculously escaped being shot, declared in any case that Roehm had respected Strasser as a level-headed, practical politician, that in the period after Strasser's downfall Roehm had tried "to change Hitler's mind about Strasser," and that he had "gone to see him in the course of a visit to Berlin." [6] Roehm is also believed to have been opposed to the suppression of the unions, initiated by Ley on orders from Hitler with the forcible occupation of the trade-union buildings on May 2, 1933. Further, Roehm seems to have disagreed with Hitler in matters of foreign policy, and favored an understanding with the Western powers, particularly France.[7] Finally, it seems likely that in the period when his relations with Hitler were becoming strained Roehm, who dreamed of a world organized along clear-cut military lines and had never ceased to be a monarchist, was beginning to have misgivings about Hitler's unrestricted dictatorial power. The "primacy of the soldier" called for different solutions.

When were Hitler's suspicions aroused? We do not know. But it is easy to see what his thoughts must have been once his attention was called to the problem. Roehm had played a unique part in Hitler's rise, and Hitler recognized the fact. Years after having him put to death he declared in a group of high party leaders that if ever the history of the rise of the National Socialist movement were written, Roehm would always have to be remembered as the second man after himself. Roehm had brought about the collaboration between the civilian nationalists of the party cells and the militant nationalists of the national defense leagues under Hitler as their common political leader. The idea of joining the party and the national defense leagues into a political movement had originated with Roehm. A brilliant organizer, he had made the SA into an instrument of power without which Hitler would not have attained his goal. On the other hand, Roehm, who was no great thinker, owed his *Weltanschauung*, the rational formulas for his emotional impulses, to his meeting with Hitler. This was the basis of Roehm's attachment to Hitler. But that attachment had never become subservience.

At least up to 1933 the two men must have been in

fundamental agreement regarding the party's political program. What led to conflict after the seizure of power was at first a question of method, which, however, as it soon developed, also involved political content. Roehm, who by his own admission divided humanity into "men who make revolutions and men who do not," [8] was an old-style revolutionary. It is unlikely that he saw the National Socialist revolution as different from the revolutions he knew from the history books; after as brief as possible a phase of violence, characterized by the storming of barricades and unavoidable bloodshed, the old order is overthrown and a new one put in its place. He never regarded the SA as anything other than the "storm battalions" of such an old-style revolution.

If Hitler ever shared these conceptions, there is no doubt that he had discarded them. More scheming, subtle, and up-to-date than the obstinate, single-minded traditionalist Roehm, he saw very different possibilities in the political situation that had arisen since he had taken over the Chancellery. The methods of cold revolution had come to him almost unawares: pseudo-legality, latent terror, carefully measured localized actions which revealed their revolutionary significance only when taken together, and a policy of deception toward friend and foe alike. Perhaps he already sensed that modern revolutions no longer storm barricades but operate through slow processes of subversion which bring deeper changes than ever before because they affect not only institutions but the human substance as well. He saw clearly that those who were clamoring for a "second revolution" wanted him to abandon the devious methods of the cold revolution and put through the unfulfilled demands of the National Socialist program—regardless of the cost in blood.

What Roehm may at first have regarded as a mere tactical disagreement was for Hitler a matter of basic principle. He opposed the demand for a "second revolution," not because he objected to its foreseeable horrors, but because he distrusted its aims. Roehm understood this too late. He, the passionate conspirator, would scarcely have preached the "second revolution" so openly if he had not been convinced that his aims were identical with Hitler's.

What alienated Hitler more than anything else was Roehm's main demand, namely, that the SA should absorb the Reichswehr and become the army of the new state. Undoubtedly this demand was consistent with the aims that had motivated both Hitler and Roehm in their struggle for power, and Hitler may well have been tempted to accede to it. For the Reichswehr could not be "integrated," and despite the complaisance of its leadership its attitude toward the new state remained equivocal. In the end, however, Hitler shrank back from integrating the Reichswehr with the help of the SA. Roehm's demand involved the old problem of the National Socialist movement, the rivalry between party and SA. To put the SA in the place of the Reichswehr would have been to give it a dominant position in the state at the expense of the party, which with the seizure of power had clearly become the political center of gravity. The leading party functionaries would have offered tenacious resistance to such a move. This in itself would hardly have deterred Hitler if the prospect of seeing Roehm in command of all the armed forces had not struck him as a threat to his own position. He had never been able to subjugate Roehm by means of the strange fascination that made all his other political intimates putty in his hands. Since the exclusion of Gregor Strasser, Roehm was indeed his only rival.

Nevertheless Hitler cannot be said to have acted on his own initiative. He was pushed into action. It was in his nature to put off unpleasant decisions for weeks or months. Here again he hesitated. But by the spring of 1934 at the latest, others took a hand in the game who had an interest in intensifying the conflict and forcing Hitler to break with Roehm. Several conversations with Roehm, the last of which took place at the beginning of June, had made it clear to him that Roehm stood by his demands. And still Hitler hesitated. But at this point the groups that had been trying for months to exacerbate the conflict, created, deliberately and with full knowledge of Hitler's mentality, a situation in which he was forced to make up his mind. When early in the morning of June 30 Hitler gave the signal for the blood purge, he presumably did not know that the circumstances which finally had touched off his action had been brought about by design, that they were a "put-up job." There is no doubt that Roehm was playing with the idea of carrying out his "second revolution" even against Hitler, for by then Hitler had in his eyes become a traitor to the National Socialist idea. But there is also no doubt that on June 30 Roehm and his fellow conspirators were far from ready for action. The testimony of one of Roehm's associates seems indicative of the state of affairs at that time: during dinner on June 28 Hitler had telephoned Roehm. Roehm had returned to table "very well pleased" by this last telephone conversation with the Führer and had informed his guests, among them General von Epp, that Hitler would attend the congress of SA leaders at Wiessee on June 30, adding that he, Roehm, "would tear the mask from Goebbels' face. He knew that he could count on his SA and the army(!)." [9] Meanwhile Roehm's enemies seem to have succeeded by adroit stage management in making Hitler believe that the "second revolution" was imminent.[10] These enemies were on the one hand the party, on the other hand the Reichswehr.

Sentiment against Roehm had a long history in the party. It went back to the beginnings of the National Socialist movement and resulted partly from the continuous rivalry between party and SA and partly from disapproval of Roehm's mode of life and that of his entourage. It soon became more intense when with the seizure of power not the SA but the party became dominant, especially so after it became clear that Roehm would not resign himself to this state of affairs. The leading party functionaries now regarded Roehm as a threat to their share of the newly acquired power. His most influential enemies in the party were Goering, Hess—the *de facto* head of the party organization—and Goebbels. In regard to Goering, who as a former SA leader had connections in both camps, one has the impression that he wished in the present instance to compensate for his past in the SA by showing particular brutality. Himmler and Heydrich, who were Goering's subordinates, also worked toward the downfall of the Chief of Staff, who was an obstacle to the plan of building up the SS as a National Socialist elite corps. Although the Schutz-Staffel, originally an emanation of the SA, had long gone its own way under Himmler, its chief, and Heydrich, his second in command in charge of the Security Service of the SS [Sicherheitsdienst, SD], it was still formally under the command of Roehm as Chief of Staff.

The reasons for the hostility of the Reichswehr are obvious. It was irritated by the amateurish competition of the SA and suspicious of its Chief of Staff. Roehm and the SA were responsible for the creeping terror of the revolution. The Reichswehr knew Roehm's plans and did not underestimate the danger they represented. The Reichswehr leaders believed that in helping to overthrow Roehm and to curtail the SA they would be extracting the revolution's poison fang. The essential was to alienate Hitler from Roehm, and to convince him that he needed the Reichswehr and could rely on it. The Reichswehr was in a favorable position to deal with Hitler because the two men who represented it in negotiations with the National Socialist leadership, Reichswehr Minister von Blomberg and von Reichenau, head of the Wehrmachtsamt (Army Office), were excepted from his usual distrust of officers. Blomberg had proved a godsend to Hitler, who had not known him when Hindenburg appointed him Reichswehr Minister on January 30, 1933. Regarded by his fellow generals as an outsider, he soon succumbed to Hitler's fascination and became his uncritical admirer, the only basis on which fruitful collaboration with Hitler was possible.[11] Still more important was Reichenau. A staunch National Socialist, he was the only highly placed officer in the Reichswehr to have maintained regular personal contact with Hitler even before 1933. He was a more modern type of officer than Blomberg, ambitious, brutal, politically gifted, and more intelligent than his minister. Under circumstances similar to those that had so long enabled Schleicher to help fashion the policy of the republic, he and not his minister determined the policy of the Reichswehr Ministry.

The tactics of the Reichswehr leadership seem to have been to point up the antagonism between the Reichswehr and the SA, and make it clear to Hitler with his tendency to steer a middle course that he would have to make up his mind. Through go-betweens, including SA Leader Lutze who was to be appointed Roehm's successor, the Reichswehr leaders knew exactly what was going on at SA headquarters and did their best to keep Hitler informed.

The details of the discussions that led Hitler to decide in favor of the Reichswehr are not known. But certain arguments can be cited that must have played a part. Hitler wanted a strong army. Rearmament had been a central point in his policy ever since the seizure of power, because Germany's freedom of movement in matters of foreign policy depended on it. Rearmament was also an internal problem insofar as it was bound to affect the political attitude of the future army. The fate of the regime and Hitler's own position might depend on it. Would the Reichswehr follow him politically? Or would it, as Roehm believed, be possible to carry out his plans only with a National Socialist army? Since the seizure of power Hitler's experience with the Reichswehr had been better than he had probably anticipated. Its leadership had proved tractable and willing. Hitler had been impressed by the intel-

ligent, efficient, politically reserved military technicians
of the officers' corps. He was well aware that rearmament
was a technical problem depending largely on the specialized techniques embodied in this officers' corps. Was he to
risk such an advantage by integrating the Reichswehr
with Roehm's SA—an operation necessarily involving violence and bloodshed—and perhaps delay rearmament
for several years, solely in order to exchange the risk of a
non-National Socialist army for the risk of a National Socialist army led by Roehm? In answering these questions
Hitler was no longer the herald and champion of a
Weltanschauung, as he had been in the course of his rise
to power, but a coldly calculating technician of power—
his own, very personal power.

Another question relating directly to Hitler's personal
position must have played a part: the question of Hindenburg's successor. Since the early spring of 1934 it had
been known to the inner circle that the President was not
likely to outlive the year. In June it became known that
the doctors gave him only a few weeks to live. The question of his successor was of vital importance for Hitler's
future position. One thing was certain in any case: since
the President's constitutional prerogatives included supreme command over the Reichswehr, no solution was
thinkable that did not meet with the approval of the
Reichswehr. The theoretical possibilities were as follows:
Hitler could assume the presidency and appoint a leading
National Socialist to the chancellorship, or else he could
restore the monarchy, a solution which had influential
partisans. The third solution, which Hitler chose, was by
far the most advantageous to himself: he would combine
the offices of President and Chancellor in his person. This
decision must have been made before June 30. Did he
purchase the assent of the Reichswehr by sacrificing
Roehm? The question remains unanswered.

It seems certain that Hitler's decision against Roehm
was arrived at in the first half of June, after his five-hour

interview with him, but that he did not immediately draw the practical consequences of his decision. It was probably the exacerbation of the conflict between Reichswehr and SA in the course of June that led him to take action. Both camps engaged in conspiratorial activity and sections at least of both Reichswehr and SA were put on the alert, each expecting the other side to strike.

The darkness surrounding the events of those days is somewhat illumined by the following testimony: "On or about June 24" the future Field Marshal von Kleist, then Reichswehr commander in Silesia, received in Breslau a warning from Fritsch, head of the army High Command, that an attack of the SA on the troops was imminent. He should therefore keep his men "as inconspicuously as possible" in readiness. In the following days Kleist received numerous reports from all manner of sources in the army, the SA, the SS, the old Stahlhelm, and from government offices and civilians, which seemed to confirm Fritsch's warning and painted a picture of feverish preparations on the part of the SA. In this tense situation Kleist, who wished to avoid a bloody clash, sent for Heines, the SA leader for Silesia and an intimate of Roehm. In a private conference Kleist spoke of the menacing preparations of the SA, and warned Heines. Heines replied that he was well aware of the measures taken by the Silesian Reichswehr, that he had interpreted them as preparation for an attack on the SA and had therefore secured his defenses. He gave Kleist his solemn word of honor that he had neither planned nor made any preparations for an attack on the army. On the night of the twenty-eighth he phoned Kleist to say that he had just learned that the Reichswehr not only in Silesia but all over Germany had been placed on the alert as of that day in expectation of an SA putsch. He declared his intention of flying to Munich on the twenty-ninth to confer with Roehm. Kleist then decided to fly to Berlin the same day. He there reported his conversations with Heines to Fritsch, chief of

the army High Command, in the presence of Beck, chief
of the General Staff. He had the impression, he added,
that a third party was spreading false reports in order to
incite the Reichswehr and the SA against each other—he
personally had Himmler in mind. Thereupon Fritsch
sent for Reichenau and had Kleist repeat his report.
Reichenau replied: "That may be true. But it's too late
now!" [12]

This surprising glimpse of the preparations for June 30
shapes the few available facts into a coherent picture.
Roehm was not planning a putsch on June 30. But sections of the SA had been alerted because the orders given
the Reichswehr on pretext that an SA putsch was imminent were interpreted as preparations for an attack on the
SA. Such a situation must have been brought about by
design. It also seems that forged alert orders had been sent
to the SA in Munich. According to the testimony of the
widow of Group Leader Schmid, who was shot on the
thirtieth, the following strange command was given during a brief absence of Schmid on the twenty-ninth: "SA,
take to the streets, the Führer is no longer for us!" Informed of this order, Schmid returned in haste and sent
couriers to all points where SA men had gathered, with
instructions "to remain peacefully in their camps and
wait for further orders." Before being summoned to Hitler early in the morning of June 30, Schmid to his horror
had noticed the absence of "two white blanks" (probably
the forged orders) that could have proved his innocence
"of Friday's events." He could think of no other explanation than that [Bavarian] Minister of the Interior Wagner, who was hostile to him, had taken them in the course
of a violent argument they had had early that morning.[13]
On the morning of June 30 an SA Oberführer, member of
the SA Jägerstandarte stationed in Bad Tölz, discovered
that two companies of the regiment had been alerted and
ordered them back to their barracks at once. He found
out that the alert order had come from the SS Officer

Training School in Bad Tölz.[14] In the excitement of those days a false news report guided into the proper channels sufficed to convince the members of the SA or Reichswehr that the other was about to launch the expected attack. This was exactly the situation required to convince Hitler that he must strike. It cannot be determined which camp first thought it had reason to fear the other's attack. Since Hitler could be certain that the Reichswehr would not attack the SA without his knowledge, he must in the end have regarded Roehm as the instigator and the alerting of sections of the SA as a signal for the "second revolution." Just this must have been the stage managers' intention.

Who they were can today hardly be held in doubt. Reichenau, as we have seen, knew what was going on and was certainly one of them. His position enabled him to involve the Reichswehr in a game which must have had the approval of Blomberg, his immediate superior, but of which Fritsch and Beck seem to have been unaware. As we know now, the Reichswehr helped to organize and carry out the action itself. Before June 30, Reichenau as its representative repeatedly discussed this collaboration with Himmler in Himmler's office, while Heydrich informed the SS Oberabschnittsführer.[15] In Dresden and Breslau, it has been proved, the SS, alerted before the action, was assembled in Reichswehr barracks.[16] In Munich, sections of the Dachau concentration camp guards, who had been mobilized on June 30 on orders from Berlin and ordered to Wiessee, were also held in readiness in order "jointly with the Reichswehr and the police" to suppress any disorders that might occur.[17] Finally, a company of the SS Guards Battalion led by Sepp Dietrich, the future Adolf Hitler Body Standard, which in the night of the twenty-ninth was sent from Berlin to a small railroad station in the immediate vicinity of Landsberg am Lech, was there met by a Reichswehr truck battalion from Ludwigsburg (Württemberg), which transported them in the direction of Wiessee.[18] In view of all this it seems quite plausible that, as Reichenau later declared, it was really not so easy to "arrange" matters in such a way as to make June 30 look like a mere inner-party incident.[19]

The main actors in the blood bath, Goering and Himmler, must also be regarded as the stage managers of the prelude. They alone possessed—in the Secret State Police [Gestapo], whose chief was Goering but which Himmler directed under his orders—the apparatus needed to stage such a scene. Their most important helper was Heydrich, whose function as chief of the Secret State Police Office [Gestapa] in Berlin placed him at the center of events. Their maneuvers attained their goal when early in the morning of June 30 Hitler gave the signal for the action against Roehm and the SA leadership.[20]

There was no attempt at legal proceedings. Everyone regarded as guilty or suspicious was shot without a trial. Hitler himself took charge in Munich, while Goering acted on his behalf in Berlin. In vain Bavarian Reichsstatthalter [Reich Provincial Governor]* von Epp, of whose staff Roehm had once been a member, tried to halt Hitler's murderous proceedings. Later in Berlin he succeeded only with great difficulty in saving Roehm's aide, SA leader Prince Isenburg, who had already been notified that he was to be shot. In Isenburg's presence Goebbels phoned Goering from Epp's office in Munich at about ten o'clock on the morning of June 30 to tell him "that most of the 'criminals' were under arrest and that he [Goering] should do his job." [21] In Berlin as in Munich the action was carried out by the SS and the police. The National Socialist leadership also took advantage of the "unique opportunity" to have troublesome political opponents murdered; members of the "Austrian Legion"

* Reichsstatthalter was the title of the newly centralized Reich administration's permanent delegates to the provincial and district governments. The office represented one more element in the process of integration.

were entrusted with this task.[22] Although the official German News Agency* reported on July 2 that the action had taken only twenty-four hours and Hitler declared in a proclamation issued the following day that it had been concluded on the night of July 1, the massacre actually went on for three days. The law of July 3 in which the cabinet legalized the murders as "emergency defense of the state" covered the "measures taken on June 30 and on July 1 and 2."

In his self-contradictory speech of justification to the Reichstag on July 13, 1934, Hitler set the number of the victims at seventy-seven. Actually at least twice and perhaps three times as many persons were murdered; it is unlikely that the exact figure will ever be established. Apart from Roehm and the SA leaders closest to him those murdered included numerous enemies of the regime or persons held in disfavor. In addition to the SA men, Hitler himself in his speech mentioned only Gregor Strasser and Generals von Schleicher and von Bredow. It was plausible to suppose that Roehm had taken Strasser, who in December 1932 had resigned from his party posts in protest against Hitler's policy, into his confidence. But except for Hitler's allegation there is no proof of it. It is certain that Hitler had never forgiven Strasser for his irresponsible negotiations with Schleicher in 1932, which had almost caused a split in the party. Presumably in the same connection Schleicher had brought on himself the irreconcilable hatred of the party. It is conceivable that as Hitler later alleged, Schleicher, who since his departure from the Chancellery had been eagerly awaiting the day of his return to politics, was also in collusion with Roehm. Here again there are no proofs, any more than for the contention that Schleicher's former associate Bredow had acted as Roehm's foreign liaison agent. A notorious lie was the official announcement that Schleicher had been shot while offering armed resistance to arrest. Schleicher and

* Product of a merger in 1933 of the WTB and TU.

his wife were murdered in cold blood in their home by SS men in civilian clothes.[23] Among those whose murder was for some time known only through rumor were former Bavarian Generalstaatskommissar von Kahr, the leader of the Berlin Catholics, Ministerialdirektor Klausener, and two close associates of Papen, his press officer Bose and the conservative publicist Edgar Jung.

The official account of the events made use of the formula "crushing of the Roehm revolt" and accused the murdered persons of high treason. The accusation of treasonable contacts with "the representatives of a foreign power"—everyone knew that André François-Poncet, the French ambassador in Berlin, was meant—was later withdrawn in a communication to the French government but of this the German public was not informed. In the newspaper stories much space was devoted to the moral depravity of Roehm and his circle, as though the facts cited in this connection had not been generally known for years and tolerated by Hitler. The reaction of the German public was chiefly one of relief that an end had been put to the creeping SA terror and to the threat of a "second revolution." Many were horrified by the brutality and bloodshed; but still more were to disregard these details and interpret the events as a victory of the good National Socialists over the bad. No one fully understood what forces had been at work and very few foresaw the consequences.

* *

June 30, 1934, meant the end of the National Socialist "revolution" in the primitive sense envisaged by its original proponents. Hitler's murder of the leaders of the "second revolution" reduced the forces of dynamic upheaval to silence. At one stroke the diverse groups and tendencies that had become fully effective with the seizure of power were established in the positions where they were to remain for years. Their attitude toward the events of June 30 assigned them their places for the future.

Hitler himself came out of the action with a significant gain in power and prestige. After ridding himself of his one rival, he had only submissive admirers in his own camp. To the very end there was no other rebel against Hitler among the leading National Socialists. After Hindenburg's death (August 2, 1934) Hitler's takeover of the presidency went off without a hitch. As chief of state and commander in chief of the Reichswehr, he had achieved a unique concentration of power. On August 19, 1934, 38.4 out of 45.5 million voters gave their "consent" to this arrangement in a plebiscite staged with virtuosity by the National Socialist regime.

On the surface the true victor of June 30 seemed to be the Reichswehr. Hitler did everything he could to make it think so. In his speech of justification on July 13 he emphatically confirmed the two prerogatives which Roehm, in the eyes of the Reichswehr leadership, had threatened; the Reichswehr, he declared, was the sole bearer of arms in the state; and under his regime it would remain a "nonpolitical instrument." At that moment the loyalty of the Reichswehr must have meant a great deal to him, for he went so far as to say that officers and soldiers could not "as individuals" be expected "to espouse our movement"! Never again did he make such a concession, which conflicted with the official fiction that all Germans were National Socialists. But the Reichswehr had little grounds for satisfaction at Hitler's demonstrations of favor. June 30 had cast a shadow on its integrity. True, it had not participated in the actual execution of the measures of June 30 and the following days. But all those who in its name had taken part in the preparations must have known that a massacre was at least possible. They cannot be cleared of responsibility. The fact that, despite indignant protest in army circles, the Reichswehr leadership took the murder of two of its generals lying down, shows that it felt compromised. The inevitable consequence was a cleavage in an officers' corps which believed that its unity was grounded first and foremost on a common ethical attitude. The cold revolution sowed the seeds of dissension in the most united social structure that still existed in Germany. That was the greatest triumph achieved by Hitler on June 30.

With justified satisfaction the party drew its conclusions from the event. The old conflict with the SA for precedence in the movement had been settled in its favor once and for all. This had its effects in the most remote villages, for now the petty party functionaries were rid of the burdensome competition of the petty SA leaders. At the highest level Hess, as leader of the Political Organization, became the party's sole representative in the Reich cabinet. The SA itself was given a new chief of staff in the person of Lutze, an agent of the Reichswehr. It soon became a mass organization without influence or political character; its past seemed to be dead.

In a decree of far-reaching consequences Hitler expressed his thanks to the SS. "In consideration of the great services rendered by the SS, especially in connection with the events of June 30," he removed it on July 20, 1934, from its position of subordination to the SA and made it an independent organization, responsible to him personally, within the framework of the NSDAP.[24] With this expression of favor began the meteoric rise of Himmler and the SS, one of the most important developments of the ensuing years.

The elevation of the SS to the rank of a powerful organization which was to set its stamp on the National Socialist regime from then on can be taken as a symbolic *pars pro toto,* for in fact June 30 changed the nature of the entire regime. Once Hitler had made cold-blooded murder the legal instrument of his policy, evil pursued him like a curse. On that day the last restraints were overcome. From then on power and violence were irrevocably joined.

NOTES

1. *Dokumente der deutschen Politik,* Vol. I, 1933. No. 36.
2. "Erklärung vor den Reichsstatthaltern vom 6. Juli 1933," *ibid.,* No. 35.
3. Ernst Roehm, *Geschichte eines Hochverräters,* 5th ed., Munich, 1934, p. 349.
4. "Gesetz zur Änderung des Gesetzes zur Sicherung der Einheit von Partei und Staat vom 5. Juli 1934," RGBl, 1934, p. 529.
5. "Befragungsniederschrift Max Jüttner (ehemaliger SA-Obergruppenführer) vom 2.4. 1952," IfZ, Munich.
6. "Aussage Robert Bergmann (ehemaliger SS-Gruppenführer) vom 14. Mai 1949." Also "Aussage des ehemaligen SA-Gruppenführer Karl Schreyer vom 23. Mai 1949."
7. *Ibid.*
8. Roehm, *op. cit.,* p. 283.
9. "Aussage Ferdinand Karl Prinz von Isenburg vom 3. Januar 1950." In view of the following day's events in Wiessee mentioned in this statement, it seems more likely that the phone call occurred on June 28, as stated on May 14, 1949, by Robert Bergmann, Roehm's aide-de-camp, than on June 29, as stated by Isenburg.
10. The supposition that Roehm had already decided on June 30 as the day of reckoning is scarcely compatible with Hitler's obvious efforts, in his telephone conversation with Roehm and in talks with his deputy Krausser, to lull the chief of staff into a sense of security. According to the statement made on May 23, 1949, by former SA Gruppenführer Schreyer (note 6, above) on the basis of statements made to him by Krausser before he was shot, Hitler "assured" Krausser during the week preceding the thirtieth that he would take advantage of the congress of SA leaders at Wiessee to have a long talk with Roehm and the group leaders and settle all differences and misunderstandings. He realized and regretted that he had not concerned himself enough with the old SA men and said he would see to it that after being prevented for many years from making a living they would be put to work again. Moreover, Hitler felt very conciliatory toward his faithful companion in arms Ernst Roehm, who would also be kept on in his post.
11. According to Friedrich Hossbach, *Zwischen Wehrmacht und Hitler,* Wolfenbüttel, 1949, p. 70, Blomberg's naval adjutant, the future Admiral von Friedeburg, was friends with Himmler.
12. "Affidavit des Generalfeldmarschalls Ewald von Kleist, abgegeben vor dem Internationalen Militärgerichtshof in Nürnberg,

1946" (unpublished). Photostat of copy in IfZ, Munich. According to the then SA member Wilhelm Ott's statement of October 12, 1949, Heines heard some days before from SA Brigade Leader von Grolmann that the Wehrmacht had been alerted against the SA. He telephoned his information to Goering and received the answer that "it was absurd, just an exercise." Ott also related that on the twenty-eighth Heines called on Kleist "who," he adds—quite plausibly in view of the subsequent turn of events—"as I later found out, misled him." Thereupon, still according to Ott, Heines sent half the relief camp [*Hilfswerklager*] and the staff guard on leave. According to Grolman's statement of June 30, 1950, he and SA Brigade Leader Freiherr von Wechmar gave Colonel Kempf, the Reichswehr commander at Schweidnitz, "an identical written declaration of loyalty."

13. Letter of Frau Martina Schmid to the Munich prosecuting attorney, June 12, 1949.

14. "Aussage Hans Hoeflmayer vom 25. November, 1949." Hoeflmayer had previously learned in Munich "that the SA was alerted last night. The SA leaders were all armed."

15. "Befragungsniederschrift Karl Wolff (ehemaliger General der Waffen-SS) vom. 7.–8. September 1952," IfZ, Munich. "Aussage Dr. Werner Best vom 1.10 1951."

16. "Aussage Friedrich Karl Freiherr von Eberstein, damals Oberabschnittsführer Dresden, vom 28. 6 1950." Eberstein "received orders from Himmler to alert the general SS and to make contact with the commander of the military district." The executions in Dresden were carried out "by the Saxony political squad [*politische Bereitschaft*], an SS formation armed and living in barracks, financed by the *Land* and serving to reinforce the *Land* police." This body was later transformed into the SS Disposition Troop in Dresden. See also "Aussage Prof. Dr. Walfried Marx vom 21. Juni, 1950."

17. "Aussage Michael Lippert, damals SS Obersturmführer und Kommandeur des SS-Wachbataillon das Konzentrationslagers Dachau vom 20. und 22. Juni 1949."

18. "Aussage Sepp Dietrich vom 18. Mai 1949." The detachment was stopped between Bad Tölz and Wiessee and ordered to Munich.

19. Hans Bernd Gisevius, *Bis zum bitteren Ende*, Zurich, 1946, Vol. I, p. 286; Hamburg, 1947, p. 250.

20. The part played by Goebbels and Hess is still obscure.

21. Cf. note 9, above.

22. "Aussagen Hermann Wild vom 4. Juli 1949 und Walter Kurreck (beide damals Angehörige des SD Oberabschnitts Süd, München) vom 13. Oktober 1949." Also "Aussage Alfred Rodenbücher, damals Führer der 'Osterreichischen Legion' ('Flüchtlings-SS'), vom 26. Juli 1950."

23. Cf. the documents on the murder of Schleicher published in No. 1 of *Vierteljahrshefte für Zeitgeschichte*.

24. Schultheiss' *Europäisches Geschichtskalender*, New Series, Vol. 50 (1934), p. 187.

The Totalitarian State:

✠ ✠ ✠

Police, Propaganda, National Expansionism, Culture

6

The Position of the SS
in the Third Reich

HANS BUCHHEIM

What was published in National Socialist Germany concerning the structure of the SS and its position in the state seldom goes beyond incidentals; even the specialized juridical literature and the works intended for the use of party functionaries provide only sporadic hints and slight glimpses, which at best give the reader an intimation of the juridical and organizational context. Consequently those contemporaries who took an interest in the matter possessed only fragmentary knowledge and nebulous or erroneous ideas. Best informed were the intelligence organizations of the Western Allies, but though the handbooks they issued for official use during the last years of the war impress one by their detailed knowledge of personalities and technical details, they fail to supply a sound over-all picture. Considerably better material is to be found in the affidavits submitted at the Nuremberg trials and the minutes of the proceedings. But in view of the tension between prosecution and defense and the consequent intermingling of constitutional and penal law, these documents do not provide an accurate idea of the institutional character of the SS. The prosecution emphasized features that seemed likely to throw responsibility on certain individuals, while the defense developed a remarkable virtuosity at dissociating elements that belonged together and in every instance pinning the responsibility on those who were not in the dock. The work of a historian is not that of a judge or attorney; it is not only his right but also his duty to forgo the categories of prosecution and defense and to leave personal, individual cases out of account. He must endeavor to draw as concrete and detailed a picture of the whole as possible; for the farther the Third Reich recedes into the past, the more people content themselves with speaking of it in vague generalities. The prevailing conceptions of the totalitarian state are based more on striking externals than on a knowledge of the causes that led to the breakdown of constitutional government. The SS was an essential factor in the totalitarian state; a knowledge of its development and character provides a basis for the investigation of the origin and true nature of such a state.

The SS was not a homogeneous organization in which all members had equal rights and duties; there were very different forms and degrees of *de jure* membership and *de facto* participation. Moreover, in the last year of the National Socialist period, the state and party jurisdictions seem to have been inextricably intertwined, so that, from the standpoint of our notions of constitutional government, the SS became a highly complex institution. Nevertheless it possessed unity, not only as an instrument of political power but also in its organizational character, which, however, cannot be discerned on the basis of a distinction between "state" and "party." All organizations subject to the authority of the Reich SS Leader [Reichsführer-SS] belonged politically and juridically to the SS, regardless of whether they had originated within the SS or been taken over by it. Consequently it is a mistake, for example, either to judge a police officer with an assimilated SS rank and an old SS "roughneck" by the same standard, or, in order to distinguish between them, to deny the unity of the institution, for there was indeed such a unity.

The source material for the study of the SS is still

scanty. The American authorities who are in possession of the German archives have not yet released the bulk of the documents relating to the SS. Many of the still surviving witnesses are exceedingly reticent. In this connection direct testimony is extremely important because nothing has been written about many vital particulars and contexts; most of the relevant data remain in a fluid, undigested state, so that a well-rounded picture can be formed only on the basis of the recollections of many witnesses. Nevertheless certain main lines of development seem to be sufficiently well established to enable us to outline the juridical position of the SS. In so doing we must take the origins of the SS as our starting point, because much in the later development of this organization can be understood only through a knowledge of its beginnings. On this foundation it will then be necessary to investigate primarily the relation between the SS and the police and the juridical position of the Waffen SS and of the Reich Commissioner for the Reinforcement of German Nationality, in other words, the points in which the position of the SS in the Third Reich is most problematic.

The Beginnings of the SS

When Hitler began to rebuild his party in the spring of 1925, he was at first unable to reconstitute the SA in the form he wished, as a body of political agitators and fighters absolutely subordinated to the party leadership. For Roehm, whom he had enlisted to reorganize the SA, demanded that it should neither be subordinated to the party leadership nor involved in the political issues of the day, but should remain independent and merely lend the party "military" support where this seemed necessary. Since no agreement was arrived at, Roehm abandoned the leadership of the SA on May 1, 1925, and went to Bolivia. All that remained of the SA was a few more or less local groups without central leadership, which could not be regarded as a useful and reliable instrument. Even earlier, in March, when an open break had not yet occurred but Roehm had already shown that he was not an absolutely subservient follower, Hitler, had thought it advisable to establish a Staff Guard [Stabswache] of some dozen wholly reliable men for his own personal protection. He turned primarily to members of his former bodyguard of 1923, the Hitler Shock Troop [Stosstrupp Hitler] and also entrusted the leadership to one of them, Julius Schreck. This Staff Guard made its first public appearance on April 16, 1925, at the funeral of Ernst Pöhner, the former Munich Police President. To right and left of the coffin marched four torchbearers, members of the Staff Guard, some of whom had until shortly before been in prison with the deceased.

Probably soon after Roehm's departure Hitler decided to set up in Munich and other localities other troops similar to the Staff Guard, and by late summer 1925 they received the name of Schutzstaffeln [Guard Squads, SS], which also included the Staff Guard. Schreck issued the first directives pertaining to the structure of these squads (it should be borne in mind that this structure was quite provisional and applies only to that particular period). Whereas the old SA was a paramilitary organization designed to take in as many members as possible, all of whom were not necessarily party members, the Schutzstaffeln were to recruit only the most active and reliable party members; the squads were not intended to be a new organization, but to remain within the party organization, though under the central command of their own Supreme Leadership [Oberleitung] in Munich. Each squad of ten was led by a squad leader and was directly under the Supreme Leadership. The organization's duties were conceived as follows: the protection of Hitler and other prominent party leaders, the defense of meetings, measures to forestall possible attacks on the party and its leaders, and, not least, the recruiting of new party members and subscribers to the *Völkischer Beobachter.* Thus the Schutzstaffeln were not in the tradition of the paramilitary organizations, but were party cadres to be used for every possible purpose, political, technical, and combative. Their insignia (black cap with death's head and black-rimmed swastika armband) expressly identified them as the successors of the Hitler Shock Troop of 1923. Even then Hitler had not felt absolutely sure of the SA, because of its close and to him rather baffling connections with the other paramilitary organizations and the Reichswehr. For this reason he had already in March 1923 set up a Staff Guard, which in May had been expanded into a Shock Troop under the leadership of Schreck and of Joseph Berchtold, but had been dissolved after the unsuccessful putsch. Berchtold had then fled to Austria, whence he now returned to take over the top leadership of the Schutzstaffeln from Schreck on April 15, 1926. At the party congress in Weimar on July 4, 1926, Berchtold received the Blood Banner of November 9, 1923, from Hitler in the name of his *Staffeln,* and swore "loyalty to the death." [1]

When on November 1, 1926, a supreme SA leadership under Captain von Pfeffer was appointed and the SA was reorganized and centralized, the Schutzstaffeln declined in importance. Over Berchtold's violent opposition, they were subordinated to the Supreme Leadership of the SA, and later when they were greatly expanded under Himmler's leadership (beginning on January 6, 1929), they were reorganized on the pattern of the SA. Yet they retained certain specific functions distinct from those of the SA as the party's army—which might best be termed "police" functions. "As distinguished from the SA, the SS is employed especially where individual men are needed," says a service regulation of 1931; the SA protects meetings, the SS provides the security service at congresses of leaders, and guards the more prominent leaders; when the SA undertakes propaganda marches, the SS cordons off the area and takes over the security service. The SS must also keep abreast of developments in other parties and is responsible for the internal security of the party; it is called upon to prevent and crush revolts within the party.[2] The Berlin SS performed this last duty to Hitler's special satisfaction when under the leadership of Daluege it helped to crush the Stennes putsch.* As a reward, Hitler at the beginning of April 1931 honored it with the motto: "SS man, your honor is loyalty."

Beginning in the autumn of 1931 an intelligence service, whose mission it was to provide the information indispensable to the security work of the SS, was organized by retired Navy Lieutenant Reinhard Heydrich. At first called "Ic Service," then, during the period (April 13 to June 14, 1932) when the SA and SS were outlawed, "Pi Service" (i.e., Press and Information Service), it formed the nucleus of the future SD [Sicherheitsdienst—Security Service].[3]

In the spring of 1933 when the SS with a membership of 50,000 and a daily afflux of new members had long ceased to be an elite troop and become a somewhat more refined variant of the SA, the events of 1923 and 1925 were repeated. On March 17, 1933, Hitler, who had just become Chancellor, provided himself in Berlin with a new Staff Guard consisting of 120 hand-picked SS men under the leadership of Sepp Dietrich; in other cities as well, reliable SS men were organized into SS special commandos and employed for police and semipolice duties. These special commandos survived the first months of National Socialist rule, first under the name of Politische Bereitschaften [Political Stand-by Teams] and later of Kasernierte Hundertschaften [Barracked Centuries], and formed the nucleus of the future *Verfügungstruppe* [Dis-

---

* Revolt planned by Walter Stennes, leader of the SA for the eastern part of Germany and a supporter of the revolutionary wing of the NSDAP.

position Troop], out of which in turn the Waffen SS developed.

Thus three times in ten years Hitler provided himself with a Staff Guard, a body of men in his personal service, characterized by absolute loyalty to him and by security duties contrasting with the aggressive tasks of the SA. These two characteristics determined the further development of the SS and its position, both *de jure* and *de facto,* in the Third Reich. This development was not consciously planned but followed logically from the organization's beginnings. In 1933 the new Staff Guard, the Politische Bereitschaften, and the SD became the mainstays of this development, while the Allgemeine SS [General SS] as it then came to be called, gradually declined in importance. To the two original characteristics of the SS, [Reich SS Leader] Himmler, who was strongly influenced by Darré,* added a third, the "elite principle": he wanted his troop not only to be politically reliable in its work for Hitler, but also to be distinguished by human qualities and abilities (according to his ideas and standards) and thus to form a leading political caste. This gave rise to a certain contradiction. For on the one hand the SS, by virtue of its absolute loyalty to Hitler and its work for his security and that of the party, was the organ and representative of his absolute dictatorship, while on the other hand the "elite principle" with its oligarchic implications contained, in germ, the idea of independence from Hitler. Though this contradiction never bore political fruit, it neverthelsss found expression in the opposition of certain sections of the SS to a merger with the police, which after all followed logically from the original tasks of the SS.

After 1933 it was possible to provide for the security of Hitler and of the National Socialist movement only by taking control of the security organs of the now con-

* Walther Richard Darré, NSDAP peasant leader and "blood and soil" ideologist.

quered state. The conditions underlying the security tasks of the SS in general and of the SD in particular had totally changed. There was no longer any need to combat active political adversaries, that is, the paramilitary organizations of the other political parties or the organs of the state, especially the police; now it became necessary to consolidate the domination of the party over the state and to make use of the organs of the state in combatting potential "ideological enemies." Moreover, there had ceased to be any serious legal barriers to this security work: any measure undertaken in the name of the security of the Führer and the movement automatically suspended all contrary laws and regulations. Thus those who were responsible for security were under obligation to exploit every single possibility, and not to rest until the last key position was in their hands and the last conceivable enemy had been eliminated or hogtied. When security becomes a principle that dominates all laws and legal principles, the man who is responsible for it is bound to strive for total domination, even if he personally is totally without ambition or will to power. It was therefore inevitable in the Third Reich that the institution which had unlimited responsibility for security should gain enormous power and not only eliminate all actual and possible competitors, but also profoundly modify the juridical foundations of the state. Thus, for example, the immoderate extension of the preventive principle in juridical practice can be traced back to the SS.

The SS and the Police

The merger of the police with the SS cannot, as is sometimes done, be disposed of as a pet idea of Himmler's which had no basis in reality and whose content never went beyond a superficial assimilation of police ranks to SS ranks. On the contrary, it was the most direct consequence of the mission assigned to the SS and also fell in with the desire of Hitler himself, who on September 10, 1937, on the occasion of a police parade at the Nuremberg party congress, said: "The German police should more and more be brought into a living union with the movement which politically not only represents the Germany of today, but also embodies and leads it."[4] There are objective reasons why, even at the end of the war, this merger had not been completed in practice; however, it was carried astonishingly far, and juridically it was completed long before the war. It resulted in a thoroughgoing centralization of the police, which became increasingly independent of the state while the SS became independent of the party and developed into an institution *sui generis*. What makes the whole process seem so extraordinarily complicated today is that it was implemented by a vast number of simple ministerial decrees, individual orders, and internal organizational and jurisdictional rulings. A seemingly insignificant order sometimes contained the seed of the most drastic institutional and administrative changes. At the same time the penal law was very gradually but fundamentally modified in such a way as to further the SS's bid for political leadership. The most important measure, crucial from the organizational standpoint, was the appointment of the Reich SS Leader as head of the German police.

Quite logically, the merger of the SS and the police began in Munich, the original home of the SS, where the SS forced its way into the functionally related Political Police. In the days before the Reichstag elections of March 5, 1933, the party seized power in those *Länder* where the coalition of the NSDAP and the DNVP, Deutschnazionale Volkspartei [German National People's Party], had not achieved a parliamentary majority, by having the central government take over the police. Invoking Article 2 of the "Decree for the Defense of Nation and State" of February 28, 1933, the Reich Minister of the Interior with a view to "the restoration of public security and order," appointed in each of these *Länder* a Reich commissioner who became the chief executive and in turn appointed other commissioners. In practice, SA leaders took control of the police everywhere except in Hesse, where the Reich commissioner appointed an SS leader as special commissioner of police, and in Bavaria. There, on March 9, Frick appointed Ritter von Epp* Reich Commissioner for Police Matters. On the same day von Epp made Himmler Police President of Munich, and on March 12 installed Heydrich as director of the political section of the Munich police. On March 16, the day the Held government† resigned, Himmler was appointed political counselor to the Bavarian Ministry of the Interior, and the entire Bavarian Political Police, as it came to be called, was placed under his command. On April 1, he finally became commander of the Bavarian Political Police.[5]

Himmler and the SS now strove to acquire a monopoly on the security activities in the entire Reich as they had in Bavaria, and to take away the leadership of the Political Police from the SA in the other German *Länder*. They succeeded within a year; Himmler became commander of the Political Police in one *Land* after another, as follows:[6]

Hamburg October 1933	Anhalt December 20, 1933
Mecklenburg December 1933	Thuringia December 1933(?)
Lübeck ?	Bremen December 23, 1933
Württemberg December 12, 1933	Oldenburg January 1934
Baden December 18, 1933	Saxony January 1934
Hessen December 20, 1933	Braunschweig January 1934

---

* Free Corps leader following the First World War; after 1928, a Nazi member of the Reichstag; made provincial governor of Bavaria on March 9, 1933.
† Headed by the founder of the Bavarian People's Party, Heinrich Held; a caretaker government since 1930.

In April 1934 Himmler finally succeeded in capturing the key positions, namely, command of the Political Police in Prussia, which Goering had already developed into an instrument of power. Just as Himmler had done in the other *Länder,* Goering in Prussia had disengaged the Political Police from the rest of the administration. Section IA of the Berlin Police Praesidium, which had been moved to a building of its own at 8 Prinz-Albrechtstrasse, provided the foundation for the Secret State Police Office [Geheimes Staatspolizeiamt, Gestapa], set up on April 26, 1933. On November 30, 1933, a law was issued proclaiming the Prussian Secret State Police [Geheime Staatspolizei, Gestapo] to be an independent branch of the interior administration, directly subordinate to the [Prussian] Prime Minister. But on April 20, 1934, Goering was obliged to accept Himmler as his deputy and had to content himself from then on with formal command. On April 22 Heydrich became chief of the Gestapo. With this the leadership of the entire German Political Police had passed into the hands of the SS.[7]

Though the Reconstruction Law of January 30, 1934, transferring the sovereignty of the *Länder* to the Reich, made the centralization of the German police inevitable, it was implemented by a decree of the Führer and Chancellor,[8] which at the same time fundamentally modified the juridical position of the police: "With a view to the unification of police missions in the Reich," it appointed a Chief of the German Police at the Reich Ministry of the Interior, who was placed in charge of all police matters in the jurisdiction of the ministry. Not only was this new position given to Himmler, but at his suggestion[9] it was officially linked with his position as Reich SS Leader. Accordingly, his new title was: Reich SS Leader and Chief of the German Police at the Reich Ministry of the Interior. According to the decree, the legal tie between the German police and the Minister of the Interior was provided by the "personal and direct" subordination of the Chief of Police to the minister; but within his jurisdiction the Chief of Police was to represent the minister in his absence and attend the sessions of the Reich cabinet whenever it took up matters within his jurisdiction, which, in view of the National Socialist conception of the role of the police, covered almost everything. How independent the position of the Reich SS Leader and Chief of Police was held to be can be seen from the circular issued by the Reich Ministry of the Interior on May 15, 1937.[10] Its purpose was to dispel the doubts that had arisen in various quarters as to whether the Reich SS Leader and Chief of the German Police at the Ministry of the Interior was entitled to make decisions which were reserved to the minister by law or other disposition. The circular stated that within his jurisdiction he was the minister's permanent representative (that is, not only in his absence as provided for in the decree), and that his decisions were in every instance ministerial decisions, regardless of whether the Reich SS Leader and Chief of the German Police acted in the name of his ministry or on his own personal authority. In other words, the position of the Chief of Police at the Ministry of the Interior was interpreted to mean not so much that the minister was in command of the police as that the Chief of Police enjoyed the same rights as the minister. On August 25, 1943, the Reich SS Leader and Chief of the German Police became himself Reich Minister of the Interior with full powers in matters of Reich administration. In November of the same year the words "at the Ministry of the Interior" were deleted from his title as Chief of Police.

Thus the subordination of the police to the Reich Minister of the Interior and hence its transfer to the jurisdiction of the state depended exclusively on the "personal and direct" subordination of the Reich SS Leader and Chief of the German Police to the minister, provided for in the decree of June 17, 1936. This subordination would seem to imply an extremely close tie; actually, in the light of the reality of National Socialist political institutions, it set the seal on the total independence of the police. For in the Third Reich it was no longer the state that wielded political power and embodied the national sovereignty, but the Führer, who was held to be the executor of the common national will.[11] In his person he encompassed the entire sovereign power of the Reich; and the entire power of the state and party derived from the indivisible and all-embracing power of the Führer. Nevertheless the party, conceived as the embodiment of the political will of the people, had priority over the state, whose function was solely "to continue the historically initiated and developed administration of the state organization."[12] The Führer's power embraced all the instruments of political action: all laws, including those that amended the constitution, were an emanation of the Führer's will, to which all Germans owed loyalty and obedience. In the later years a command of the Führer's came to be recognized as the highest form of political act, overriding all written law to the contrary in accordance with the principle that all measures of the political leadership possessed legislative force and took priority over regulations made by the administration.[13] Similarly, in the structure of the state, the organs of the political leadership enjoyed priority over administrative organs; and among the organs of the political leadership, those that were closest to the Führer and most directly associated with him enjoyed priority over the others. Thus the Reich SS Leader as representative of a typical institution of political leadership enjoyed juridical priority over the Minister of the Interior as head of a typical administrative department; and this priority was not diminished but rather confirmed by the "personal and direct subordination" of the former to the latter. In itself this form of subordination would imply the closest control of the superior over the subordinate, because the subordinate would not be able to invoke objective rights and duties inherent in his position, which the superior would also have to respect. But as soon as the subordinate is "personally and directly" responsible to two superiors, the higher superior has priority in every instance and the lower superior is in no position to invoke the objective obligations imposed on his subordinate by departmental discipline. He can only attempt to assert his personal authority over against that of the other superior. But since the Reich SS Leader, who institutionally was one with the Chief of the German Police, was personally and directly subordinate to the Führer,[14] the Minister of the Interior was unable, in conflicts over the management of the police, either to invoke the jurisdiction of his ministry or to insist on his authority over his personal and direct "subordinate," because in so doing he would have been impinging on the authority of the Führer. Thus the "personal and direct" subordination of the Chief of Police to the Minister of the Interior meant that his command over the police was based, not on administrative law, but on the new legal order of the leadership state. But since in this sphere the Minister of the Interior was in competition with the Führer, his rights could only take their place within the framework of the Führer's higher rights. Thus the police was only indirectly subordinate to the Minister of the Interior, and it was only indirectly an organ of the state; but it was directly an organ of the sovereign Führer, standing above state and party. In practice it was a part of the SS, through which it was more directly connected with the Führer than through the minister. As a rule, moreover, Hitler sent his instructions to the Reich SS Leader and Chief of the German Police directly and not by way of the minister; when Minister Frick once complained to Hitler of the autocratic behavior of his "subordinate," he was told to allow the Reich SS Leader all possible freedom because with him the police was in good hands.[15]

This position of the police, institutionally connected with the SS and juridically "denationalized," was in keeping with the new ideas concerning the legality of police measures. The police acted legally not only when it acted in accordance with existing laws and regulations, but also when it acted as an instrument of the political leadership and carried out its will. Consequently, the actions of the Gestapo, which already made an administrative practice of what in principle applied to the entire police, were not subject to review by the courts; the only possible way of obtaining redress was by a complaint to the higher authorities of the Gestapo itself: it was no longer possible to determine whether a branch of the police had acted legally in the "old-fashioned" sense or had acted according to the will of its superiors, that is, of the supreme political leadership. The political leadership, from which the police derived its new powers and its related juridical position, was Hitler himself or the Reich SS Leader, and in no event the Minister of the Interior.[16]

But in spite of everything, this secondary subordination to the Minister of the Interior was not entirely pointless. For one thing, it was an arrangement typical of the development of National Socialist institutions. The Weimar constitution had never been explicitly abrogated but had merely been shorn of all substance and rendered meaningless by a series of new laws and decrees. Officially, the rights and jurisdictions of the already existing government agencies were almost always supposed to "remain unaffected" by the many new agencies that were constantly being set up under the Third Reich; the flow of business was merely diverted and the old river bed left to dry out. Secondly, the *de facto* removal of the police from state jurisdiction was far from severing all administrative and operational ties between the police, especially those sections of it that had relatively little political importance, and the state. Only very gradually was it possible to adapt the police administration and its financial and organizational setup to the very different forms and regulations of the SS. Thus a good many things continued to be done as before, but always on a temporary basis, that is, only so long as the old routine did not conflict with the aims and measures of the political leadership. And lastly, without his secondary authority over the police the Minister of the Interior would have had no way of making use of it, even for purposes that had nothing to do with politics.

Though the *Führerverfassung* [legal order of the leadership state] could only be implemented in part and strictly speaking had nothing to do either with law or with order,[17] it was not a mere propagandist phrase but the cornerstone of what passed for law in the Third Reich; it was not only politically effective but also exerted a decisive influence on the legislation and jurisprudence of the day. Accordingly, we cannot simply ignore it and look upon those vestiges of constitutional government that "remained unaffected" by it as the sole reality. Because the National Socialist legal system was only in small part formulated in laws (and then as a general rule indirectly) there is a tendency today to overlook it and to interpret the administrative realities of the time on the basis of the administrative law which was still in part governed by the old constitutional tradition. But the more one applies the old traditional categories that have now regained their validity to the realities of that time, the less one will perceive of the unusual and illegal element in the National Socialist state. The result will be an unintentional but nevertheless dangerous embellishment and justification of the Third Reich. It is inadmissible that the relationship between the Reich SS Leader and Chief of the German Police and the Minister of the Interior should today be disposed of in a scientific paper with the following remarks:

> Of course it is known that the Reich SS Leader tried to make of the police an instrument of power subject exclusively to his command. It is also known how well he succeeded in this, thanks to the weak character of Doctor

Frick, the Minister of the Interior. But this does not alter the fact that the Ministry of Police was under the Ministry of the Interior, and that legally the Chief of the German Police remained subordinate to the Minister of the Interior.[18]

Even if one takes the words "at the Ministry of the Interior" in the title of the "Reich SS Leader and Chief of the German Police at the Ministry of the Interior" at their face value, one cannot help being taken aback by the combination: "Reich SS Leader and Chief of the German Police," which, from the standpoint of constitutional jurisprudence, is a complex conception. The union cannot be taken as merely personal, because there is no proof of such a contention; but if it is taken as institutional, the whole question of the *Führerverfassung* is necessarily opened, and seen from that point of view the words "at the Ministry of the Interior" also appear in a new light.[19] The literature of the time provides valuable contributions to a solution of these problems. "The title Reich SS Leader and Chief of the German Police," we are told, for example, indicates that the desideratum is not a passing personal union but a lasting bond between police and SS,[20] and that the significance of the fact that the German police under the leadership of the Reich SS Leader has become the point of intersection between the movement and the state cannot be overestimated.[21] Elsewhere it is stressed that a body that has grown as powerful as the German police, whose members moreover are bound together by the charisma of a personal leader and a bond of inviolable loyalty, takes on a juridical weight of its own.[22] Though meant as a panegyric, this is closer to reality than an attempt to explain the position of the police in the Third Reich on the basis of its rudimentary subordination to the Ministry of the Interior.

The Waffen SS

At the party congress of 1933 the Staff Guard re-established on March 17 of that year was given the name of Adolf Hitler Body Standard [Leibstandarte Adolf Hitler] and on November 9 took the loyalty oath to Hitler in person. It is unlikely that many Germans then suspected the implications of this oath. The Body Standard with its commander, Sepp Dietrich, was thus withdrawn from the command of the Reich SS Leader and so ceased to be part of a section of the NSDAP; moreover, it was subordinate neither to the Reichswehr nor to any other state institution, but exclusively to Hitler in person. As long as Hitler was only the leader of the party and was not even a German citizen, a personal commitment on the part of his former Staff Guards was rather in the nature of a romantic act; in any case it was without significance. But after he had become Chancellor and still more so after he had become Chief of State in 1934, an oath sworn to him in person took on a unique juridical significance. For in this way the Chancellor, or Chief of State, acting not on the strength of his office but as an individual, established a sphere of personal sovereignty and private law separate from the party and all state institutions. In this sphere of new law—into which were absorbed, in the course of a few years, the police, the military detachments of the SS, and the office of the Reich SS Leader with all its subordinate agencies—the *Führerverfassung* found its logical realization. It was a domain distinct from party and state, where the civil servant's duty to the state and the party member's duty to the party were overshadowed by an exclusive obligation to the Führer and his appointee, the Reich SS Leader, whose orders, in case of conflict, suspended all duty or loyalty toward the state or party. This prepared the way for what was actually meant by the

"Reich" in National Socialist terminology, a superordinate political form which nullified the German State and the National Socialist Party.

In spring 1933, simultaneously with the Staff Guard, SS commandos for special missions were set up in various German cities, for example, in Berlin, Dresden, Munich, Hamburg, and Ellwangen.[23] As a rule they were financed by the party, and by the *Länder* or townships only in exceptional cases, that is, when the uses to which they were put could be defined as state business. These SS commandos continued under the name of Political Stand-by Teams or Barracked Centuries and in the course of the years 1933 and 1934 were expanded along the lines of the Body Standard. By March 1935, when universal military service was introduced, they formed a disposition troop [*Verfügungstruppe*] consisting of nine *Sturmbanne* [battalions], an engineer battalion, and an intelligence section, under the supreme command of the Reich SS Leader. An "Inspection Section of the Disposition Troop," responsible for the administration and training of the active SS units was set up on October 1, 1936, and the *Sturmbanne* were grouped into *Standarten* [regiments]. In the summer of 1939 the Disposition Troop consisted of the following units:

Adolf Hitler Body Standard
Deutschland Standard, in Munich
Germania Standard, in Hamburg
Der Führer Standard, in Vienna, Graz, and Klagenfurt
Intelligence Battalion, in Unna
Engineer Battalion, in Dresden
Nuremberg Battalion (est. August 1936)
VT Medical Section
Artillery Standard (est. summer, 1939)
Tölz Officers' Training School (est. in 1934)
Braunschweig Officers' Training School (est. in 1935)
Klagenfurt Officers' Training School

Troops were recruited through three recruiting offices,

each covering a particular district; these offices were in Berlin (Military Districts 1–4 and 8), Hamburg (Military Districts 4 and 9–11), and Munich (Military Districts 5, 7, 12, and 13). Only the Body Standard was permitted to make use of all three recruiting offices, while to each of the other units a particular recruiting office was assigned.

In addition to the Disposition Troop there were the so-called Death's Head Units. These were emanations of the SS commando under Theodor Eicke, which guarded the Dachau concentration camp in 1933. In 1934 Hitler had commissioned Eicke to form a unified organization of the guards of all the concentration camps, whereupon, in the course of 1935, Eicke had grouped these units into five *Sturmbanne,* which he placed under the command of the Office of the Inspector of the SS Death's Head Units. These were the I "Upper Bavaria," II "Elbe," III "Saxony," IV "East Frisia," and V "Brandenburg" *Sturmbanne.* Since guarding the concentration camps was held to be state business, the Death's Head Units were at first financed by the governments of the various German *Länder.* On April 1, 1936, they and the Disposition Troop as well came under the jurisdiction of the Ministry of the Interior. At the same time Eicke obtained the title "Leader of the SS Death's Head Units and of the Concentration Camps." In April 1937, the five *Sturmbanne* were reorganized into three *Standarten,* which bore the names "Upper Bavaria," "Brandenburg," and "Thuringia." Their headquarters were at first Dachau, Oranienburg (Sachsenhausen), and Frankenberg; in the summer of 1937 the Thuringia Standard was moved from Frankenberg to Weimar (Buchenwald). In the autumn of 1938 a fourth, the Ostmark Standard was set up in Linz. Sections of the Death's Head Units took part in the marches into Austria and Czechoslovakia. Meanwhile those *Sturmbanne* which had remained behind at headquarters administered a brief course of training to members of the

General SS belonging to the classes of 1894 and more recent years. These trainees were designated as police reinforcements.

Incorporated into larger units of the regular army, the *Standarten* of the Disposition Troop took part in the Polish campaign. The Body Standard engaged in the Western campaign as an enlarged regiment and was expanded into a division only in 1941. The other three *Standarten* of the Disposition Troop, however, were grouped into the "SS Disposition Division" immediately after the Polish campaign. This division later released the Germania Standard, which formed the nucleus of the new "Viking" division, and itself was given the name of "Reich" division. It is not possible to determine exactly when the term "Waffen SS" first made its appearance. The comprehensive report of the Wehrmacht High Command on the Polish campaign (September 23, 1939) still speaks of the "SS Disposition Troop." But an order of the Reich Treasurer of the NSDAP, dated March 2, 1940, already uses the designation "Waffen SS." The name became official when Hitler used it in his speech to the Reichstag of July 19, 1940, after the French campaign. The change of name brought with it no institutional changes of any kind.[24]

In October 1939 the armored SS Death's Head Division was formed out of the 6,500 men of the four Death's Head Standards, complemented by the men who had been trained as "police reinforcements." It was a part of the Waffen SS. The Waffen SS also included the fourteen additional Death's Head Standards set up at the beginning of the war; consisting chiefly of men who had been trained as "police reinforcements," they were later dissolved or incorporated into new Waffen SS divisions. For the guarding of the concentration camps the "Death's Head Guard *Sturmbanne*" were formed; their personnel, consisting in part of men unfit for military service, was recruited from the General SS. Unlike the Death's Head Standards before 1939, they were under direct orders of the respective camp commanders. From March 3, 1942 on, both categories of concentration camp guard troops belonged to Group D of the Central Economic and Administrative Office of the SS. In the last years of the war, the guard *Sturmbanne* recruited chiefly overage SA men, wounded soldiers, men unfit for military service, and SS members belonging to German populations outside the Reich [*Volksdeutsche*].

The juridical position of the Disposition Troop and of the Death's Head Units (or later of the Waffen SS) was first of all characterized by the fact that they were not sections of the party. According to the official definition,[25] "sections" [*Gliederungen*] were those National Socialist organizations which, unlike the so-called "affiliated organizations" [*angeschlossene Verbände*] possessed no juridical personality of their own, but were legally and financially identical with the NSDAP. As the Führer's agent and in a sense the "authorized representative" of the party, the Reich Treasurer controlled the financing and supervised the budgets of the sections; he was answerable for damages caused by members of the sections in the performance of their duty and through no fault of their own.[26] Characteristically, this terminology, which presupposes that the party (as the sum of the registered party members) was the sole representative of the "movement" (as the totality of all National Socialists in any way organized) and determined its political, ideological, and juridical development, came into existence in the spring of 1935. For at that time the SA had lost its political importance, while the SS had barely embarked on the development that brought with it a fusion of the state and the political leadership. Different conceptions of the "unity of party and state" had prevailed in the first years of the Third Reich. They were regarded as "inseparably connected" yet clearly distinct institutions; in theory the party "only" exercised political leadership, while the state "only" carried out its decisions. To be sure, Hitler's dual position as "Führer and Chancellor" made for a fusion of the two, but this tendency was deliberately attenuated by the appointment of a Deputy of the Führer. Not Hitler himself but his deputy was the "representative of the movement as a whole" vis-à-vis the Reich government and its agencies. Hitler was the embodiment of National Socialist Germany, but the National Socialist movement was represented in Germany by the Führer's Deputy. Since this deputy also represented those National Socialist organizations that were independent juridical persons, it was he who enforced "the party principle that all the parts are subject to a single central leadership and that the interests of the movement as a whole are above those of its individual institutions." [27]

In the course of the National Socialist period, the SS units disengaged themselves both from the juridical unity of the party represented by the Treasurer and from its organizational unity as represented by the Führer's Deputy. Its break with the financial organization of the party, of which it thus ceased to be a section, is demonstrated by the "Communication Concerning Financial Liability in SS Matters," published in 1936 by Brigade Leader Pohl, Chief Administrator of the SS.[28] According to this document, the General SS was a section of the NSDAP, but "the SS Disposition Troop and the Death's Head Units were parts of the Schutzstaffel, whose financial liabilities are subscribed by the Minister of the Interior." Thus in civil lawsuits resulting from the negligence of a member of the Disposition Troop or of the Death's Head Units in the performance of his official duties, complaints were to be made exclusively "against the German Reich represented by the Minister of the Interior, in turn represented by the Chief Administrator of the Schutzstaffeln of the NSDAP." Despite the juridical separation between the Disposition Troop and the Death's Head Units on the one hand and the General SS on the other expressed in this statement, the three formed a unit not only politically but also in their internal administration. They were all under the financial administration of the Chief Administrator of the SS (after April 1939 of the Central Office for Finance and Administration), who at the same time was Reich Treasurer of the NSDAP (for the General SS) and department head at the Ministry of the Interior (for the armed SS). Both formations were under the orders of Himmler, who both in respect to the General SS and to the armed SS units was directly subordinate to Hitler and responsible to him alone.[29]

By 1936, to judge by Pohl's "Communication," the only tie between the armed SS units and the party derived from the powers of the Führer's Deputy, who represented the unity of the movement vis-à-vis the state, regardless of the juridical forms of the particular parts of the movement. The position of the Führer's Deputy, however, ceased to exist on May 10, 1941, when Rudolf Hess flew to Britain. His successor, Martin Bormann, took over all the rights that Hitler's deputy had enjoyed vis-à-vis the agencies of the state, but he no longer bore his title and was no longer the "representative of the movement as a whole," either vis-à-vis the state or within the movement, but was merely "Director of the Party Chancellery." Hitler himself took back the leadership of the party, as was stated in a circular issued by Bormann on April 2, 1942:[30] "The Party Chancellery is an office of the Führer. He makes use of it for the leadership of the NSDAP, which he resumed completely and exclusively on May 12, 1941."

The appointment of Bormann as Secretary to the Führer on April 12, 1943, merely confirms the fact that he did not possess the partial sovereignty of a Deputy of the Führer.[31] Thus there was no longer a separate representation of the party, its sections and attached organizations, but only the all-embracing representation of the entire National Socialist movement and of the German state by Hitler alone. Now only the Führer in person embodied the unity of the National Socialist movement, and under his supreme leadership the party and the SS were organizations on an equal footing but of different character. On the side of the SS the fusion of movement and state was far advanced, while on the side of the party it had just begun. In 1941 the party chancellery was again instructed to make certain that the National Socialist movement should contribute to the framing of state legislation.[32] But this had almost become an anachronism at a time when the movement, through the executive, was already exerting a more and more persistent influence on state legislation thanks to the unity between the SS and the police. Another vestige of an obsolete conception was that in the war years the General SS continued to be administered as a section of the NSDAP; it would have been more realistic to call it a section of the total community of the SS, whose center of gravity resided in the "emancipated" SS. To this "emancipated" SS belonged not only the armed units and the sections that had merged with the German police, but also the staffs of the central SS headquarters and the sections and subsections of the General SS, which "in view of the special political tasks on the home front" should, in case of mobilization, "be preserved for police duty," and whose personnel for this reason should be exempt from wartime duty in the Wehrmacht.[33]

The relation of the armed SS, dissociated from the NSDAP, to the state and to particular state institutions, is explicitly described in an order issued by Hitler on August 17, 1938.[34] The preamble and most vital sections of this unusually informative document are as follows:

> By my appointment of the Reich SS Leader and Chief of the German Police at the Ministry of the Interior on June 17, 1936 (*Reichsgesetzblatt* I, p. 487), I laid the foundation for the unification and reorganization of the German police.
> Thereby the Schutzstaffeln of the NSDAP, which were

already under the command of the Reich SS Leader and
Chief of the German Police entered into close connection with the tasks of the German police.

By way of regulating these tasks and defining the common tasks of the SS and the Wehrmacht, I issue the following comprehensive and basic instructions:

1. The SS in its totality, as a political organization of
the NSDAP, required no military organization or training for the political tasks incumbent on it. It is unarmed.

2. For special internal political tasks of the Reich SS
Leader and Chief of the German Police, which I reserve
the right to assign him as the occasion arises, or for mobilization within the framework of the Army (SS Disposition Force) the following SS units, already existing or to
be set up in case of mobilization, are excepted from the
ruling stated in Par. I:

The SS Disposition Force,

The SS Officers' Training Schools,

The SS Death's Head Units,

The Reinforcements for the SS Death's Head Units
(Police Reinforcements).

In peacetime these units are under the command of
the Reich SS Leader and Chief of the German Police, who
. . . bears sole responsibility for their organization, training, armament, and complete fitness for duty in connection with the internal political tasks assigned to him by
me, . . . The SS Disposition Force is a part neither of
the Wehrmacht nor of the police. It is a standing armed
force at my exclusive disposition.

The legal requirements of active military service (§8
of the Defense Law) is held to be met by an equal term
of service in the SS Disposition Force.

The SS Disposition Force is financed through the
Ministry of the Interior. Its budget must be reviewed by
the High Command of the Wehrmacht . . .

In case of mobilization the SS Disposition Force can
be utilized in two ways:

1. By the Commander in Chief of the Army within
the framework of the Armed Forces. In this case it is

subject exclusively to military laws and regulations but remains politically a section of the NSDAP.

2. In case of internal need, according to my instructions. It is then under the command of the Reich SS Leader and Chief of the German Police.

The SS Death's Head Units are a part neither of the Wehrmacht nor of the police. They are a standing armed force of the SS for the performance of special tasks of a police nature, which I reserve the right to assign as the occasion arises. . . . They are under the command of the Reich SS Leader and Chief of the German Police, who is responsible to me for their organization, training, armament, and complete fitness for duty.

This order, which is unclear and contradictory in crucial points, is without precise juridical significance, and, in the last analysis, can be explained only from a political and tactical point of view. It is certain, however, that it sanctioned a state of affairs that had been in force for some four years: The Disposition Force was a standing armed unit without being part of the Wehrmacht; under the command of the Reich SS Leader and Chief of the German Police, it was at Hitler's sole disposition, and service in it was considered equivalent to military service as defined in the Defense Law. Moreover (this the order does not state), the Disposition Force and the Waffen SS which emanated from it took the oath to Hitler personally as "Führer and Chancellor," and not in his quality of Commander in Chief of the Wehrmacht. The oath formula was as follows:[35] "I swear to you, Adolf Hitler, as Führer and Chancellor of the Reich, to be loyal and brave. To you and to the superiors appointed by you I swear obedience unto death, so help me God."

Under this oath and in accordance with the stipulations stated in the order of August 1938, the Disposition Force was organized on the model of the Body Standard. Through the oath it entered the sphere where the

Führerverfassung based on Hitler's personal sovereignty began to take body. A member of the Disposition Force in the Waffen SS ceased to be subject to state military service, that most tangible manifestation of state sovereignty; his sole allegiance was to Hitler in person, and this was more true of him than of the usual party member. For although the party had claimed from the outset to be sovereign vis-à-vis the state, every party member without exception remained subject to the laws of the state, so that there was no guarantee that he would not come under the jurisdiction of the essentially non-National Socialist Wehrmacht.

If the order specified that the Disposition Force (as later the Waffen SS) was to be financed through the Ministry of the Interior, it was because the armed SS, as several passages of the order clearly show, was regarded as a police unit. For this reason its budget was attached to the police budget and was drawn up at the Ministry of the Interior by the Director of the Police Budget.[36] Any legal tie with the ministry that might have been created by the budget was superseded by the superordinate tie with the Führer for the reasons discussed in connection with the juridical position of the police. In view of the original functions of the SS, the characterization of the Disposition Force as a police unit (an idea which was also to be the foundation of the "Führer's statement concerning the future state police," issued on August 6, 1940)[37] was not entirely unwarranted; in all probability, however, its motivation was largely tactical. In view of Hitler's policy, it is understandable that he should have mentioned the Disposition Force neither in the Proclamation of Universal Conscription of March 16, 1935, nor in his Reichstag speech of May 21, 1935, nor in the Defense Law of the same date.[38] Unable to build a brand-new National Socialist army in the course of a few years, Hitler was obliged to take the old army as he found it and try to win it over. For this reason he declared several times in 1934 that the

Wehrmacht was the nation's sole armed force (for example, on August 17 and 20 and on September 3).[39] Under these circumstances armed SS units could only be set up and developed under the head of that institution which, because of its functions, the Wehrmacht was obliged to recognize as also entitled to bear arms, namely, the police. The fact that the order of August 1938 concerning the armed SS units several times associates them with the police, but expressly states that neither the Disposition Force nor the Death's Head Units were parts of the police, merely proves that this association had rather a tactical than a practical significance.

It must also have been tactical considerations that led Hitler to point out several times in the order that politically the Disposition Force and the Death's Head Units remained sections of the NSDAP. In the light of Pohl's "Communication Concerning Financial Liability in SS Matters," this could only mean that these units remained parts of the National Socialist movement and would not be taken over by the state.

The status of the Death's Head Units was not the same as that of the Disposition Force. True, they too were a "standing armed force," belonging "neither to the Wehrmacht nor to the police," and their missions were also assigned by Hitler himself; but they were not at Hitler's "exclusive disposition." Accordingly, duty in the Death's Head Units was not regarded as military service, and those members of the Death's Head Units who had not yet performed their military service were drafted into the Wehrmacht or the Disposition Force. The fact that a body so closely related to the Disposition Force in other respects lacked this most important privilege underscores the special juridical position of the Disposition Force deriving from the notion of "exclusive disposition." Later on those Death's Head Units that were taken into the Waffen SS also obtained this special position.

In line with this special position of the armed SS, it was

not incorporated into the Wehrmacht, but remained an independent body on an equal footing with the Wehrmacht and organized along parallel lines. Whenever the armed SS obtained equal legal rights with the Wehrmacht in any domain, it was given the institutions it needed to exercise these rights independently. Thus the Disposition Force was included in the Wehrmacht Welfare and Social Service Law [Fürsorge- und Versorgungsgesetz] of August 26, 1938,[40] but on the basis of the Implementation Order of November 10, 1938, a separate SS welfare office was set up.[41] By an order of October 17, 1939, the SS obtained its own penal jurisdiction, covering offenses for which Wehrmacht members were tried in Wehrmacht courts, and the judicial apparatus it entailed.[42] From the very start not only the members of the Waffen SS, but also the personnel of the Officers' Training Schools, of the police units on special duty, and of the Reich SS headquarters, insofar as SS duty was their principal activity, were subject to this jurisdiction. Later it was extended to all those whose work with the SD was their main occupation and to all active members of the police, because during the war these were regarded as permanently mobilized.[43] A jurisdiction of its own meant for the SS a new sovereign right which confirmed its independence of the Wehrmacht. It is a mistake to argue that the SS had moved closer to the Wehrmacht because it was now organized along similar lines. Only during the Polish campaign were the units of the Disposition Force not only tactically but also for disciplinary purposes subordinated to the army units within which they functioned. Partly because certain disciplinary cases had given rise to conflicts between the SS and the Wehrmacht, the SS was given a judicial apparatus of its own, and a tie which had indeed existed for a long time was explicitly severed.[44]

In the course of the war, the concentration camp guards, the personnel of the General SS headquarters and of certain other agencies were given Waffen SS pay books.

In view of the special position of the Waffen SS, this measure presented other advantages besides organizational efficiency. Far from being purely administrative it had its juridical consequences and a considerable political significance. For anyone who carried a Waffen SS pay book (which, as stipulated in an order of the Reich SS Leader of August 1, 1944, contained a picture of the Führer)[45] was wholly exempted from the jurisdictions of state and party and obtained privileges that were extremely useful to the SS in the pursuit of its policies. Without special permission of the military authorities members of the Waffen SS could enter territories designated as "operational zones" and as such closed even to high state officials and party dignitaries. This, for example, gave the Reich SS Leader in his capacity of Reich Commissioner for the Reinforcement of German Nationality great advantages over various agencies with which he was in competition. For if he listed his agents as members of the Waffen SS, they were able to press his interests in the territories immediately behind the front before the agents of state and party were even admitted to these zones.

The actual military activity of the Waffen SS in the Second World War provides substantial arguments for the view that this body, or at least its combat troops, were for practical purposes a part of the Wehrmacht. For one thing, the Waffen SS had no General Staff and was not able to set up units capable of operating independently. Second, from the summer of 1934 on, more and more recruits were drafted into the Waffen SS and from July 1942 on, the fitness requirements ceased to be more stringent than those of the Wehrmacht.[46] Third, the soldiers of the Waffen SS who had been fighting for years in the units of the army could not help feeling that they were a part of the German Wehrmacht. All these arguments seem to provide justification for those who today characterize the members of the Waffen SS combat units as "soldiers like the rest" [47] and treat them accordingly. Be that as it may, the Waffen SS was legally quite distinct from the Wehrmacht; and it is also inaccurate to call it the "fourth arm of the Wehrmacht," because the three arms of the Wehrmacht—army, navy, and air force—were differentiated according to the element they fought in, and the Waffen SS did not fight in a fourth element. The Waffen SS remained a part, or perhaps even the core, of the "emancipated" SS, a body at the exclusive disposition of the Führer. Its soldiers, whether volunteers or not, had to take an oath that was different from the oath taken by the other three arms of the Wehrmacht.[48] They swore allegiance not to the Commander in Chief of the Wehrmacht and not to the *German* Reich and *Nation,* but to Hitler personally "as Führer and Chancellor of the Reich." This oath contained no express reference to the German state or the German nation, but related rather to that Reich which the Führer, by the right of his sovereignty, was trying to erect outside of party and state and beyond the frontiers of Germany.* Finally, in the intention also of the National Socialist leaders, the Waffen SS was not a part of the Wehrmacht, but was the military force with which the party hoped gradually to become independent of the Wehrmacht. Striking evidence of this is provided by the speech which the Reich SS Leader made on August 3, 1944, to the district leaders of the NSDAP.[49]

---

* The reader may recall earlier commentary on this subject in the Bracher essay (pages 126–27), and may find the substantive difference between the SS and Wehrmacht oaths difficult to perceive. We admit to the same difficulty, and can only suggest that this is a fascinating area for further study, as even a cursory comparison of these oaths with earlier German versions and with military oaths of other nations will indicate.

The Reich Commissioner for the Reinforcement
of German Nationality
[Reichskommissar für die Festigung deutschen
Volkstums, RKF]

In a decree of October 7, 1939 (not published at the time), Hitler directed the Reich SS Leader to take measures for the "Reinforcement of German Nationality," that is, to "bring back those German nationals and ethnic Germans residing abroad who are eligible for definitive return to the Reich," to settle them in certain zones of occupied Poland, and to eliminate from those zones "the harmful influence of alien populations representing a danger for the Reich and for the German national community." In the execution of this task the Reich SS Leader was empowered to issue general instructions and take sweeping administrative measures, to make use of "the existing agencies and institutions of the Reich," and (in cooperation with the Foreign Minister) to negotiate with foreign governments and agencies. The Finance Minister was to supply necessary funds.[50]

This new mission made no essential change in the position of the Reich SS Leader and of the organizations under him within the National Socialist system, but it did confirm and consolidate that position. The "emancipated" SS had set aside the distinction between state and party and also the resultant principle that the function of the party was to provide political leadership while the function of the state was purely executive. The institutional merger of the SS and the police had already presupposed a new conception, namely, that at politically crucial points the National Socialist movement would itself have to take over the executive function. And both in theory and in practice the police adhered to the principle that measures serving to carry out the political will of the leadership did not require review by the courts, in other words, that it was not permissible to appraise them by the standard of the prevailing laws. It was now only logical to go still further and conclude that the "political tasks" laid down by the leadership could not be carried out by the state administration acting within its customary legal framework. The new missions assigned the Reich SS Leader provide characteristic examples of what was meant by "political tasks": the resettlement of German populations and the elimination of the harmful influence of alien ethnic groups, in other words "human mobilization" [*Menscheneinsatz*], the over-all term applied to this branch of activity.[51] It was held that the rules of the state administration were too narrow to permit of a real solution to these problems consonant with the Führer's intentions, that they would only impede and stifle creative political action. Moreover the civil service was thought to lack the ideological firmness requisite to the relentless pursuit of the appointed political aims. In this spirit the Chief of the SS Race and Settlement Bureau [SS-Rasse-und Siedlungsamt] wrote as follows in a letter of March 31, 1939, to the Chief of the Security Police and SD:[52]

> Since in my opinion the settlement problem, especially outside the old Reich borders, is primarily a political one, I am convinced that only a political organization—namely, the SS—can deal with it, and not the ministerial departments which have thus far proved largely unfit for the execution of political tasks.

This was the view of an individual, but it reflected a widespread conviction, as is amply confirmed by the Reich SS Leader's activity as Reich Commissioner for the Reinforcement of German Nationality.

The Reich SS Leader, it should be stated, was not given the title of "Reich Commissioner" in the Führer's decree of October 7, 1939, although he claimed that this was the case in his first order laying the organizational foundations for the execution of his mission. In actual fact, as the Reich Minister of Food Supply stated in a circular of January 17, 1940, it was the Reich SS Leader himself who established the Reich Commissariat for the Reinforcement of German Nationality with a view to carrying out the mission assigned him.[53] At first this Reich Commissariat was not conceived as an agency which would itself carry out its assignment, but rather as a staff headquarters empowered to enlist the services of already existing agencies as needed. This probably accounts for the name "Reich Commissariat"; for, though on a much smaller scale, the Reich Commissioners of the Weimar Republic had similar powers. A comparison might also be drawn with the far-reaching rights of the Plenipotentiary [*Beauftragter*] for the Four-Year Plan,[54] but here there was a fundamental difference; Goering held his powers personally, not in one of his official capacities, and his position was clearly a state position. In the present case the Reich SS Leader held his power as the embodiment of an institution, and the enormous power he brought to bear in the performance of his new tasks was based more on his special position than on the terms of the decree of October 7. This is one of the cases typical of the practice of National Socialist government, in which an authorization given in very general terms derived its concrete content from the use which the authorized person was able to make of it on the strength of his political influence.

The headquarters of the Reich Commissar for the Reinforcement of German Nationality (RKF) did not require to be set up, but was already in existence; it was the Bureau for Immigration and Return to the Reich [Leitstelle für Ein- und Rückwanderung], founded on June 23, 1939, to arrange for the resettlement of German nationals and ethnic Germans from the South Tyrol.[55] Renamed RKF Bureau, it remained as before attached to the personal headquarters of the Reich SS Leader. In June 1941, when the administrative apparatus of the

RKF, which had meanwhile grown enormously, was reorganized, the bureau was transformed into an RKF Staff Headquarters, which "in respect to SS matters (was) placed on an equal footing with the main offices of the Reich SS leadership." Thus the position of the RKF was equivalent to that of the top staff of the SS: since not Himmler as a private person but the Reich SS Leader had received Hitler's assignment, there was no need for his new agency to be incorporated into the state administration; instead, it was attached to the already existing institutions under the orders of the Reich SS Leader. Over against this fact, certain elements of state administration in the RKF were of a very secondary nature. The main reason for them was that the Finance Ministry, which provided the Reich Commissioner with funds, demanded an accounting in accordance with the regulations governing Reich agencies.

It soon turned out that the tasks taken in hand were too enormous and too novel to be performed on the side by already existing government departments and agencies. Accordingly, the staff headquarters itself had to be enlarged and numerous new bureaus founded, which busied themselves exclusively with the work of the RKF. Side by side there were bureaus that worked only partly and temporarily for the RKF, others that were exclusively RKF offices from the very start, and still others that became so in the course of time. The coexistence of these different types of bureaus made the institution as a whole extremely complicated both juridically and otherwise. One of the bureaus that had lost its original independent status and become almost exclusively a section of the RKF was the Center for Ethnic Germans [Volksdeutsche Mittelstelle—Vomi], whose development is typical of the position of the SS in the Third Reich.

Vomi was founded by the NSDAP in 1936 as a center for all financial and political dealings with ethnic Germans abroad, that is, all those who were German in descent and language but held foreign citizenship.⁵⁶ On the ground that the shortage of foreign currency made it necessary to distribute the aid funds raised in the Reich rationally and equitably and to set up a centralized system for procuring foreign currency, Vomi was charged with the administration of all funds destined for ethnic Germans. This enabled it to subject the entire nationality policy to National Socialist control; for Vomi was in a position on the one hand to "integrate" the aid organizations within the Reich and on the other hand to introduce National Socialist sympathizers into the leadership of the German groups residing abroad. Furthermore, all transactions between Germans living abroad and the state or party agencies in the Reich (the volume of these transactions had increased enormously) passed through its hands because, since the "ethnic Germans" held foreign citizenship, neither the German diplomatic missions nor the foreign organizations of the NSDAP were permitted to handle such transactions.

The organizational picture of Vomi is confused: it was founded as a bureau of the NSDAP and this it remained in part to the last; as late as 1944 it was still a section of the Brown House local group of the NSDAP,⁵⁷ which exclusively comprised bureaus of the Reich NSDAP leadership, and not bureaus under the Reich SS Leader. But it also became a main office of the SS, and there is no doubt that it had certain of the secondary characteristics of a state agency. For example, it made use of the Reich official seal and its director flew the Reich standard; yet as of January 10, 1938, SS Obergruppenführer Lorenz, who on January 1, 1937, had taken over the leadership of Vomi from a department head in the Ministry of the Interior, possessed the disciplinary prerogatives of an SS Oberabschnittsführer. On its founding, Vomi had been placed under the command of the Führer's Deputy, which made it part of the "general sphere" of the NSDAP. In 1938, however, it was transferred to the personal command of

Hitler, so entering the domain directly under the Führer and Chancellor, where a distinction between state and party institutions was no longer possible.

This brought with it important political advantages: Vomi could exert the powers of a government department but was not absolutely bound by the regulations applicable to such departments; in its dealings with foreign countries, it could take an official attitude or not, as the situation demanded. When exposed to political attack, it represented itself as an official department of the Reich which it was not permissible to criticize; when it dealt with "ethnic Germans" over the heads of the governments of the countries where they resided, it stressed its political rather than its official aspect. On the whole it was an institution typical of the *Führerverfassung* that was gradually taking form. For whereas in dealing with German nationals living abroad it was still necessary to make a distinction between state and party, the one being represented by the Foreign Ministry, the other by the foreign organizations of the NSDAP, it was held that for the ethnic Germans there should only be the "Reich," which was represented to them as a fusion of the German State and the National Socialist Party, embodied precisely by Vomi.

Even before the war Vomi, thanks to the disciplinary subordination of its head to the Reich SS Leader, was not only under the political influence of the SS but also juridically its subsidiary. But its dependence on the SS was limited by its direct subordination to Hitler. In October 1939, Lorenz was personally and directly instructed by Hitler to organize the resettlement of the Baltic Germans. Soon thereafter, however, his direct tie with Hitler in all matters of resettlement was withdrawn and he was put under the command of the Reich SS Leader as Reich Commisioner for the Reinforcement of German Nationality.[58] Thus by way of its immediate subordination to Hitler, Vomi had been transformed from a party agency to an SS agency. Within the SS it had jurisdiction over resettlement and developed into a giant organization; but at the same time it gradually lost its political importance, largely because, as the war progressed, there came to be less and less need for the delicate operations that had characterized its beginnings.

In the long run jurisdictional conflicts and political differences were bound to arise between the Reich SS Leader in his quality of Reich Commissioner and the party; they stemmed primarily from the activity of Vomi and of the SS Race and Resettlement Bureau within the RKF organization. One of Vomi's functions was to "foster Germanism" among the people being resettled, in other words, to "bring back to Germanism" those persons of foreign origin who were "susceptible of Germanization"; the NSDAP, however, insisted on its monopoly on National Socialist leadership. The NSDAP Office for Racial Policy felt that the SS Race and Resettlement Bureau infringed on its jurisdiction. At first the Führer's Deputy tried to settle these disputes. He decreed that since the Führer had appointed the Reich SS Leader as his responsible agent, he was also the agent of the Führer's Deputy and hence of the party.[59] Thereupon the Reich SS Leader set up an NSDAP Bureau for Nationality Questions, which however had no other function than to forward to the proper SS office all communications concerning nationality policy addressed to the NSDAP; moreover, an SS leader was placed in charge of each of the four departments of this bureau. Bormann seems to have complained to Hitler about this arrangement on the ground that it discriminated against the party, for in a decree of March 12, 1942, Hitler confirmed the Reich SS Leader as his authorized agent in the matter, but decreed that a Central Office for Nationality Questions should be set up at Reich NSDAP headquarters, which office should be directed by the Reich SS Leader, acting not as RKF but as an agent of the NSDAP. In practice little was changed. The Reich SS

Leader retained a virtual monopoly on nationality policy, but had now been appointed to his position in a manner compatible with the prestige of the party.

This arrangement was far from doing away with all friction, as is demonstrated by a dispute between Vomi and Bohle's Foreign Organization as to whether those ethnic Germans of Northern France who had been given German citizenship should or should not remain subject to the authority of Vomi.[60] Bohle argued that there could not be two classes of German nationals and that all ethnic Germans who had acquired German citizenship therefore belonged to the Foreign Organization. Vomi countered that the naturalized ethnic Germans must remain in an educational community [*Erziehungsgemeinschaft*] along with those who had not been naturalized, his main argument being that the juridical act of naturalization was no proof of their Germanization. The Reich SS Leader finally decided in favor of Vomi, which was able to advance two additional considerations of great weight: one, the first persons to be naturalized were the leaders of the ethnic groups; to abandon these to the Foreign Organization would be to lose control of the ethnic Germans altogether; and two, something had to be done to prevent the Foreign Organization from laying claim to all those who as members of non-German SS units automatically received German citizenship in accordance with the Führer's decree of May 19, 1943.

The Reich SS Leader also emerged victorious from the conflicts into which he, acting as RKF, entered with the state authorities. An example: On July 17, 1941, Rosenberg was appointed Reich Minister for the Occupied Eastern Territories. On that same day the Reich SS Leader in his capacity of Chief of the German Police obtained full police power in these same territories, and moreover it was expressly specified that he should receive his instructions directly from the Führer. Thus the authority of the minister, who in theory also enjoyed full powers, was very limited from the start. The Reich SS Leader believed that the powers vested in him for the eastern territories were sufficient to allow him, acting in his capacity as RKF and without consulting the minister, to set up an office in August 1941 in Riga, which was still in the zone of operations and which for that reason the civilian officials of the Ministry for Occupied Eastern Territories were not permitted to enter. When Rosenberg complained to Hitler, Hitler expressly confirmed that the jurisdiction of the RKF included the "occupied Eastern territories," so that in all questions of "human mobilization" the minister lost the power of decision and execution to the Reich SS Leader.[61]

In Poland the RKF was expected to "Germanize" not only the country but also such parts of the Polish population as in his opinion had sufficient German blood to "out-Mendel" the foreign component. The Ministry of the Interior as the department in charge of citizenship questions participated in this work and was even put "in charge." But this did not alter the primacy of the organ of political leadership over the administrative department. For the Ministry of the Interior was permitted to naturalize only those whom the RKF had previously declared "worthy of Germanization." The right to confer naturalization was reduced to a mere bureaucratic rubber stamp, no longer involving the slightest political decision. In a decree of September 12, 1940, the Reich SS Leader laid down the principles of his repopulation policy. Essentially, the corresponding order of the Minister of the Interior, dated March 4, 1941, was little more than a paraphrase and bureaucratic variant of the above-mentioned decree. The RKF issued all its further directives on his own authority, while the minister was always obliged to consult him before drawing up the necessary implementation orders. In every particular instance the RKF exerted the power of final decision through a High Court of Review for Questions of Ethnic Appurtenance; presided over by the RKF in person, this body had seven other members, two representing the former German ethnic group in Poland, two the party, two the SS, and only one the Minister of the Interior.[62]

All the disagreements between the Reich SS Leader as RKF and the NSDAP revolved around jurisdiction in questions of political leadership. But no such disagreement would have been possible on the subject if, as is sometimes claimed on the strength of the title "Reich Commissioner," the RKF had been a government agency. Moreover, the primacy of the RKF over the Reich authorities and its right to make political decisions without consulting them proves conclusively that it was an organ of political leadership. Though the RKF demonstrably possessed certain characteristics of a government agency, though a number of its tasks, functions, and rights were incontestably of a governmental nature, it was never, and never could have become, a government department. For the foundations of the National Socialist system and rule would have been shattered if the party had ceded any of the prerogatives of political leadership to another organization and if this organization had been taken over by the state. Thus the amalgamation of functions of political leadership with functions of state administration in the RKF can only be properly understood if we recognize the RKF to be part of the Führer-system that was growing up outside the confines of party and state. Standing above state and party, the sovereign Führer was free to assign the tasks of political leadership to anyone he pleased. And when necessary he could endow the institution to which he assigned "political tasks" that he did not wish to entrust to the state administration, with governmental rights and powers, not in order to turn it into a government agency, but in order to give it an official status equal or superior to that of the government organs.

* *

The three phenomena we have discussed—the rapidly advancing fusion of the police with the SS, the genesis of the Waffen SS, and the consequences of the powers of the Reich SS Leader as RKF—all clearly show common trends of development. But although in each case the same purposes and manner of thinking were at work, the methods and points of application varied with the political possibilities. For this reason, each of these developments has been described in its concrete reality, and not derived theoretically from the common foundations; for the whole should not be made to look more symmetrical than it actually was. Nevertheless I believe that the common denominator has been made sufficiently clear.

NOTES

1. Concerning the early history of the SS, cf. *Völkischer Beobachter*, April 18, September 23, and December 9, 1925, January 29 and July 7, 1926; *Augsburger Postzeitung*, April 29, 1924; d'Alquen, *Die SS*, Berlin, 1939; Rühle, *Das Dritte Reich, Die Kampfjahre*, Berlin, 1936; Volz, *Daten der Geschichte der NSDAP*, Berlin and Leipzig, 1938; *Lehrplan für zwölfwöchige Schulung*, published by SS Hauptamt, n.d. Cf. also the relevant passages in the various editions of the work of Konrad Heiden.

2. *Dienstvorschrift für die SA der NSDAP*, Diessen near Munich, 1931, Part I, pp. 44 ff.

3. D'Alquen, *op. cit.*, p. 22; *Nachruf für Reinhard Heydrich*, published by the Reichssicherheitshauptamt, Berlin, 1942.

4. *Der Parteitag der Arbeit vom 6, bis 13. Sept, 1937. Offizieller Bericht*, Munich, 1938, p. 194.

5. *Völkischer Beobachter*, March 10 and April 2, 1933; *Nachruf für Heydrich; Das Deutsche Führerlexikon*, Berlin, 1934.

6. The sequence has been compiled from partly inaccurate and mutually contradictory statements in the *Völkischer Beobachter*, in *Keesings Archiv*, the *Deutsches Führerlexikon* of 1934 and the National Socialist publication *Das Archiv*, edited by A. I. Berndt. Apart from Thuringia and Lübeck, it can however be regarded as reliable.

7. Cf. the testimony of Goering and Gisevius at the Nuremberg war crimes trials; Diels, *Lucifer ante portas*, Stuttgart, 1950; *Zeugenschrifttum im Institut für Zeitgeschichte*, Nos. 16, 303, and 537.

8. RGBl I, p. 487.

9. Testimony of Lammers at the Nuremberg trials, April 8, 1946 (IMT XI, p. 70).

10. RMBl IV, p. 788.

11. Cf. Huber, *Verfassungsrecht des Grossdeutschen Reiches,* Hamburg, 1939, pp. 230 ff, 56 f.

12. Hitler at the 1935 party congress; quoted in Gottfried Neesse, *Partei und Staat,* Hamburg, 1936, p. 49.

13. Damage suits were not permitted in the case of damages caused by members of the NSDAP or of its affiliations in the execution of decisions of the political leadership. For damage suits would have led to a review of political decisions of the leadership, and such a review would have been incompatible with the character of a "leadership state." Cf. Haidn-Fischer, *Das Recht der NSDAP,* Munich, 1936, p. 87.

14. Decree of July 20, 1934, whereby the SS was proclaimed an independent organization within the framework of the NSDAP (reprinted in Rühle, *Das Dritte Reich,* 1934, Vol. II, p. 237.

15. Lammers, *op. cit.,* p. 71. Evidence that the Minister of the Interior did not control the police is to be found in the recollections of an official of the Reich Church Administration of the time, who writes: "I noticed of course that an appeal to Reich Minister Frick concerning the behavior of the State Police never brought results. Such petitions were handled not by Frick but by the Reich Central Security Office [Reichssicherheitshauptamt], which thus proved to be the supreme authority." It is interesting to note that the Reich SS Leader as Chief of the German Police received equal pay with the Chief of the Wehrmacht High Command; cf. Maunz, *Gestalt und Reicht der Polizei,* Hamburg, 1943, p. 6.

16. Cf. Maunz, *op. cit.,* pp. 26 ff., and Best, *Die Deutsche Polizei,* Darmstadt, 1940, pp. 14 ff.

17. Here we cannot discuss the question of why the *Führerverfassung* was not, strictly speaking, a form of law; our investigation is concerned not with the essence of National Socialist institutions but with their consequences.

18. W. Kalisch, "Die Weiterverwendung vertriebener Reichspolizeibeamter in Niedersachsen 1945," in *Mensch und Staat in Recht und Geschichte, Festschrift für Herbert Kraus,* Kitzingen, 1954, pp. 96 f.

19. It should not be overlooked that the structure of the administration in a constitutional state is not only an organic structure but also a juridical structure derived from the sovereignty of the state, but that in the Third Reich this structure retained only a technical character. The state was reduced to an administrative apparatus and its legal system to a table of organization.

20. Best, *op. cit.,* p. 85.

21. Best, *Deutsches Recht,* 1936, p. 258. Although Kalisch him-

self (*loc. cit.*, pp. 97–98) calls Best the most reliable authority on the conditions of the time, he takes no account of the passages we have cited. Instead he writes (*loc. cit.*, p. 101): "Drastically as the transformation begun in 1933 affected the inner structure of the German state, there can be no doubt that this transformation applied more to the ideational foundation, that is, the National Socialist concept of the state, than to the outward organization of the traditional branches of the administration, which were everywhere taken over as such, and where, on the medium and local level, little was changed except for the introduction of the 'leadership principle.' Even the centralization [*Verreichlichung*] of the police and the appointment of the Chief of the German Police at the Ministry of the Interior brought no very far-reaching change in administrative structure. . . ." He fails to take into account that between the "ideational foundation" of the principle of the state and the "outward organization of the traditional branches of the administration" there was also a system [*Verfassung*], which undoubtedly underwent far-reaching changes as a result of the introduction of the leadership principle.

22. Maunz, *op. cit.*, p. 64.

23. In connection with the following account of the development of the Waffen SS units, cf. Tiemann-Schropp, *Die Arbeits- und Wehrdienstpflichtfibel;* Boberski, *Die Versorgungsgesetze des Grossdeutschen Reichs; Verordnungsblatt der Waffen-SS;* d'Alquen, *op. cit.;* Best, *Die Deutsche Polizei; Anlage zum Plaidoyer des Verteidigers der SS, Rechtsanwalt Dr. Pelckmann:* "Die Entwicklung der Allgemeinen und der Waffen-SS und ihr Verhältnis zu anderen Organisationen in Himmlers Machtbereich"; Hausser, *Waffen-SS im Einsatz,* 4th ed., Göttingen, 1954.

24. *Erlasse des Reichsschatzmeisters der NSDAP, 1940; Schultheiss' Europäischer Geschichtskalender, 1940.*

25. Par. 4 of the "Verordnung vom 29. März, 1935 zur Durchführung des Gesetzes zur Sicherung der Einheit von Partei und Staat vom 1. Deg. 1933" (RGBl I, p. 502).

26. On the exceptions cf. note 13, above.

27. Gauweiler, *Rechtseinrichtungen und Rechtsaufgaben der Bewegung,* Munich, 1939, pp. 12, 16 ff; Haidn-Fischer, *loc. cit.,* pp. 58 f.

28. *Juristische Wochenschrift,* p. 2696.

29. "Verfügung vom 20. Juli 1934" (cf. note 4 above) and "Anordnung vom 17. August, 1938" (Nuremberg Document PS–647); cf. below, pages 275–77.

30. *Verfügungen, Anordnungen und Bekanntgaben der Parteikanzlei,* Vol. I, pp. 4, 6.

31. *Ibid.,* Vol. IV, p. 1.

32. *Ibid.,* Vol. I, p. 5.

33. "Anordnung vom 17. August, 1938."

34. Nuremberg Document PS–647 (IMT XXVI, pp. 190 f.).

35. *Dich ruft die SS,* a recruiting pamphlet for the SS, published by the SS-Hauptamt, Berlin, n.d.

36. The right of the Wehrmacht High Command to review this budget did not apply to decisions as to what was to be procured, but only to the appropriateness of the sums proposed. The budget of the Waffen SS was not published (*Zeugenschrifttum des Instituts für Zeitgeschichte,* Nos. 178 and 511; Nuremberg Document NG–4392).

37. Nuremberg Document 665–D (IMT XXXV, pp. 535 ff.)

38. I have been unable to find any corroboration of Hausser's contention (*op. cit.,* p. 11) that in reasserting Germany's military sovereignty Hitler also announced the formation of an SS division. It does not seem very likely that he did so because such a step would have antagonized the Wehrmacht.

39. Foertsch, *Wehrpflichtfibel,* Berlin, n.d., pp. 30 ff.; *Schultheiss' Europäischer Geschichtskalender 1934,* p. 219.

40. Sec. 201 (RGBl I, p. 1077).

41. RGBl I, p. 1607. On April 18, 1937, the Order Concerning the Use of Arms by the Wehrmacht of January 17, 1936 (RGBl I, p. 39) was extended to the Disposition Force and the Death's Head Units (RGBl I, 1937, p. 545). It is interesting to note that through the Order Concerning Road Traffic of November 13, 1937, (RGBl I, p. 1254) the SS obtained a new emblem for their trucks (the runic double S)—a privilege that was never accorded the party.

42. RGBl I, p. 2107.

43. Lastly, on September 1, 1942, to the entire police (cf. Maunz, *loc cit.,* p. 32).

44. Cf. *Zeugenschrifttum des Instituts für Zeitgeschichte,* No. 240.

45. *Verordnungsblatt der Waffen SS,* August 1, 1944, p. 112.

46. *Verordnungsblatt der Waffen SS,* July 15, 1942. The conflict between the Wehrmacht and the SS over promising recruits continued to the end of the war (*Verfügungen, Anordnungen und Bekanntgaben der Parteikanzlei,* Vol. VII, p. 306).

47. Such as Chancellor Konrad Adenauer, in a speech delivered in Hanover on August 30, 1953.

48. The oath of the Wehrmacht soldiers ran: "I swear by God this sacred oath, that I will obey Adolf Hitler, Führer of the German Reich and Nation and Commander in Chief of the Wehrmacht, without condition and will be a brave soldier, ready at all times to stake my life for this oath."

49. *Vierteljahrshefte für Zeitgeschichte,* No. 4, 1955.

50. Nuremberg Documents PS–686; (IMT XXVI, pp. 255 ff.) NO–3075; NG–962.

51. The orders of the RKF were published in a collection entitled *Der Menscheneinsatz* (published by the Stabshauptamt des RKF, December 1940 and December 1941).

52. Nuremberg Document NO–3162.

53. Nuremberg Documents NO–3078, NG–937.

54. RGBl I, 1936, p. 887.

55. *Menscheneinsatz*, Vol. I, pp. 3, 141, 144. Cf. note 51. *Zeugenschrifttum im Institut für Zeitgeschichte*, No. 317.

56. Nuremberg Documents NO–5591, NO–4701, NO–3981; VIII. Trial Minutes, pp. 1265, 2605, 2608, 2611 ff., 2850 ff.; and *Verteidigungsdokumentenbuch I für Lorenz*, passim.

57. Nuremberg Document NO–3981.

58. VIII. *Nürenberger Prozess*, Prot. pp. 2619 ff.

59. *Verfügungen, Anordnungen, und Bekanntmachungen der Parteikanzlei*, Vol. II, pp. 159 ff. and Nuremberg Document NO–4237.

60. Nuremberg Documents NO–2575, NO–2553, NO–2533.

61. Nuremberg Documents NO–3726, PS–1997, NG–951; Bräutigam, *Überblick über die besetzten Ostgebiete während des 2. Weltkrieges*, published by the Institut für Besatzungsfragen, Tübingen, January 1954, pp. 10 f.

62. Nuremberg Document NO–3531; RGBl I, 1941, p. 118.

7

Goebbels' Speech on Total War, February 18, 1943

GÜNTER MOLTMANN

Ordinarily a historian must concern himself with a confusing multiplicity of initiatives, ideas, and conceptions, analyze their interpenetration and reciprocal influence, and investigate their political effect. But this applies only in a limited sense to the historian who deals with the history of the Third Reich. For in the totalitarian state there is one compulsory ideology to which every sphere of public and as far as possible also of private life is aligned. For the historian, consequently, the study of ideas is overshadowed by the more urgent question of how it was possible to impose this *one* point of view. He must determine what methods of intellectual "integration" were used and how the population reacted to totalitarian pressures.

Side by side with outward coercion, the extent of which varied from year to year, mass suggestion was an essential factor in the National Socialist system of domination. Propagandist activity became most intense at times when grave crises threatened to undermine the loyalty of the followers to the leadership. Thus after the defeat of Stalingrad the regime launched one of its largest propaganda campaigns in order to overcome the disillusionment and discouragement of the population and bind it as firmly as possible to the leadership. At a mass meeting in the Berlin

Sportpalast on February 18, 1943, Propaganda Minister Goebbels called on his listeners to come out in support of "total war."

In the historical literature Goebbels' speech is considered from the most divergent viewpoints and interpreted in different ways. Most authors are agreed that Goebbels showed extraordinary demagogic skill in stirring his audience to acclaim total war. Some of the popular monographs about the Second World War express the opinion that the Allied demand for unconditional surrender, put forward on January 24, 1943, three and a half weeks before the meeting at the Sportpalast, had prepared the German people to support total war: "If even their statesmen . . . were demanding unconditional surrender . . . how could the masses of the German people see a way out at this late hour?" [1] Or, expressed in a succinct formula: "In any case Roosevelt and Churchill could have done Goebbels no greater favor, . . . bolstering up his 'hold-out-to-the-end' propaganda than they did with their demand for unconditional surrender." [2]

Speaking as an expert in public relations, Walter Hagemann provides a more thorough analysis of the speech.[3] As might be expected, he is interested chiefly in Goebbels' psychological technique. He sums up as follows: "This speech was one of the best Goebbels had delivered since 1933. It made use of all the tested tricks of mass suggestion and was helped by careful selection of the audience and careful staging." As for the audience, Goebbels spoke to a "like-minded public," consisting of the "old Berlin party guard" and a few thousand trusted supporters who had been brought in "from all over Germany by train and bus" and who had received instructions "with a view to the projected demonstration." As for the "staging," the hall was decorated with an enormous streamer, most of the audience for visual reasons were made to wear civilian clothes rather than uniforms, and songs, applause, shouts of approval, and speaking choruses were suitably orchestrated. Hagemann then gives a few excerpts from the speech, accompanied by sound psychological comments and superficial polemical remarks. Differing with other authors, he takes a very skeptical view of the general effect of the speech: not only on anti-Nazis, but also on "neutral bystanders" in and outside of Germany, and even on "likeminded" radio listeners, he tells us, the "hysterical screaming and yelling of the masses had a repellent effect" and was interpreted as a "symptom of the progressive mental disintegration of the regime."

Allied observers at the time were not so skeptical of Goebbels' propagandist success. This is shown, for example, by Alexander L. George's study of the inferences drawn by the Allies from German propaganda.[4] He too holds that the meeting was "carefully staged by Goebbels": enough supporters had been assembled to provide an "effective claque." George holds, however, that the Allied intelligence services were wrong in supposing that Goebbels had merely wished to whip up sentiment for a new type of war that the National Socialist regime had already decided on. They overlooked, he believes, that Goebbels wished to exploit his position as Propaganda Minister to shape top-level policy in accordance with his own views and to advance his private political ambitions. This interpretation is not new. George refers to the diary of Rudolf Semler, Goebbels' press officer, excerpts of which were published in 1947.[5] Goebbels' biographers quite naturally stressed the importance of the Sportpalast speech for Goebbels' position and career.[6] On the basis of Semler's notes and preserved fragments of Goebbels' own diary, they described the "struggle behind the throne," that is, the intrigues among the National Socialist leaders at the end of 1942 and the beginning of 1943, and placed the Sportpalast speech in the context of Goebbels' ambition to hold the second place in the state. According to this theory Goebbels, in opposition to Bormann, Keitel,

and Lammers,* whom Hitler had commissioned to work
out the guidelines for total war, and to Ribbentrop and
Rosenberg† as well, had tried to thrust himself into the
foreground and with the help of Goering, Speer, Funk,
and Ley‡ to take the initiative for mobilizing the masses.
But despite his success at the Sportpalast in 1943 he had
not succeeded in improving his position with Hitler.
Only after July 20, 1944, when Goebbels was appointed
"Plenipotentiary for Total War Commitment," did he
achieve the aim for which he had been striving.

Yet despite George's exaggerated formulations these
two interpretations—Goebbels as a wily but unsuccessful
careerist or as a conscientious minister successfully promoting the regime and its increased war effort—are not
irreconcilable. It is merely necessary to establish dividing
lines and put the accent's in the right places. Still, our
short survey of the varying interpretations indicates a lack
of clarity in many points that makes a systematic inquiry
seem worthwhile. The reasons for the enthusiasm of the
audience have not been sufficiently clarified, nor have the
speaker's propaganda methods been satisfactorily analyzed. The demagogue's motives and intentions and his
relationship with Hitler—was Goebbels obeying Hitler's
orders or taking him by surprise?—are also deserving of
closer attention.

Although the records of the Reich Propaganda Ministry have been preserved only in scattered remnants,[7]
ample sources are available for such a study. Not long ago
some pages from Goebbels' diary at the time of the speech
(February 14 to 23, 1943) came to light, partly filling the

* Field Marshal Wilhelm Keitel, Supreme Commander of the Wehr-
macht, and Hans Heinrich Lammers, Minister without Portfolio and
Director of the Reich Chancellery.
† Foreign Minister Joachim von Ribbentrop, and party ideologist and
Minister for the Occupied Eastern Territories Alfred Rosenberg.
‡ Reich Minister for Armament and War Production Albert Speer,
Minister of Economics Walter Funk, and German Labor Front chief
Robert Ley.

regrettable gap from December 21, 1942, to February 28, 1943.[8] Valuable insights are provided by the published notes and memoirs of men who worked with Goebbels[9] and by more recent information obtained from newspapermen and members of Goebbels' staff who attended the meetings as observers.[10] Moreover, recordings have been preserved which not only indicate deviations of the spoken text from the official wording,[11] but also provide an authentic auditory picture of the meeting.[12] Thus the rhetorical effect of the speech and the reaction of the audience can be analyzed in detail. A valuable complement to these documents is provided by the *Deutsche Wochenschau* (newsreel) of February 24, 1943,[13] and by press photos taken during the meeting, which add the visual to the auditory element. Such material, it is true, creates a special problem: films and sound recordings bring this intense experience so close to us that it is difficult to regain the historical perspective prerequisite to sober analysis.

* *

As is generally known, the idea of total war was not invented by Goebbels but made its appearance before the Second World War. The "theory of total war" originated in the mid-thirties. The progress of aviation had led air strategists to the view that the entire territory of a belligerent power must be regarded as a theater of war.[14] But far more influential than the speculations of technicians was Ludendorff's book *Total War* (1935), which had sold 100,000 copies in two years. The book is important in the present context because it came very close to certain theses—and sometimes even to formulations—which Goebbels was to set forth eight years later.[15]

In the last analysis what is decisive for the outcome of this [total] war for the preservation of the nation is moral unity, for today no state will let its army lack

armament, training, and equipment. Moral unity alone
enables the people to supply the embattled army with
ever renewed strength, to work for the army, and confident of victory to withstand the hardships of war and the
impact of enemy action.

These ideas of Ludendorff's sprang not so much from considerations of military strategy as from his nationalist
[*völkisch*] ideology. The strength of a nation, he believed, lay in its unity. From this standpoint he developed
a program for the war of the future: The "moral unity of
the people," he wrote, must be achieved "through a unity
of racial heritage and faith, and through careful consideration of the biological and spiritual laws and qualities of
the racial heritage"; it is preserved by the "mortal peril
and suffering of the people and by the right kind of propaganda; indeed it can become still more intense."

Ludendorff's ideas about industrial mobilization and
troop commitment in total war seem very schematic and
old-fashioned compared to the demands put forward by
Goebbels in 1943. But the invocation of nation and race
was also to be a major component of the Sportpalast
speech. This speech was definitely "the right kind of
propaganda" in Ludendorff's perspective; there was a
similarity in the two men's propaganda techniques. According to Ludendorff, "an adult people . . . demands
truth from its government, and not only in peace time; it
is in war that it really insists on knowing the truth of its
situation; otherwise things are made too easy for the 'mal-
contents' and rumor mongers." In the preamble to his
speech Goebbels showed himself to be Ludendorff's apt
pupil, declaring: "The German people, raised, schooled,
and disciplined in National Socialism, can bear the
truth." Though he did not go on to tell the full truth—
Ludendorff had not done so either in the First World War
—nevertheless his admission that Germany had entered
into a critical phase of the war was calculated to take the

wind out of his critics' sails. At the same time he flattered the people by declaring them adult enough to listen to frank words and to act accordingly.

The National Socialist movement broke with Ludendorff, but the theory of total war continued to exert an influence. In an article on "Wartime as a Problem of Organization" by the Wehrmacht Chief of Staff (April 19, 1938) we read:

> It is contrary to the principles of the total war of the future to regard "conduct of armed warfare," "adjustment of psychological and economic warfare to the aims of armed warfare" and "organization of the embattled nation in support of armed warfare" as separate tasks. . . . Only the unity of state, army, and people offers a guarantee of success in war. . . . Thus army, homeland, and people interact and are woven into an inseparable whole.[16]

"Total war," to be sure, is not a clearly definable concept. Though "totality" in the strict sense of the word is not subject to gradation, there are in practice many "degrees of total war." They hinge on various factors: the military situation of the moment, the technical limits to the exploitation of the national potential, and the willingness of the people to be integrated in the war effort. Thus during the blitzkrieg in the first phase of the war the total enemy potential was combatted and after the enemy's defeat exploited, yet there was still no thought of total mobilization inside Germany and no one had very clear ideas on the subject. It was still possible to meet the needs of the war by a very limited conversion of the economy.

It was the end of the blitzkrieg and the first serious difficulties on the Eastern Front that first necessitated large-scale mobilization. But characteristically the conversion of the war machine was undertaken only very hesitantly, although the leading circles were better aware of what was going on than the population at large. The contrast between the constant victory propaganda, which could not be turned off, and the actual crisis of the winter of 1941–1942 gave rise to a dilemma, reflected in half-measures that could not produce lasting results. If Goebbels had had his way, "total war" would have been proclaimed at that time; he seems to have felt that he could make the shift acceptable by means of propaganda. Goebbels developed his ideas on total war in "repeated conversations" with Moritz von Schirmeister, his personal press secretary, who had returned to Berlin on January 16, 1942, after a few months of war duty in Russia.[17] His plan was that "the entire industrial potential should be concentrated on bona fide war production to the neglect or exclusion of all items that were not vitally necessary. This would at the same time liberate manpower for the Wehrmacht." According to Schirmeister, Goebbels submitted his plan to Hitler at the time, but failed to obtain his approval, "primarily because of Goering, who persuaded Hitler that all this was not necessary, that we would win the war with the present methods." "In a rage" Goebbels said to Schirmeister: "The German people will never hold it up to us if they have to go in rags for a few months; but they will never forgive us if they have to lead the life of a beggar all their lives!" [18]

Of course this early initiative on Goebbels' part may have been inspired by a desire to improve his position within the National Socialist leadership. As propaganda minister he naturally saw a personal opportunity in total mobilization for a new kind of warfare. But the fact that more than a year before the Sportpalast speech he was already agitating for the new style of warfare and had found his chief obstacle in Goering, with whom in 1943 he would ally himself against Bormann, suggests that the speech of February 1943 should not be interpreted too one-sidedly as a mere move in the "battle behind the throne." It is hard to believe that this fanatic's unremitting advocacy of a cause which did after all concern the preservation of the entire regime stemmed from nothing more than private intrigue.

After his unsuccessful attempt to gain Hitler's support for his ideas Goebbels could do nothing until new and more serious reverses had occurred on the war fronts. But soon the military situation did indeed deteriorate and Goebbels was able to resume his efforts. In the summer of 1942 Japan incurred its first defeats in the Pacific; in October the British launched their successful counterattack in North Africa; in November Allied troops landed in Morocco and Algeria; and—still worse for Germany— after the German offensive was stalled in the Caucasus, the Red Army surrounded the German troops in Stalingrad. In this same year Ludwig Beck,* speaking at the Berlin Wednesday Club, attacked Ludendorff's ideas on the absolute necessity of total warfare.[19] "Unfortunately," he declared, "we are obliged to ask ourselves at the present time . . . whether in view of modern total warfare it is still possible to draw a distinction between the wars of civilized and uncivilized peoples." "Woe to us," he warned, "if politics not only continues to follow in the wake of total war, but actively prepares the way for it." He concluded that "a new ethical idealism is indispensable if we are to rid ourselves of the idea that total war is an inescapable necessity."

It goes without saying that Beck's remarks had no appeal for a radical fanatic and shrewd demagogue like Goebbels, who moreover was intelligent enough to draw the logical conclusions from his ideology. The grave crisis on the war fronts gave new timeliness to his ideas on increasing the war effort and it now became possible to use the watchword of "total war," whose propaganda value was not yet exhausted, to good effect. Contrary to the opinion of some biographers,[20] Goebbels had decided by the middle of December 1942 to resume his activities in this di-

* Army Chief of Staff who opposed Hitler's war plans, resigned, and was instrumental in organizing the resistance.

rection. The significance of the Stalingrad crisis was already clear to Goebbels.[21] The diary entries for the first half of December show no great alarm. On the 16th Press Secretary Semler, who had just returned from Stalingrad, reported to him on the intensity of the battle. On the 18th and 20th Goebbels noted in almost identical words that developments in Stalingrad gave ground for a "certain concern." On the 26th, according to Semler, he was "greatly worried." During this period he was not inactive. In mid-December he had submitted to Hitler proposals for increasing the war effort on the home front and Hitler had found them acceptable.[22] On the 16th the introduction of an auxiliary air force service made up of boys and girls from the secondary schools came under discussion, but the idea of "universal conscription for women without family or children" still met with Goering's opposition.[23] On the 28th Goebbels conferred with Bormann; they agreed that it was necessary to lower the standard of living and demand "special sacrifices on the part of the top ten thousand," in order to obtain manpower and materials for the war effort.[24]

Thus in the second half of December it was decided that the war effort must be increased, that the war must become "total." From the very start Goebbels must have contemplated a mass meeting to whip up enthusiasm. As early as December 7, before he suspected that catastrophe was imminent in Stalingrad, he had noted: "We really ought to speak in public more often than we have done up to now." And on December 12: "We really ought to make the gravity of the situation clear to the German people." [25] The material that has come down to us makes it clear that Goebbels was a force, and probably *the* driving force, behind the new measures. But it is equally clear that the group "behind the throne" which was to play a determining role in the controversies of the coming months, had not yet crystallized. Goering, Goebbels' future ally with whom he had achieved a momentary *rap-*

prochement in the spring of 1942,[26] still shrank back from radical measures as he had done at the beginning of the year. On the other hand, relations between Goebbels and Bormann do not seem to have been as strained as in the ensuing months. In reporting the conversation of December 28, Semler makes no mention of differences of opinion. There is no doubt that for the present the party leadership was more concerned with the need for increased mobilization than with the internal struggle for power.

Early in 1943 preparations for total mobilization were begun, soon followed by propaganda for the "new course" and official decrees. On January 4 Goebbels delivered a lecture in his ministry, which was interpreted by his staff as an "unofficial signal for total war." [27] "I hope," he declared, "that I and everyone else in the ministry will get the idea out of our heads that we cannot lose the war. Of course we can lose the war. The war can be lost by a people that does not want to exert itself; it will be won by those who make the greatest effort. We must not believe passively in a sure victory, but must resolve to conquer." The present standard of living, he went on, was incompatible with the hardship suffered at the front. On January 6 Sauckel, the Commissioner for Labor Mobilization, addressing a meeting of some eight hundred members of his Labor Mobilization Staffs in Weimar, spoke of "total labor mobilization for victory" and demanded that labor service on the part of workers from occupied territories should cease to be voluntary and made compulsory; this he termed the "iron law of the year 1943." [28] In mid-January Hitler set up the Committee of Three, consisting of Lammers, director of the Reich Chancellery, Bormann, director of the party chancellery, and Keitel, Chief of the Wehrmacht High Command, to inaugurate measures for total war.[29] Goebbels, it was decided, should be called in in an advisory capacity. On January 27, a "Decree Concerning the Reporting of Men and Women for Defense

Tasks" was published in the *Reichsgesetzblatt*. Men from sixteen to sixty-five and women from seventeen to forty-five were to report to the labor offices by March 31. Pleasure establishments, bars, candy stores, jewelry stores, and other branches of business were closed.

On January 30, immediately before the fall of Stalingrad, Goebbels read a proclamation by Hitler at a meeting in the Sportpalast.[30] "The heroic struggle of our soldiers on the Volga," said the proclamation, "must be an admonition to each one of us to do his utmost in the struggle for the freedom of Germany and the future of our people and thus, more generally speaking, for the preservation of our entire continent." And Goebbels added grandiloquently: "From the breadths and depths of our people a cry for the most total war effort in the widest sense of the word rises to our ears." On the same day Goering delivered his feeble "Leonidas Speech" and Minister of Economics Funk, writing in the *Völkischer Beobachter*, demanded an increase of productivity in the defense industries. There followed numerous proclamations, orders, decrees, speeches, congresses, and publications which cannot be listed here. Everything was done to create a new style of warfare. And the climax of this campaign was Goebbels' speech of February 18, the origins of which we shall now examine more closely.

It was the appointment of the Committee of Three that first led Goebbels to personal considerations in connection with his efforts to speed up the mobilization of the people. Semler tells us how bitterly disappointed Goebbels was at the subordinate role assigned him, at the fact that he who had done the planning was not to have a greater voice in the execution.[31] He complained to Hitler, and beginning at the first session of the committee on January 20 violently criticized the irresolution of its principal members. The "bureaucrats," he said, "were destroying the whole conception," while he had to defend it before the public; he would organize a mass meeting on

his own initiative to further the cause. Semler puts it suc-
cinctly: "Goebbels is contemplating a daring plan. He
wants to put pressure on Hitler by stating radical demands in a speech at the Sportpalast. The crowd will applaud wildly. In this way he hopes to force Hitler to put
an end to the half-measures. If his demands were not met,
the government would be compromised. This the Führer
could not afford at the present moment." These notes lay
bare the extreme ambition that motivated Goebbels' action. In order to put through his plan, he intended not
only to obtain Hitler's sponsorship but to put pressure on
him. Undoubtedly the Propaganda Minister regarded
himself as the right man to hold the reins.

But it seems evident that Goebbels also attached the utmost importance to the cause itself. Within the narrow
limits of National Socialist ideology and war policy, he
had realized sooner and more radically than anyone else
what had to be done in the crisis. Now he saw that his
ideas were being watered down. He also knew that an increase in the people's willingness to make sacrifices for the
war effort could not be obtained by decrees alone, that it
was essentially a matter of propaganda, a field in which he
possessed both authority and ability. Consequently he was
bound to regard the appointment of Keitel, Bormann,
and Lammers, who moreover were all stationed far away
at the Führer's headquarters, as a political and personal
mistake. His experience with the Committee of Three
confirmed his fears. Thus his reaction, first emotional,
then calculated, seems to have sprung from two inseparably linked motives: personal ambition and fanatical devotion to the cause.

But what was the nature of Goebbels' relations with
Hitler at this juncture and how did Hitler take the Sportpalast speech? Semler's note on the speech of February 18
("Goebbels went much further than Hitler had approved") makes it appear that the Propaganda Minister
had acted entirely on his own.[32] But the independence of

his action should not be dramatized inordinately. For one thing, Hitler's reaction to the speech, expressed to Goebbels at an interview on March 3, was positive:[33]

> My measures in connection with total war are fully approved by the Führer. He speaks in terms most flattering to myself of my Sportpalast speech, which he calls a masterpiece of psychology and propaganda. He told me he had studied it attentively from beginning to end and had come to the conclusion that with it we had struck at the heart of the matter. He is positively enthusiastic about the effect produced.

Even if we concede that this entry shows a certain smugness and that Goebbels may have exaggerated to some extent, the impression remains that Hitler did not feel that his hand was being forced, but fully approved Goebbels' action. Moreover, Semler's belief that Goebbels had meant to present Hitler with a *fait accompli* was not shared by all the members of Goebbels' staff. According to Schirmeister, Goebbels "obviously spoke only after obtaining Hitler's authorization . . . never throughout the war did Goebbels act in such decisive questions without Hitler's express consent." [34] On the strength of his knowledge of Goebbels' working methods, Stephan, though without direct evidence that the Propaganda Minister received instructions from higher authority in this instance, regards it "as certain that after the catastrophe of Stalingrad he [Goebbels] submitted every particular to the 'Führer' and obtained his approval." [35]

A satisfactory answer to the question of Hitler's authorization calls for a slight digression. Despite the distance between the Propaganda Ministry and the Führer's headquarters, there is no doubt that Goebbels had kept in close touch with Hitler since the beginning of the war. In addition to communications by telephone, telegraph, and courier, Goebbels had made frequent visits to the Führer's headquarters. The diary entries in our possession alone note nine meetings in 1942 and 1943. Thus there was room for an intensive exchange of ideas; undoubtedly Goebbels made suggestions and Hitler gave instructions. Nowhere do the diaries indicate any appreciable friction between the two men; they indicate rather that Goebbels was utterly loyal and devoted and that his share of responsibility increased as time went on. From 1942 on Hitler's public appearances became more and more infrequent. In the first four months of the war he made five big speeches, in 1940 nine, and in 1941 seven. But in 1942 he made only five. Without contact with the population, he contented himself more and more with speaking on the radio, reading proclamations, or having them read by others. Thus while preserving his unassailable position at the head of the state and of the party hierarchy, he exposed himself less to the criticism which, in view of the deteriorating military and political situation and the regime's desperate countermeasures, might well have set in. The appointment of the incompetent Committee of Three was not necessarily an affront to Goebbels but is rather to be explained by the narrowness of Hitler's horizon since he had been spending his days in his underground retreat.

As Hitler became increasingly isolated, Goebbels became his deputy in matters of propaganda. It was only natural that as time went on he was given more and more opportunity to act on his own initiative. The functionary who had merely followed instructions became Hitler's aide, giving him suggestions, sometimes "benevolently" correcting him, but never taking the attitude of a hostile critic or rebelling against him. In the field of propaganda he outdistanced all other functionaries; he became the leader and pacemaker. But his personal rise did not lead him to question his dependence on Hitler. Though he ceased to ask others for advice, he continued to ask, time and time again, for pointers "from above." His visits to the Führer's headquarters bolstered up his self-confidence.

With only slight fluctuations he remained under Hitler's spell to the very end.

Today certain details have become known to us about the preparation of the Sportpalast speech.[36] On the afternoon of February 14 Goebbels dictated a draft and started correcting it that same evening. In the intention of producing "a masterpiece of his eloquence," he reworked it several times in the following days. On February 17, he toned down "a few excessively violent passages" and submitted the parts dealing with foreign policy to the Foreign Office for review. By now he felt that the speech was indeed a masterpiece and was convinced that it would be a "great success." Hitler, who at that time was staying at his headquarters near Vinnitsa in the Ukraine, was too busy to listen to the broadcast of the speech and asked to have the text sent to him afterward. But this does not preclude the possibility that he had been informed at an early date of its intention, conception, and broad outlines and had given his blanket approval. On February 18 Goebbels remarked that it was difficult at the time to communicate directly with Hitler, but that this was not absolutely necessary, since "the guidelines for internal policy and for external propaganda as well" had been pretty well established.

Moreover it is hard to see what significant cuts Hitler would have made. He might conceivably have had reservations about Goebbels' unvarnished account of the crisis, but he expressly approved of this in his subsequent interview with Goebbels.[37] In general the speech did not demand anything more than the measures that were soon to be taken or had already been taken. Its main purpose, to prove that the masses were ready to accept total war, had already been very largely anticipated by Goebbels' commentary on Hitler's proclamation of January 30. ("From the breadths and depths of our people a cry for the most total war effort in the widest sense of the word rises to our ears.") The crux of the speech was not so much the content as the rhetorical tactics and technique of suggestion employed to whip up the audience to frantic applause. In this domain Hitler could hardly have given directives. Thus it is unlikely that Goebbels exceeded or disregarded instructions. In all probability Hitler basically approved Goebbels' action and to a very great extent left him a free hand to develop his demagogy as he saw fit.

Before we analyze the speech, a brief survey of the ensuing months may serve to round out the context.[38] Goebbels' diary for the period of the speech reveals little concerning the conflict within the party or the execution of the new war measures. Goebbels spent the evening of February 18 with Milch,* Speer, Ley, Stuckart,† Thierack,‡ State Secretary Körner, and others. The opinion was expressed that the speech had been "a kind of tacit *coup d'état.*" The butt of the *coup d'état,* however, was said to be not any particular person or persons, but the bureaucrats in general. No member of the leadership, it was thought, would now be able to oppose the project for total warfare. And Goebbels hoped to be able to bring Goering over to his side.

It was not until March 1943 that the signs of a "struggle behind the throne" became evident. On March 2, Goering was won over to a harder line. It was decided that Hitler's "eyes should be opened" to the incapacity of the Committee of Three, that Goering should activate the Council of Ministers for Defense, of which he was chairman, and draw Himmler, Ley, and Speer into its work. Goebbels was chosen for the post of deputy chairman. This plot failed, however, when in the course of conferences with Hitler in April it turned out that Goering's authority had been greatly overestimated. Goebbels too had had illusions about Goering's energy, activity, and reliability. De-

* Field Marshal Erhard Milch, air transport specialist and member of the Central Planning Board.
† Wilhelm Stuckart, State Secretary in the Reich Education Ministry and the Prussian Ministry of the Interior.
‡ Otto Thierack, Reich Justice Minister.

spite this miscalculation he continued to feel responsible for the conduct of the campaign. He obtained some reduction in the personnel of nonessential industries despite considerable opposition.

He encountered other obstacles as well. His efforts to shake the masses out of their peaceful habits of life led here and there to excesses that had almost a character of class struggle. The new directives were not uniformly followed. Some *Gauleiter,* Schirach for example, attempted, apparently for reasons of local egoism, to attenuate the measures in their districts. But most of all the organization was deficient. The Wehrmacht was in no hurry to recruit the men who had been laid off by industry and the labor offices' efforts to impress those ineligible for military service into defense work were not satisfactory. The new policy proclaimed by the high functionaries was only partially carried out because the bureaucratic apparatus was too cumbersome. As late as September 29, 1943, Goebbels and Speer were still deciding "really to put the total war policy into effect with the help of certain seemingly unsensational measures." This suggests a very negative balance. Yet it should not be supposed that the proclamation of total war at the beginning of the year brought no results at all. The regime had weathered the Stalingrad crisis without any appreciable inner strain, and the war effort had increased. The Sportpalast speech had played a considerable part in this achievement.

Some of Goebbels' biographers provide further information about how he worked on his speech up to the morning hours of February 18 and about his behavior after the meeting.[39] For our present purposes such details are significant only insofar as they show that he was clearly conscious of his aim—to hypnotize the masses—and of the methods by which to achieve it. He is quoted as saying to the members of his entourage after the meeting: "What an hour of idiocy! If I had told these people to jump from the fourth floor of the Columbus House, they

would have done it." [40] What were then the methods
which so hypnotized the crowd that they replied in the
affirmative even to such questions as: "Do you want total
war? Do you want it, if necessary, to be even more total
and radical than can even be imagined today?" and "Do
you accept the fact that anyone who detracts from the war
effort will lose his head?"

For an understanding of the reaction of the audience, a
knowledge of its composition is important. Hagemann's
observation that apart from the "Berlin party guard"
Goebbels had brought in "a few thousand trusted supporters from all over Germany by train and bus" and that
well-rehearsed groups had formed a claque[41] would provide a simple solution, but it cannot be accepted uncritically. The original text of the speech suggests that the
meeting was not attended by any appreciable number of
non-Berliners; a number of passages were obviously made
to order for a Berlin audience. If such passages were deleted from the official text, this was only to give the acclaim an appearance of wider validity. After the speech,
moreover, Goebbels remarked that "the Berliners" had
been "marvelous" and that they were "the most political
audience we now possess in the Reich." [42]

As to whether the groups that made up the audience
received previous instructions, the opinions of persons
who were present or who had close knowledge of the situation vary.[43] Stephan thinks it possible "that functionaries
were brought in to bolster up the enthusiasm" and "that
the Berlin District may have rehearsed some of the speaking choruses." Von Schirmeister believes that "there was
always something of a 'claque' at these big Sportpalast
meetings . . . a few hundred persons were quite sufficient." Doctor Fritz Hippler, former director of the film
section of the Propaganda Ministry, regards it as "unlikely" that members of the audience had received previous instructions, while Friedrich-Christian, Prince of
Schaumburg-Lippe, who was a propaganda speaker him-

self at the time, claims that it was expressly forbidden by the party to "steer groups at meetings." But all agreed that whether a claque was actually present or not, there was no need for one. Journalists who attended the meeting as observers had the same impression.

This is confirmed by the newsreel strips at our disposal. Here we see masses of people only too willing to applaud. They required no direction from rehearsed groups but took the signal for applause directly from the speaker, who adroitly worked up the excitement before giving the audience an opportunity to express its approval. The reactions—the jumping up from benches, the raising of arms, the shouts, and the speaking choruses ("Führer, command, we will follow!")—came spontaneously from the entire hall. And the applause was far more self-expression on the part of the audience than approval of the speaker. More and more the masses were thrown into a state of ecstasy verging on drunkenness. Hippler remarks: "Goebbels had so formulated his key sentences and questions, he had placed his rhetorical accents in such a way, that in *this* historical situation [after Stalingrad] and before *this* audience spontaneous acclamation could be expected with a probability bordering on certainty; if it took forms bordering on hysteria this was overcompensation for the first stirrings of despair."

Thus we cannot be certain whether or not there was a claque, but the question proves to be unimportant. As to the composition of the audience, Goebbels noted in his diary that almost the entire Reich cabinet, a number of *Reichsleiter* and *Gauleiter,* and almost all the state secretaries were present. In the speech itself he mentioned Speer, Ley, and Sauckel, who also appear in the film. He also spoke of wounded, Red Cross nurses, bearers of the Oak Leaves and the Knight's Cross, defense workers, party members, soldiers, doctors, scientists, artists, engineers, architects, teachers, civil servants, and white-collar workers and of women, children, and old people. He described the audience as a "cross section of the entire German people" and called on the audience to show that this was the case.[44]

Of course these representatives of the people had not gathered at random. In several instances Goebbels himself remarked that they had been "invited." Presumably the invitations, as usual on such occasions, had been sent out by the party organizations in accordance with a plan that is reflected in Goebbels' listing. Hospitals, army headquarters, National Socialist subsections, and professional organizations were included.[45] This provided an audience that—even without precise directives—was quite willing to "join in." Critics of the regime, the disillusioned or indifferent, did not attend, or at most formed a vanishing minority in the conformist crowd. The composition of the audience was an important factor in the propagandist success, though of course far more was needed to throw them into a state of ecstasy.

The reactions of those members of the audience who were conspicuous for their popularity—scientists, artists, and especially actors—were perhaps less spontaneous. From the very start it had been the practice of National Socialist propaganda to enlist the support of such personalities, and noncompliance could have unpleasant consequences. Despite the contempt that Hitler and his party never ceased to display for the intelligentsia, Goebbels attached special importance to the attendance of the leading representatives of cultural life at his meetings.[46] But even in these circles there were many who shared in the ecstasy, as is shown by the example of the actor Heinrich George, who during the speech "could not control his enthusiasm, climbed up on a chair, tore off his necktie, and waved it."

Another important factor was the setting. The film strips and photographs provide partial and panoramic views of the scene. In front was the broad speaker's platform, decorated only with swastika flags; behind the plat-

form hung the only streamer in the entire hall, inscribed
with the words: "Total war = shortest war." Otherwise
there was little decoration except for garlands. The bare-
ness of the hall was in keeping with the occasion and favored the absolute concentration indispensable to hypnotic suggestion. This was one more example of the special
gift that the National Socialists had developed in their
early years for obtaining strong propaganda effects by visual means.[47] Another important psychological factor was
the size of the crowd. According to the press reports
15,000 persons were assembled.[48] This gave the participants the feeling of being part of a great organization
expressing a single undivided will. What can throw an individualist into a panic gives conformists a boundless sense
of power. The crowd's identification with the hypnotic
speaker transformed the audience itself into a single living organism and this sense of unity threw it into
ecstasy.[49]

Thus a specific audience and a specific atmosphere provided the basis for the success of the speech itself, which in
turn was shrewdly calculated. Content, structure, formulations, rhetoric, and gesture were of a nature to sweep
the audience off its feet. Goebbels began with a reference
to his speech of January 30, 1943, which the last defenders
of Stalingrad had heard over the radio; after praising the
soldiers, he went on to say that it was every German's duty
to bear misfortune and to overcome it. In passing he
touched on the dogma that a people which performed this
duty was unconquerable. After this introduction he
promised to give an "unvarnished picture of the situation" and laid a foundation for confidence with the remark that the "schooled and disciplined German people"
could "bear to hear the whole truth." Anticipating possible questions that might be lurking in the minds of his
audience—such as, Who was to blame for Stalingrad and
what purpose was served by the sacrifice?—he said that
the time for such questions had not yet come and that the

future would prove that Stalingrad had "not been in vain." He admitted however that the events in the East had been a serious blow: "The steppes" had launched an unconscionably violent "attack on our vulnerable continent." Thus Goebbels interpreted the threat to Germany, National Socialism, and the regime as a threat to the whole Occident, so appealing indirectly to traditional sentiment, pride, and sense of responsibility. And he alluded to the historical mission of Germany and its satellites by declaring that the German army with its allies was "the only conceivable bulwark" against this onslaught.

In the next section of the speech this contention is repeated, but now it is argued systematically. Goebbels points out: (1) Europe was faced with the threat of world Bolshevism, which was synonymous with a "world revolution of the Jews"; there was a threat of "Bolshevist-capitalist tyranny," which meant "terror and anarchy," "hunger," "misery," and "forced labor." (2) No other country was capable of resisting "the divisions of motorized robots." In England Bolshevism was already gaining ground and "Jewry," here in "plutocratic-capitalist" dress, had already "infiltrated" the Anglo-Saxon countries to a very great extent. Thus there was only one choice: "between a Europe under the military protection of the Axis and a Bolshevist Europe." From these two premises he derived his third thesis: "We must act quickly and radically, otherwise it will be too late." This was his transition to the next section of the speech, which was devoted to the requirements of "total war."

But before going into the details of the new mode of life, Goebbels prepared his listeners for drastic measures. He subtly exploited class antagonisms ("the time has come to say goodbye to bourgeois squeamishness . . . to take off our kid gloves and bandage our fists"), pointed out that the end justified the means ("and so the question is not whether the methods we employ are good or bad, but whether they bring results"), and made it clear that the workers were the driving force behind the government's measures, for they had accused the government of not being "ruthless enough." After repeating the slogan adorning the front of the hall: "Total war = shortest war," he proceeded to pillory the scapegoats, the idlers and slackers. Adroitly attuning his words to the popular criticism of certain dark sides of German public life, he attacked the people who "sit around in places of amusement," who regard "the care of their stomachs as their main task in life," who stood around in luxury stores and had nothing to sell, but would deign only to exchange goods for butter and eggs. He criticized the useless beauty cult carried on in beauty parlors and hairdressing establishments and the bureaucracy that spent whole weeks on "absurd occupations" such as the Germanization of foreign words. Every morning in the Tiergarten, he declared, you could still see "cavalcades" of horsemen riding by; in the watering places people "lounged around for weeks doing nothing but exchanging rumors"; "unemployed tourists" were taking up room in the trains. Of course, he added by way of consolation, such places of popular cultural recreation as the theaters, movie houses, and concert halls would not be closed (which would have curtailed the possibilities for propaganda).

Assuming a graver tone, Goebbels went on to comment on the most important measures that had been taken: the compression of economic life, the conversion of the labor force (new workers to the defense industries, released workers to the front), and compulsory labor service for women. After flattering the women and praising their capacity for work, he ventured to observe that "doctor's certificates will not be taken at face value" and that so-called "alibi work" (at the place of work of friends and relatives) could not be accepted. All this because—and here again he anticipated the applause—the people want "quick and radical action."

After the familiar historical pseudo-parallel between

the Second World War and the Seven Years' War, Goebbels finally embarked on the last section of the speech, climaxing in the ten questions. The crowd confirmed their faith in victory; their willingness to fight; their determination to work harder and produce more; their will to total war; their absolute confidence in the Führer; their readiness to reinforce the Eastern Front with men and arms; the obligation of the home front to give the army everything it needed for victory ("a sacred oath"); the necessity of labor service for women; the necessity of the most radical measures against "slackers and profiteers"; the necessity of making equal demands on all Germans behind the lines. In leading up to the questions Goebbels showed great psychological astuteness. He motivated them by alleged statements in the English and American press to the effect that the Germans were unprepared for the present crisis. Of course he had no need "to prove the contrary," but he would nevertheless ask questions to "bring out the truth." Each of the first five questions was introduced by a provocative assertion allegedly taken from the English press. In addition, though this was hardly necessary in view of the enthusiasm that had long since set in, Goebbels predisposed the audience to answer enthusiastically by his above-mentioned reference to its representative composition, which made them feel that they were speaking for the German nation. After the questions were answered, Goebbels expressed his satisfaction in a grandiloquent summary (again in the form of an oath of the home front to the fighting forces), brushed in an optimistic picture of the future, with victory "tangibly near," and concluded with a quotation from Körner: "Now people, arise, and let the storm winds blow!"

Thus the speech can be broken down as follows: invocation of the danger threatening the Occident from the East—the need for painful measures affecting the private and public lives of the population—confirmation of the people's absolute willingness for "total war." It is interest-

ing to note that the much discussed principle of unconditional surrender, proclaimed by Roosevelt shortly before,
was not used to enlist unconditional support of the war,
and indeed was not even mentioned in the speech. This in
itself casts doubt on the thesis that Roosevelt and Churchill in Casablanca had provided grist for the German propaganda mill. It will be worth our while to inquire why no
use was made of the Casablanca formula at this time. The
first answer is to be found in the speech itself: Goebbels
had concentrated the attention of his audience on the
danger from the East; after the catastrophe of Stalingrad
this promised better results than any reference to vague
threats that might materialize in the distant future. True,
he also spoke of alleged Western war aims, but only insofar as they concerned the "Bolshevization of Europe"—
which brought him back to his main theme.

The second and more decisive reason why the demand
for unconditional surrender was ignored was that—Western views to the contrary—[50] those responsible for German propaganda did not regard this principle as useful
for propaganda purposes and at first did not even understand it. This is made clear by the extant directives of the
Propaganda Ministry to the German press for January
and February 1943.[51] On January 27, three days after the
demand for unconditional surrender was issued, the journalists were informed that "Roosevelt has referred to the
Casablanca conference as the 'unconditional surrender
conference'. This was probably an allusion to the treason
of the French generals [after the Allied invasion of North
Africa]. It would be a mistake to speak of this too ironically, but also to take it too seriously." On February 11
Churchill reported on the conference to the House of
Commons and made it very plain that unconditional surrender had been demanded; yet on the evening of the
same day a spokesman for the Propaganda Ministry made
the following statement at a press conference: "The
points to be noted in Churchill's speech are his remarks

(a) on the U-boat threat, (b) on the appointment of Ei-
senhower as commander in chief. . . . These two points
are at the center of the polemical discussions with
Churchill, the Soviet stooge of London. They are to be
treated without special emphasis." On February 13, after
Roosevelt had also publicly repeated the Casablanca formula, the Propaganda Ministry described his speech as
"not very significant in content and exclusively propagandist in design." "Consequently the speech should be dealt
with only briefly in the German press. . . ."

Thus the Casablanca formula cannot be said to have
given Goebbels welcome help at the time of his speech.
And how indeed could any propaganda effect have been
derived from reference to an Allied statement that possessed little more than formal significance and that did
not even specify how Germany was to be treated after the
peace, when alleged Western plans for the extermination
of Germany had long been a standard item in Goebbels'
propaganda? [52] Measured against such plans the demand
for unconditional surrender would have come as an anti-
climax. Of course critics of the regime who read between
the lines and realized that propaganda was propaganda,
may well have attached more importance to the Allied
proclamation. But the Casablanca formula scarcely made
a dent on the consciousness of the general public, so that
in view of its composition the audience at the Sportpalast
cannot have been seriously influenced by it. If the reaction of the crowd was a product of despair, this despair
was brought on by Stalingrad and not by Casablanca, and
Goebbels had chosen the right approach.[53]

His tactic of characterizing the catastrophe as such and
making no attempt to embellish it (though of course he
did not admit the mistakes of the leadership) was well
calculated. In the first three years of the war the population had been showered with jubilant victory communiqués. Such crises as that of the first winter campaign

in Russia were made light of, and time and again new victories seemed to justify the optimism of the propaganda mill. Admission of the defeat of Stalingrad was bound to shock the credulous souls whose wits had been dulled by habitual good news, and shake them out of their lethargy. Since the pessimistic note had been struck not by the so-called defeatists but by the government itself, the same credulous souls felt confident that the government's directives would turn the tide in favor of the Axis powers. Vacillation between faith in optimistic propaganda and doubt that the victories would continue could now give way to the reassuring thought that the German people were not unaware of their vulnerability but looked the danger square in the face. This took the wind out of the sails of the "grumblers." In reality, of course, one self-deception had merely given way to another: those who had formerly believed that the war was going well now believed that once the danger was recognized and the nation's reserves more fully mobilized new victories would be assured. At this point Goebbels ceased to tell the "unvarnished truth." With the assertion that "a danger recognized is a danger half overcome" (still stronger in the official text: ". . . a danger recognized is a danger soon overcome . . .") he launched on a new type of optimistic misrepresentation and continued to build alluring castles in the air.[54] Goebbels' "truth" was purely tactical; that is one essential difference between it and Churchill's "blood, sweat, and tears" of spring, 1940.

Goebbels attached great importance to this "truth"; up to a certain point he welcomed the setbacks at the front. This is made evident by two unpublished passages in his diary. On March 1, 1943, he dictated:

It is no longer possible for us to play the pessimistic game. Consequently we sound a few hopeful notes. I do this with one tearful and one laughing eye. I should prefer to go on giving a somewhat black picture; for then

it will be easier to make the German people and especially the leading classes accept the totalization measures.

Two days later:

> A Spanish newspaper writes correctly that in contrast to
> the first half of the war, in which propaganda was made
> with optimism, now propaganda would be made with
> pessimism. . . . This view is not so mistaken. In any
> case, as the Spanish paper observes, while formerly one
> had to deduct 50 percent from the good news, one is now
> obliged to deduct 50 percent from the bad news. Other
> days, other ways.

The foregoing brief summary of the speech might make it
appear as though Goebbels had organized his ideas logically and so convinced his audience by rational means.
This is not the case. The speech does indeed consist of
three main sections. But this structure is based more on
psychological than on objective factors. On closer scrutiny
it is easy to see that identical theses are repeated in all
parts of the speech and that sections which appear to be
delimited on a logical basis have essentially the same content. Repeated references are made to the "movement's
days of struggle" which supposedly proved that determination brings success, and to the duty of saving the Occident from Bolshevism; similarly repeated are the clichés
to the effect that the same "Jewish world conspiracy" was
at work in both Bolshevism and the "plutocracy," the demand that "Bolshevist methods" be met with similar
methods, and the contention that the people had already
made clear its readiness to accept total war, etc. The same
few ideas are repeated over and over again in varied form.

The "three theses concerning the battle in the East"
were not clearly distinguished but closely intermingled
and sometimes used interchangeably, as for example: "If
the German army were not able to ward off the danger
from the East, the Reich and soon thereafter all Europe
would fall a prey to Bolshevism," and "Only the Germany

army and the German people with their allies have the
power to save Europe lastingly from this threat." Repeatedly he shifted the accents slightly, each time adding
a little something new. Even the ten questions—actually
eleven, because the first was formulated in two sentences
and answered in two sentences—merge and overlap. Thus
support of the Führer was demanded in questions 1 to 3
and again in question 5. In question 3 Goebbels called
for support of his demand that the population work up
to sixteen hours a day and "give their utmost for victory"; immediately thereafter he demanded approval of
total war, which implied the same thing, and in question
7 he once again demanded that the people give the army
everything it needed for victory.

Thus the entire speech was demagogic and calculated
for emotional effect; it did not develop ideas and arguments. The three sections of the speech can best be titled
as follows: a theoretical-pedagogic statement of premises; a
moralistic picture of the consequences following from
these premises; a call to deliver a profession of faith. The
propagandist suggestiveness of the whole was further intensified by particular formulations, choice of words, and
sentence structure. Every rhetorical trick that Goebbels
had learned in years of propagandist activity was brought
to bear. The speech progressed like a display of fireworks
with effects rising to a climax. From the start he appealed
not to reason but to the emotions of his audience. "I
should like my words to be a message from my innermost
heart to yours . . . I will therefore clothe my remarks in
holy earnestness and perfect frankness." At the beginning
he addressed the audience by the polite *Sie* but soon he
slipped into the familiar second person plural: "I ask
you . . ." [*Ich frage Euch*], and by the end of the speech
speaker and audience were one. "All of us, children of
our people, welded together with the people . . . we
swear. . . ."

Goebbels knew how to touch the militant, revolutionary chord in his listeners: All "difficulties and obstacles" could be overcome by the "power" of the masses, by "militance of thought and action" and by "revolutionary drive." From the very start the speech was larded with sacral elements which gave the meeting the character of a religious rite: Goebbels promised to speak with "holy earnestness"; he proclaimed a struggle for the "most sacred possessions" of the German people, for "its families, its women and its children, the beauty and innocence of the landscape"; our people "would stake their priceless blood" to defend the women's "most sacred treasures," their children; the present struggle was a "historic mission." And the ten questions demanded "trusting faith" and a "sacred oath."

Another factor was the appeal to responsibility, which instilled in the audience a feeling that their consent and support were important. Goebbels spoke of the "profound, fateful significance" of the times, of the "earnestness of the fateful problem," of "fateful struggle," "historical task," and of the "greatest and most fateful hour of our national history." These formulations were motivated by the repeated references to the duty of Germany and its allies to the Occident: "The edifice which it has taken Western man two thousand years to build" was in danger; if this threat were not countered, "this most venerable continent would be shaken to its foundations and the historic heritage of Western mankind would be buried beneath its ruins." Everything depended on the decision of the moment. The whole was punctuated with short sentences emphasizing the urgency of the present action: "The hour presses," "There is no time to be lost," "Total war is the need of the hour," "It is time to whip up the stragglers . . . We cannot wait," "Strike while the iron is hot," etc.

Striking a note of class struggle, Goebbels appealed to social justice. He contrasted "the broad toiling masses" of the people "with a certain class" which still clung to a "high, almost peacetime standard of living." "National Socialist justice," he declared, "is no respecter of class or profession. Poor and rich, high and low must be subjected to the same demands." He attacked "a small passive part" of the population, which "is trying to shirk its wartime responsibilities." Women, "even if they belong to the privileged classes," must offer their services. Precisely because it had been ignored in the Third Reich, this socialist note, familiar to Goebbels from the early years of the movement, met with enthusiastic response.

Goebbels assumed as a matter of course that the masses had long been spontaneously willing to support a total war program: The German people "wants a Spartan mode of life," and "many millions of the best German women . . . are waiting impatiently for their ranks to be swelled by new recruits." He said that he was "happy to submit this program of victory [!] to a people which not only willingly accepts these measures but demands them, and demands them more urgently than has ever been the case since the beginning of the war. The people demands quick and radical action." By thus making himself the spokesman for the alleged opinions of the people, Goebbels planted the idea of confident consensus between people and leadership in the minds of his audience and flattered the people by indirect praise. Allegedly the public's eagerness to volunteer for extra work was already overwhelming, but this did not prevent him from trying to whip it up a little more: "This does not mean that only those who are mentioned in the law are privileged to work. We welcome everyone. . . . The government can provide only over-all framework laws. To give these framework laws content and life is the task of the toiling masses, and this must be done under the inspiring leadership of the party."

These appeals were supported by moralistic admonitions such as "The homeland in its entirety must remain clean and unsullied" and "All of us who are active in the service of the people must at all times, both in our work and in our inward attitudes, set a shining example to the people." The audience took such remarks not as a reproach but as encouragement, because, since their good will had already been certified, they had no reason to feel that any reproaches applied to them. For the same reason Goebbels was able to obtain stormy applause even with threats: It would be necessary to take "draconic measures" against slackers, for in the present situation "indulgence would be out of place." The fourth question demanding acceptance of "radical measures against a small group of slackers and profiteers" and of the fact that "anyone who detracts from the war effort will lose his head" was answered in the affirmative no less loudly and spontaneously than the others. And incongruous as it may seem after his assurances that with few exceptions the masses were already willing, Goebbels was even able to issue commands. The German woman, for example, "must . . . spontaneously show her solidarity, she must fall into the ranks . . . better tomorrow than the day after." And "I expect innumerable women and men too, men especially . . . to report."

Over and over again Goebbels lent emphasis to these encouragements, admonitions, threats, and commands by describing what would happen if the total mobilization should fail: "Bolshevization of the Reich," "liquidation of our entire intelligentsia and leadership class," "forced labor battalions for the Siberian tundra," "Jewish liquidation commandos," "terror, the specter of mass starvation and total anarchy," "the greatest national calamity," etc. Then after brandishing the whip he held out a sugar bun, if only in the form of glowing pictures of the future: "After the war we will return to the principle of live and let live"; "after the war we will be gourmets again"; fashion shops "will reappear . . . after the war—why, of course"; "our women and young girls have nothing to fear; they will appeal to our victorious homecoming sol-

diers even without peacetime frills"; "after the war we
will . . . build bigger and more beautiful houses than
ever and the state will lend a helping hand," etc. And besides, "in order not to create a gray, wintry mood," the
theaters, movie houses, and concert halls would remain
open, the radio would even expand its programs. And another word of assurance: no one expected "a woman not
physically equipped for it to do heavy work, in a tank factory, for instance," and the leaders would do their utmost
to "reduce the sacrifices to a minimum."

Goebbels also made use of the usual stock in trade of
National Socialist propaganda. He excoriated the standard scapegoats: the "international plutocracy," "international Bolshevism," and above all "international Jewry"
as the "incarnation of evil," the "demon of decay," the
"herald of an international culture-destroying chaos,"
the "world plague"; he scoffed at Germany's Western adversaries, the "lamenting lords and archbishops," and glorified the German leadership, first and foremost the
Führer himself. He did not hesitate to throw the spotlight
on his own person, to represent himself as a "spokesman
of the people" and as "responsible spokesman for the
leading country of this continent." His lack of restraint in
speaking of himself demonstrates his absolute self-
assurance and certainty of having the audience behind
him. He did not speak of the government as such. By
doing so he might have aroused certain doubts, and moreover his position as the promoter of the total war program
would not have stood out as prominently as his own interests demanded. But Hitler's infallibility was stressed all
the more; he was the shining example for the people to
look up to: "Since the beginning of the war and even
long before, the Führer has not had a single day's vaca-
tion"; the road to victory "is built on faith in the
Führer"; "we will not fall short of his demands"; "the
Führer has commanded, we will obey." In the prevailing
atmosphere there was no need to embellish the old Na-

tional Socialist maxim that "the people want to be led."
Even Goebbels' occasional slips were accepted and did not
detract from the applause. "If the Führer can do that," he
declared, "his paid servants can do it too." In the official
version of the speech this was changed to: "the servants of
the state can do it too." The listeners were in no mood to
criticize the content of the speech; all they wanted was to
profess their faith.

Many more pages could be filled if to this analysis of
the contents of Goebbels' speech we wished to add a detailed formal analysis. Let a few indications suffice: The
number of superlatives used exceeded all measure. Goebbels employed sentences such as "Today the most radical
is barely radical enough and the most total barely total
enough to lead to victory." Ample use was made of adjec-
tives from the standard vocabulary of National Socialism:
"heroic," "steeled," "gigantic." Goebbels showed a special
penchant for alternatives such as: "not victors and van-
quished, but only the surviving and the destroyed" will
issue forth from the war; "we would rather wear patched
clothes for a few years than run around in rags for a few
centuries." He made ample use of rhetorical questions,
such as: "What German woman could bring herself to
evade . . . such an appeal?" There was a sprinkling of
pithy puns: "We are not spoilsports, but neither will we
let our sport be spoiled." Sententious phrases are frequent:
"The people do not exist for the benefit of officeholders,
officeholders exist for the benefit of the people," or "he
who gives himself quickly gives himself doubly." Barba-
rous turns of phrase were effective in spite of, or rather
because of, their very banality. He appealed to the popular taste with homespun utterances such as: "When
Daddy comes home, Mama hasn't always got dinner on
the table." Catchword after catchword thundered into the
hall. The speech was a gold mine for the weekly "Political
Quotation Service." [55]

The effectiveness of Goebbels' speech also owed a good

deal to his delivery, mimicry, and gestures. Volume, pitch, and rhythm were skillfully controlled. His tone was grave, imploring, moralizing, severe, challenging, scornful, amused, ironical, incendiary, or monotonous as the occasion demanded. His voice was so shrill that it sometimes seemed about to crack, but even when he was screaming it was always self-assured, controlled, and clearly understandable. Pithy phrases, especially sententious utterances, were spoken slowly, with emphasis on every syllable. Striking words, especially superlatives, were drawn out and strongly accentuated. Before important passages he paused. When making challenging statements he spoke so fast that the words almost ran together, and moved closer to the microphone so as to increase the volume. He had a special way of heightening applause by continuing to speak for a moment after it had begun. He intensified the reaction to his questions by shouting such terse phrases as "Are you for it?" or "Are you willing?" in the midst of the applause.

His facial expression was tense and energetic as always when he spoke in public. Important passages were underlined with movements of his hands which heightened his expression of determination. The films show how this physically unimpressive man was able by his words, voice, and gestures to exert such a fascination that his audience looked up to him as though spellbound, and reacted blindly. Word, tone, and gesture seemed to emanate from a single center and thus appealed not separately to the eyes, ears, or reason, but to the whole man. Goebbels' personality was infectious. Many of his rhetorical refinements were not new; they belong to the repertory of every experienced speaker. What was unique in this speech was its perfect fusion of all the means at the orator's disposal.

The pictures and sound recordings also give us an idea of the reaction of the public. Though the speech lasted some two hours, the audience showed no sign of fatigue. When the listeners remained quiet for any considerable time, it was only because the speaker's words did not call for applause, for example, when he brought up historical reminiscences from the early days of the National Socialist movement or the Seven Years' War. But when the applause resumed, it was all the more impressive. The desire of the audience to applaud required the merest spark to set it off. The speech was interrupted more than two hundred times by cheers, laughter, storms of applause, and speaking choruses, by clapping, inarticulate cries, shouts of "Yes!" "Bravo!" "Phooey!" "Never!" and rhythmic slogans such as *"Sieg heil!"* and "Führer, command, we will obey!" At times every sentence was received by applause, sometimes a single sentence was interrupted two or three times. Though Goebbels sometimes deliberately invited applause and paused for it, he also attempted occasionally, with or without success, to choke off applause by continuing to speak. The speech would have taken several hours more if the frenzied public had always been given its way. One of the journalists present recalls: "During the second part of the speech a kind of frenzy gripped the audience. . . . On our little press platform foreign journalists from neutral countries jumped up spontaneously to applaud Goebbels." [56]

In order fully to understand the historical importance of the speech, we must also consider its propagandist impact on the country at large. The German radio stations transmitted it directly, so that every radio listener was able to participate in the event. The text of the speech was wired to the press by noon of February 18.[57] At the same time the newspapers received the following directives:

> The speech . . . will be featured in the early editions of the Friday morning papers. The parts dealing with Bolshevism and total war deserve to be specially stressed. In the headlines of the text and in the human-interest stories, the response of the people to the questions asked them is to be characterized as an expression of the entire

nation's will. . . . The terminology of the days of struggle is in order. The two main themes . . . must be discussed in detail in tomorrow's editorials. The Minister
addresses ten questions to the meeting, which it answers.
This must be described clearly and impressively. The
photographs used in the press should concentrate on the
meeting, not on the speaker.

On the following day newspapermen were notified that
"the great effect of Goebbels' speech on the German people must be stressed in their comments." "They should
indicate that a meeting like yesterday's is possible today in
any German city, and that the people would everywhere
react in the same way. Foreign reactions should not be
dealt with until tomorrow's evening papers; then feature
those from Italy, but also mention those from neutral
countries." Only on February 21 was the following directive sent out: "Let the foreign echo of Goebbels' speech
gradually fade out. Do not take up Swiss opinions to the
effect that Goebbels is the intellectual helmsman of the
Reich."

On February 24, six days after the meeting, the German newsreel appeared. Some 240 feet of film were devoted to the Sportpalast meeting. In rapid sequence the
film showed general views, the speaker's platform, the
crowd, the speaker alone, sections of the audience, individuals in the audience, familiar faces, outstretched
hands. The interaction between the speaker and the audience was captured from different camera angles. The
sound men had received a manuscript of the most important passages in advance.[58] Special camera men had been
assigned to catching the positive reactions of the prominent members of the audience. Particular stress was laid on
filming individual and group expressions of approval.
The cutting was done under instructions from the Propaganda Ministry, and Goebbels as usual had both the silent
rough copy and the finished copy with music and provisional commentary run off for him before the film was

submitted for censorship. Before the newsreel was released, it was sent to Führer's headquarters for approval.

* *

From our investigation of the background of the Sportpalast speech and analysis of the speech itself the following inferences can be drawn: Goebbels was motivated in
part by ambition, by the desire to improve his position in
the National Socialist hierarchy. But it would be unduly
one-sided to suppose that this was his only motive. At the
end of 1942, when the total war program was conceived,
the "battle behind the throne" against the Committee of
Three had not yet broken out. It entered its decisive phase
only in spring, 1943, after the mass meeting. Goebbels'
personal ambitions cannot be dissociated from his desire
to preserve the National Socialist regime against dangers
which he saw more clearly than others. He attacked those
who wanted to water down his ideas, but he was not a
rebel against Hitler.

The unreserved acclaim of the audience, which seems
puzzling in retrospect, is explained primarily by its composition. The audience was prepared in advance to approve. It did not represent the entire German nation, but
does not seem to have received any particular advance instructions. There was no need of a claque to induce the
desired reaction. It was not the Allied demand for unconditional surrender but the catastrophe of Stalingrad that
had given rise to the mood of despair on which Goebbels
played so skillfully in his speech. The speech as a whole,
with its appeals to the emotions, to the sense of responsibility, and to class-struggle impulses, its encouragements,
admonitions, and threats, and finally with its copious repertory of rhetorical tricks, threw the audience into a state
of ecstatic intoxication in which they were prepared to
agree to anything.

It is not necessary to regard the Sportpalast meeting as a
miracle that defies rational explanation, nor is it correct

to explain the audience reaction by state direction and outward pressures alone. On February 18, 1943, Goebbels performed a feat of mass hypnosis by methods that become perfectly clear on analysis. The event was significant because it helped the regime to weather the post-Stalingrad crisis and to carry on the war to the bitter end. There is no doubt that propaganda was an essential factor in National Socialism domination and contributed materially to prolonging the war.

NOTES

1. Walter Görlitz, *Der zweite Weltkrieg 1939–1945*, Stuttgart, 1951, Vol. I, p. 417. This assertion contrasts strangely with the author's previous observation that the catastrophe of Stalingrad had brought about a significant change in the internal scene by reviving the anti-Nazi resistance movement in the army (p. 415).

2. Rudolf Fiedler, *Im Teufelskreis, Krieg ohne Frieden. Der zweite Weltkrieg und seine Folgen*, Munich, 1960, p. 145. A connection between "unconditional surrender" and the Sportpalast speech is also drawn in the biography of Goebbels written by Werner Stephan, personal adviser to Reich Press Secretary Otto Dietrich, *Joseph Goebbels, Dämon einer Diktatur*, Stuttgart, 1949, pp. 256 f. Cf. also Günter Moltmann, "Die Genesis der Uncondition-Surrender-Forderung," *Wehrwissenschaftliche Rundschau*, Vol. 6 (1956), p. 118. (See correction in note 53, below.)

3. Walter Hagemann, *Publizistik im Dritten Reich, Ein Beitrag zur Methodik der Massenführung*, Hamburg, 1948, pp. 464–473.

4. Alexander L. George, *Propaganda Analysis. A Study of Inferences Made from Nazi Propaganda in World War II*, Evanston, Ill. and White Plains, N.Y., 1959, p. 69.

5. Rudolf Semler, *Goebbels—The Man Next to Hitler*, with an introduction by D. McMachlan and notes by G. S. Wagner, London, 1947, pp. 68 f.

6. Curt Reiss, *Joseph Goebbels, Eine Biographie*, Baden-Baden, 1950, p. 345; going even further in the same direction: Roger Manvell and Heinrich Fraenkel, *Doctor Goebbels, His Life and Death*, London, 1960. A well-balanced account is provided by Helmut Heiber, *Joseph Goebbels*, Berlin, 1962, pp. 328 ff.

7. "Records of the Reich Ministry for Public Enlightenment and Propaganda," *Guides to German Records Microfilmed at Alexandria, Va.*, No. 22, Washington, The National Archives and Record Service, General Service Administration, 1961; *Übersicht über die*

Bestände des Deutschen Zentralarchivs Postdam, Schriftenreihe des Deutschen Zentralarchivs No. 1, Berlin, 1957, p. 111. Further documents are to be found in the Hauptarchiv in Berlin-Dahlem and in the American Document Center in Berlin.

8. Originals of the war diary pages that have thus far come to light in the Hoover Institution, Stanford University, Palo Alto, California. A part of them were published by Louis P. Lochner, *Goebbels Tagebücher aus den Jahren 1942–1943,* Zurich, 1948. Diary entries for February 14–23 at Institut für Zeitgeschichte, Munich.

9. Stephan, *op. cit.;* Semler, *op. cit.* The diaries of Wilfried von Oven, *Mit Goebbels bis zum Ende,* 2 vols., Buenos Aires, 1949 f., are useless for our present purposes because they are complete only from the middle of 1943 on.

10. Such information has already been utilized in the secondary literature. In addition, the author has drawn on letters from Werner Stephan, Doctor Fritz Hippler, Moritz von Schirmeister, and Prince Friedrich-Christian zu Schaumburg-Lippe, to whom he expresses his thanks. He wishes also to thank Fritz Sänger, Doctor Hans-Joachim Kausch, and Peter Raunau, who attended the Sportpalast meeting as journalists and have generously provided information.

11. Cf. also the German newspapers for February 19, 1943; also Alfred-Ingemar Berndt and von Wedel (eds.), *Deutschland im Kampf,* No. 83/84, Berlin, February 1943, pp. 80 ff., and Alfred-Ingemar Berndt (ed.), *Das Archiv, Nachschlagewerk für Politik, Wirtschaft, Kulture,* Vols. 103–108, Berlin, 1942–43, pp. 975 ff., in which, however, the official notes on the applause and interruptions of the audience are lacking.

12. A recording of roughly the last two-thirds of the speech is in the possession of the British Broadcasting Corporation in London, and a copy in the Lautarchiv of the Deutscher Rundfunk in Frankfurt a.M. listed as N. 53 A 688. Doctor M. Kunath, director of the "Spoken Word" section of the Lautarchiv, informs me that this is a so-called "black pressing" made at the time by the Reichs-Rundfunk-Gesellschaft from a broadcast. Occasional static does not prevent one from listening consecutively to the speech. Recently the Bundesarchiv in Koblenz acquired a complete recording (black pressing) returned by the Americans with other articles requisitioned during the war (No. 120 in the list of recordings). But it had not yet been recut when this article was written. Its value as a document is considerably diminished by sound control and by editing of the applause sequences, but its authenticity cannot be held in doubt. On source criticism of sound recordings, cf. *Tondokumente zur Zeitgeschichte, Politik und Wirtschaft 1901–1933,* hrsg. vom Lautarchiv des Deutschen Rundfunks, Frankfurt a.M., April 1958 (mimeographed), p. 5.

13. BA Koblenz No. 650/1945. The source value of the newsreel scenes is diminished far more than that of the sound recordings by

perspective cutting. Cf. Fritz Terveen, "Der Film als historisches Dokument, Grenzen und Möglichkeiten," *Vierteljahrshefte für Zeitgeschichte,* No. 3, 1955, pp. 57 ff.; Wilhelm Treue, "Das Filmdokument als Geschichtsquelle," HZ, Vol. 186 (1958), pp. 308 ff. The original sequences from which the newsreel of February 24, 1942, was composed were destroyed in the war. A description of this newsreel in *Filmkurier,* February 24, 1943.

14. The leading exponent of this conception was the Italian General G. Douhet in his book *La guerra integrale,* Rome, 1936.

15. The following quotations from Erich Ludendorff, *Der totale Krieg,* Munich, 1935; 2nd ed., 1937, pp. 5, 11, 20 f., 103, 26.

16. *Der Prozess gegen die Hauptkriegsverbrecher vor dem Internationalen Militärgerichtshof Nürnberg,* November 14, 1945–October 1, 1946, Nuremberg, 1947 ff., Vol. XXXVIII, Document L–211, pp. 35 ff.

17. Communication from Herr von Schirmeister, Viña del Mar, Chile, to the author, June 8, 1959.

18. The Goebbels' diaries that have come down to us begin on January 1, 1942. The intentions expressed to Schirmeister are reflected to a certain extent in the entries of January 21 and 23, 1941, cf. Lochner, *op. cit.,* pp. 44 f., 48 f. On the 21st Goebbels spoke with Lieutenant Colonel Martin, Wehrmacht liaison officer, against a "defeatist mood in the armed forces High Command and the army High Command" and with his State Secretary Gutterer about measures "against defeatism in the Berlin government quarter." According to the diary, Goebbels suppressed news reports that "would arouse excessive hopes in the German people. . . . The German people should adjust itself to the war situation and not feed its heart on empty hopes. . . ." Not fully compatible with Schirmeister's statement is the sentence: "Thank God, I have met with the Füherer's full support in the course I have taken. That is comforting and inspiring." On the 23rd he wrote: "I am engaged at the Ministry in releasing some 300 members of the personnel for the Wehrmacht and war industry, and replacing them with women." And further on: ". . . the grumblers and pessimists are legion in so-called government circles. . . . Precisely they are the most vulnerable, which is why they must be screened against defeatist currents and rumors."

19. Ludwig Beck, *Studien, hrsg. und eingeleitet von Hans Speidel,* Stuttgart, 1955, pp. 227–258, esp. pp. 253, 255, 258. Cf. also Wolfgang Foerster, *Generaloberst Ludwig Beck, Sein Kampf gegen den Krieg, Aus nachgelassenen Papieren des Generalstabschefs,* Munich, 1953, pp. 158 ff.

20. Stephan, *op. cit.,* p. 254; Riess, *op. cit.,* p. 345; Manvell/Fraenkel, *op. cit.,* p. 298. All ignore the events of December 1942

21. Cf. Lochner, *op. cit.,* pp. 217 ff.; Semler, *op. cit.,* pp. 59, 62.

22. Semler, *op. cit.,* pp. 62 f.

23. From the unpublished parts of Goebbels' diary. Cf. also the

entry for December 17, 1943. Lochner, *op. cit.,* p. 228. Two months later the male air force auxiliaries were mobilized.

24. Semler, *op. cit.,* p. 62.

25. Lochner, *op. cit.,* pp. 217 f., 220.

26. *Ibid.* This early *rapprochement* did not last as long as maintained in Manvell/Fraenkel, *op. cit.,* p. 280.

27. Semler, *op. cit.,* pp. 63 f.

28. Excerpts in *Prozess gegen die Hauptkriegsverbrecher,* Vol. XLI, "Dokument Sauckel–82," pp. 225 ff.

29. Semler noted this on January 18, 1943, in his diary, *op. cit.,* p. 66.

30. Berndt/Wedel, *op. cit.,* p. 73. The following quotation, *ibid.,* p. 60.

31. On this and the following, Semler, *op. cit.,* pp. 66 ff.

32. *Ibid.,* p. 69. Also Riess, *op. cit.,* p. 351: "This is rather a risky undertaking. Hitler does not like to be confronted with a *fait accompli.*"

33. Lochner, *op. cit.,* p. 259.

34. Communication to the author of June 8, 1959.

35. Communication to the author of May 14, 1959.

36. Cf. Goebbels' diary for February 14–23, 1943 (unpublished), and the accounts in Manvell/Fraenkel, *op. cit.,* p. 298 (where the dating, based on Semler, is wrong: February 13 instead of 18, 1943); Riess, *op. cit.,* p. 351; Heiber, *op. cit.,* p. 328.

37. Lochner, *op. cit.,* p. 259.

38. The following according to Goebbels' diary for February 19, 1943 (unpublished).

39. Stephan, *op. cit.,* p. 260; Riess, *op. cit.,* pp. 299 f.

40. Riess, *op. cit.,* p. 356; similarly Manvell/Fraenkel, *op. cit.,* p. 299.

41. Hagemann, *op. cit.,* p. 464. Also Riess, *op. cit.,* p. 351, claims that "a claque of a few hundred men was installed . . . as, incidentally, at all his [Goebbels'] speeches."

42. Goebbels' diary for February 19, 1943 (unpublished).

43. The following, according to communications to the author: Werner Stephan (May 14, 1959), Moritz von Schirmeister (June 8, 1959), Doctor Fritz Hippler (June 7, 1959), Friedrich-Christian Prinz zu Schaumburg-Lippe (June 23, 1959), Fritz Sänger, (March 24, 1961), Doctor Hans-Joachim Kausch (March 28, 1962), Peter Raunau (March 30, 1962).

44. The slip in the spoken text: "Jews, it is true, are not represented here"—which logically implied their membership in the German nation—is lacking in the official text.

45. This can also be inferred from the communications to the author mentioned in note 43, above.

46. This is attested with specific reference to the meeting of February 18, 1943, by the communication from Herr von Schirmeister mentioned in note 43. A photograph in the *Hamburger*

Tageblatt for February 19, 1943, shows the following "representatives of the art world" at the meeting: Eugen Klöpfer, Theodor Loos, and Franz Grothe.

47. Cf. Karlheinz Schmeer, *Die Regie des öffentlichen Lebens im Dritten Reich,* Munich, 1956, pp. 122 f.

48. Cf. *Völkischer Beobachter,* February 20, 1943. According to the press bureau of the Sportpalast the hall can today seat a maximum of 9,000 persons (at boxing matches).

49. A good characterization of this method is to be found in Adolf Hitler, *Mein Kampf,* pp. 536 f.; cf. also Schmeer, *op. cit.,* pp. 44 f.

50. According to the *Völkischer Beobachter* for February 21, 1943, p. 2, the Swedish newspaper *Aftonbladet* had reported that Goebbels' speech was regarded in London "as the German answer to the demand for 'unconditional surrender' proclaimed by the Anglo-Americans in Casablanca." Cf. also Churchill's statement in Casablanca on January 23, 1943: "Excellent! I can imagine how Goebbels and the whole gang will fume." From Elliott Roosevelt, *Wie er es sah,* Zürich, 1947, pp. 151 f.

51. The following from the thus far unpublished instructions of the Propaganda Ministry to the press. These are in the possession of Herr Fritz Sänger, whom I thank for allowing me to consult them.

52. It would be worthwhile to study these instructions to the press to see what use may have been made of the formula later. But it is obvious that the formula was not taken up in the weeks following its actual proclamation, whereas twenty months later considerable propagandist use was made of the Morgenthau Plan, which had only allegedly been signed.

53. My former view that Goebbels' propaganda made effective use of the unconditional surrender demand (cf. note 2, above) must here be revised. The Goebbels diary entries for March 21, 26, and 27 which I then cited (Lochner, *op. cit.,* pp. 136, 140, 142) relate primarily to a speech by Vansittart in the House of Lords and moreover date from the year before the Sportpalast speech. In them Goebbels points out (as he often does later on) that he derived great benefit from Western propaganda, which was directed in part against Germany. I applied this overhastily to the unconditional surrender demand. The diary entries for 1943 show no appreciable reaction to the Casablanca formula, and this supports the negative inferences drawn from the instructions to the press. Cf. also Anne Armstrong, *Unconditional Surrender. The Impact of the Casablanca Policy upon World War II,* New Brunswick, N.J., 1961, a comprehensive but unfortunately superficial investigation.

54. Cf. also Stephan, *op. cit.,* pp. 260, 277.

55. Fourteen especially pithy sentences from the Sportpalast speech were included in it; see *Politischer Zitatendienst, hrsg. von Walther Koerber and Hans Zugschwert, Regierungsräte im Reichsministerium für Volksaufklärung und Propaganda,* Vol. 2, No. 13, Berlin, March 10, 1943, pp. 1686–1689.

56. Communication of March 28, 1962, from Doctor Hans-Joachim Kausch to the author.

57. This and the following from secret instructions to the press (cf. note 51, above). In view of the precise directives the pleasure which, according to his diary, Goebbels experienced at the reactions of the domestic press seems grotesque. To Goebbels' extreme annoyance a Security Service report had also noted negative reactions among the German public.

58. This and the following according to a communication of June 7, 1959, from Doctor Fritz Hippels to the author. On February 20, 1943, Goebbels noted in his diary: "In the evening we finished the new newsreel. It came out magnificently . . . a real masterpiece of the visual rendition of a mass meeting."

8

National Socialist Europe Ideology

PAUL KLUKE

Soon after the end of the war an important book appeared which undertook to provide an interpretation of recent events from a lofty historical standpoint: Ludwig Dehio's *Gleichgewicht oder Hegemonie* (Balance of Power or Hegemony).[1] In it the author represented National Socialist policy as an attempt to create a hegemony over Europe, a phenomenon preceded by a series of similar attempts on the part of other nations, which Europe had defeated time and time again in the course of the last few centuries, but each time with a greater expenditure of energy and finally only by recourse to extra-European powers. In this series Hitler's venture is seen as the most radical, the most destructive, and at the same time the last possible attempt to achieve a position of hegemony, an attempt which led to the breakdown of the European system and threw the Continent into a field of extra-European forces that had now become predominant. Not with the same intensity of thought but also saturated with the history of the old Continent and enriched by the breadth of vision gained through looking at the old Continent from the vantage point of his second home across the seas, Hajo Holborn[2] has described the collapse of Europe as an irrevocable fact, initiated by the First World War with its shattering of the stable order but definitely completed only by "Hitler's war"[3] and the absence of energy and ideas in Western Europe.[4] Though the accents are differently distributed, both authors show clearly that Europe itself was responsible for its political demise.

The causes of the great political transformations we are witnessing in our time are sought in a different quarter by Otto Westphal, who "as a former fascist" has undertaken "to reconstruct the architecture of history." [5] With an ingenuity equaled only by his arbitrariness he examines the changing relations among European states and tries to show how an autochthonous European order was wrecked by the rise of the two world powers, the United States and Russia. Thus, in contrast to the two other authors, Westphal finds the dynamic in the enemy camp; Europe, he holds, is on the defensive, and he tries to explain the emergence of Hitler in this light. The First World War, he maintains, gave rise to a horizontal world axis extending from Washington to Asia and hemming Europe in. In 1918, however, after the collapse of the Central Powers and the triumph of Bolshevism in Russia, this axis had broken down. The ensuing period, during which new groupings were possible, coincided with the rise of Hitler, whose guiding idea, according to this interpretation, was that Germany must take its place in the great anti-Soviet combination that was then taking form and thus ward off the danger, which had already become discernible in the First World War, that Europe would be destroyed by its eastern neighbor. That the leadership of the Continent would then fall to Germany "was indeed foreseeable; but whether Hitler at the bottom of his heart regarded this German leadership as his goal and not merely as a means to an end, whether, to oversimplify, he was not even more an anti-Marxist European than a Pan-German imperialist," is, according to Westphal, a matter well worth investigating.[6] Westphal's thesis is indeed deserving of serious scrutiny. All the more so because a number of other authors have expressed themselves less profoundly than Westphal but all the more vociferously in the same direc-

tion, declaring that in the Second World War Germany
was only rendering a service to Europe by combatting the
Bolshevist world-enemy. Often, to be sure, the personal or
partisan motivation behind this interpretation is only too
evident. But this has not prevented it from finding wide
acceptance, as seems only natural when we consider that
the experience of the postwar period and the consequences of Hitler's policy of aggression have brought
both the threat of the Bolshevist world power and the
need for a European policy to general awareness. In view
of the ease with which the insights and aims of the day are
projected, consciously or not, into the past, particularly
into a past that is still so close to us,[7] there is a distinct
danger that preoccupation with a European or Occidental
mission may blind the public eye to the purely destructive forces at work in the National Socialist leadership.
Thus in confronting Westphal's ingeniously expounded
theory it will be useful to ply the historian's trade with
caution and deliberation and to inquire within the limits
of the space available to us how the concept of Europe
arose in the National Socialist mind, what it meant to the
National Socialists, and how it expressed itself in their
policy.

Of course, there is a certain difficulty in making statements about National Socialist opinion, because the
movement consisted of many groups, often in conflict
with each other. But in the period when the party was
being consolidated and its power secured, the more independent individuals who had been welcomed with open
arms during the years of struggle were forced by Hitler
and the group of leaders subservient to him to join the
mainstream, and repressed or eliminated if they declined
to do so. It was only in the last phase of the National Socialist Reich, when chaos and doom were approaching
and Hitler's charisma was paling even in the minds of his
closest followers, that deviating opinions were able to
venture forth again. These remarks apply also to the Na-

tional Socialist views on Europe. They reveal certain shadings; in the early as well as the late period we find hopeful idealism, clear insights, sober reflection, and painstakingly camouflaged or naked Machiavellism. Apologists for the Third Reich or for their own past are concerned only with evidence of a policy such as is being demanded today, and undoubtedly some evidence can be found. But a historical judgment must be based first and foremost on the conceptions and actions of Hitler himself and his entourage, since by and large they alone determined the course of events. Consequently the present investigation will be devoted chiefly to them.

When the party was founded in Munich, the most powerful factor in the experience of that period of ferment was the defeat in the West and resentment of the peace treaty imposed at Versailles. Thus the party took a position of hostility toward France and England, and speakers at the earliest meetings of which we have record went so far as to demand contacts with "a healthy Russia, and in general an Eastern orientation." [8] Hitler's ideas had not yet crystallized; he too toyed with this trend and for a time was the proponent of a highly primitive version of the Bismarck tradition.[9] But very soon various other influences crowded out this painstakingly reactivated archetype from the mind of the young agitator who was learning fast and already possessed a keen instinct for mass appeal. Connections with leading Austrian and Sudeten-German National Socialists as well as White Russian *émigrés* contributed to his increasing hostility to Bolshevism. *The Protocols of the Elders of Zion,* which he read during this period, also helped to provide the anti-Semitism he had brought with him from Vienna with a psuedo-scientific political underpinning. He became acquainted with the Nordic myth, probably through the Thule Society, and in his first article for the *Völkischer Beobachter,*[10] which the party had just acquired, Hitler declared that the movement would create a "Germanic

Reich of the German Nation." For the present, however, he was concerned chiefly with the struggle for internal power, so that considerations of foreign policy seemed unimportant. As early as 1920 Hitler had said: "Nations become capable of a great ascent only when they have undergone internal reforms which make it possible to concentrate the whole race behind foreign-policy goals." [11]

Thus the party still had no need to advance a comprehensive foreign program. Hitler was himself to develop such a program only in the leisure of Landsberg prison. Its foundation is the doctrine, advanced with utter candor and for that reason so seldom taken seriously, of a biologically grounded fight for land as the most sacred right on this earth. This sacred right could not be fulfilled in Cameroons, but "by and large only at the expense of Russia." [12] This idea, fundamental to all Hitler's thinking on foreign policy, occurs only in the second volume of *Mein Kampf*, which appeared two years later. It merely provides further arguments, drawn from history and an analysis of the contemporary situation, in favor of the radical cure he had in mind for the spatially underprivileged German national organism, and various prescriptions for treatment.

The rabid anti-Semitism of his remarks only thinly veils his deepest, ultimate goal. For to his way of thinking destiny had given the German people a sign when with the Bolshevik Revolution "the inexorable world-Jew" had taken power in Russia,[13] thence to acquire world supremacy. Thus Germany's historic mission to save the entire non-Bolshevik world, by making war against a Jewish Bolshevism striving for world supremacy, was clearly linked with the fundamental German problem of acquiring living space. The very chronology of the development of this "granite foundation" of Hitler's thinking makes it quite clear that to Hitler this mission was only a way station, the means to an end, and not the end itself.

The same mentality led Hitler to reject and despise the

League of Nations. Later on he was not to take it into account in framing his policies, but only to combat it. Already in his book he scoffed at the sentimental fools who suggested that Germany should oppose the League of the hitherto dominant victor powers by taking the lead in a "League of Oppressed Nations." [14] Similarly the party rejected Briand's plan for Europe out of hand, terming it a means of denationalizing the German people. To these efforts of an undoubtedly constructive statesmanship the National Socialists opposed the determination of the "coming German national state" "to demand as much power and as much space for the German people as necessary to secure its future." [15]

It is hard to see how in the following years Hitler succeeded time and time again in deceiving both his supporters and his adversaries as to his true purposes from which he never swerved. One explanation perhaps is that his extreme singleness of purpose left room for extreme flexibility in his day-to-day tactics, all the more so as he was never impeded by petty considerations of honor, justice, or tradition. His living-space theory is credibly attested time and time again by his statements to intimates from whom he felt no need to conceal his innermost thoughts. We have, for example, his conversations with Rauschning during the summer before the seizure of power, in which he made it clear that a Germany under National Socialist rule was destined to set its stamp on the new era and gain supremacy over Europe.[16] And above all we have the policy statement he made immediately after his appointment to the chancellorship, in which he declared his intention of rebuilding the political power of Germany by an internal policy of terror, after which it would be possible to conquer new living space in the East and ruthlessly Germanize it.[17] There is no mention of Europe in this astonishing document whose brutal frankness can be explained only by his euphoria at the moment of finally acceding to power. But the official party position on foreign policy for

the consumption of its members and many sincere supporters consisted in the Pan-German policy set forth in
the party program. To be sure, Gottfried Feder had put a
radical interpretation on this policy as early as 1928, when
he demanded the union of all "who are of German blood,
regardless of whether they now live under Danish, Polish,
Czech, Italian (sic!) or French sovereignty . . . in one
German Reich." [18]

Alfred Rosenberg, on the other hand, tried to link the
National Socialist doctrine with older conceptions. Taking the nation as the unalterable foundation of all political development,[19] he cast his eyes over Europe and assigned the highest rank to four nations which in the course
of centuries of struggle had proved to be creative of culture, states, and prototypes, namely, Italy, France, England, and Germany. They had given Europe a fourfold
vitality of mind and soul, whereas Russia had now reverted to Central Asia. These four great nationalisms, said
Rosenberg, must be regarded as given by destiny, and
preserved. Europe, which is "not a crude aggregate but
organic unity and forceful multiplicity, is fulfilled in the
creative exchange and interaction among them." The destruction of any of these nations would bring about a
chaos to which the others would also inevitably succumb.
The smaller and smallest peoples were not equal in rank
to these great nations, as the League of Nations tried mechanically to maintain, but they too had their special values; side by side with the culture-souls of the great nations
they had weaker, less highly developed, but characteristic
souls, and they had a right "to fulfill their existence on
their own soil." [20] It was indeed an ethical imperative[21] to
respect every nationhood. In these ideas we can still discern, under the abstruse cloak of the racial myth, a certain
echo of the spirit-of-peoples doctrine of Herder and the
Romantics, and of Ranke's moral energies embodied in a
society of great powers. A credible Europe ideology involving a European mission to combat Bolshevist Russia

might conceivably have been developed on this basis. But Rosenberg was a paper theoretician of foreign policy. As early as 1932 Theodor Heuss very astutely ridiculed Rosenberg as a literary jester, tolerated in the party because no one took him seriously, and warned the public not to attach much importance to his outpourings.[22]

More characteristic of the immoderate foreign designs of an internally victorious German nationalism is a statement written amid the exuberance of 1933 by a man who was not even a "native" National Socialist but more of a free-lance mercenary, to wit, F. W. Heinz, who later broke with National Socialism and entered into contact with the German opposition:

> German nationalism is the conscious and unrestricted claim of the German people to fulfill politically, culturally, and economically its personality—determined by unity of faith, blood, history, country, and language—in an *unlimited* area of supremacy the center of which is constituted by a German Reich encompassing every branch of the German nation.[23]

But such voices of minor supporters could always be disavowed. At the time, the Chancellor of the Third Reich was far more concerned with consolidating his position on the right and left by protestations of peaceful intentions. In an interview with de Brinon, the first French journalist to call on him, he went so far as to say that he did not even aim at an Austrian *Anschluss*.[24] In the next few years he even paid lip service to the idea of Europe. At the very time when he was tearing up the Locarno Treaty, Hitler issued a warning against plunging this Europe, a family of nations whose boundaries had become immutable, into hate-filled conflicts by unreason and decisions born of passion.[25] Holborn has pointed out quite correctly[26] that the abandonment of the Locarno system without resistance had destroyed all French aspirations to European leadership; that from then on Paris followed in the wake of British diplomacy. With his unerring flair for his adversaries' weaknesses and in general for the chinks in the armor of Western democracy, Hitler exploited this decline of French energy for an attempt to take the reins in hand himself, allegedly in order to defend Europe against Bolshevism. Democracy, Hitler declared, had paralyzed a part of the Continent in its resistance to "the greatest world danger of this declining second millennium of our Christian [sic!] history," while he, by curing the democratic disease in Germany had proved to be a better European, "in any case a more sensible one." [27] Now he demanded an immunization of the European states against the danger of Bolshevist contagion, spoke of the need "to combat the international source of infection itself," and found friendly words for a "national" France as a member of the European family of nations.[28]

To his great satisfaction these words made a favorable impression in England, now the leader of the Western camp. When Lord Halifax visited Hitler in Berchtesgaden, he recognized Germany as the "bulwark of the West against Bolshevism" and declared his willingness to abandon adherence to the Central European status quo in favor of peaceful efforts to realize the German claim to self-determination.[29] But this appeasement policy of Neville Chamberlain and of his friend and Foreign Minister Lord Halifax in 1937 and 1938 cannot be explained solely by a desire to abandon with dignity a morally weak position stemming from the errors of Versailles (while quietly rearming on the side). Its chief motivation was rather a new concept of Europe which was making its way against the League of Nations ideology hitherto prevailing at the Foreign Office. This new concept aimed at a concert of great powers, England, France, Germany, and Italy. The support of the last two was to be obtained by appreciable concessions, while the Soviet Union, which since 1934 had been moving toward the West, the League of Nations, and the theory and practice of collective security, was once more to be rebuffed.[30]

This was the historical moment when, if Hitler had not been Hitler, the nationalist policy of the Third Reich might have developed into a European policy along the lines of Westphal's thesis and the propaganda of the years from 1936 to 1938. On March 3, 1938, the British ambassador made Hitler an official proposition, holding out the prospect that Germany might not only participate in safeguarding the peace and security of Europe but also obtain a share in the colonial system, hence an outlet for its economic energies.[31] Hitler made light of this offer. Despite his vocifereous colonial demands, he was not interested in overseas colonies, the development of which would have brought with it German cooperation with Europe but also, through the economic ties it entailed, have made Germany dependent on the West. He preferred to launch his dynamic policy in Eastern Europe. After the Austrian *Anschluss*[32] he turned to Czechoslovakia. He still made use of Pan-German formulas for external consumption, but there is ample documentary evidence from the period of the prolonged summer crisis of 1938 that he had already swung from the *Volkstum* policy, which he had thus far found so convenient in his progress toward his ultimate goal, to a policy of pure expansionism. The Sudeten Germans served as a pretext for the destruction of Czechoslovakia and as a basis for agitation.[33] Hence his insistence on a military solution of the conflict, his rage (at first repressed with difficulty) at the Munich Pact despite the enormous success it represented, and a few months later his march on Prague.[34]

It was consistent with this line that the VDA [Verein für das Deutschtum im Ausland—Association for Germanism in Foreign Countries] was now "integrated." Since its foundation and most recently under the leadership of the Austrian-German Hans Steinacher, the VDA had sought to reinforce the cultural bond between all persons of German blood, but had recognized the politi-

cal map of Europe. Soon after 1933 many leading figures
in the organization had been expelled. Finally at the end
of 1937 Steinacher too was eliminated. Now the VDA became an instrument of the SS and its Volksdeutsche Mittelstelle [Center for Ethnic Germans], which made use of
German ethnic groups to subvert foreign states.[35] At the
same time the Germans ceased to collaborate with the European Congress of Nationalities, in which the German
groups had played a leading role and which had exerted a
considerable influence for the last decade under the leadership of Doctor Ewald Ammende.[36] And indeed, what
interest could the National Socialists have had in an institution that championed the cultural autonomy of *all* ethnic groups in Europe and defended them against forced re-
education by national states of any form whatsoever? The
Congress of Nationalities demanded legal status for national groups; it wished to establish in Europe a corporate
order of nationalities and so relax the sclerotic frontiers of
the national states. In short, it defended the right to live
of large and small groups alike, in the realization that
"Europe is a great bracket binding together an immense
wealth of nations." [37] Such thinking was of course radically repugnant to the National Socialists; it meant not
only that small nations should be given the same possibility of developing as large ones, but above all that the German groups in foreign countries should not be used as instruments of centralistic power politics. The leadership of
the German national groups was integrated when in November 1936 Konrad Henlein was made head of their organization. Those who declined to follow the new course
were reduced to impotence. From his headquarters in Vienna the Baltic-German Paul Schiemann, an authentic
liberal, tried in vain to propagate a minorities policy independent of Berlin.[38] During the death agony of the
League of Nations, the Congress of Nationalities met
once again in London in 1937 and then in 1938 in Stock-

holm, and already sensing the imminent crisis, delivered itself of a few last forlorn speeches that were ignored in Berlin.

In diametrical contrast to such endeavors Konrad Henlein, in the summer of 1938, had administered the Sudeten German group in accordance with direct instructions from Berlin and so done his bit to further Hitler's policy of smashing the Czechoslovakian barrier. After his overwhelming success in obtaining the Munich Pact, Hitler's thoughts turned at once to his living-space plans in the East, and Ribbentrop's diplomacy attempted to gain Poland as a compliant satellite by vague promises of Ukrainian territory.[39] Here we need not go into the reasons why these plans failed and why in a diplomatic revolution Hitler suddenly presented himself to the world as the ally of Bolshevist Russia. This step, incompatible with the declared principles of National Socialism, was not only designed to isolate and destroy Poland; it also meant the elimination of the entire chain of buffer states which had been placed around the Soviet Union after 1918 and which had been rendered viable only by the political and diplomatic support it had thus far received from the European continent. As a counterweight to Bolshevism this chain of states had moved the European order forward into regions which since the eighteenth century had succumbed to tsarist expansionism. The all-European function of these territories was now abandoned for the sake of a momentary diplomatic gain. In the secret clauses to the German-Soviet pact and in the friendship treaty, Central and Eastern Europe were divided into spheres of interest of the two great powers, and "all interference of third powers in this settlement" [40] was excluded. Thus as a first step Europe was banished from this region. When after his victory over Poland Hitler inaugurated his peace offensive, he very considerably tempered his language in speaking of Russia, now Germany's friend and diplomatic ally. In his speech to the Reichstag on October 6, 1939, he spoke of the "task of establishing a farsighted order of European life" and, in a wonderfully mealy-mouthed account of National Socialist policy toward defeated Poland, declared that his contribution to the performance of this task was to create better ethnographic conditions in Poland by a resettlement of nationalities, which would also have to include the no longer viable parcels of Germans in the East and Southeast.[41] Thus he still tried to maintain a semblance of nationality policy and even restricted his intentions to a "practicable order in the Central European area." [42]

The German victory over France in the following summer gave Hitler—now the most powerful man on the European continent—new possibilities and responsibilities. One of the main aims proclaimed in *Mein Kampf* had been achieved: the only military power comparable to that of Germany was eliminated. From the Atlantic to the borders of the still allied Soviet Union, Hitler's will was supreme. At the time of this great victory the leading weekly of the war years made its appearance. Its name, *Das Reich*,[43] is characteristic of National Socialist intentions. After the triumph of the sword, it proclaimed to the world the party's ideas for a new political order of Europe. The first word that meets the eye is not "Europe"; the "Reich" takes precedence over the idea of Europe; it is the gateway through which all ideas, discussions, proposals relating to a new European order must pass. But what is the content of the word "Reich"? Some time before, Hitler had expressly forbidden further use of the term "Third Reich." Lammers had still used it deliberately in 1938 in a lecture on "Statesmanship and the Third Reich" and interpreted it as follows: "Combining the ideas of state and nation, the term 'Third Reich' of the Germans also seems to me to have profound significance from the standpoint of political law, and for the first time to provide a correct designation for the German state." [44] Hitler's prohibition[45] was designed no doubt to extirpate that root of the National Socialist movement which had sprung from the soil of Young Conservative thought. Hitler wished now to dissociate himself from the formulation of Möller van den Bruck.* Another linguistic decree prescribed that the word "Reich" was to be applied solely to the German Reich and to no other political formation; there were many states but only one Reich.[46] If for the moment we disregard the later National Socialist interpretation of the word, this much is evident: it suggested an association with the medieval Reich [the Holy Roman Empire], and such an association no doubt existed among the broad masses. Divested in the religious void of National Socialism of its essential original content, namely, symbiosis with Christianity, the resonance of the word—a venerable tradition, the richness and radiance of a millennial history—was expected to induce a mystical ecstasy. But above all, blatantly ignoring the total change that had taken place in the content of all political functions, the National Socialists were enabled, by evoking the old Reich's role of leadership, to put forward their own claim to the European succession while maintaining an attitude of vagueness about the many territories that had long been outside the boundaries of a German or even a Greater German state. The Reich they spoke of was no longer "holy," it was "eternal"; and the more National Socialism laid bare its aims, the more clearly race, the so-called Nordic component, entered into the concept of the Reich.[47]

The National Socialist ideologists looked out beyond the "Reich"; they carefully, perhaps out of regard for the Soviet ally and its not yet clearly defined aims, avoided using the word "Europe" or any definite geographical terms. They preferred to speak of the "new order" that

---

* Artur Möller van den Bruck, author and critic who was a major intellectual mentor to the corporativist Young Conservative movement until his suicide in 1925. In 1923 he had published a book entitled *The Third Reich*.

was now to be established on the Continent.[48] But the basis of this new European order was economic. As far as we can determine, the term "true European order" was first used in 1939 by Darré in a speech on agricultural policy.[49] At that time Darré believed that while the energies of England, France, and Russia were pushing out beyond Europe, the task of Germany was to establish, through spiritual leadership and not with the methods of nineteenth-century political and economic imperialism, an equilibrated economic bloc in Central Europe. "If Greater Germany succeeds in this ordering task, other states will crystallize as of their own accord around this Central European 'ordering bloc' with its well-balanced and continuous economic relations, and thus the basis for a true new European order will have been created." [50]

Now after the victory these ideas were taken up again, though with little regard for the above-cited rejection of economic imperialism. The aim of the new order was to replace a system dependent on trade with England by an autarkic planned European economy modeled on the German economy and immune to blockade.[51] This program directed against England and the hitherto prevailing economic system was put forward in a number of variations.[52] At length Economic Minister Funk, in a message to the world press, spoke of the new order in resolute, but practical, down-to-earth terms, avoiding flights of fancy.[53] Foreign trade, said Funk, should be increased in accordance with the methods of the prevailing system of payments, facilitated only by a shift from a bilateral to a multilateral basis; the reichsmark which had been so strengthened by the war would be the regulatory currency and Berlin the new money market. Funk rejected any violation of natural realities such as a general European customs or currency union. He held that the necessary new economic forms had already been embodied in the relations between the Reich and Southeastern Europe.[54]

The National Socialist press also believed firmly in a new social order of Europe that would imitate the German model. But it took good care not to come out with any concrete political proposals. Only once was an occasional contributor to *Das Reich* permitted to develop his dreams and to predict that the internal boundaries of Europe would lose their political reality, "except for the Alpine frontier at which the Germanic Reich of the North and the Roman Reich of the South do not divide but meet in friendship." [55] Here we gain a glimpse of a large European area, inhabited by a few foreign peoples taken under German protection and rendered harmless, to be exploited by National Socialist economic imperialism with its centralized administration. Meanwhile Darré's blood-and-soil circle were already announcing a program of expansion based on peasant colonists.[56]

Strangely enough, no mention was made of France in these discussions of a new order. The victory over this great military power was so overwhelming and had been gained so quickly that even the leadership needed time to think out the political possibilities. When on June 19, 1940, an inventory of the spoils of victory was drawn up at Goering's headquarters,[57] the National Socialist leadership luxuriated in plans for a thoroughgoing transformation of the map of Europe. While Holland was to be left a certain independence, Norway and Luxembourg were to be incorporated into the Reich, Alsace-Lorraine reintegrated, and Brittany made an independent state. As to the fate of Belgium with its Flemings and of Burgundy, a decision was held in abeyance. At that time Hitler even considered annexing North Africa and, bypassing the Foreign Office, commissioned Undersecretary Stuckart of the Ministry of the Interior to draft a plan.[58]

These were the weeks in which Hitler still expected that England, having been driven off the Continent, would sue for peace or soon be defeated. After this victory he planned to set up a Greater German Reich taking in the predominantly Germanic parts of Western Europe as well as Scandinavia. France as a whole had no place in this structure; it would lead an uninteresting, impotent existence in the southwest, doomed to biological decline and negrification. England's perseverence and the frustration of his hopes of invading the island compelled Hitler to temporize. In the late summer of 1940 two possible means of continuing the struggle presented themselves and were discussed in diplomatic and military circles. These two possibilities were war in the Mediterranean Basin and Africa, and a campaign against the East. In the first case Hitler needed France, still an important colonial and naval power; in the second, France would at least have to keep quiet.

But though in 1939 Hitler had had no qualms about conciliating Russia for the sake of his Polish campaign, now he was too set in his conception of France as a degenerate nation, too drunk on the magnitude of the German victory, too intent on his prospect of displacing frontiers on an "ethnic" basis, to recognize the unique and short-lived opportunity to gain the support of the French and in collaboration with them to build a continental order deserving of the name. After the day of Mers-el-Kebir, when the greater part of the French fleet was shot to pieces by the Royal Navy, there was more bitterness in the country against the former ally than against the victor. But now, with German preparations for an invasion of England under way, when Laval offered to bring France into the war, Brauchitsch refused his offer with contempt: "We have no need of your help, which in any case would not amount to much." [59] Whereupon Vichy embarked on a policy of *attentisme* and diplomatic duplicity. Communications with London were restored by way of Madrid and Lisbon, and shortly after the Montoire meeting (between Hitler and Pétain) Professor Louis Rougier, an intimate of the French Foreign Minister, held secret talks with Churchill. He returned from

London with Churchill's undertaking to restore the pre-war borders of France, provided France gave no help to the totalitarian powers. In possession of this statement Pétain informed Laval on November 10, 1940, that he would never tolerate French participation in a war between England and Germany.[60]

But the problem of French *attentisme* does not concern us here; what is important in our context is that a reconciliation between the two great nations, indispensable to the realization of any genuine conception of "Europe," was never seriously contemplated by Hitler or the National Socialist leadership. The reasons for this attitude are not to be sought in justified distrust of the political action of the defeated enemy or of the sincerity of his offers. They lay deeper.

To the National Socialist mind the defeat of France was a triumph in three respects. First, it was the end of a struggle over the Rhine frontier, which had raged for three centuries and in the course of which one chunk after another had been torn out of the German Reich.[61]

Second, it was regarded as a victory over the "discarded ideals" of 1789, that "revolution of subhumans" [62] with its rights of man, parliamentary government, and democracy, its "mild ideals and brutal reality." [63] In the National Socialist view the total defeat of the country where those hated ideals had originated demonstrated to the whole world that National Socialism was a conquering political principle, the form of government suited to young warlike peoples.[64] And this National Socialist judgment on France did not change when Pétain in Vichy tried to establish a new form of state, the *état français*. True, the doctrine of this "national revolution" in France[65] was a far cry from National Socialism, and the Marshal's own attempt[66] to draw an analogy with National Socialism was not convincing. But in Germany we find not so much as an attempt to take this new political formation seriously. While preserving a certain respect for the aged Marshal, the National Socialists laughed it off as a superficial imitation.

Thirdly, the victory of 1940 was regarded as a complete triumph over the author and guardian of the order of Europe established in Versailles, an order characterized by the fuss and bustle of small countries that preened themselves on their sovereignty, though they had no true political existence, and by a League of Nations controlled by England and France and served by their clientele of petty states, which for two decades had arrogated to itself the right to determine the face of Europe and to hold down the Reich.

Immediately after the armistice the controlled press was full of articles insisting that this victory of German arms, of German history, of the German political system must under no circumstances be given away[67] or watered down by false sentimentality.[68] France had light-mindedly brought about the war and must not be discharged from its responsibility.[69] When a few weeks later it seemed advisable to take a somewhat more diplomatic attitude toward France, the newspapers directed their antidemocratic venom against England, the birthplace of parliamentarianism. *Schwarzes Korps* declared that "a new order can only be an order without England." [70] But even in this situation France was still excluded. Responsibility for the new order rested on the shoulders of the two stronger nations of the Center, which were fighting for the freedom of Europe. "The destiny of France," it was agreed "is necessarily marginal to this era." [71]

Amid this euphoria of victory the plans for a partition of France, which in June had been discussed in small circles, even found literary expression. The Breton project, however, proved short-lived. A Breton national congress arranged to hold a demonstration in favor of Breton autonomy on July 3, 1940, in Pontivy, but the outcome was a demonstration against the Germans. In what degree this whole affair was a mere puppet show staged by the

occupying power,[72] we do not know. In view of the strict
government control over all literary production it is of
course no accident that a book by a Celtologist on the
Breton autonomy movement should have appeared just
then, in the summer of 1940.[73] A similar movement in
Burgundy had a more lasting echo. For some years Burgundian regionalism, a sentiment that Burgundy had
been disenfranchised and culturally drained by Parisian
centralism, had found a literary champion in France in
the person of Johannès Thomasset, who in disgust at the
Paris Moloch, murderer of the provinces, had given up
his academic career and retired as a peasant to his homeland, where he poured forth his complaints in lyrical
prose: descriptions of the landscape, visions saturated
with Germanic mythology, and invocations of the heroes
of Burgundian history.[74] A collection of his writings was
now in 1940 brought out in German translation.[75] When
the book appeared, *Schwarzes Korps* devoted a whole
page to this "seer from Burgundy"; the reviewer proclaimed that the despiritualization and racial degradation
of the French provinces had come to an end and that Burgundy, this historic country of German imprint, would
now be restored to its national existence. The article concluded with one of Thomasset's visions: after miraculous
victories an Emperor Ulrich liberates France from its
usurping masters, the power of Paris is eliminated, and
the old provinces are grouped into three spheres of influence, each under a kindred protector. The Celtic sphere
centering on Brittany is nominally attached to Ireland, its
racial sister; the Germanic sphere, consisting of Alsace-
Lorraine, Champagne, and the two Burgundies, is placed
under the protectorate of the Holy Empire, while the first
steps of the Latin sphere are guided by Italy. Thus in
the noncommittal form of an anonymous article and a
vision,[76] the SS published its most secret thoughts. In the
ensuing years interest in Burgundy was fed by reports of
all kinds, and in the midst of the war a learned book on

Burgundy, the millennial land of destiny at the border, appeared under the sponsorship of the German military governor of France.[77] Small wonder, for that is where Himmler wished to settle the Germans of the South Tyrol. But when a new home for them appeared to have become available in the Crimea, he declared nonchalantly: "Then we shall just have to find a different people or population for Burgundy." [78]

Though all this never went beyond plans and literary intimations, the implications for France of the National Socialist New Order were made very clear by the measures regarding Alsace-Lorraine. The demand for its reintegration was motivated in equal degree by the desire to repair the injustices of 1681 and 1918 and by the Germanic blood-and-race myth. A policy of reannexation was discernible in the very first ordinances issued by the German military government in the summer of 1940, when a distinction was drawn between the old established population and the French who had immigrated since November 1918. The term "ethnic German" of Alsace-Lorraine was introduced and on the strength of it persons who had long been living in France proper were summoned to return home.[79] In order to prevent a sense of common destiny from arising in the population of the two provinces and to facilitate incorporation with the neighboring National Socialist *Gaue* of Baden and Saar-Palatinate, the press was instructed at the end of August [80] to stop using the artificial over-all term "Alsace-Lorraine" and to refer to the two components separately "along the lines of the natural development following the introduction of the civil administration." Vichy issued a solemn protest against the preparations for annexation.[81] A few weeks later the German armistice commission in Wiesbaden demanded the immediate discharge of all still mobilized French soldiers of Alsace-Lorraine origin. At the same time Gauleiter Bürckel of Lorraine demanded the expulsion of tens of thousands of Lorrainers who in his opinion were not fit for

Germanization. On November 3 they were obliged on only a few hours' notice to leave home with only the most indispensable hand baggage for unoccupied France where no preparations whatever had been made for their reception. The simultaneity of the military and civil ordinances shows that these measures were part of a systematic policy ordered by the supreme National Socialist leadership.[82] Yet a few days earlier Hitler had informed Marshal Pétain in Montoire that the German peace was not a peace of vengeance and that France would occupy its warranted place in the New Order.[83] There can be no better illustration of National Socialist contempt for France than this coincidence of word and deed.

In the ensuing period Alsace-Lorraine became a field of experimentation for the resettlement fanatics of the SS, whose internal instructions throw a significant light on the Germanization and racial betterment policy. Their aim was to separate this territory radically from France, and they did everything in their power to render the barrier insurmountable. It was planned as early as 1941 that the Alsatians and Lorrainers living in unoccupied France should as ethnic Germans be returned to their native land: some 50,000 Alsatians and 23,000 Lorrainers were expected.[84] In August 1942, Stuttgart Gauleiter Murr went with Himmler to see Hitler, who spoke of his plans for the political transformation of Western Europe. The problem of Alsace, Hitler is quoted as saying, would be solved by "deporting to France all asocial and criminal elements" as well as those of inferior, non-German stock.[85] Those who did not fall into this lower group but for whom there was no place in the Alsatian border territory would be resettled in the old Reich, but racially valuable elements would be given the special privilege of settling in the conquered East.[86] In November 1942 similar measures concerning Lorraine were discussed at SS staff headquarters, where it was decided that "racially unfit groups" were to retain French nationality and "be deported at a date to be announced." [87] Thus while the plans to dismember the rest of France were postponed and perhaps abandoned, a rigid ethnic frontier was set up and preparations made for a division deeply humiliating to Germany's western neighbor.

Our discussion of Alsace-Lorraine has gone ahead of our general investigation. In the autumn of 1940 it became evident that Hitler's none too seriously envisaged plans of combatting England by way of the Mediterranean were impracticable, perhaps because of irremediable conflicts of interest between the three Latin Mediterranean states, and perhaps also because such an African policy would have required the participation on an equal footing of France and hence its recognition as a great power. War against Russia, seriously considered as early as July, now became the sole basis of orientation, and with this the New Order and the idea of Europe took on a new form in National Socialist propaganda. Immediately after the meeting at Montoire the press was instructed to attach no great importance to this event. Under no circumstances must attention be focused on the relations between Germany and France. "Reports which might be offensive to France or which on the other hand might give the impression that we had become the servants of French interests are not to be published." [88] The German press was attuned to a policy of *attentisme:* "No statements that can be interpreted as promises!" [89] Finally, immediately before Molotov's visit to Berlin (November 12, 1940), discussion of "Europe" was barred entirely from the daily and periodical press. The watchword now became: "We are fighting primarily not for a new order of Europe but for the defense and safeguard of our own vital interests." [90] This admission concluded the first phase of the propagandist effort with which National Socialism, after its brilliant and yet so deceptive partial victory, attempted to gain world support for its Central European policy.

It is sufficiently known with what overweening optimism Hitler prepared for his Russian campaign, which was begun on the anniversary of the day in 1812 when Napoleon crossed the Russian border. By way of explaining to the people why they had been thrown into this hardest of wars, the censored press had for the present to content itself with Hitler's statement, contained in his proclamation, that this step had been absolutely necessary. Above all, the new move was to be represented as part and parcel of the war against England, while in the Propaganda Ministry's first instructions to the press the theme of a union of all European peoples against Bolshevism was sounded only in passing.[91] It almost seems as though the National Socialist leadership itself had been surprised by the enthusiasm which the war against the Soviet Union aroused among the anti-Communist elements of Europe. It was only later that the Propaganda Ministry found the right tune and began to celebrate "the campaign of all Europe against Bolshevism" and to laud Hitler as the banner bearer of Europe and of its common culture and civilization.[92]

How little sincerity there was in such propaganda is shown by the instructions issued at the same time to soft-pedal this "European campaign" in the domestic press: on July 7, the press received instructions that news reports on the French volunteer battalions being enlisted to fight Bolshevism were "not to be printed outside of France." [93] Reports of the volunteers from smaller European states that were being enrolled in SS formations were likewise suppressed.[94]

Hitler himself now reverted to his original version of the aims of the Russian campaign proclaimed years before. Once the armored advances of the first few weeks seemed to show that his predictions of victory had again been justified, he felt that his now unlimited power enabled him to speak freely. His outlook had not changed. He believed that his central problem—not that of "Eu-

rope" but that of gaining new living space for Germany—
was about to be solved. The essential, he held, was "to
slice the enormous cake handily, so as to be able first to
control it, second to administer it, and third to exploit it."
He did not wish to make things harder for himself with
superfluous explanations and preferred to motivate his
steps in the eyes of the world "by tactical considerations." [95]

A coherent picture of his ideas about Europe at that
time, at the peak of his career, can be obtained from his
free and easy conversations with friends at table.[96] Nowhere in these conversations does he speak of Europe as
the home of a family of nations with a distinct cultural
and political heritage, molded by antiquity, Christianity,
and the interworking of the Germanic and Latin spirits,
as a community of states, each with its specific function
and right to exist and develop. Hitler's conception of Europe derives exclusively from his racial ideas. Europe in
his definition "is not a geographic concept, but a concept
conditioned by blood." [97] And along similar lines: "The
true boundary between Asia and Europe is the boundary
which divides the Germanic from the Slavic world," and
consequently "it is our duty to put that boundary where
we want it." [98] But the "Slavic world" also includes the
West and South Slavs, who thus apparently have no part
in the coming Europe. In speaking to Halder about preparations for war in the East, Hitler came out with an un-
intentionally revealing formulation: Once Europe was
defeated, Germany would be master of Europe *and* the
Balkans;[99] thus to his way of thinking the Balkans were
not part of Europe.

This exclusion of the Slavs from the world Hitler
wished to create justified in his eyes the policy of brutality
toward the Slavic peoples implemented by Gauleiter
Erich Koch, Reich Commissioner of the Ukraine. Alfred
Rosenberg, in whom we have already discerned a feeble
glimmer of the older, romantic-conservative views on

problems of nationality, favored a policy of "national de-composition" [100] in the East. He wished to grant the peoples under German occupation a certain autonomy and so to a certain degree include them in the new European order. Under his leadership a number of experts, familiar with the East and its complex nationality problems, advocated a more humane and politically wiser policy. It is highly significant that Hitler with his intuitive understanding of men should have placed this weak-kneed writer and teacher at the head of the Ministry for [the Occupied] Eastern Territories. As Hitler surely foresaw, Rosenberg was powerless to put through his ideas over the opposition of his more powerful rivals or even of Erich Koch, who was formally his subordinate. The members of the ministry staff wrote memorandum after memorandum but never succeeded in modifying Hitler's policy. Even the experience of two years of war could not divert the terrible conqueror of living space from his obsessions. He had only contempt for Rosenberg and his "political underworld shop dating back to his own *émigré* days." He reluctantly allowed propaganda to be carried on among the Eastern peoples, but only on the express condition "that not the slightest practical inferences be drawn from it." [101]

The Latin peoples also had no place in Hitler's so-called Europe. The three great nations without which the history and achievement of Europe are unthinkable stood in very different relations to the Reich—Italy was its friend and ally, Spain was neutral, and France defeated—yet there was an unmistakable similarity in his attitude of coolness toward all three; all were looked upon as alien and excluded from his plans for the future. He had long ceased to look up to Mussolini as a model; he had become a partner in need of support, virtually a satellite. Hitler had tried for years to delude himself and others about the Italian potential, disregarding early objective reports by German observers.[102] Overestimating his ally[103] and not wishing to impair his prestige, he had not insisted on a coordinated war effort of the Axis powers but had allowed Italy to carry on its parallel war;[104] the allies took pleasure in surprising each other with their actions. The profound reason for this attitude was, however, that Hitler took no political interest in the Mediterranean region;[105] this was Italy's living space, of which Il Duce was entitled to dispose as high-handedly as Hitler did of the Greater German Reich.[106] German propaganda had always stressed the equal status of the two powers; the "pact of steel" had defined their respective living spaces.[107] Soon after Italy's entry into the war, however, Hitler could not help perceiving his ally's weakness. In intimate conversation he admitted that the Italians might wreck the nerves of the German soldiers,[108] or that after Hungary Italy was socially the sickest community in the new Europe.[109] He never permitted himself however to make such an admission publicly. In the language of the new diplomacy, Italy would enjoy an independent position side by side with Germany in the new Europe, for "it was entitled to its own living space, which it will freely shape politically, economically, and culturally in the interests of Europe as a whole." [110] But the low opinion in which the ally was held can be seen from the fact that in the resettlement plans of the SS aimed at betterment of the race the Italians were not excepted from the humiliating provisions for segregation from the German racial group.[111] The weaker the position of Italy became in the course of the war, the more the Italians, fearing that they too might become victims of the new order guided by the Reich, became bitterly distrustful of "Europe ideology." [112]

But when Italy dropped out of the war, the ideology of the two living spaces collapsed like a house of cards, and suddenly, in this late phase of the war, unrestricted expansion became the avowed policy of the Reich. Not only did the National Socialist leadership decide that the ethnic frontier of South Tyrol would be restored; they also dug up all the old claims dating from the Habsburg era with a view to situating the southern frontier of the Reich south of Venezia. Such ideas, which we first encounter in Goebbels,[113] were also taken up by Hitler, who thought of including Venezia in a loose federation that would become part of the Reich.[114] Unhampered by any sense of tradition, the champions of propagandist obfuscation and rabid power lust—while allegedly endeavoring to build a new continental order that would endure for thousands of years—were quick to abandon an axiom of their political creed.

The National Socialists had never given much thought to Spain. In 1937–1938 it had offered a convenient testing ground for new weapons and military tactics. In 1940, when Hitler was at the peak of his success, Franco turned a deaf ear to his appeals. Strikingly enough, we find in Hitler's *Table Talk* no complaints about Franco's refusal to go along with the "Felix" plan to seize Gibraltar. But Hitler regarded Spain as an utterly alien country, perhaps the only one in Europe that he would never visit.[115] For Spain was a land of religious bigotry; regardless of form of government, it had time and time again harnessed itself to the secular aims of the Church, which by that time had ceased to be anything more than a joint stock company for the exploitation of human stupidity.[116] Since Franco too recognized its power in the state, the national revolution had not yet won out and Hitler was counting on a second revolution of the Falange in Spain. For this eventuality he believed that not only the Blue Division under Muñoz Grande, then fighting on the Eastern Front, but also the 40,000 Spanish Reds still imprisoned in French camps should be held in readiness.[117] How, in view of such an outlook, could Spain, which in dissonance and harmony is an indispensable voice in the melody of Europe, have found even the most modest place in the New Order?

The same question may be asked in connection with

the central problem of the National Socialist Europe ideology, the question of the relation between Germany and France. The cultural and artistic achievements of France did not interest Hitler in the least; at the most the architectural monuments of Paris found grace in his eyes. He judged France exclusively from the standpoint of power politics, and in this respect the Russian war brought no change in his views. In those months the French made repeated attempts at *rapprochement*, based on the idea of Franco-German collaboration in building a European community; all were rebuffed. In April 1941 a few of the younger members of Darlan's cabinet suggested that a renovated France might serve "as a bridgehead and shield of Europe on the Atlantic," while the French economy would be integrated with the European economy; Hitler did not even deign to reply.[118] Similarly Pétain's attempt to obtain a German statement on the position of France was arrogantly dismissed by Ribbentrop with the observation that the attention of the leading members of the Reich government was entirely taken up by operations in the East and that there could consequently be no discussion of the questions pending between Germany and France.[119] In the eyes of Hitler and Ribbentrop such French attempts to invoke the idea of Europe and a European war on Bolshevism were a mere stratagem aimed at radically modifying the political relations between Germany and France, or worse, a barefaced insinuation that France should share in the spoils of conquest.[120] Not even the experience of the first Russian winter could move Hitler to take the slightest consideration of these French initiatives which continued until the spring of 1942.[121] He was convinced that he did not require the help of Frence arms, he regarded the French people as sick and corrupt, and he was determined to hold on to his trump cards. "We must"—this was Hitler's view according to Goebbels' diary—"exclude the military and political power of France once and for all from the future European play of forces." [122] Neither Hitler nor Goebbels ever abandoned the intention of making France pay dearly for the war; if possible the boundary of 1500 would be restored, so that "Burgundy comes back to the Reich . . . all this talk of collaboration is intended just for the moment." [123] How could a constructive policy toward France have developed from such views and intentions?

Thus Hitler's racial ideas and the political practice of his most successful years gave rise to an extremely narrow conception of Europe, a Europe confined to the part of the Continent held to be Germanic, which would be made over into the "Germanic Reich of the German Nation" and extended to the east. This would be the Reich of which he had first spoken in 1921 and which, in addressing the young National Socialist cadres at the castle of Sonthofen, in November 1937, he had declared to be the goal of German history.[124] In other words, when Hitler said Europe, he had in mind the center, north and northwest of the Continent plus an eastern hinterland, the territories where in his view the propagators of the Nordic race lived or were destined to rule. The Slavic and Latin peoples, apart from certain isolated individuals and the "Germanic" territories incorporated into France, were all racially alien; since the bloodstream was the nature-given immutable constant, these peoples were not "nationally transformable" (*umvolkbar*), hence they were useless for the German-Germanic Reich. At best they—the subjugated Slavic peoples, for example—were raw material, useful for menial labor and as a market for the cheap mass-produced articles turned out by Western industry; or if it seemed advisable, they could be ruthlessly driven out.[125]

But even in this "Germanic Reich of the German nation" which had replaced the broader idea of Europe, the accent rests clearly on the word "German." No new idea is developed; the German nation is merely extended to a wider territory. In his conception of the Reich as in his entire world outlook Hitler clung to the shallow conceptions of the late nineteenth century and in particular to the most extreme biological nationalism. The primary factor in this Germanic Reich of the German nation was to be "a self-contained national community." [126] Any number of Hitler's statements make it clear that in his opinion any attempt to reach out toward a larger supranational community was treason against one's own nation. He attacked the officials of the League of Nations who, like the rajahs of India bought out by England, or the princes of the Rhenish League in their day, let themselves be seduced by high salaries and neglected their duties to their own nation in favor of this institution.[127] He did not allow the Ministry for Eastern Affairs to employ advisers of foreign nationality. For, he explained, if they worked against their country they would be without character, while if they worked for it, they would be dangerous.[128] He believed that even the seemingly valuable members of other nationalities who fought in the legions of the Waffen SS must undergo thorough ideological schooling before being committed, because "each one of these legionaries must feel like a traitor to his own people unless he is imbued with the feeling that he belongs by blood to the great new Germanic Reich that is in the making." [129] He was skeptical of Himmler's endeavors to "fish" bearers of Nordic blood from among other peoples and of his attempts to Germanize the Dutch;[130] he wished to confine the settlement of areas made available in the East essentially to Germans and make use of members of other Germanic peoples only in numbers small enough to "be digested." [131] For this reason the press was forbidden to publish reports on the Dutch settlers in the East.[132]

When Hitler reflected on the transformation of Germany into a Germanic Reich, it was always in images originating in Bismarck's founding of the German Empire.[133] The Bismarckean empire, however, with its unique regard for all justified diversity was not his ultimate goal, but only a station on the way to his own centralistic dictatorship. And Hitler's Europe could not have differed from Hitler's Germany. True, he gave little thought to administrative or constitutional questions, the solutions envisaged were always of a centralistic nature, concentrating all the power in his hands. This by no means excluded the more or less autonomous regimes of satraps such as Erich Koch acting in defiance of the ministerial bureaucracy of the capital, provided they were devoted to him and pursued or even anticipated his plans; but it did exclude any genuine self-government. "The fact is that community can only be created and maintained by force," he proclaimed to his table companions,[134] and "a particularly high level of culture is characterized not by individual freedom but by the restriction of individual freedom through an organization comprising as many individuals as possible of like race." "Self-government leads to independence; you cannot keep with democratic institutions what you have taken by force." [135] Along the same lines he informed his eager listeners that the Dominions would support the British Empire only so long "as a strong central power can force them to." [136] And in the same spirit, from the directive of March 1942 to party organizers: "Employing the word 'Empire' the British were able to make their national possessions, extending around the globe, known to the whole world as a unified state. We must strive, with the word '*Reich*,' to make the new Germany with all its possessions known to world opinion as a self-contained political unit." [137] This positively classical inability to gain so much as an inkling of the spirit and character of the British Commonwealth (its name is not even mentioned) gives a good indication of the system of domination to be embodied in the new Reich. The "bric-a-brac of small states" would be liquidated as quickly as possible; a united Europe would "obtain a clear organization through the Germans alone." [138]

The ideas of his chief companions in arms differ only slightly from Hitler's. Goebbels' lust for conquest, it would seem, drew more on historical reminiscences and for that reason was oriented more toward the West or toward Italy,[139] whereas in regard to the East he was somewhat more perspicacious than Hitler, the fighter for living space. The ideas of the blood-and-soil ideologists surrounding Darré did not go far beyond peasant resettlement; the importance of German colonization for Europe was repeatedly stressed. Goering took an interest in the economic exploitation of all occupied territories, and Ribbentrop contented himself with loudly repeating the ideas he had gathered from the Führer.

Among the top National Socialist leaders Himmler alone showed signs of a more independent policy reflecting a somewhat different attitude. Unburdened by imagination but endowed with the primitive logic of a born policeman, he was seldom attracted to an idea, but when he was, he followed it out with fanatical method. One such idea was that the Nordic peoples constituted a master race and that all Germanic strains were of high value. Ingenuously equating German with Germanic, he believed sincerely in the possibility of a greater Germanic community and tried to pave the way for it with his SS. He wished the Waffen SS to become a Germanic fighting force.[140] More than any other top National Socialist leader he believed that Nordic elements could be sifted out from among non-German populations; this was the purpose of his biological "fishing expeditions" of which Hitler became increasingly skeptical. On occasion he revealed an almost childlike pleasure at having managed to settle a group of Germanic non-Germans somewhere in the East.[141] For these ideas he won a few supporters in other countries, even in Switzerland, and his attempts to forge a more enlightened policy are still cited in the diehard rehabilitation literature as evidence of the laudable intentions of the entire Black elite.

It is quite clear, however, that the SS as a whole did not depart from the general National Socialist attitude. This for a number of reasons. To begin with the simplest human motives, prolonged immersion in Pan-German ideas prevented the German officers and noncommissioned officers of the volunteer formations from recognizing the claim of any foreign nationality to equal rights within a greater community.[142] The chief obstacle lay in the biological nationalism at the base of the ideology of these groups. The party's supporters in other countries also wanted to eliminate the hitherto prevailing democratic, parliamentary form of government; they wanted a national renewal, first and foremost a stronger state at home and only then collaboration with a larger political community. Thus even a Quisling, a Mussert, or the Flemings with their *dietschen Staat* came into a conflict with the National Socialist conceptions of a New Order; consequently they were snubbed by Himmler's men, rival groups or individuals were favored; in other words, the friendly movements in other countries were undermined from within by their German teachers. Finally, the dual character of the SS, at once elite organization and terroristic police, also made itself felt in the non-German formations. Thus the "Germanic" volunteers were utilized from France (Joseph Darnand)[143] to Denmark (the Schalburg Corps)[144] to terrorize their own people. Soon they were hopelessly discredited, and with them everything that might have been fruitful in the German ideology. In the end "volunteers" were recruited in foreign countries (often by force) for only one reason, to provide more cannon fodder. Whatever ideological motive there may have been for such recruiting at the start, in the late period the sole motive for the recruiting of French volunteers is formulated in Gottlob Berger's* revolting words: "Every foreigner who falls means one less weeping German mother." [145] At this stage the SS formations took in everyone they could lay hands on; it was no longer possi-

---

* Chief of the SS Head Office and Himmler's representative in the Ministry for Occupied Eastern Territories.

ble to take so-called Germanic superiority into consideration or to pursue any farsighted political aims.

In view of such blatant Machiavellism it was not easy
for National Socialist propaganda to present the great
struggle in a light that would appeal to other European
peoples. Every castle in the air erected by the propagan-
dists, every promise they made, was likely to arouse ex-
pectations that the National Socialist leadership had no
intention whatever of fulfilling. But the more desperate
the struggle became, the more Hitler rejected all constructive ideas; he took "no great interest in positive plans
for building the future Europe." [146] Thus the press was
able to offer nothing more than vague generalities,
though the tone varied with the fortunes of war.[147] At first
the new continental order was interpreted very concretely
as a "war for grain and bread, for a well-stocked larder." [148]
At this time the accent was still on the claim of the
stronger to leadership and on the necessary subordination
to his law of all other aspirations on the Continent;[149] the
neutral dwarf nations were contemptuously conceded the
right to carry on "beyond good and evil their modest self-
satisfied existence of watchmaking, tourist trade, and
chocolate manufacturing." [150]

If one listens closely, the nationalistic leitmotiv is always unmistakable.[151] There is always a strong anti-
English note. England represented balance-of-power politics, internationally colored ideology, and defense of the
bourgeois-liberal world.[152]

The press was not allowed to publish serious discussions
of the future form of Europe, or the position in it of the
various nations.[153] No mention was to be made of any
autonomist strivings among the guided or conquered nations of the East or West. Time and time again orders
were issued forbidding discussion of the national policies
of the smaller nations of the Continent or of the relations
between them.[154]

After the Stalingrad tragedy, the propaganda machine

abandoned the conquest of living space and the well-stocked larder and discovered the "crisis of Europe." [155] It goes without saying that the European order was equated with the political system of the Axis powers which it was necessary to defend against Bolshevism and plutocracy, both offshoots "of a period of liberal democratic degeneration." But since the understandable reluctance of the National Socialists to divulge their true war aims resulted in an absence of political values and ideas, Goebbels' propaganda mill revived the anti-Semitic note, combining it with anti-Bolshevist propaganda to provide an emotional stimulus for the will to fight.[156] It was only when the possibility of defeat came to be taken seriously that even Hitler, in his more and more infrequent public appearances, remembered the "European family of nations" and "the oldest continent of culture" which "the German army and the countries allied with us and hence Europe" were defending.[157] And the Reich press chief saw fit to open a European congress of journalists with a plea for "the great culture-creating nations of the Continent." [158] And now even a renovated France was invited "to take its place" in the new Europe, "for the welfare of the totality and of every individual." [159] Such late lip service to "Europe" could no longer convince anyone. And yet it is only logical that in the period of decline National Socialist propaganda should have returned to the gentler strains and amiable generalities with which in happier days it had spread a veil of innocence over the menacing accumulation of German power.

In conclusion let us see what the works of National Socialist writers on political law had to say of the projected new order. Astonishingly enough, their organ, the periodical *Reich, Volksordnung, Lebensraum,* founded in 1941,[160] was allowed to engage in ideological discussion. As the title indicates, "Europe" was not among its preoccupations. Its ideas revolved rather around the Reich as the "goal of all German striving" [161] and around the con-

cept of *Grossraum,* which was to supersede the old conceptions of international law and sovereign national
states. Its contributors went so far as to develop a whole
philosophy of "space as the shaper of domestic and foreign
policy." [162]

The *Grossraum* concept as such is of pre-National Socialist origin and was at first purely economic in content.
It arose in connection with endeavors to restore the economic ties developed in the Habsburg Empire and
abruptly broke off when the empire was broken down into
separate states by the Paris treaties of 1919.[163] But in the
late thirties the idea was taken up from the standpoint of
international law. Carl Schmitt among others attacked
existing international law as obsolete and unrealistic because it adhered to the universal concept "state" and the
juridical equality of all sovereign states.[164] Schmitt however wished only to modify international law, not to destroy it; he recognized that the hitherto prevailing concept
of "state" implied the minimum of calculable organization and inner discipline which must be regarded as the
foundation of any concrete "community of nations."

The more strictly National Socialist authorities on political law went further. They criticized Schmitt's identification with the outworn "individualistic state and individualistic legal system." [165] Carrying his ideas further,
they conceived of a *"Grossraum* order based on nationalistic [*völkish*] political theory." [166] Though Höhn, director of the Intitute for Political Research at the University
of Berlin, did not for the present venture to formulate a
complete doctrine and discipline, former Ambassador
Werner Daitz did just that: he gave the *Grossraum* theory
biological content and defined a *Grossraum* as the natural
living space of a family of nations or race.[167] In this
perspective he found six greater living areas [*Grossle-
bensräume*]: that of the East Asians, that of the Indo-
Malayan family of peoples, that of the black race, North
America, South America, and that of the European fam-

ily of nations, which extended from Gibraltar to the Urals and from North Cape to the coast of North Africa. Along with the notion of "biological Monroe Doctrines" he proclaimed a new economic ethic, to wit, that each nation should satisfy its needs in its own greater living space and should also give political and cultural preference to its own living space.[168] Within each *Grossraum* there was to be a "family-of-nations law" [*Völkerfamilienrecht*] while its external relations were to be governed by an "inter-*Grossraum* law" [*Zwischengrossraumrecht*]. Both internally and externally the family of nations is the bearer of the supreme will and sovereignty of the *Grossraum;* as a rule, however, the primary representative of this will and sovereignty is the leading power within the family of nations.[169] Within each *Grossraum,* "the future juridical and political order will have to take the achievement of the different nations as the measure of their political structure, i.e. of their freedom within the common bond." [170] According to a long Western tradition, international law, that normative principle rising above the laws of separate states, is grounded in divine decree or in natural law; now the National Socialist jurists, going even further than positivist legal theory, robbed it of its universal validity, fragmented and biologized it, making it the instrument of a "realistic" order governed by the day-to-day struggle for power. Now the small nations are deprived not only of the protection of a universally valid concept of justice, but even of the possibility of asking the assistance of an outside power; they are at the mercy, for better or for worse, of the nation that is the guardian and leader of their *Grossraum.* The economic policy of the New Order already demanded the adjustment of all nations to the needs of the German economy, and now the authorities on political law were doing their bit to complete the dependency of those subjected to German leadership.

It goes without saying that such a political theory rejects the idea of a balance of power as a regulative. Balance is understood only in terms of a mechanical, quantitative measurement of power after the manner of the eighteenth-century financiers, and is criticized for its destructive, fragmenting effect in history.

> Such a mechanical unit, built slowly of quantitatively determined elements is . . . necessarily without leadership. Its unity results exclusively from the automatic workings of certain laws, not from conscious, personal action. The unity of this totality has consequently no visible and effective representation in a leading power, it is merely an imaginary point, that is, precisely, the pivot of a scales.[171]

These writers deliberately ignore the very concrete content which the balance-of-power principle gave the European concert of nations in the nineteenth century, namely, recognition of an idea regulating the entire community of states, so that limits were set to the expansion of any one state and many nations were enabled to develop freely, each in its own way. They ignore everything which for a whole century made the balance of power the guarantor of a rich, highly differentiated European development.[172] But National Socialist political theory saw its own function precisely in destroying the diversity of political forms and hence also the concept of sovereignty which safeguarded the existence of small states. The doctrine of sovereignty is condemned both for its historical crimes and for its disastrous effects in the present. Not only did it destroy the Holy Roman Empire but even today it makes all true leadership and followership in the life of nations impossible, that is, "it paralyzes the foreign policy of leading nations and prevents them from building empires." The idea of sovereignty also inoculates the small nations with ruinous presumption, takes up too much of their attention, and prevents them from taking their "natural and appropriate place in the order of nations." [173]

Once deprived of the concept of sovereignty as a safeguard against the superior power of the empire nation
[*Reichsvolk*], the subject peoples could not look to the
theory of human rights for salvation. National Socialism
had robbed the members of its own nation of their universal dignity and degraded them into "national comrades," whose rank and worth were measured exclusively
by their utility to the National Socialist community. The
citizen no longer found fulfillment as a subject of the political community but had become an object; he was
"taken over" [*erfasst*]. The state

> systematically takes over the human beings subject to
> it, in order to employ them rationally for its purposes.
> . . . In the future the German state will never again be
> of the opinion that mere formal integration with the
> state structure provides it with citizens; only a man who
> has been taken over in nature and spirit, that is, in-
> wardly and completely, will be regarded as a true citizen
> of the Reich.[174]

This sentence which a National Socialist professor at a
German university penned in cold blood, without blush-
ing for shame at his own degradation, designates very
clearly the deepest problem attendant on this Reich
building. Even members of the Reich are appraised by
several different standards. The perspectives of the *Grossraum* theorists were not narrowed by the Nordic racial
fanaticism we have encountered in Hitler. They looked
upon all European peoples, with the exception of the
Jews of course, as racially close enough to them to be fellow members and bearers of the Reich.[175] They proclaimed respect for foreign nationality,[176] promised the
peoples in the *Grossraum* protected by the Reich "freedom to maintain their mode of life and cultural
activity." [177] But if the peoples were permitted to develop
in accordance with their own will and feeling, how could
they be taken over body and soul like good National Socialist citizens? Thus either these nations, where they

were not reduced to the level of helots, were condemned to live on the political outskirts in reservations that the Reich deigned to grant them, a possibility open only to insignificant groups; or else they would have to renounce their individuality and allow themselves to be fully taken over in order to become citizens. The total leadership state is capable of development only toward more efficient means of coercion and subjugation, not in the direction of equal rights and coexistence. Quite understandably, the *Grossraum* theoreticians were no more able than any other National Socialist to solve the dilemma. Whenever the problem came up, they spoke of the living dynamic of the Reich that would benefit all the nations that joined it in the struggle, and, in the hope of diverting their thoughts from the caged existence in store for them, attempted to lure the subordinate nations with the undreamed-of economic upsurge guaranteed by the still untapped raw materials that would become available in the colonial lands to the east.

From whatever angle one approaches the problem, the practical policies of those years and, once the thin veil of propaganda is pierced, the National Socialist mind, disclose not a concern for Europe but a radical, unrestricted nationalist drive for conquest and domination.

Hitler's career suggests a comparison with the great Corsican conqueror who over a century ago subjected Europe to his military domination and met his doom in the snowy wastes of Russia; the comparison is all too obvious, for which reason Hitler himself, even at the peak of his success in the East, was not at all pleased with the publication of Bouhler's book on Napoleon, fearing that the modern reader, letting his thoughts pursue their own course, might envision a similar doom for the modern conqueror. But even on superficial observation the fundamental difference between the two men is evident. Napoleon tamed the French Revolution, but he also perpetuated its ideas and carried them out; he was inspired by

the Revolution and also bound by it; in his conquests, as
has rightly been said, he shattered states but liberated
peoples. Hitler, on the other hand, was not the creature of
the Brown Revolution; he was at all times in command of
it. The ideology he created was merely for his own benefit. Guided exclusively by the calculations of the moment,
he looked on ideas as mere expedients and for this very
reason regarded himself as the greatest of practical politicians. Despite his initial success he left nothing behind
him but ruins—like all adepts of cheap Machiavellism.
When Napoleon found himself obliged to end his days on
a rocky island far out in the Atlantic, he gave free rein to
his imagination and painted a picture of his "true" aims,
which he had been prevented from carrying out. This
Mémorial de Sainte-Hélène was the spiritual foundation
of the *Idées Napoleoniennes,* that gospel of the liberation
of Europe from reactionary oppression and arbitrary dis-
memberment, with which his nephew paved the way for
his rise to power. While preparing for the death that he
himself had chosen, Hitler too wrote a political testament.
Apart from protestations of innocence and a last outburst
of hatred against the Jews, it contained nothing but a
summons to the people and army he had led to their ruin
to resist to the death, in order that their bloody sacrifices
might provide the seed for a radiant rebirth of the National Socialist movement. To attempt, on the strength of
this legacy, to build up a legend to the effect that Hitler's
"true" aim, which he had been prevented from carrying
out, was a European community secure against Bolshevism, is to ask too much of human forgetfulness. If we are
looking for a European idea in the Germany of that time,
a sense of responsibility for the old Continent and its im-
perishable though always threatened values, we shall have
to turn not to National Socialism but to the German resistance movement.

NOTES

1. Ludwig Dehio, *Gleichgewicht oder Hegemonie*, Krefeld, 1948.
2. Hajo Holborn, *The Political Collapse of Europe*, New York, 1951.
3. *Ibid.*, pp. 138 ff.
4. *Ibid.*, p. 148. Great Britain and France "had no conception of a political system in which Germany would have full equality of status without being able to gain supremacy."
5. Otto Westphal, *Weltgeschichte der Neuzeit 1750–1950*, Stuttgart, 1953.
6. *Ibid.*, p. 327.
7. In a recently published article, which must however have been conceived some years ago, Geoffrey Barraclough has called attention to the dangers of historical misunderstanding inherent in the explanation of Germany's action by an "Occidental" mission: "Geschichtschreibung und Politik im neuen Deutschland," *Aussenpolitik*, November 1954, pp. 720–729.
8. Meeting of the Deutsche Arbeiterpartei on February 11, 1919. Photocopy at Institut für Zeitgeschichte. See also W. W. Pese, "Hitler und Italien" in *Vierteljahrshefte für Zeitgeschichte*, No. 3, 1955, pp. 120 f.
9. Report on a meeting at the Kindl-Keller on January 4, in *Völkischer Beobachter* (hereinafter cited as VB) for January 9, 1921, and on a celebration of the foundation of the German Empire, *ibid.*, January 20, 1921.
10. VB, January 1, 1921.
11. At the Hofbräuhaus on November 19, 1920, *ibid.*, 1920, No. 102.
12. *Mein Kampf*, 1st ed., 1925, Vol. I, p. 147; popular edition, p. 154.
13. *Mein Kampf*, Vol. II, 1927, pp. 312, 316; popular edition, pp. 738, 742.
14. *Mein Kampf*, Vol. II, p. 319; popular edition, p. 747.
15. VB, May 20, 1930.
16. Hermann Rauschning, *Gespräche mit Hitler*, pp. 30, 44 ff.
17. "Neue Dokumente zur Geschichte der Reichswehr 1930–1933. Kommentiert von Thilo Vogelsang," *Vierteljahrshefte für Zeitgeschichte*, No. 2, 1954, p. 434.
18. Gottfried Feder, *Das Programm der NSDAP und seine weltanschaulichen Grundgedanken*, 3rd ed., Munich, 1928, p. 19. Hitler had already abandoned his claims to the South Tyrol. Cf. Pese, *op. cit.*, pp. 118, 121 ff.
19. Rosenberg developed his ideas most clearly in a speech on

"Krisis und Neugeburt Europas" delivered at the "Volta-Congress" of the Royal Italian Academy in Rome in November 1932. Reprinted in *Blut und Ehre,* Vol. I, pp. 296 ff.

20. *Ibid.,* p. 311.

21. He still spoke in these terms in his speech on "Altes und neues Europa" in Vienna on March 13, 1940. Rosenberg, *Tradition und Gegenwart,* Munich, 1941, Vol. IV, pp. 359 ff.

22. Theodor Heuss, *Hitlers Weg,* Stuttgart, Berlin and Leipzig, 1932, p. 102.

23. F. W. Heinz, *Die Nation greift an. Geschichte und Kritik des soldatischen Nationalismus,* Berlin, 1933, p. 9. Italics added.

24. The interview took place on September 9, 1933, in Berchtesgaden. A stenographic transcript of sorts is in the records of the trial of de Brinon for collaboration, published in *Les Procès de Collaboration,* Paris, 1948, pp. 78–80. De Brinon published a sensational article on the interview in *Le Matin,* while characteristically VB did not devote a single line to it.

25. Speech of March 7, 1936, and especially the "great Karlsruhe peace speech" of March 13, each published in VB for the following day.

26. *Op. cit.,* p. 145.

27. Concluding speech at the Nuremberg party congress of 1936. *Der Parteitag der Ehre,* Munich, 1936, p. 303.

28. VB, September 15, 1937.

29. *Akten zur deutschen auswärtigen Politik 1918–1945, Serie D* (hereinafter cited as DD), Vol. I, pp. 47–49.

30. Cf. Keith Feiling, *The Life of Neville Chamberlain,* London, 1946, Chaps. 23, 24; Craig-Gilbert, *The Diplomats,* pp. 548 ff.; DD, Vol. I, p. 217 (thus this was even Ribbentrop's impression!) and pp. 223–225.

31. DD, Vol. I, No. 138.

32. The way in which it was carried out was distasteful even to leading Austrians in the Greater German camp, such as Seyss-Inquart and Wolf.

33. E.g., in a communication to the Hungarians of September 20, 1938, DD, Vol. II, No. 554.

34. In his first report from Berlin on December 15, 1938, the new French ambassador, Robert Coulondre, astutely recognized that this was a consistent step in the carrying out of an unswerving policy, that there had merely been a change of emphasis. He wrote: *"La première partie du programme de Mr. Hitler—intégration du Deutschtum dans le Reich—est exécutée dans son ensemble: c'est maintenant l'heure du 'Lebensraum' qui sonne." Le Livre Jaune Français, Documents diplomatiques 1938–1940.* Ministère des Affaires etrangères, Paris, 1939, No. 33, p. 45.

35. *Verpflichtendes Erbe. Volkstum im Ringen um seinen Bestand und seine Anerkennung,* Kiel, 1954, esp. pp. 44 ff.

36. Cf. Kurt Trampler, *Die Krise des Nationalstaates. Das Nation-*

alitätenproblem im neuen Europa, Munich, 1932. Also the magazine *Nation und Staat. Deutsche Zeitschrift für das europäische Nationalitätenproblem,* published by Braumüller-Verlag, Vienna.

37. The words of Pastor Schmidt-Wodder at the 12th Congress of Nationalities in Geneva, 1936. A paper on "Das Lebensrecht der Völker" read at the congress was published in *Nation und Staat,* Vol. X, p. 12.

38. Cf. H. von Rimscha, "Paul Schiemann," in *Jahrbücher für die Geschichte Osteuropas,* New Series, Vol. II, pp. 475 ff. In 1938 Schiemann returned disillusioned to his home in Riga and did not participate in the Baltic resettlement of 1939.

39. DD, Vol. V, p. 112, 119 f., 126.

40. Article II of the treaty of September 28, 1939. Carroll-Epstein, *Deutschland und die Sowietunion 1939–1941,* p. 117.

41. "Der grossdeutsche Freiheitskampf," in *Reden Adolf Hitler,* Munich, 1940, Vol. I, p. 82.

42. *Ibid.,* p. 90.

43. The first issue appeared on May 26, 1940.

44. Address at a congress of the Austrian Academy of Administration (cf. VB, September 2 and 4, 1938). Also Carl Schmitt, "Der Reichsbegriff im Völkerrecht," in *Positionen und Begriffe,* Hamburg, 1940, p. 307.

45. In "Verfügung R. 121/39" of June 13, 1939. *Verfügungen, Anordnungen, Bekanntgaben,* Munich, n.d., Vol. I, p. 206.

46. "Verfügung V. I 23/306" of March 21, 1942, *loc. cit.,* p. 206.

47. E.g., Seyss-Inquart in his book *Idee und Gestalt des Reiches,* published without indication of place or date, apparently (cf. p. 26) immediately after the outbreak of the war with Russia.

48. E.g., Eugen Mündler, editor in chief, in *Das Reich* for June 30, 1940.

49. R. W. Darré, "Die Marktordnung der NS-Agrarpolitik als Schrittmacher einer neuen europäischen Aussenhandelsordnung. Rede vom 25.1.1939 vor der Kommission für Wirtschaftspolitik." Reprinted in Darré, *Blut und Boden,* Munich, 1940, pp. 511 ff.

50. *Ibid.,* p. 519.

51. Economic editor Doctor John Brech, "Europa findet sich. Konturen künftiger Festlandswirtschaft," *Das Reich,* 1st issue, May 26, 1940.

52. John Brech, "Europa ohne Übersee," *Das Reich,* June 16, 1940. Brech, "Raumplanung. Wirtschaftliche Neuausrichtung der Erdteile," *Das Reich,* June 30, 1940. Eugen Mündler in the leading article of the same issue, etc.

53. VB, July 26, 1940; cf. also *Hitler's Europe. Survey of International Affairs 1939–1946,* ed. Alfred and Veronica Toynbee, London, 1945, pp. 47 f. I owe a number of ideas to this collection.

54. "Rede in Wien," *Das Reich,* September 8, 1940.

55. Max Clauss, "Tatsache Europa," *Das Reich,* October 20, 1940.

56. Anton Reinthaler (Assistant Secretary in the Reich Food

Ministry), "Deutschen Lebensraum. Voraussetzungen nationalsoz-ialistischer Grosswirtschaft," *Das Reich,* August 4, 1940.

57. Nuremberg Document 1155–PS, IMT XXVII, pp. 28 ff.

58. "Aussagen Dr. Globke vom 25.9.1945," Nuremberg Document 513–F, IMT XXXVII, pp. 218 f. Doctor Globke's memory seems to have played him false. These plans were drawn up in the summer of 1940 and not at the end of the year as he states.

59. Entry for August 30, 1940, in diary of Foreign Minister Paul Baudouin. *The Private Diaries of Paul Baudouin,* London, 1948, p. 224.

60. *Ibid.,* p. 274. At the time of publication, I was not yet able to consult Louis Rougier, *Les accords secrets franco-britanniques,* Paris, 1954.

61. As late as the period of the *Sitzkrieg* two pamphlets were de-voted to this subject: Arnst Anrich, *Die Bedrohung Europas durch Frankreich. 300 Jahre Hegemoniestreben aus Anmassung und Angst,* Berlin, 1940, and Wolfgang von Franqué, *Deutschland und Frank-reich. Eine wertende Rückschau,* Bonn, 1940.

62. *Schwarzes Korps,* August 22, 1940.

63. Eugen Mündler in *Das Reich,* July 21, 1940. On July 4 *Schwarzes Korps* wrote: "With the bastion of Paris the last demo-cratic nest of resistance on the European mainland has fallen. . . . Democracy returns dying whence it came [to England]."

64. Reinhard Höhn, *Frankreichs Demokratie und ihr geistiger Zusammenbruch,* Darmstadt, 1940, 76 ff. This pamphlet was written in April 1940. In September 1940 there appeared by the same author: *Frankreichs demokratische Mission in Europa und ihr Ende.* Darmstadt, 2nd ed., 1941, 222 ff.

65. In his *Histoire de Vichy 1940–1944,* Paris, 1954, pp. 196–217, Robert Aron points to the antidemocratic nationalism of the Action française, the personalism of the young Catholics, and an economic corporatism as the foundations of this "national revolution." There is no doubt that Christian belief in the image and value of the personality remained an indestructible force in this revolution, and in the economic sphere the development of the "corporations" was designed as a safeguard against excessive government intervention.

66. In an article in *La Revue des deux mondes,* September 15, 1940; Aron, *op. cit.,* p. 215.

67. Leading editorial in *Schwarzes Korps,* July 11, 1940.

68. "Michel ist geheilt," *Schwarzes Korps,* June 6, 1940.

69. At the end of July the Reich Press Propaganda Office issued the following directive: "We no more forget the guilt of present-day France toward Germany than that of past generations. . . . France as a great power has been destroyed and will never be restored." "Geheimes Presserundschreiben II/384/40," unpublished, Archiv des Instituts für Zeitgeschichte (hereinafter cited as Archiv des IfZ).

70. *Schwarzes Korps,* October 3, 1940.
71. *Das Reich,* August 25, 1940.
72. This is the opinion of Robert Aron, *op. cit.,* pp. 101 f. Unfortunately he does not indicate his source.
73. Willy Krogmann, *Breiz da Vreiziz. Die Bretagne der Bretonen. Zeugnisse zum Freiheitskampf der Bretonen,* Halle, 1940. As early as September the periodicals were forbidden to review the book: "Vertrauliche Informationen für Zeutschriften No. 114/40," unpublished, Archiv des IfZ.
74. On Thomasset, M. H. Böhm, *Geheimnisvolles Burgund. Werden und Vergehen eines europäischen Schicksalslandes,* Munich, 1944, pp. 389 f.
75. J. Thomasset, *Verhülltes Licht,* Berlin, 1940, a translation of *Pages bourguignonnes,* Brussels, 1938.
76. According to oral information received from Doctor Ludwig Jedlicka of Vienna, the Haus-, Hof- und Staatsarchiv in Vienna was commissioned in 1940 to compile from source material in the Burgundian Chancellery a memorandum demonstrating the Reich's historical claim to Burgundy.
77. Böhm, *Geheimnisvolles Burgund,* see note 74 above.
78. "Himmler an Frauenfeld 10.7.42," Nuremberg Document No.–2417 (unpublished).
79. Eugene Schaeffer, *L'Alsace et la Lorraine 1940–1945. Leur occupation en droit et en fait,* Paris, 1953, esp. pp. 73 ff.
80. "Vertrauliche Informationen für Zeitschriften No. 101/40," unpublished, Archiv des IfZ.
81. Baudouin, *op. cit.,* pp. 216, 229.
82. Ambassador Abetz, to be sure, claims that Bürckel's stupidity was responsible for the deportations from Lorraine: Otto Abetz, *Das offene Problem,* Cologne, 1951, pp. 166 ff.
83. Baudouin, *op. cit.,* p. 276.
84. Nuremberg Document NO–3531 (unpublished). Reichskommissar für die Festigung deutschen Volkstums, *Der Menscheneinsatz. Grundsätze, Anordnungen und Richtlinien,* 1st supplement, published September 1941, pp. 39 ff.
85. Nuremberg Document 1470–PS (unpublished).
86. Nuremberg Document NO–1600 (unpublished), September–October 1942.
87. Nuremberg Document NO–5211 (unpublished), December 5, 1942.
88. "Vertauliche Informationen für Zeitschriften 121/40," n.d. Circular 122/40 gives directives for the evaluation of the meeting between Hitler and Mussolini in Florence on October 27, 1940. Every meeting between the two statesmen, so the circular declared, had made a contribution to the creation of a new Europe which was engaged in freeing itself from British imperialism.
89. *Ibid.,* 125/40.

90. Reichspropagandaamt, "Geheimes Presserundschreiben II/ 466/40," dated November 6, 1940.

91. "Vertrauliche Informationen für Zeitschriften R. Spr. No. 275, Inf. No. 48," June 26, 1941.

92. "Vertrauliche Informationen R. Spr. No. 137, Inf. No. 49," June 30, 1941: "Reports from all sides indicate an unprecedented campaign of all Europe against Bolshevism. Europe is marching against the common enemy in unparalleled solidarity, rising up as it were against the oppressor of all human culture and civilization. This birth of the new Europe is taking place without command or coercion on the part of the Germans. Small nations, even the smallest, are showing that they have understood the common European task by summoning their peoples to sacrifice the blood of their sons for the common ideal. For this reason we will not speak of a crusade. This situation confronts the periodical press with an enormous task, for precisely in respect to America it is indispensable that the unanimity of Europe in the struggle against Bolshevism should be clearly expressed for the benefit of the New World. And now moreover the great hour has come for puncturing the English phrase and contention that Adolf Hitler is a dictator who like a modern Genghis Khan hurries restlessly from country to country because his aggression spurs him on to new and vaster fields. On the contrary, Adolf Hitler has shown himself to be the standard-bearer of Europe for a common culture and civilization, and as such is meeting with the enthusiastic approval of the entire European world."

93. *Ibid.*, "Inf. No. 52."

94. *Ibid.*, "Inf. No. 5/41."

95. Nuremberg Document L–221, IMT, XXXVIII, p. 88.

96. The incorrigible Hans Grimm holds that the *Tischgespräche* "with their South German slovenliness" can be excluded as a historical source and prefers to take the Winter Aid speech of October 8, 1942, as a source for Hitler's aims. Hans Grimm, *Warum-Woher—Aber wohin?* Lippoldsberg, 1954, p. 402.

97. Henry Picker, *Hitlers Tischepräche im Führerhauptquartier 1941–1942*, Bonn, 1951, p. 45 (conversations of November 8–11, 1941).

98. *Hitler's Table Talk 1941–1944*, London, 1953, p. 37 (conversation of September 23, 1941). Hitler spoke in a similar vein in the conference of July 16, 1941, Nuremberg Document L–221, see note 95 above.

99. Franz Halder, diary entry for July 7, 1940.

100. This is the formulation of Peter Kleist, *Zwischen Hitler und Stalin*, Bonn, 1950, p. 141.

101. "Besprechung Hitlers mit Keitel vom 8.6.1943," reprinted in George Fischer, "Vlasov und Hitler," *Journal of Modern History*, 1951, pp. 58 ff. Cf. "Dokumentation zu Hitlers Ostpolitik im Som-

mer 1943," in *Vierteljahrshefte für Zeitgeschichte,* No. 2, 1954, pp. 307 ff.

102. Von Rintelen, the German military attaché, tells us that a memorandum on the Italian army and its armament prepared by him for the German General Staff in the winter of 1938–1939 was pulped by orders from above. Enno von Rintelen, *Mussolini als Bundesgenosse,* Tübingen, 1951, p. 55.

103. *Ibid.,* p. 89.

104. *Ibid.,* pp. 87–136. Also Elizabeth Wiskemann, *The Rome-Berlin Axis,* London, 1949; S. Westphal, *Heer in Fesseln,* Berlin, 1950, p. 154.

105. Cf. von Rintelen, *op. cit.,* p. 92.

106. As late as May 13, 1942, Hitler recognized that he had no interests in the Mediterranean. *Table Talk,* p. 479.

107. In the third paragraph of the preamble to the treaty of alliance of May 1939. *Reichsgesetzblatt,* 1939, Part II, p. 826.

108. *Table Talk,* p. 660.

109. *Ibid.,* p. 117.

110. "Standard-Thesen und Richtlinien für die deutsche Auslandspropaganda. Geheime Reichssache. These Nr. 25, 4, angeordnet am 5.11.1942."

111. Gauleiter Murr on August 17, 1942: No exceptions to be made of Italians in the deportations from Alsace, Nuremberg Document 1470–PS (unpublished); on projected deportation of Italians from Luxemburg at the end of the war, Nuremberg Document NO–1792 (unpublished).

112. Cf. Abetz, *Das offene Problem,* pp. 200, 234.

113. *Goebbels Tagebücher aus den Jahren 1942–1943,* ed. Louis P. Lochner, Zürich, 1948, p. 408. Goebbels' justification: "By their disloyalty and treachery the Italians have lost all claim to be a modern national state."

114. *Ibid.,* p. 441. The tourist trade from the Reich would serve as a sop to Venice.

115. *Table Talk,* p. 515.

116. *Ibid.,* p. 607.

117. *Ibid.,* pp. 520, 568, 607. *Tischgespräche,* p. 108.

118. *Memorandum d'Abetz sur les Rapports Franco-Allemands,* Paris, 1948, pp. 79 ff.

119. Verbal note from Pétain of July 14 and Instruction from Ribbentrop to Abetz of August 13, 1941. Abetz, *Das offene Problem,* pp. 197 ff., and *Memorandum d'Abetz,* pp. 107–116.

120. Cf. Hitler's remarks in the same above-mentioned conference of July 16, 1941, Nuremberg Document L–221, IMT, Vol. XXXVIII.

121. *Memorandum d'Abetz,* pp. 117–140; Robert Aron, *Histoire de Vichy 1940–1944,* Paris, 1954, pp. 425 ff., 502, 511 ff.

122. *Goebbels Tagebücher,* March 7, 1942, p. 114; cf. also p. 150.

123. *Goebbels Tagebücher*, April 26, 1942, p. 177. The same attitude is shown in an entry for May 5, 1943; unpublished photocopy of the diaries, Vol. 23, p. 2262, Archiv des IfZ.

124. Hitler's speech of November 23, 1937, is reprinted as an appendix to the *Tischgespräche*, pp. 443 ff.

125. The racial doctrine is summed up in a politically utilizable form in Egon Leuschner's book, sponsored by the Rassenpolitisches Amt: *Nationalsozialismus—Fremdvolkpolitik.* Undated, presumably published before the Russian campaign.

126. Sonthofen speech (cf. note 124, above), *loc. cit.*, p. 446.

127. *Tischgespräche*, p. 54.

128. Note by Hewel on a visit by Rosenberg to the Führer's headquarters on May 19, 1943. Nuremburg Document NG–3288 (unpublished).

129. *Tischgespräche*, p. 68.

130. *Ibid.*, p. 66.

131. Nuremberg Document 1520–PS, IMT, Vol. XXVII, p. 288. Cf. also *Table Talk*, p. 16.

132. *Presserundschreiben* II/26/42 of June 15, 1942.

133. *Tischgespräche*, pp. 98, 102.

134. On April 11, 1942. *Tischgespräche*, p. 71.

135. *Ibid.*, p. 50.

136. *Ibid.*, p. 47. In March 1940 he put hopes in the increase of imperialist sentiment in the United States and hence in a demand for the annexation of Canada. Interview with Colin Rose on March 12, 1940, German diplomatic records, Series D, Vol. VIII, London, 1954, No. 671.

137. *Verfügungen, Anordnungen und Bekanntgaben*, Vol. I, p. 206.

138. Hitler's address to the *Reichsleiter* and *Gauleiter* after the official funeral ceremony at the Chancellery (May 1943) for Lutze, who had been killed in an accident. Goebbels gives the content of the speech in his diary, *op. cit.*, pp. 322 ff.

139. See page 370 above. Robert Coulondre reports that in his Summer Solstice speech of 1939 Goebbels declared (the sentence was of course suppressed in the official record of the festival) that Germany intended to recover all the countries that had belonged to it in the course of history. Report to Paris of June 22, 1939. *Livre Jaune*, No. 143, p. 194.

140. As early as April 13, 1940, instructions went out to recruit troops in Denmark and Norway. Nuremberg Document NO–5897; on May 13, 1940, Berger met with Dutch National Socialists in Düsseldorf, and on May 25, 1940, Hitler issued the order to found the Dutch "Westland" Standard, Documents NO–5717 and 5742. By December 1940, Berger took measures to establish SS formations in Flanders, Document NG–3481 (all unpublished).

141. For example, in a letter of January 3, 1943, to Generalgouverneur Frank, Document NO–2444 (unpublished).

142. Cf., for example, the complaints of the Flemings about the German officers of their unit, Nuremberg Document NO–942 (unpublished).

143. Cf. the record of the trial of Darnand in the collection *Les Procès de la Collaboration*, pp. 243–347.

144. Cf. Nuremberg Document NG–3910, NO–607, NO–914 (unpublished).

145. "Berger an den Höheren SS- und Polizeiführer Frankreich am 8. February 1944," Nuremberg Document NO–5618 (unpublished).

146. "Goebbels-Tagebuch zum 21.5.1945," unpublished, photocopy in Archiv des IfZ, Vol. 25, p. 2446.

147. This development can be most readily followed in *Das Reich*, which set the tone for the controlled press and whose leading editorial was regularly supplied by Goebbels from the end of 1940 on.

148. Goebbels in the leading editorial "Wofür?" in *Das Reich*, May 31, 1942.

149. "Das neue Europa," *ibid.*, October 4, 1942.

150. *Ibid.*, November 8, 1942.

151. "Vom Sinn des Krieges," *ibid.*, August 23, 1942: The national living-space thesis. "Der Segen der Erde," *ibid.*, October 18, 1942: We are living in the century of national development. "Die neue Ordnung," *ibid.*, November 15, 1942: The German nation is only in the making, etc.

152. "Die Vision eines neuen Europa," *ibid.*, December 6, 1942.

153. Confidential instructions to the press of June 9, 1941: "Remarks on the future forms of coexistence of the nations in general or from particular points of view are to be avoided."

154. As already in "Anweisung vom 26.6.1941, J Nr. 48": "Strivings for independence of nationalities within the Soviet Union are not to be mentioned . . . Nationality maps are not authorized." Similar instructions in "Geheime Presserundschrieben des Reichspropagandaamtes" vom 3.2.1942, II/6/42; vom 23.11.1942, II/48/42; vom 25.2.1943, II/4/43; vom 15.11.1943, II.4043. Archiv des IfZ.

155. *Das Reich*, February 28, 1942.

156. "Geheime Presseanweisung II/12/43" of May 3, 1943: "Reports which do not on the face of them offer an anti-Semitic possibility are to be made into such anti-Semitic propaganda." An example of how this is to be done follows. And as late as May 1944 the Propaganda Ministry reminded the press that the anti-Semitic and anti-Bolshevist campaign was still in the public interest. *Ibid.*, II/II, 14.

157. "Proklamation zum 31.1.1943," *Keesings Archiv*, p. 5808; similarly in a speech to officer candidates on November 29, 1943, *ibid.*, p. 6184; and in his radio address of January 30, 1944, *ibid.*, pp. 6256 ff.

158. *Das Reich*, June 27, 1943.

159. Reichspressechef Dietrich at a press conference in Paris on January 15, 1944. VB, January 16, 1944.

160. *Reich, Volksordnung, Lebensraum, Zeitschrift für völkische Verfassung und Verwaltung. Herausgegeben von Wilhelm Stuckart, Werner Best, Gerhard Klopfer, Rudolf Lehmann, Reinhard Höhn.* Most of the significant articles are in the first two volumes, which appeared in 1941. The last volume to appear was Vol. VI, in 1943.

161. "Geleitwort der Herausbeber," in *ibid.,* Vol. I.

162. This was the title of an article by Herbert Krüger in *ibid.,* Vol. I.

163. R. Höhn, "Grossraumordnung und völkisches Rechtsdenken," *ibid.,* Vol. I, p. 260, contains a reference to *Grossraumwirtschaft,* a compendium edited in 1931 by Gürz and Grotkopp.

164. Carl Schmitt, "Der Reichsbegriff im Völkerrecht" (1939), in *Positionen und Begriffe,* pp. 303 ff.

165. Höhn, "Grossraumordnung und völkisches Rechtsdenken," *loc. cit.,* Vol. I, p. 281.

166. *Ibid.,* pp. 284 ff.

167. Werner Daitz, "Echte und unechte Grossraume, *ibid.,* Vol. II, pp. 75–96, esp. pp. 81, 83.

168. *Ibid.,* p. 88.

169. *Ibid.,* p. 92.

170. *Ibid.,* p. 91.

171. H. Krüger, "Der Raum als Gestalter der Innen- und Aussen-politik," *ibid.,* Vol. I, p. 135.

172. An appreciation of the function of a balance of power is well expressed by the foreign minister of a small state: Grigore Gafencu, *Vorspiel zum Krieg im Osten,* Zürich, 1944; cf. esp. p. 49, where he demands that the idea of a balance of power preside over the reconstruction of Europe: "A balance of power in the interior of the Continent in order to secure unity and justice and respect for the rights of each country; a balance of power on the outer confines of the Continent, where the border states must be restored and grouped, in order to secure and defend the interests and essential positions of universal peace; balance and moderation in the definition of European intentions and demands, which must be directed against no one and opposed to no other continent."

173. Krüger, *loc. cit.,* Vol. I, pp. 158 f.

174. *Ibid.,* pp. 125–127.

175. *Ibid.,* p. 164; Daitz, *loc. cit.,* Vol. II, pp. 85–86; Höhn, *loc. cit.,* Vol. II, p. 219.

176. W. Stuckert, "Die Neuordnung der Kontinente und die Zusammenarbeit auf dem Gebiete der Verwaltung," *loc. cit.,* Vol. I, pp. 3–28.

177. Höhn, *loc. cit.,* Vol. II, p. 225.

9

Art in the Political Power Struggle
of 1933 and 1934

HILDEGARD BRENNER

The decisions on what powers were to formulate and exe-
cute National Socialist policy on art were made in 1933
and 1934. This phase sets in with the establishment of the
Reichsministerium für Volksaufklärung und Propaganda
[RMVAP, Reich Ministry for Popular Enlightenment
and Propaganda] on March 11, 1933. The appointment
of Goebbels as Reich Minister, the cultural character of
his political mission ("competent for tasks concerning the
cultural molding of the nation"), the ostentatious title of
the new ministry—these three elements initiated not only
a "transformation of public opinion" (Hitler) but also,
to this end, a "transformation" in the style of culture-
political leadership. The conquest of power in the realm
of culture seemed to call for new methods, more dynamic
than those hitherto employed by the groups terming
themselves "folkish" [*völkisch:* national, ethnic, folk, of
the people]. One of the most urgent tasks of the new ministry was to devise such methods.

In the political sphere the National Socialists had
broken with the old folkish tradition by 1928 at the latest.[1] Now they were determined to do so in their policy
with regard to culture and art.

The appointment of Goebbels came as no surprise to
him.[2] It was also a repudiation of Alfred Rosenberg's

claim to leadership in the cultural sphere, a repudiation which Rosenberg, a strong believer in principles, was far from willing to accept. The basis of his claim was the fact that he had been founder and director of the Kampfbund für Deutsche Kultur [Combat League for German Culture], which had hitherto been the representative National Socialist cultural organization, and in it had trained the culture-political cadres of the new Reich. Founded in August 1927 as the National Scientific Society[3] the Kampfbund had been taken over as such into the organizational structure of the NSDAP.[4] Motivated largely by resentment, individuals, groups, and beginning in 1931 whole organizations had flocked to it. Throughout Germany a network of headquarters had been set up. In its numerous militantly conducted actions the Kampfbund's main purpose was to revile the Weimar Republic (as for example by such horror shows as "Government Art from 1918 to 1933," "Spirit of November, Art in the Service of Sedition," "Art Bolshevism," etc.). It maintained close organizational, personal, and ideational ties with the Frick regime in Thuringia* (1929–1933), whose cultural policy was identical with its own. What Rosenberg's Kampfbund with its headquarters in Munich had proclaimed was decreed in Thuringia, the laboratory of National Socialist culture and art policy (e.g., the decree "Against Negro Culture, for German *Volkstum*" of April 5, 1930) and carried out in the form of books and film censorship, "purges" of museums, dismissal of undesirable artists and officials of artistic institutions, etc. The National Socialist cultural offensive of 1931 had emanated from Thuringia.[5]

Thus up to 1933 anything that could claim to be a Na-

---

* The National Socialists emerged from the *Landtag* election on December 8, 1929, with 11.3 percent of the vote. A month later they formed a government together with the right-of-center and agrarian parties. Wilhelm Frick became Minister of the Interior and Minister of Popular Education.

tional Socialist art policy had hinged on the Munich-Weimar axis. This policy was called "folkish" because its beginnings were inseparably bound up with the intense culture-political activity of the folkish groups which in 1927 were still largely independent. This activity had been transposed unchanged into new organizational forms and into the cultural reconstruction of Thuringia, so that at the end of 1932 the folkish element provided both the general public of the National Socialist culture policy and its spokesmen (A. Bartels, Schultze-Naumburg, H. F. K. Günther, Darré, H. S. Ziegler, etc.)

As late as January 30, 1933, all indications were that the folkish policy would be taken as a model and extended to the whole country. Doctor Frick, Thuringian Minister of the Interior and Minister of Popular Education, had become Reich Minister of the Interior. He brought his cultural functionaries with him to Berlin, including Professor Schultze-Naumburg, who again became his adviser in artistic questions. The Kampfbund für Deutsche Kultur had prepared for the seizure of power. From January 30, the feverish activity carried on even at its remotest outposts bore witness to a plan to occupy the cultural key positions with its members. A number of activities pointing in this direction are mentioned in the correspondence of the Reich Kampfbund's central office,[6] which also shows, however, that the Kampfbund's cultural seizure of power was already meeting with the opposition of competing institutions, the Reichsbund Volkstum und Heimat [Reich Folkhood and Home League] with its highly active leader Professor Karl Alexander von Müller,[7] the National Socialist Association of Teachers, and, still more important, the cultural section of the NSDAP. But it was the founding of the RMVAP that raised the first serious threat to the folkish power strategy. Undoubtedly the appointment of Goebbels was viewed as a particular affront because Goebbels already occupied two high party positions including that of Reich propaganda leader of the NSDAP, but was without either power or achievement in the realm of culture. He embarked on his culture-political functions as a king without a country.

The establishment of this second culture-political command post gave rise to a well-nigh inextricable conflict between practice and ideology, reality and program—a conflict reflected in a continuous rain of slogans, polemics, etc. Behind these manifestations and to some extent through them, the complex process of power consolidation within the party went on. While the outward political events were marking the stages of integration [*Gleichschaltung*], the well-known struggles for power were taking place within the party. It was in the course of these struggles that the official National Socialist art policy took form.

Art policy became a factor in the struggle for power, all the more so because the "program" which became identified with Goebbels was eminently an instrument of domination. Its intent was not to lay down a line in art policy, or to develop a National Socialist art program with secure ideological underpinning, but rather to adapt the slogans and practices of the "days of struggle" to the political conditions created by the conquest, to refurbish and apply them. Thus, in the realm of culture and art policy, the "systematization of the irrational" (Theodor Heuss) meant first of all the elimination of doctrinaire positions. And these positions were held by Rosenberg's folkish wing.

In this conflict the political interest groups were mobilized above all by one question, which led to a bitter confrontation. This was the question of modernism, particularly in the fine arts.

The rivalries between the high party leaders were widely known and gave rise to hopes in artistic circles. During the first few months of National Socialist rule, when public discussion was still relatively possible, these rivalries encouraged an oppositional tendency that—failing to realize that the power-political situation was the one thing that really counted—thought it could exert an influence on the art policy of the future. When these hopes spread even to leading circles of the National Socialist Students Association, who carried their opposition to the point of open revolt, the party leadership was faced with the need to make a fundamental decision.

Hitler put an end to the discussion; all that he retained of it was fuel for his own criticism of the folkish faction. The battle over modern art was laughed off as a mere episode in the history of the Third Reich. And intrinsically that is what it was. Yet it has a broader significance: the controversy over German expressionism and Italian futurism shows how integration, the imposition of controls, etc., developed as it were from within, as a dynamic process full of contradictions, tactical attitudes, and tolerances stemming from the power constellation of the moment. It also shows how the National Socialist art policy was refashioned in the course of the struggles between high party leaders, and how these tensions ultimately became factors in new forms of domination. Precisely because the art controversy was a circumscribed episode within the over-all process of political consolidation, we are able to view it as a whole and so arrive at richly differentiated insights into the process of totalitarian integration leading from the conquest to the consolidation of power.

*   *

It remains an open question why the government's art policy aroused opposition precisely in the fine arts and why no other opposition in the art field gained public notice in that early phase of political and cultural integration.

The first complaints were uttered when after January 30, 1933, Alfred Rosenberg's Kampfbund developed its activities on a broad scale and it seemed likely that the art policy of the Thuringian National Socialists would become the general model. In the big cities there was talk of "reactionary art policy," of "excesses in the provinces." It became known that political commissars had begun to "purge" the contents and personnel of the state museums. Undesirable teachers at art academies were boycotted, private exhibitors threatened, modern works of art in public buildings destroyed. The museums of Karlsruhe, Halle, and Mannheim set up the first so-called chambers of horrors:[8] art works belonging to private collections and erotic drawings confiscated in private studios were put on exhibition to show what trash the museums were squandering public funds on. This vandalism had the desired effect on the public, which felt cheated.

Who were the persons who openly called such an art policy "reactionary"? All young people: painters, sculptors, graphic artists, students and young fine-arts instructors, art critics. These members of the first postwar generation looked on the German expressionists, the "Brücke" and "Blaue Reiter" groups, as their most vital artistic experience. In their minds "quality" and "truth" were identified with the names of Kirchner, Heckel, Schmidt-Rottluff, Barlach, and Nolde. Their own work was in this tradition and was unthinkable without it.

These so vulnerable opponents of the folkish art policy gathered in and around the National Socialist Students Association. The center of their activity was Berlin. Their spokesman was the painter Otto Schreiber, the deputy leader of District 10 (Berlin) of the National Socialist Students Association. He had come to the NSDAP from the Jesuit "New Germany" society by way of the SA. The "conquest" of the Hochschule für Kunsterzeihung [Superior School for Art Training] in Berlin-Schöneberg[9] was attributed to him, and in the spring of 1933 he represented the four Berlin art schools in the National Socialist Students Association. The fact that these young people were National Socialist in their political convictions, that they did not in their discussions criticize the party's political and racial dogmas, made it possible for them to set their theses on art policy before the public. High hopes were placed in them, especially in circles with liberal artistic views.

Their opposition centered around the watchword "national." In this it did not differ from the attempts of certain bourgeois circles, widely echoed in the press during these first four months, to justify modern art. In order to put as broad as possible a definition on the works of art that would be admissible in the future, these bourgeois critics pointed to the "national" character of endangered works, which might reside in their subject matter, color quality, or composition. The "experience of the front" played a leading role. By way of protecting at least the older expressionists from the threatened ban, an extensive literature was devoted to "the Nordic in them." What distinguished the student opposition from these defensive tendencies was that it aspired to extend the National Socialist *revolution* to the field of art.

This linking of art policy with a revolutionary political and ideological thesis gave a powerful impulse to their action and moreover identified it with a political movement, the "Berlin opposition," which was feared within the party, though every effort was made to conceal its existence from the public. The political demonstration of National Socialist students outside the Berlin stock exchange and the "Worker and Student" demonstration at Tempelhof Airfield had been directed against Hitler's alliance with Hugenberg and Papen.[10] The spokesmen of this "Berlin opposition," who never fully succeeded in concealing their left-wing origins,[11] were Doctor Fritz Hippler, leader of the Berlin National Socialist Students Association and Doctor Johann von Leers, his educational director.

Though Hippler and Leers were not personally interested in questions of art policy, they sponsored discussions on the subject. Otto Andreas Schreiber spoke on the subject at a number of student congresses and meetings.[12] After reporting the excesses of the Kampfbund in the provinces and the blacklisting of artists, he characterized the development that was threatening Germany: "The *Gartenlaube* artist* and the 'literary painter' are having their great day; the former imitates nature and claims that the people understand him, and the latter paints Germanic subjects and claims that his art is folkish." Schreiber quoted from the letter rejecting Nolde's application for admission to the Kampfbund and termed the systematic defamation of Barlach, Heckel, Kirchner, Müller, Schmidt-Rottluff, and Nolde a "crime against German culture." He called Rosenberg's Kampfbund an "organization of cantankerous daubers" and deliberately provoking it declared: "We will not let them sell us any National Socialist artists."

The decisive mass meeting, which was to earn its speakers the name of an artistic "Otto-Strasser movement," was held on June 29 in the main auditorium of Humboldt University in Berlin.[13] For days red posters had announced the demonstration with the slogan: "Youth Fights for German Art." Personal invitations had also been sent out, signed by Fritz Hippler and the National Socialist Students Association. In the presence of an overcrowded auditorium, Hippler and Leers delivered speeches attacking the restoration of Wilhelminian academicism and all regulation of art. Some papers by art critics in defense of modern art were read [14] and then Otto Andreas Schreiber, the last speaker, took up the problems of the day. "The attempt of uncreative persons to lay down dogmas in art criticism is a nightmare to all the young artists in our movement. . . ." "The National Socialist students are fighting against reaction in art, because they believe in art as a living force of development

---

* The family weekly *Gartenlaube* had the reputation of catering to the taste and sentiment of the German Philistine.

and because they wish to prevent the previous generation of German artists from being disavowed. The National Socialist youth . . . believes in nothing so firmly as in the *triumph of quality and truth.*" "The vital element of art is freedom. . . ." [15] Nolde, Barlach, Heckel, and Schmidt-Rottluff were glorified and taken as the basis of a program. Their tradition was to be the foundation of a "new German art." In conclusion, Schreiber declared the Rosenberg Kampfbund groups at the Berlin academies and art schools dissolved and announced an exhibition of modern German artists under the special protection of the National Socialist Students Association.

The audience, including Geheimrat Ludwig Justi,[16] applauded wildly. The revolt seemed to be a great success. The first declarations of solidarity from other university towns arrived. "The National Socialist student body of Halle proclaims its enthusiastic support of the demonstration of the National Socialist students of Berlin against reaction in art. The SA man's battle in the street must not be betrayed in the field of culture. Long live the *complete National Socialist revolution.*" [17]

With this a nation-wide forum was established. Referring explicitly to the "culture-creating mission of National Socialism," members of the National Socialist organization had rejected the claim of the folkish faction to leadership in the realm of art.

The liberal bourgeois press reacted with curious optimism. Declarations of solidarity such as that from Halle were published verbatim.[18] The *Deutsche Allgemeine Zeitung* printed Otto Andreas Schreiber's theses a second time.[19] Professor Karl Hofer published an article.[20] Speculation was rife in artistic circles: Would this public airing of the question bring about a liberalization of the government's art policy? Rumors went around, many of them well founded: Hitler regretted the breach with Barlach and was already trying to reconcile him with the new regime;[21] Reich Minister Rust had privately declared Nolde to be "the greatest living German painter";[22] Goebbels had even hung several Nolde originals from the Nationalgalerie in his home;[23] the same Goebbels, moreover, had come to regard the burning of the books (May 10, 1933), the initiative for which he had claimed at the last minute, as a "mistake";[24] and so on. Much of this partly fanciful speculation hinged on Goebbels, his person and his office. In the end it was inferred that he followed the activities of the art opposition with a certain sympathy, which was true, though the motives for his sympathy were misinterpreted. This belief was so widespread that it even found an echo in the foreign press.[25]

The activities of the National Socialist students had in particular two results that did much to determine the further development of the art opposition: First, the meeting at Humboldt University had attracted the interest of the influential and energetic circle around the Kronprinzenpalais Museum in Berlin. Secondly, one of the many new sympathizers with the movement was an art critic at the RMVAP, a painter by the name of Hans Weidemann, one of the politically tested [26] and artistically ambitious young men whom Goebbels had sought out to help build up his ministry. (Weidemann's career was to culminate in the vice-presidency of the Reich Chamber of Fine Arts, a post which he was obliged to abandon in November 1933 at Hitler's express wish because, among other things, he had dared to suggest Nolde as president.) Weidemann was thought to be influential with Goebbels. His willingness to support the struggle for modern art, if only unofficially, encouraged the belief that Goebbels had decided to pursue a new nonfolkish course in art policy.

*   *

While the leaders of the Berlin Socialist Students Association were working with Hans Weidemann on the forthcoming exhibition of modern German painting and sculpture at the Ferdinand Moeller Gallery and Professor

Alois Schardt, director of the Berlin Nationalgalerie, was "reorganizing" the Kronprinzenpalais in accordance with his instructions,[27] the folkish faction was mustering its forces for a counterthrust. In the following months their action was reflected in Rosenberg's "encirclement" policy, which finally triumphed when the function of supervision in artistic matters was officially conferred on Rosenberg (January 1934).

This policy was furthered, at least indirectly, by Hitler's declaration (speeches of July 1 and 6) that the National Socialist revolution was ended. This deprived the student opposition of their political argument in defense of modern art.

And it was in this new political and ideological light that Rosenberg opened his campaign against the student revolt. In two leading editorials, "Revolution in the Fine Arts" (VB, July 6, 1933) and "Revolution for Its Own Sake!" (VB, July 14, 1933), he resumed his programmatic vilification of Barlach and Nolde; now it was his turn to invoke the SA, declaring that "any healthy SA man" would agree with him, and denouncing Otto Andreas Schreiber, the spokesman of the art opposition, as "a cultural Otto Strasser." This "Otto Strasser of the 'Black Front,'" he declared, regards himself "as the true representative of 'revolutionary National Socialism.' In the political field we have already had an Otto Strasser tendency and combated it, as we believe, to the benefit of the movement." [28] At the Bachsaal, the Kampfbund's meeting place in West Berlin, Rosenberg again stated his position on the revolution in the fine arts in a speech entitled "Tradition and New Art" (July 14, 1933). He came out strongly against a "battle of concepts." "It is inadvisable," he declared, "to transpose terms originating in the political struggle for power . . . to the struggle over creation in the plastic arts." Wading through the swamp of pseudo-concepts, he went on to speak of continuity in art as "a trend close to our hearts." The only point of interest in this speech later published by Eher is that in an address devoted to culture at the party congress of 1933 Hitler took over Rosenberg's attack on the "slippery dialecticians" of a "folkish expressionism" almost word for word.

In other quarters as well, the Berlin student revolt had been identified with political revolt. Walter Hansen, later one of the initiators of the "Degenerate Art" exhibition, termed the meeting at Humboldt University "an effective blow against the art policy of the Führer and of Rosenberg," [29] "a maneuver of falsification directed against national art and the racial principle," and an "act of sabotage." [30] And the *Magazine for National Socialist Education,* edited by Hans Schemm, the Bavarian Minister of Education, stigmatized it as an "open attack on the sovereignty of the party." [31]

Insofar as it was manifested in the press the controversy between Rosenberg and the leaders of the National Socialist Students Association of Berlin came to an end for the time being after the *Deutsche Allgemeine Zeitung* for July 14 had published a statement in which Schreiber "gave his word of honor . . . that the student youth stand irrevocably by their convictions in matters of art policy, but that . . . the student youth . . . are not attacking his [Rosenberg's] personal view of art." The fact that in this statement Schreiber no longer spoke in the name of the National Socialist Students Association shows how, through political defamation, the opposition had been forced to relinquish its claim of representing the party. State Commissioner Hans Hinkel threatened "severe measures against all discussions among National Socialist artists," insofar as they were directed "against each other." Further, disciplinary action would be taken against "all those who twist the words of sincere National Socialists and so attempt to bring division into the front of the true new German art." [32]

The Kampfbund's efforts to prevent the exhibition at the Ferdinand Moeller Gallery were unsuccessful. On

July 22 this much discussed showing of "thirty German artists," officially sponsored by the National Socialist Students Association, opened. Again representative works of Rohlfs, Pechstein, Macke, Schmidt-Rottluff, Nolde, and Barlach were shown. Formal extremes were avoided. A few works of the younger generation, including Schreiber and Weidemann, suggested a moderate continuation of the controversial tradition. The critics responded favorably. One of them wrote: "Gratifyingly animated by a desire for quality and actuality." [33] But only three days later, on July 25, Doctor Frick, Minister of the Interior, closed the exhibition. Two SS men guarded the entrance. Hippler and Schreiber were expelled from the National Socialist Students Association. When about a week later the exhibition was permitted to reopen, it was no longer sponsored by the National Socialist Students Association.[34]

Meanwhile Professor Schardt, with the help of loans from private collections, had reorganized the leading German collection of modern painting at the Kronprinzenpalais in Berlin, and was waiting for permission to admit the public. Himself a passionate advocate of expressionism, he had worked out a historical method of justifying modern art, which he represented as a protest against "international encroachment," "rationalism," etc.

In a sensational lecture entitled "What Is German Art?" Schardt set forth his program (July 10, 1933). The *Neue Zürcher Zeitung* wrote:

> For him [Schardt] the specific character of the Germanic, of the German-national, is to be sought in the ecstatic and prophetic. To his mind there is a connection between the nonobjective ornament of the German bronze age and the painting of the German expressionists (e.g., of a Nolde, Marc, or Feininger)! According to Schardt, the decline of German art began as early as 1431 with the incursion of naturalism. He holds that the German art produced after the first third of the fifteenth century, that is, from the sixteenth to the nineteenth cen-

tury, is without value except as a historical document, and is fundamentally un-German. . . .[35]

Here the history of art was employed in defense of art. Meanwhile, in other quarters the history of art was being employed in defense of the new art *policy*.[36]

Eyewitnesses[37] to Schardt's new arrangement of the Kronprinzenpalais report that few pictures were hung on the pastel-tinted walls: on the ground floor the German romantics Caspar David Friedrich and Blechen; on the first floor chiefly Hans von Marées, selected works of Feuerbach, etc.; on the top floor Barlach, Nolde, Lehmbruck, and Feininger, the "Blaue Reiter" and "Brücke" painters.

> The arrangement seemed strange, was understood by only a few, and failed to convince even all the friends of modern art, for it was doubted whether the omission of so many representative artists and an almost esoteric attempt to interpret art by creating a mystical atmosphere were the right thing for a world capital like Berlin.[38]

The examining commission headed by Rust prohibited the exhibition. Schardt had disappointed the confidence placed in him by the party. He was not confirmed as director of the Nationalgalerie and was also prevented from returning to Halle. (When in 1936 he opened an exhibition of Franz Marc, he was arrested in the gallery by the Gestapo. Released, he fled to the United States.) With the appointment of Doctor Eberhard Hanfstaengl the excitement over the Kronprinzenpalais subsided.

*   *

The beginning of 1934 was marked by a change in the art policy situation, brought about by Hitler's decision. He had established an Office for the Supervision of the Entire Cultural and Ideological Education and Training of the NSDAP and appointed Rosenberg (January 1, 1934) as its director. Thus far we have little definite knowledge of the reasons for setting up this monstrous office. It is surely no mistake to consider the question against the background of the new phase in the National Socialist conquest of power and to draw a connection between Hitler's authoritarian halting of the revolution and the tasks of the new office. Seen in this light, the above-described events of the previous summer may well have contributed to convince Hitler of the expedience of such an organ of party supervision.

The work of the Kampfbund and its emanation the Reichsverband Deutsche Bühne [German Theater League] in the realm of art and culture now obtained the institutional support that Alfred Rosenberg had kept asking for since January 1, 1933.[39] Thus Hitler had taken account of an existing relation of forces.

But the establishment of Rosenberg's office also made it clear how Hitler wished to decide the competition between Goebbels and Rosenberg in the field of culture. The very wording of the document defining the tasks of the new office[40] shows that here again he followed the principle of dividing the power he delegated, in order to keep it the more firmly under his own control. Whether Goebbels' headstart in this tug of war over National Socialist culture and art policy would serve as a corrective to the folkish conception, only the future could show. For the present the institutionalization of Rosenberg's claims to leadership undoubtedly meant a strengthening of the folkish wing, its practice and its ideology.

Rosenberg's initially hesitant and unimaginative handling of his office was solely to blame if the opposition was able to muster its forces a second time and to engage in activities that attracted considerable attention.

This new mustering of the opposition began in the fall of 1933. After Rosenberg had succeeded in depriving the first wave of opposition of its claim to represent the party, its initiators found themselves reduced to private actions. Under the protective name of Der Norden (North), the painters formed a group. Their program included the statement: "We reject all pedantic norms, formalism, intolerance, and trademarks." [41] The group was made up of pupils of Otto Mueller, Moll, Rohlfs, and Thorn-Prikker, among them Otto Andreas Schreiber and Hans Weidemann. They showed at the Ferdinand Moeller Gallery and later at van der Heyde's. It was Ferdinand Moeller who, before it was too late, called the attention of the young National Socialist art oppositionists to the fact that it would soon be necessary to obtain a permit for new periodicals. To anticipate this regulation, and because meanwhile all art periodicals favoring modern art had been obliged to suspend publication, the magazine *Kunst der Nation* [Art of the Nation] was founded at the end of October. Hartmann, the former director of *Weltkunst* [World Art] and Otto Andreas Schreiber were its business and editorial directors. This excellently written magazine was able to appear for almost two years. Although the butt of much hostility, the editors managed to come out openly and militantly for expressionism without being prosecuted for opposition to the party.   The contributors included Werner Haftmann, Bruno E. Werner, Griebitzsch, Pinder, F. A. Dargel, Wilhelm von Schramm, and Hans Schwippert. *Kunst der Nation* had become a forum of modern art. (When it was suppressed in 1935 it had 3,500 subscribers. But its circulation was larger, since it was also sold at newspaper stands.[42])

Again the National Socialist art avant-garde acquired official positions. Inspired by vague notions of "workers' culture," Doctor Robert Ley, leader of the "Strength Through Joy" movement, wished his movement to have its own cultural organization and asked Goebbels to appoint one of his staff as its director.[43] Goebbels delegated his art expert Hans Weidemann and under his direction Otto Andreas Schreiber organized the Fine Arts section of the Strength Through Joy cultural organization. A competition was scheduled for that December, with a jury in-

cluding Erich Heckel, Mies van der Rohe, Paul Hinde-
mith, and Richard Strauss.[44] And toward the end of 1933
the Fine Arts section began to organize Strength Through
Joy factory exhibitions. These exhibitions, closed to the
general public, were to be the last refuge of the National
Socialist art avant-garde.

The private art galleries supported the new effort:
group shows of Barlach, Nolde, Feininger, etc. were held
in Berlin and here and there in other German cities. The
bourgeois-national press published favorable reviews.

In the weekly *Deutsche Zukunft* [German Future] for
November 5, 1933, Gottfried Benn wrote an "Apology
for Expressionism" as the "last great resurgence of art in
Europe," whose "antiliberal function" was a prelude to
National Socialism and its logical accompaniment, cultural naturalism ("Propaganda touches germ cells, the
word grazes the sex glands . . ."). In *Deutsche Zukunft* (January 7, 1934), Max Sauerlandt rehabilitated
the war generation of expressionists—"they painted in
the spirit of the national movement"—and with them the
student opposition of the preceding summer: "To have
made the first attempt to clear the way for these most authentic among the artists of the recent past and to have set
them apart from the mass of 'incompetents and charla-
tans' will redound to the eternal credit of the National
Socialist Students Association and its leaders."

Soon the *Völkischer Beobachter* was expressing alarm
at this revival of public discussion, this powerful though
unorganized pressure from below. The newspaper's art
critic, a strong proponent of Rosenberg's policy, pointed a
finger at "cliques of saboteurs who completely distort the
Führer's Nuremberg culture proclamation"; once again
he made open and veiled allusions to the student revolt
and to the incorrigible "circle around the Berlin Kronprinzenpalais." "A bitter and systematic resistance has
been organized against the new National Socialist ideal of
a spiritually healthy art anchored in the race." "Almost as

in the heyday of Marxism . . . decadent art is everywhere on the rise." [45]

Even the public at large was discussing the question of
"two kinds of art in Germany."

The climax of this second phase of the conflict came
with the exhibition of Italian futurist painting (*aeropittura*) in March 1934. It is hard to say how much justification there was for the widely vented suspicion that this
exhibition was a systematic attempt to improve the standing of modern German art by calling attention the officially accredited art of friendly Fascist Italy. Be that as it
may, the *aeropittura* show came to Germany at a time
when the struggle over modern art left no room for a neutral position. Even Goebbels exposed himself for the first
time. As a member of the government he, along with
Goering and Rust, belonged to the committee of honor,
which on the German side also included Professor Eugen
Höning, president of the Reich Chamber of Fine Arts,
and Doctor Eberhard Hanfstaengl, the new director of
the Berlin Nationalgalerie; and on the Italian side, Marinetti, Mussolini's comrade in arms, Ruggero Vasari, and
Ambassadress Cerutti.

Despite this official protection the exhibition began
with a scandal. On the morning of the opening (March
28) Robert Scholz, the spokesman for Rosenberg's art
policy, wrote in the *Völkischer Beobachter* that the exhibition was a second instance of foreign interference.[46]
"The conspicuous interest of certain circles at the present
moment" was calculated "to throw contempt on the main
body of German art." In reality, Scholz went on, young
Fascist Italy "formed a solid front" with the young generation of German artists "who are fighting for the development of an indigenous art"; by contrast, this "so-called
'futurism' " was a "movement without significance in
Italy itself;" the Fascist revolution had long since brought
about a "clarification," a "total transformation" of this
tendency. In connection with a previous exhibition at the

Hamburg Kunstverein, Ruggero Vasari had given the *Hamburger Nachrichten* an interview in which he defended himself against accusations of "artistic Bolshevism." The *Völkischer Beobachter* now repeated these accusations and described the Italian guest exhibition as an "attempt at propaganda." It may have been this article that finally decided the representatives of the Reich government to stay away from the exhibition.

The reception at the former Galerie Flechtheim on Lützowufer developed into a demonstration—a kind of artistic tribunal. In his welcoming address Rudolf Blümner, formerly close to the "Sturm" group and to Dada, declared that it was false to call futurism a seditious movement. He referred to the German abstract painters who, he said, were related to the futurists: both had succeeded, on the strength of a new approach, a new *stato d'animo*, in apprehending the spirit of the epoch as a meaningful unity, something that realistic painting had proved incapable of doing. In his essay, "Aerial Painting, Modern Art, and Reaction," [47] Ruggero Vasari reviewed the development of futurism from the publication of the first manifesto in *Le Figaro* to *aeropittura*. He termed the "devious reactionary attempts" to stigmatize futurism as an art of Bolshevist origin, a "falsification of art history." He cited Gauguin: "In art there are only revolutionaries and plagiarists!" and invoking the authority of Mussolini proclaimed: "A new state, a new nation can thrive only if the whole of art is revolutionized." [48] Marinetti then defined the position of this new Italian futurist painting in cultural history, representing it as a national and heroic form of life and art, irrevocably bound up with the race. "Airborne power," he declared, bore witness to a new spirituality, a vitalization of existence in the rhythm of machines, motors, and geometric forms. In the leitmotiv-like figurations of storm troops and Fascist legions he found futurist apotheoses of the Fascist idea. This, he maintained, was a "dynamic conception" as opposed to the "static conception" which insists one-sidedly on so-called enduring contents, representations, etc. Finally, Gottfried Benn, as vice-president of the Union of National Authors, conjured up his "imperative world Reich." In the realm of art as elsewhere, "discipline and form as symbols of domination" must mold the "cold style of the future." [49]

The show itself did not justify all this to-do. The examples of *aeropittura* were disappointing. Even its best representatives, Prampolini, Ambrosi, and Gitio, made no new contribution to futurist painting. Nevertheless, wrote *Weltkunst* (April 8, 1934), the exhibition was of "inestimable" importance "as an indication of the tie between the political forces and artistic endeavors of an allied nation." It had once more called Rosenberg's dogmatization of art into question and refuted its arguments; it seemed to rehabilitate the student opposition of the previous year by demonstrating that Mussolini had declared futurism to be the art of the Fascist state.

A new wave of articles appeared. "Mussolini is the political futurist," wrote G. H. Theunissen in *Kunst der Nation,* April 15, 1934.

> Without him Italy today would be a dusty picture postcard. Marinetti and his disciples of the Manifesto are the artistic incarnations of an idea, born about 1909 from the Vesuvius of Marinetti's mind and the inferno of his heart. This idea was to capture time, time as such, to seize it by the hair as it speeds over Europe's asphalt roads, polished smooth by balloon tires . . . the new continent is inhabited by airplanes, automobiles and Marinettis. . . . We hail the futurist exhibition on Lützowufer . . . as welcome testimony to the many-sidedness of artistic endeavors and to the justification of this many-sidedness.

Again the eloquent Andreas Schreiber lauded the Italian example of an art movement consistent with the modern era. Then, after a strategic retreat in which he took ac-

count of the concrete German situation, he came out all
the more emphatically in favor of expressionism as the
historic parallel to Italian futurism, appropriate to the
"German North." *Aeropittura,* Schreiber conceded to
the official critics, was "too Latin a conception," but then
went on to plead his own cause: Whereas Italian futurism
endeavors to implement only *one* method of artistic realization, "we maintain that surface, color and vision (inward and outward) remain *the* categories of painting and
furthermore that to reject any subject matter as a matter
of principle in an antiartistic approach." Calling for a
"continuation of expressionism," Schreiber heralded a
German painting of the future, for which expressionism
itself would be only a beginning, a transitional stage:

> . . . the young painters of today . . . continue to build
> on the artistic experience of color and form which they
> found present. On the strength of this organic continuity
> a higher development of German painting is to be hoped
> for. But apart from this they refuse to be harnessed to
> any school or "style," and go forward relying on their
> own powers in order that painting may go forward.[50]

In April the Ferdinand Moeller Gallery in Berlin
showed over sixty water colors and lithographs by Nolde.
Exhibitions of Feininger and Schmidt-Rottluff were held
in other cities.

*   *

This second attempt to demolish the folkish position
and incline National Socialist art policy in favor of modernism confronted the supreme authorities with the necessity of making decisions. The decisions were announced and explained by Hitler himself at the party
congress of September 1934. In a report to the "forum of
the hundred thousand" on the consolidation of National
Socialist power, Hitler rejected the renewed attempt at a
liberalization of art policy and went further. He took the

occasion to reformulate National Socialist art policy, introducing the correctives which would at last make it an effective modern instrument of political power.

We possess a number of records of the inner-party situation leading up to these decisions. On June 5, 1934, Alfred Rosenberg noted in his diary:

> A veritable tug of war is now beginning in cultural questions. Wherever I go I hear a unanimous complaint about the lack of direction in the Reich Chamber of Culture [Reichskulturkammer]. This shows that the people at large realize what an omnium gatherum it is. The old Jewish crowd as presidents, Rotary Club lawyers in key positions, incompetent "National Socialists," and a sprinkling of good men who feel uncomfortable to say the least. On top of it all Goebbels makes speeches without content, in the smooth manner, evading all problems. A dismal situation.[51]

Rosenberg was prepared to take drastic measures to correct this "situation." "Our people set their hopes in me, but the fact that a National Socialist is president of the Reichskulturkammer makes it hard for the party to set up another organization without the Kammer or against it."

Further we possess the heated correspondence carried on by Rosenberg and Goebbels in the fall of 1934,[52] which Rosenberg, as he himself stated,[53] occasionally forwarded to the "Führer's deputy." In this duel Rosenberg had taken the first step. Goebbels answered coolly, pointing out obvious errors and ignoring most of Rosenberg's accusations. In the end he protested "energetically" against "unfounded assertions, which on closer examination had proved to be completely inaccurate" and "which can accomplish nothing but to denigrate me and my work, or to foment between you and me an epistolary war for which I have neither time nor inclination." [54] In an aggressive tone Rosenberg denounced Goebbels and sang his own praises. His thinking was still dominated by the "achievements" and methods of the "days of struggle":

The Kampfbund für Deutsche Kultur came into being at a time of severe political struggles; it sprang from the idea that the cultural aspect of the movement also requires attention and that it was necessary to seek out men who would be able to carry on this cultural work later on. At that time next to no one concerned himself with the cultural questions of National Socialism; nor did you, Doctor Goebbels, for those were the days when you chose Hans Heinz Ewers, author of *Alraune* and *Der Vampir,* and Arnolt Bronnen, author of *September-novelle,* as your artistic associates. . . .

And later on in the same letter, alluding to Richard Strauss but indirectly implicating Goebbels:

Either one accepts a high position and honors in the Third Reich, and then one must forgo Bruno Walter, Hoffmannsthal, and Zweig, or one sticks to one's old friendships and forgoes representative and culture-determining positions in the Third Reich. I feel it is the duty of the President of the Reichskulturkammer to watch these things. . . . I can assure you that the conduct of the Theaterkammer and certain other developments, in the fine arts and the cinema, for example, have shaken a good many people's faith in the firmness of the National Socialist philosophy and philosophy of culture in Germany. . . . The "high point" was unquestionably the successful attempt to put on a futurist exhibition of Berlin art Bolshevists by the detour of Italy, sponsored by you among others, evidently in ignorance of the trends represented. Perhaps indeed it was unknown to you that the organizer of this exhibition was for many years active in Berlin as an art Bolshevist and spokesman of the "Sturm" group. I can assure you that this fact was appropriately deplored among National Socialist artists. . . .[55]

What had led these two high party leaders to attack each other in this way?

When Alfred Rosenberg was charged with the "supervision of the entire cultural and philosophical training

and education of the NSDAP" (January 1934), this had
placed him formally on a level with Goebbels in the domain of cultural affairs. The tasks entrusted to the supervisory office confirmed the priority of cultural work. But
with respect to actual power, Goebbels had taken a lead
that Rosenberg strove in vain to make good. For this
there were several reasons: in the Reichskulturkammer
Goebbels had created an institution that attached all
those engaged in the production, reproduction, and distribution of art both economically and socially to the
Propaganda Ministry. Thus he had not only made inroads
on the jurisdiction of the Prussian Ministry of Education
and Cultural Affairs [Kultusministerium],[56] but had also,
after this ministry was transformed into the Ministry of
Science, Education, and Popular Education, been able to
increase the scope of his power though he had been
obliged to accept certain compromises;[57] four implementation decrees attaching to the Reichskulturkammer Law,
a special agreement with the Labor Front (DAF), and
two "notices concerning the jurisdiction of the Reichskulturkammer" had not sufficed to define its expanding
jurisdiction. Then there was the style of his administration which owed much of its success to its appearance of
relative unorthodoxy, especially in matters of art. It was
this that attracted members of the intelligentsia who were
still willing to serve in leading positions. Thus Goebbels
had staffed the cultural sections of his ministry largely,
and the Reichskulturkammer almost exclusively, with
professional artists. In order to encourage artistic activity,
he took a sympathetic attitude toward the economic situation and working conditions of artists and was realistic in
his artistic judgments. He advocated quality in art ("Art
means know-how") over against the flood of political
Kitsch.[58] He was equally broad-minded in his dealings
with people. He requested that potential refugees stay in
Germany,[59] and tried with some success to persuade prominent refugees to return.[60] He did everything possible to

further the development of a politically utilizable art. Considerations of publicity played an essential role in this policy even in its beginnings. Goebbels admired Italian architecture because it was "impressive";[61] he admired the Italian film policy, because Fascism had "attempted for the first time to place the cinema directly in the service of the state."[62] Similarly Goebbels had once praised the "healthy views" of expressionism,[63] and lauded neo-objectivism [*die neue Sachlichkeit*] as the "German art of the next decade."[64] And only a few days before Hitler made his pronouncement to the contrary, Goebbels had proclaimed that the "laws of revolution" were a National Socialist "principle of state." The slogan became: "The poet shall go hand in hand with the statesman,"[65] and with seeming generosity he offered the artists the role of an avant-garde in this "revolution."[66]

The artists seemed to take such speeches less literally than Goebbels' opponents in his own political camp, first and foremost Alfred Rosenberg who in Goebbels' tactical maneuvers suspected an ideological diversion. An intervention with the party chancellery was virtually the only way in which Rosenberg could hope to gain official support for his supervisory activity. He was a man of principle; his mission, as he saw it, was to "keep the National Socialist party line pure."[67] Stubbornly he insisted that his negative principle of selection was the only means of regulating the party's cultural and art policy. "We have no thought of proclaiming any dogma of art," he declared in his programmatic speech of February 22, 1934; "the future direction of creative activity will follow from the critique of opposing currents."[68] For "the individual does not always . . . know what he wants in a positive sense, but he is always instinctively aware of what he does not want; his innermost nature will lead him to what is in keeping with this will, this innermost nature."[69] Unmodified but rendered more fanatical by intraparty rivalries, the folkish "anticonceptions" of the days of struggle had become a doctrine. They determined the style of Rosenberg's administration. Under his direct or indirect management so-called "shame exhibitions" [*Schandausstellungen*] traveled from city to city. In accordance with the Thuringian model, exhibits calculated to discredit museum directors were shown in shop windows. Professor Schulze-Naumburg delivered lectures at which he displayed ideal images (e.g., the "Bamburger Reiter") to serve "as standards of racial selection for all." [70] "Selection for and selection against the North," or "antithetical selections" were the categories with which he rewrote the history of German art. Under the motto "Let us build with our hearts!" well-known architects[71] delivered lecture series for the Kampfbund, attacking the Bauhaus as "architectural Bolshevism" and neo-objectivism as "November architecture." In connection with art the word "German" was on its way to becoming synonymous with "regional" in the sense of anti-international. The "folkish" value of this art was measured by the extent to which it was not understood on the "outside." [72] Displayed as "German" painters, as painters of the "country," and "of the unspoiled instinct of the simple man" were Leibl and the Dachau group, the Bodensee-Bund, Hans Thoma of the Black Forest, the Tyrolean Egger-Lienz, and the "arch-Germanic" painters Henrich, Stassen, Fidus, and Fahrenkrog. Insofar as the regulative intentions of Rosenberg's art policy were susceptible of formulation, Doctor Ernst Hanfstaengl, the foreign press secretary, stated them in an interview with the international *Weltkunst* (January 14, 1934): "Germany, which has learned to feel so supranationally, will have to learn to feel intranationally on the basis of a folkish national state. The German must be subjected to a nationalistic cure, so to speak. —A kind of extra drill! —A blood cure! . . ."

Meanwhile the organizational basis for an intensification of Rosenberg's cultural policy had been provided. On June 4, 1934, the Reichsverband Deutsche Bühne

[German Theater Association] and the Kampfbund für Deutsche Kultur, both with large memberships, were merged into an over-all cultural organization, the NS-Kulturgemeinde [National Socialist Cultural Community], which in turn was subordinated in the summer of 1934 to the Amt für Kunstpflege [Office for the Cultivation of Art] and thus anchored in the Reich leadership of the NSDAP. But even this step of Rosenberg's seems to have been determined less by a practicable program than by the notion that the NS-Kulturgemeinde would become an institution opposed to Goebbels' Reichskulturkammer, and equally effective in its own way. The diary entry in which Rosenberg himself expresses this idea dates from the day before the (official) foundation of the NS-Kulturgemeinde. Moreover, as prearranged, Rosenberg's organizations enjoyed exclusive control over the field of cultural publicity (Goebbels possessed direct access to it only through his position as Reich propaganda leader of the NSDAP and did not avail himself of this possibility until after 1935). The explanation for Rosenberg's lack of initiative in the internal struggle for political power must be sought in his ideological preoccupation with "selection" or "purification" and in his adherence to the old folkish practices.

Hitler's remarks at the Reich party congress of 1934 take on their full significance against this background of an insufficiently stabilized cultural policy. Characteristically he attacked on two fronts.

Immediately before Hitler's speech Alfred Rosenberg had invoked the "culture-political" situation. After citing Hitler's words at the party congress of the preceding year—"Under no circumstances must the representatives of decay . . . suddenly become the banner bearers of the future"—he had once again evoked the events of summer, 1933: "National Socialism," he declared, "must energetically oppose all importunate efforts . . . to talk us into regarding the pseudo-ecstatic . . . artists of the last decades as our revolutionaries." In the preceding year, unfortunately, "there had been a visible attempt, by means of slippery dialectics, to smuggle the outworn spirit, which had been driven out of the political sphere, back into the cultural field." [73] This was addressed to the rebellious students. And then for the benefit of the Italian "friends" of Germany: "The great cultural and spiritual rebirth of Germany that is now in progress has the right to expect people abroad to take it seriously into consideration when they speak of National Socialism." "But unfortunately the most unobjective attempts have been made precisely in recent months to represent the great struggle of the German people as 'barbarism.'" [74] Rosenberg then devoted a few words to "hostile critics" and continued: "We respect the genuine art works of all peoples, but we expect the same respect for ourselves from their spokesmen." [75]

Thereupon Hitler, addressing himself to the arts, spoke of "two dangers" which National Socialism must "today . . . overcome." First, the antitraditional "spoilers of art," the "cubists, futurists, dadaists, etc.," who threatened the development of National Socialist art. This "cultural auxiliary to political destruction" was "tolerable neither from the racial . . . nor from the national point of view"; for it threatened the "healthy unspoiled instinct" of the National Socialist movement. They must be told clearly and unmistakably that "not only the political but also the cultural line of the Third Reich is determined by those who created it."

> The charlatans are mistaken if they think the creators of the Third Reich are foolish or cowardly enough to let themselves be befuddled or intimidated by their chatter. They will see that perhaps the greatest cultural and artistic mission of all times will go about its business, ignoring them as though they had never existed.[76]

Thus far Hitler reaffirmed Rosenberg's judgment. But then he spoke of a "danger" Rosenberg had not mentioned, and here his warning was addressed to Rosenberg.

Second, the National Socialist state must defend itself against the sudden emergence of those backward-lookers who imagine that they can impose on the National Socialist revolution, as a binding heritage for the future, a "Teutonic art" sprung from the fuzzy world of their own romantic conceptions. . . .[77]

What Rosenberg had neglected to do was now done by Hitler himself. He disposed of the spokesmen of the folkish faction. He mentioned no names. But everyone interested in such matters knew whom he meant: all the folkish reformers of architecture, language, literature, and fashions, the Fiduses, Fahrenkrogs, and Lanzingers, the old guard who in 1934 made up Rosenberg's camp.

Hitler did not content himself with dismissing them from his service. Only a few days later Walter Frank* contemptuously bade the "national" intelligentsia—once so welcome an adjunct to the building of the party's organs of leadership—return "over the patriotic asses' bridge" by which they had come.[78] And now Hitler himself, setting the keynote for this about-face, slandered his most faithful henchmen politically. "They were never National Socialists," he declared.

Either they dwelt in the hermitages of a Germanic dream world which even Jews found ridiculous, or they trotted along pious and harmless amid the angelic hosts of a bourgeois Renaissance. . . . When . . . after our victory . . . they hurried down from the loft of their bourgeois party stable to offer their services as political minds and strategists to the National Socialist movement . . . they had no understanding for the magnitude of the upheaval that had meanwhile taken place in the German people. So today they offer us railroad stations in original German Renaissance style, street signs and typewriter keyboards with genuine Gothic letters, song tests freely imitated from Walther von der Vogelweide, fashions borrowed from Gretchen and Faust, pictures of the

---

* Professor, President of the Reich Institute for the History of the New Germany.

"Trompeter von Säckingen" type. Perhaps they would like us to defend ourselves with shields and crossbows.

It was high time, he went on, that "these petrified backward-lookers" should retire to the museums and cease to "spook about molesting people and giving them the shudders." [79]

Hitler termed both the modernist and the folkish trend "dangers to National Socialism."

What were the motives behind this exaggerated formulation? With regard to the modernists the question is easily answered. Hitler with his unschooled taste had always rejected modern art, and more important, he had never overestimated the political importance of such intellectual groups. Those who insisted that art should reflect the complexity of modern life were an insignificant minority. At the party congress of 1934 Hitler laid down an educational program for the nation, summing up his views in the slogan: "To be German means to be clear!" To Hitler clarity meant consciousness of political purpose. Within this political scheme the arts like everything else had their fixed place. Anything that might seem confusing, not to say ridiculous, endangered the political program. What the student revolt and the Kronprinzenpalais circle had demanded and what Rudolf Blümner, Marinetti, Vasari, Gottfried Benn, and *Kunst der Nation* were again producing—all this was of a nature to muddle the "artistic line of march." "As long as I am leading it," Hitler had written to Goebbels in 1939 in connection with the Strasser affair, "the National Socialist party will not be a debating club for uprooted litterati or drawing-room Bolshevists, but will remain what it is today: a disciplined organization. . . ." [80] It was for the sake of this "discipline" that Hitler settled the art controversy in favor of Rosenberg's policy because he was convinced that the modern art campaign had been "sabotage" and that its spokesmen were "cultural Bolshevists." [81]

It was a different matter with the members of the folkish wing. He had tolerated them, obviously for tactical reasons; now he ceased to do so. His basic attitude had not changed. What he said in September 1934 had already been stated in *Mein Kampf* (1924) and in almost the same words.[82] But what had motivated the party's forbearance in the intervening years? [83]

Unlike the modern art group the folkish wing represented a numerically important body of National Socialist supporters. All the early independent folkish groups had had their cultural programs. Though the political ambitions of the folkish groups had been disappointed at an early date, there is little doubt that their cultural ideas and activities had contributed very considerably to winning popular support for the party and swelling the National Socialist vote. Thus it was only natural that these groups should urge their cultural ideas to be put into practice, as the Frick regime in Thuringia had already adopted some of them. Thus if Hitler hesitated to repudiate them in the cultural field as he had repudiated them politically in the middle twenties, the main reason is doubtless to be sought in the fact that their cultural movement represented a political force.

Once Hitler had seized power, he no longer needed the support of the folkish faction. But he did not break with them at once because in 1933 and 1934 the consolidation of National Socialist power was not yet complete. Moreover, in temporarily favoring Goebbels' cultural policy over against Rosenberg's folkish conception, he had hoped that the situation would regulate itself. But this had not happened.

In his speech at the party congress of 1934 Hitler spoke at conspicuous length of the party, its organization, and tactics. In stressing once again that the NSDAP must be a disciplined elite party trained to dominate the masses, Hitler was merely restating one of his most important ideas concerning the stabilization of political power. But this lesson in political leadership was set before the public

888

at a time when this type of leadership had already been largely put into practice and institutionally anchored at least in the social and cultural spheres. Thus Hitler's intervention in the realm of art policy merely added the finishing touches which confirmed and consolidated the National Socialist art policy.

1. The still divergent practice in matters of art policy was adjusted to the balance of power that had already found its institutional expression (Goebbels' ministry, Rosenberg's supervisory office). Hitler's intervention smoothed over certain power conflicts, but at the same time confirmed the principle of rivalry[84] within the culture-political and art-political leadership. The stabilizing function of this principle had proved its worth, the swing to the new style of leadership had in no small part been effected through rivalries.

2. The folkish spokesmen who had prevented Rosenberg from carrying on an effective art policy had been eliminated. The last doctrinaire positions had fallen. Rosenberg inclined, and the orientation of his cultural policy became more pragmatic and political than ever. Nothing more was heard of Professor Schultze-Naumburg and his "comrades in struggle." [85] Minister Frick ceased to concern himself with cultural policy. The winter art season of 1934–1935 in Berlin with its model exhibits of the National Socialist Cultural Community was soon to show how effectively Rosenberg had been pressed into forward flight.

3. National Socialist art policy had been defined. Modern art was excluded once and for all. It seems possible that Goebbels, though he had never committed himself in artistic matters, would have preferred a more liberal, flexible attitude toward modern art, if only in order to have a more varied assortment of publicistic weapons at his disposal.

Hitler's decision spelled the end of the art-political opposition. *Kunst der Nation* was suppressed at the beginning of 1935. Otto Andreas Schreiber and Hans Weidemann retreated to the last line of defense: under the sponsorship and protection of the Strength Through Joy movement, they organized internal factory exhibitions. Well into the war years they managed from time to time to show Nolde, Pechstein, Pankok, and Schmidt-Rottluff.[86] But the public heard nothing of it.

Thus at the end of 1934 the National Socialist art policy was adapted to the requirements of political power. The rejection of modern art showed that measured by these requirements even regard for a friendly foreign power (Italy) or for world opinion was secondary.

As already indicated by the reappearance of "Agitation and Propaganda" under the thin disguise of "Popular Enlightenment and Propaganda," the National Socialist cultural organization with its accent on political domination bore a Leninist imprint. It was distinguished from its model only by the markedly one-sided, undialectical, and in this sense total character of its functionalization, its unlimited exploitation of culture and art as one sphere of power among others. While in the "days of struggle" and even later the National Socialist cultural and art policy had still operated in accordance with programmatic principles, ideological positions, etc., these were liquidated by the swing to the new style of leadership. Without fixed aims, without political theory or principles, without educational program or ideology, National Socialist art policy had ceased to be anything other than a political weapon. Thus the measures, practices, and tendencies that now constituted the art policy of the Third Reich can no longer be discussed in terms of cultural history. This policy was a break with all historical contents. Instead, politics was decreed to be "art." Traditional concepts are inapplicable to such a situation, and this makes it difficult to analyze or formulate National Socialist art policy. The historian can only observe its functioning and attempt to derive from it new categories with which to define it.

428   *Hildegard Brenner*

This is what was done by the National Socialist art policy itself: soon it was discovered that the arts could serve as an instrument of social control. The road was clear for the development of new and effective forms of "art-political" action.

NOTES

This paper is based largely on unpublished material. The only work published since 1945 to touch on the events which here concern us is that of P. O. Rave. They are mentioned in the memoirs of a few artists (Schlemmer, Moholy-Nagy). Indications of the chronology of the events and statements are contained in German newspapers and periodicals of the years 1933 and 1934, particularly the *Völkischer Beobachter* (VB), the *Deutsche Allgemeine Zeitung* (DAZ), and *Kunst der Nation*. Important source material concerning the political implications of artistic discussion were found, though in dispersed form, in archives some of which have not yet been exploited, as for example: a part of the epistolary controversy between Rosenberg and Goebbels in the Centre de Documentation Juive Contemporaine, Paris (cited in the following notes as CDJC), and a part at the Berlin Documentation Center (BDC) and Bundesarchiv Koblenz (BA). Certain primary source material has also been obtained from private persons. Finally, direct and indirect participants in the events were questioned. Their statements were taken down in writing (cited in the following as "Prot.," the Roman numeral being the code for the name of the person questioned). These can be consulted in the archives of the Institut für Zeitgeschichte in Munich.

1. Martin Broszat, *Der Nazionalsozialismus*, Stuttgart, 1960, pp. 21 ff.

2. Werner Stephan, *Joseph Goebbels. Dämon einer Diktatur*, Stuttgart, 1949; Heinrich Fraenkel and Roger Manvell, *Goebbels. Eine Biographie*, Cologne and Berlin, 1960.

3. CDJC, CXLV–618.

4. "The Kampfbund für Deutsche Kultur undertakes to gather together the treasures of folkish culture and its bearers. From this reservoir the NSDAP Section of Popular Education communicates the best to the people in the form of education.

"The culture-political organizations in the districts are enlisted on the service of this section of the Kampfbund." From "Dienstvorschrift für die Politische Organisation der NSDAP."

5. An account of the art policy of Rosenberg and Frick before

1933 is provided in my book, *Die Kunstpolitik des Nazionalsozialismus* (Rowohlt).

6. BDC/Akte, "K.f.D.K. Reichsleitung."

7. In October 1933 Professor K. A. von Müller resigned from the position of Reich leader of the Reichsbund Volkstum und Heimat. Alfred Rosenberg took his place and quietly incorporated the organization into the Kampfbund. BDC/Akte, "K.f.D.K. Reichsleitung."

8. Paul Ortwin Rave, *Kunstdiktatur im Dritten Reich,* Hamburg, 1949, pp. 24 f.

9. At the end of February 1933, a propaganda team of the National Socialist Students Association "occupied" the Hochschule für Kunsterziehung in Berlin-Schöneberg, locked the faculty in the vestibule, and hoisted the swastika flag on the roof. Reich Minister Rust ordered an investigation of the incident.

10. The demonstration outside the Berlin stock exchange, in which a number of windows were broken, took place one afternoon in February or March 1933; the "Worker and Student" demonstration occurred some time between March and June 1933 (some 20,000 students and Young National Socialist Workers are thought to have participated). There were other demonstrations of this kind. The official hushing-up of these incidents makes a reconstruction difficult.

11. Their other connections have not been established. There is no proof of a link with Strasser or Roehm. Prot. III, 2, 4, 7, 12, 13; V, 1, and XII, 1. Leers's posthumous papers (DZA Potsdam) also contain no information on the matter.

12. Prot. III, 2, 3, 9, and BDC/Akten, "Hinkel."

13. Prot. III, 1, 2, 3, 7, 22.

14. Their author, the Berlin art critic Doctor Schwark, was not named. Prot. III, 2.

15. DAZ, July 10, 1933. Italics in original text.

16. Geheimrat Justi offered to finance the speakers' trips if they wished to speak in other cities. Prot. III, 1, and correspondence of the Berlin Nationalgalerie.

17. Signed "Schimmerohn." Italics in original.

18. DAZ, July 10, 1933.

19. *Ibid.*

20. DAZ, July 13, 1933.

21. Barlach rejected this offer of reconciliation. Prot. II, 1.

22. Prot. VI, 1.

23. Rave, *op. cit.,* p. 42, and Prot. III, 2.

24. The reaction abroad was unexpectedly violent and the new Reich's reputation suffered. Moreover, the burning of the books set off the third wave of emigration, which cost Germany an appreciable part of its intellectual class. See also Fraenkel-Manvell, *op. cit.,* p. 191.

25. E.g., *Basler National-Zeitung,* April 30, 1934.
26. Since 1930 Weidemann had directed party propaganda in the Essen-Ruhr district. In March 1933 he became a section head at the Reich headquarters of the NSDAP—Sec. II, Propaganda.
27. Professor Schardt was "specially charged with examining the art works in the possession of the Kronprinzenpalais." (BA/Akten Reichskanzlei, R. 43 II/1235, "Schreiben vom 11.7. 1933."
28. VB, July 14, 1933.
29. "Parteiinterner Informationsbericht über Dr. Johann von Leers aus dem Jahre 1936," Prot. III, 1, 5.
30. Handwritten manuscript in the archives of the Berlin Nationalgalerie; also VB, January 16, 1934; *Hansische Hochschulzeitung,* No. 10, 1936; *Die Bewegung,* No. 15 of April 8, 1936; *Das Bild,* February 2, 1937.
31. No. 15 of July 10, 1933.
32. VB, July 16–17, 1933.
33. DAZ, July 22, 1933.
34. Prot. III, 1.
35. *Neue Zürcher Zeitung,* August 28, 1933. See also Oskar Schlemmer, *Briefe und Tagebücher,* Munich, 1958, pp. 313 f. Paul Ferdinand Schmidt made a similar attempt to justify modern art in *Deutsches Volkstum,* 2nd October issue, 1933.
36. Perhaps the most instructive example of this is the falsification of art history in Kurt Karl Eberlein's polemic, *Was ist deutsch in der deutschen Kunst? Schriften zur deutschen Lebenssicht,* published by Erich Rothacker, Bonn and Leipzig, 1934. Cf. Wilhelm Pinder's reply in *Zeitschrift für Kunstgeschichte* 1934/II, pp. 53 ff.
37. Rave, *op. cit.,* pp. 33 f.; Prot. VI, 1, and IV, 1.
38. Rave, *op. cit.,* p. 54.
39. "After repeated discussions with Party Comrade Hess, Party Comrade Rosenberg has written an extensive memorandum explaining in detail why (Hess) should request the Führer to grant the KfDK official recognition as the National Socialist cultural organization in the near future." (From "Rundschreiben N. 17. An alle Landesleiter KfDK," February 12, 1933) BDC/Akte, "KfDK Reichsleitung." See also Document PS–048 in *Das politische Tagebuch Alfred Rosenbergs aus den Jahren 1934/35 and 1939/40,* published by Hans-Günther Seraphim. Berlin and Frankfurt, 1956, p. 129.
40. BDC/HA–NSDAP, Akte No. 169.
41. Prot. III, 1.
42. Prot. III, 1.
43. Prot. III, 22.
44. Prot. III, 22.
45. VB, March 16, 1934.
46. An exhibition of Italian architecture "in the Bauhaus style," had been held previously in Berlin (VB).
47. Printed in Leipzig in 1934.

48. Quoted from *Kunst der Nation*, April 15, 1934. Italics in original. Also *Frankfurter Zeitung*, April 7, 1934.

49. *Ibid.*

50. *Kunst der Nation*, April 1, 1934.

51. Rosenberg, *op. cit.* (see note 39, above), p. 26.

52. CDJC, CXLII–246: Rosenberg's letter to Goebbels, August 8, 1934, 8 pp.; Goebbels' letter to Rosenberg, September 25, 1934, 6 pp. The correspondence seems to have closed with these two letters.

53. Rosenberg's letter to Goebbels of August 30, 1934, concludes with the remark: "I have sent copies of your letters and mine to the Führer's deputy."

54. CDJC, CXLII, letter of September 25, 1934.

55. CDJC, CXLII, letter of August 30, 1934.

56. This was also the occasion of his part in stormy arguments with Goering (over the Prussian theater commission).

57. The art teachers who had hitherto been under the exclusive jurisdiction of the Kultusministerium were now given compulsory membership in the Reichskammer der bildenden Künste. Despite Goebbels' demand, the museum directors remained under the Kultusministerium (edict of May 15, 1934).

58. "Rede vor den Theaterleitern, 8.5. 1933," in *Dokumente der Deutschen Politik*, Berlin, 1939, Vol. I, p. 321.

59. Prot. XI, 1.

60. The attempt in 1934 to persuade Thomas Mann to return to Germany was unsuccessful. Marlene Dietrich was the object of far more persistent but equally unsuccessful efforts.

61. Speech at Humboldt University in Berlin, end of May 1933. Quoted from *Angriff*, July 1, 1933.

62. *Ibid.*

63. "Rede vor den Theaterleitern," *loc. cit.*, p. 321 (see note 58).

64. *Ibid.*, p. 322.

65. "Rede Dr. Fricks über die neue Erziehung, 9.5.1933," in *Dokumente der Deutschen Politik*, p. 326.

66. "Rede zur Eröffnung der Reichskulturkammer 15.11.1933," *ibid.*, p. 365.

67. "Das politische Tagebuch Alfred Rosenbergs," *ibid.*, p. 49.

68. *Dokumente der Deutschen Politik*, Vol. II, p. 324.

69. Alfred Rosenberg, *Gesinnung und Kunst*, 1935.

70. Paul Schultze-Naumburg, *Kunst und Rasse*, Munich, 1928.

71. Speakers, according to Schultze-Naumburg, were Professor Paul Schmitthenner, Reich group leader of the "Fine Arts Section" of the Kampfbund, and Doctor Nonn, director of the "Architects and Engineers" group. See also Schlemmer, *op. cit.*, pp. 313 f.

72. "Art is always the creation of one particular blood, and the form-bound essence of an art is truly understood only by creatures of like blood; to others it means less or nothing at all. . . ." From

Alfred Rosenberg, *Der Mythos des 20. Jahrhunderts*, Munich, 1935, p. 120.

73. Speech in Nuremberg, September 5, 1934. Quoted from *Reichstagung in Nürnberg 1934, herausgegeben im Auftrag des Frankenführers Julius Streicher*, Berlin, 1934.

74. In his interview with the *Hamburger Nachrichten* (February 2, 1934) Doctor Ruggero Vasari spoke ironically of the recent exhibition of German art in Florence. Rosenberg's invocation of the "Greek tradition," i.e., the anti-Roman implications of his search for artistic ancestors, had provoked public protest in Rome.

75. Speech in Nuremberg, *loc. cit.*

76. Speech in Nuremberg, *loc. cit.*

77. *Ibid.*

78. "Rede auf einer Kundgebung der Reichsjugendführung in Berlin am 15.9.1934 anlässlich des 100. Geburtstags Heinrich von Treitschke," in Walter Frank, *Kämpfende Wissenschaft*, Hamburg, 1934, pp. 30 ff.

79. Speech in Nuremberg, September 5, 1934, *loc. cit.*

80. "Brief Hitlers an Goebbels vom 30.6.1930." BDC/Akte, "Gregor Strasser."

81. VB, January 16, 1934, and speech in Nuremberg, September 5, 1934.

82. See the chapter on "Weltanschauung und Organisation."

83. Only Goebbels made an exception. The *"völkische Wanderapostel"* were featured in his one-man show at the Pharus-Säle in North Berlin.

Goebbels spoke as follows of the folkish spokesmen's latent threat to the NSDAP: "As long as the party is occupied with great political tasks, these [folkish] efforts represent no danger at all to its development. They become dangerous only in times of party crisis caused by prohibitions or internal difficulties. Then a field of activity is thrown open to these specialists whose interest is *solely* anti-Semitic or racial." (From *Kampf um Berlin*, Vol. I, *Der Anfang (1926–1927)*, Munich, 1932, p. 217.

84. The struggles for power were carried on on this basis. In 1934 (presumably toward the end of the year) Rosenberg and Goebbels sent Hitler a "pact" they had drawn up jointly. It requested for Rosenberg a "Reichskulturamt" within the *Reichsleitung* of the NSDAP and for Goebbels as an equivalent an additional "Reichskammer für Kulturpflege." CDJC, CXLV–581.

85. Adolf Bartels was the only one of them ever to be retrieved from oblivion. This occurred in 1937 when as the "oldest folkish cultural pioneer of the present day," he received "in recognition . . . of his work for the folkish cultural renewal" the Reich's highest award for cultural achievement, the Adlerschild des Deutschen Reiches.

86. Prot. III, 14, 19, 21.

The Origins of
Inhumanity

✠ ✠ ✠

10

Social Darwinism in Germany, Seen as a Historical Problem

HANS-GÜNTER ZMARZLIK
(For Gerhard Ritter on His Seventy-fifth Birthday)

Social Darwinism is one of the more recent "isms" in our field. Though used by biologists as early as 1906,[1] the term did not gain general acceptance among historians until 1944, when Richard Hofstadter published his *Social Darwinism in American Thought.*

In Germany since then the critical study of National Socialism has given additional weight to the term and the concept it stands for. Under the Third Reich millions have been systematically murdered in the name of the German people. A historian trying to account for this monstrous reality must take all manner of factors into consideration. Among the most important of these are certain ideological components: a biologistic dogma of racial inequality; a moral nihilism invoking the "struggle for existence" and the "survival of the fittest" as a universal law of nature; and—resulting from both of these—the conviction that radical extermination of the racially inferior elements and the selection of racially superior elements are justified by the fact that these policies are a vital necessity to a people that wishes to be strong.

"Struggle for existence," "extermination," and "selection" are terms of Darwinist origin, and this is no accident; a glance at Hitler's *Mein Kampf* shows that a

monism tinged with popular Darwinism figured prominently in the outlook of the National Socialist leadership.
It was one of the few ideological elements that dominated
Hitler's thinking throughout his political career and that
he did not manipulate in accordance with tactical needs.
Thus it becomes incumbent upon the history of ideas to
investigate the origin and meaning of this Darwinism.[2]
But the question is not only where Hitler and his closer
collaborators derived this ideology. It must also be asked
whether this Darwinism is a primitive version of conceptions that can be found elsewhere, for example, in bourgeois rightist circles. For if this were true, we might perhaps more readily understand why the inhuman theory
and practice of Hitler and his party did not in these
circles arouse the opposition that their intellectual and
ethical level might have led one to expect. And the scope
of our inquiry must be broadened still further. For if we
wish to appreciate the full historical importance of Social
Darwinism, we cannot confine ourselves to the prehistory
of the Third Reich, but must study the social consequences of the Darwinian theory from the very beginning.

So broad an undertaking confronts us at the start with a
confusing picture. For Darwinism has been invoked in
support of very divergent interpretations of the social
process. The proponents both of an altruistic ethic and
of a brutal master-race morality take it as a foundation; it
was invoked by liberal believers in progress, but also by
the spokesmen of a crass historical fatalism, by the champions of egalitarian socialism but also by those who
formulated doctrines of racial inequality. A closer look at
the developments and their chronology enables us, however, to reduce the countless variants of Social Darwinism
to two basic forms, the one determined primarily by the
idea of evolution and the other by the principle of selection. What is meant by this will, it is to be hoped, be
shown by the following remarks, in which I shall first at-

tempt to give a descriptive analysis of the principal vari-
eties of Social Darwinist thinking, and then take up the
question of their historical importance.

The story begins in 1859 with the appearance of Darwin's chief work, *On the Origin of Species by means of
Natural Selection, or the Preservation of Favoured Races
in the Struggle for Life.* This book was eminently timely;
within a few years it not only revolutionized the science of
biology but aroused passionate interest far beyond the
confines of biology. With the precision characteristic of
Darwin, the title indicates the thesis at the core of his
theory: it combines the idea of a cohesion in the developments of all living creatures—an idea repeatedly put forward since Buffon and Lamarck but never adequately explained—with a theory of selection, that is, the idea that
the species had evolved through selection among varied
offspring in the course of the struggle for life.

The explosive force of this cool, scientific formulation
becomes apparent when we consider the prevailing conceptions of the time. To simplify, the biological thinking
of the pre-Darwinian was based on two metaphysical assumptions: the notion of universal prototypes, which has
its purest expression in Plato's theory of ideas, and that of
individual final causes after the manner of the Aristo-
telian entelechies.[3] In one form or another these conceptions presided over all attempts to interpret the wealth of
data brought to light in the first half of the nineteenth
century in the fields of zoology, botany, embryology,
paleontology, and related sciences. Darwin now opposed a
mechanical explanation, capable of dispensing with all
extranatural and supernatural factors, to these idealistic
principles, which imposed a pre-established intellectual
form on the events of the natural process, so predicating
the existence of a formative hand behind the phenomena,
of a power which determined the direction of development in accordance with a preconceived plan, in short, of
a higher unity amid empirical multiplicity. Up until then

the awe-inspiring "fitness" of living creatures, their meaningful integration with their environments, had been regarded as the work of a superior guiding power, or in
Christian terms, as the natural manifestation of God's cre-
ativeness. Now this fitness was no longer to be conceived
as the product of causes operating in accordance with
some higher purposes, but as the result of a vast number
of possibilities of adaptation which served no transcen-
dent aim but were selected or rejected on the basis of
their aptitude for preserving and promoting the viability
of individuals and groups from moment to moment. The
developments of organisms could now be understood as a
sum of improvisations unrelated to any ideal plan, and
the natural cosmos as a product of chance.

Thus Darwin took the magic and metaphysics out of
the natural process by reducing it to interactions that
could be understood in scientific terms: he naturalized biology and at the same time made it accessible to a historical method, that is, he immersed the species, which until
then had been universally regarded as constant, in a
stream of development descending from a past whose
remoteness had never before been suspected and contended that all the innumerable species had risen gradually from the simplest forms. And far from being a mere
hypothesis, Darwin's theory was supported by a wealth of
convincing empirical evidence.

Darwin's book gave the idea of evolution a hitherto undreamed-of force. It exerted a profound influence on all
the sciences[4] and indirectly on every sphere of social life.
But here we shall not speak of these indirect emanations.
The social dynamic of Darwin's doctrine expressed itself
directly in the violent controversies that arose almost immediately between Darwinists and spokesmen for the
churches. The stumbling block was the fact that the theory of evolution did not stop with animals but offered
compelling proof that man was descended from the animal kingdom. Though Darwin had said nothing conclu-

sive about the origin or specific character of the qualities which gave man his special position as a thinking being, nevertheless, by effacing the dividing line between man and animal, his proof of the natural connection between them struck a violent blow at the traditional concept of man.

The controversy began when a monism of Darwinist inspiration attacked the biblical doctrine of Creation and Christian dogma in general. The leader in this assault was Professor Ernst Haeckel of Jena, whose brilliance as a zoologist was matched by his naiveté as a natural philosopher. Haeckel did not content himself with the empirical and analytical methods to which nineteenth-century science owed its extraordinary progress. In Darwin's theory of descendance he saw a means of providing a unified interpretation of physical, biological, and psychological phenomena, of arriving at a synthesis of the specialized sciences and on this foundation of building a universal philosophy. This was a crude abuse of Darwin's theory and was condemned by the leading natural scientists of the day, Rudolf Virchow in the lead. But Haeckel was not to be discouraged. He became the prophet of a monist nature religion based on Darwinism—which disposed of the belief in a personal God and Creator as an old wives' tale.

Despite his radical attack on the dogmas of the Christian churches, Haeckel did not criticize the ethical norms of Christian origin by which Western man had hitherto oriented his social conduct. To be sure, side by side with the need to love one's neighbor he stressed the duty of self-preservation and self-assertion in accordance with the natural law of the struggle for life. But he did not reject altruistic, humanitarian attitudes. On the contrary: only when a balance between struggle and harmonious order such as that revealed in nature had been recognized as the universal law of life and embodied in the will of the individual would mankind come of age and thus become capable of fulfilling the maxim: "Let man be noble, helpful, and good." Thus Haeckel amalgamated the naturalistic determinism of his mechanical concept of development with the ideas of a pre-established harmony between individual strivings and general development and of progress toward ever higher ethical perfection.

At the same time attempts were made to include sociology in a monist synthesis based on Darwinism. These "bioorganic" social theories, by far the most significant of which was developed by Herbert Spencer, rested on the assumption that society was a special kind of organism, similar to a biological organism in constitution and function and hence subject to the same laws. Society was regarded as an aggregate whose nature results from the nature of its units, that is, human individuals. The physiologically demonstrable tendency of organisms to develop into more highly differentiated and integrated species was interpreted as a trend toward perfection and explained in man by gradual adaptation to an increasingly complex social environment. Thus a virtually automatic progressive evolution was regarded as the fundamental law governing the natural and the social process alike, so that the competitive struggle between individuals became a guarantee of continuous progress in ethics and civilization. Seen as the power behind human progress, struggle lost its sting and became an impersonal natural force.

The evolutionary optimism that characterized the first phase in the application of Darwinist principles to natural philosophy, social theory, and ethics was far more an expression of the liberal, rationalist doctrines of the time than of Darwin's theory. For the core of the Darwinian theory is a process of selection in which value judgments play no part. Although in the "improvement of most organisms in respect of their aptitude for life" [5] Darwin saw a certain trend of the evolutionary process toward higher and more efficient types, he avoided deriving criteria of value from this view. As a keen-sighted and incorruptible observer he perceived that development in nature is not necessarily upward. Strictly speaking, his theory states merely that success in the struggle for existence signifies biological fitness for the living conditions prevailing at a particular time and place. Thus Social Darwinism in the more specific sense did not come into being until development ceased to be equated with progress and the theory of natural selection was taken as the principal model for social and political thinking. Only then did the special feature of Darwin's theory, the mechanical explanation of natural development by processes of selection and extermination in disregard of all teleology, achieve its full effect.

A shift of accent in this direction took place when in a period characterized by the second industrial revolution, by imperialism and the national uprisings in eastern Central Europe, the doctrine of liberalism and with it men's confidence in the natural harmony and automatic upward trend of the social process ceased to be dominant. This change of climate which began in the seventies throughout the Western world and became more pronounced in the nineties was marked by a "naturalization" of political thinking and a brutalization of political methods. This is clearly shown in the writings of Social Darwinist authors. What only a short while before was interpreted as a free competition of individuals, with the prize going to the ablest and ethically best, was now looked upon literally as "struggle for existence"—a permanent struggle for self-assertion through increased power—and not primarily between individuals but between collectivities: social interest groups, nations, and races.

Thus the theory of natural selection assumed central importance in Social Darwinist thinking; the struggle for existence was taken as a fundamental law and from it was derived a system of Darwinist social ethics in which the accent was put on the instincts of self-preservation and self-assertion. The proponents of this ethic postulated the right of the stronger and thus sanctioned the egoistic power drive of the group, nation, or race to which they belonged. From here it was only a step to the condemnation of Christian ethics and the humanitarianism based on natural law that was the heritage of the Enlightenment. Certain authors spoke openly of a "morality of pity" or "humanitarian babbling," out of keeping with the new, harder era.

The nineteenth century had owed the greater part of its scientific achievement to the "naturalistic revolution against metaphysical tradition," [6] a revolution in which Darwin, Comte, and Marx had played leading roles. But now the extreme radicalization of Darwinist principles[7] gives us an intimation of the threat to social praxis inherent in this same revolution. Of this the Social Darwinists were scarcely aware; in any case it meant little to them compared with the proud certainty of having at last fathomed the realities of the politicosocial process.

In this second stage of Social Darwinist thinking a new school made its appearance. At the turn of the twentieth century the new school broke with the crude naturalistic monism of the older school characterized above, which held that supposedly all-embracing natural laws were at work in human society and that all social phenomena derived from the operation of these laws. This view had been rendered obsolete by the neo-Kantian theory of knowledge and untenable by the progress in biology. The younger Social Darwinists inquired into the relations between social processes and the biological development of man. Essentially this offered a promising field for research. But unfortunately, the younger Social Darwinists, instead of contenting themselves with analyzing and interpreting empirical phenomena, derived from their analyses prescriptions for a new social order and felt called upon to pave the way for such an order.

This was typical of the activism that became widespread at the end of the nineteenth century. In at-

tempting to give an "Over-all Picture of the Cultural
Development" shortly before the First World War, a contemporary wrote as follows:

> The gigantic development of technology and industry
> has . . . not only basically changed the externals of
> the world but also produced a new type of man who is
> keenly aware that, as Marx . . . put it, the essential is
> not to give a different interpretaton of the world, but
> to change it. In other words: the rise of technology and
> industry has created a new relationship between theory
> and practice. And between the past and future as well.
> Formerly men of the past, we have become men of the
> future. Comte's maxim: *Savoir c'est voir pour prévoir*
> has become the watchword of our day.[8]

This attitude did not spring only from the sense of
power inspired by the enormously increased scientific and
technical tools now at man's disposal, but also from a critique of the times, that is to say, a will to assume responsibility for the future because men had lost confidence in a
self-evident and automatic progress. The Marxists had
still concerned themselves primarily with a critique of
false consciousness, an attempt to correct the concious-
ness of the masses and so give increased impetus to a trend
that was already inherent in the historical process. The
young Social Darwinists formulated the problem more
radically. They started from the assumption that modern
civilization involved mortal dangers to human society because it vitiated man's biological substance—a diagnosis
based on the conviction that the achievement of individuals and social groups hinged essentially on their inherited racial constitution. Hitherto, they held, natural selection had seen to it that by and large the biologically
superior individuals should occupy the leading positions
in society. But now this regulator had been dangerously
impaired. Consequently it was necessary to complement
natural selection by a socially guided selection, for otherwise a general "vulgarization," that is, qualitative deteri-

oration, of the human substance was inevitable, with disastrous consequences for the group's cultural creativity and capacity for political self-assertion.

Thus the Social Darwinists held that it was the responsibility of the collectivity to control spheres of individual life which in the era of the liberal constitutional state had been excluded from the public jurisdiction. Certain consequences of the industrial revolution had, it is true, long since made it necessary to "organize a fight for public health." [9] Thanks to progress in science and medicine this fight had been largely successful. But this was merely a matter of combating visible evils by preventive measures of social hygiene, so providing humanly acceptable living conditions in the present. The younger Social Darwinists, however, considered it vitally important to put through the systematic application of sociobiological practices whose benefits would be reaped only by future generations and whose urgency most contemporaries found it hard to understand. Their program implied an extremely far-reaching departure from the conceptions regarding the relations between the state and individual that the nineteenth century had imprinted on the public mind. This becomes still more evident when we consider the two main and distinct Social Darwinist orientations: racial anthropology and racial hygiene.

The racial anthropologists took the difference between races as their point of departure. They tried to provide the speculative racial theories of the nineteenth century, in particular that of Gobineau, with a scientific foundation, and to develop them further. With the help of skull and body measurements and pigment specifications, in other words, with the methods of so-called physical anthropology,[10] they determined and described certain racial types. Behind the divergent physical characteristics they sought, and believed they found, divergent intellectual and psychological qualities. The highest rank and hence the right to social leadership were attributed to the North

Germanic race. Thus the biological care of this race, the preservation of its purity, seemed the most urgent task, and the most vital politicosocial goal was held to be a social organism in which the bearers of the most valuable racial heritage formed the ruling class.

Thus these Social Darwinists invoked the highest authority of the late nineteenth century, namely science, as a justification for deriving from the empirically demonstrable diversity of human groups a strict dogma of inequality and for denying the claim of all individuals to equal social and political opportunities. Opposing modern industrial society with its tendency toward mobility and democratization, they embarked on a social-reactionary course which inevitably led them to regard the implementation of racial-biological demands at the expense of individual liberties as at least a necessary evil.

It is perfectly obvious that the claim of the racial anthropologists to have found a scientific foundation for their theses rested on a massive self-delusion. For—quite aside from the fact that they vastly underestimated the role of environment—the concept of race with which they operated obliged them to oversimplify the complex relations between phenotype and genotype so as to make it appear as though certain outward characteristics were invariably associated with certain intellectual and psychological characteristics. Looking as they did upon the races as distinct, self-enclosed units and accordingly "explaining the warlike and cultural achievements of the various states by their physiological characters and the inequality of their social substances," [11] they were obliged to misinterpret biological and social reality and force it into a bed of Procrustes.[12] And indeed the proponents of racial anthropology were dilettantish free-lance scholars with inadequate scientific training.

Not so the racial hygienists. Here the tone was set by university men who, in studying social processes from a sociological point of view, made a serious effort to confine themselves to demonstrable facts. They were concerned mainly with the problems of racial degeneration which, they held, entailed a qualitative population policy. While the racial anthropologists put the accent on "Nordification," the racial hygienists, for the most part, stressed the need of improving the race. The science of genetics had made enormous progress thanks to Weismann's germ-plasm theory, the rediscovery of the Mendelian laws of heredity, de Vries' investigations of mutations, etc. But this progress had brought with it a decision of fundamental importance, which had the effect of radicalizing Darwin's principle of selection. Hitherto biologists had assumed with Lamarck that acquired characteristics could be inherited, and Darwin himself had accepted this thesis. Now it came to be generally recognized that hereditary characters were passed down from generation to generation substantially unaffected by external influences and underwent change only through mutations, that is, abrupt modification of the germ plasm.

The racial hygienists inferred that if individually acquired characteristics could not be transmitted, then the qualities that individuals acquired by training and social influence would die with them unless the hereditary substance could be preserved from harm. Thus, to their minds, the progress of civilization, in which their contemporaries took such pride, was a series of Pyrrhic victories, because the joint effects of modern civilization and of Christian humanitarian ethics were harmful from the standpoint of racial biology. Constitutionally feeble persons and sufferers from hereditary ailments, who in former times would not even have attained the age of reproduction, were now able to bring forth numerous offspring, while the most gifted, socially superior classes tended to limit the size of their families. Both social institutions and public opinion, the racial hygienists held, were dominated by extreme individualist conceptions. Thus the duty to preserve the species, that is, the individual's biological obligation to the people as a whole, had been criminally neglected.

Reflections of this kind were at that time current in all industrial countries and led scientists to concern themselves increasingly with biosocial problems. The racial hygienists made valuable contributions to this body of thought. Unfortunately their scientific discipline did not preserve them from the fundamental error of the other Social Darwinist schools, namely, drawing inferences about the nature of man as such from scientifically verifiable data concerning partial aspects of man. Though they tried to avoid unwarranted generalizations and were well aware that standards of social conduct cannot be derived from the scientific observation of natural processes, their belief that the quality and viability of human society depended essentially on the hereditary, biological factor led them to regard racial hygiene as a matter of life and death, far more important than all other existing problems. Thus, for example, Fritz Lenz, professor of racial hygiene at the University of Munich and one of the most strictly scientific proponents of the racial hygiene school, wrote: "The question of the genetic quality of the coming generations is a hundred times more important than the conflict between capitalism and socialism and a thousand times more important than the struggle between black-white-red and black-red-gold." * [13] Countless such statements might be cited. They all call for a new philosophy of life hinging on considerations of racial hygiene.

The consequence of this orientation was that among the racial hygienists we find the same critique of civilization as among the racial anthropologists, though on an intellectually far higher level. Condemning modern in-

---

* Black, white, and red had been the colors of the Bismarck Empire; black, red, and gold, of the student movement and the liberal democratic revolution of 1848. The Weimar Republic adopted the latter for its national flag but the former for its commercial flag, and thereby practically institutionalized the national divisions and the bitter conflicts which the colors symbolized.

448   *Hans-Günter Zmarzlik*

dustrial society and disparaging democracy, its political correlate, as a leveler, they idealized rural life and a social structure based on strictly defined classes. Some of them even held that the Nordic-Germanic race is the most valuable factor in the European cultural sphere. They criticized individual racial anthropologists for their lack of scientific method, but regarded their work as a whole as deserving and worth encouraging.

Under these circumstances the unquestionable idealism of the younger Social Darwinists can only be called misguided. They desired a better future for their own people, and indeed for all mankind, and wished to observe humanitarian principles in putting through their aims. They earnestly and with subjective sincerity wished to save the health of the nation from the harmful influence of modern life. But in actual fact they favored the emergence of dangers far worse than those they wished to prevent.

This last statement, to be sure, anticipates our findings. Thus far we have merely shown that a certain group of ideas can be singled out from the realm of ideas in general and described with the help of the concept of Social Darwinism. This demonstrates the historical existence of our subject. But what of its historical significance?

An answer must be based on two criteria: (1) What has been the historical influence of Social Darwinism? (2) What light does it throw, as a *pars pro toto,* on the general history of the era?

The question of how and to what extent ideas exert a historical influence soon leads from the realm of demonstrable fact to that of conjecture and opinion. This is especially true in the case of Social Darwinism. For here we are not dealing—as in Marxism, for example—with a logically self-contained ideology that interprets every sphere of life from a unified point of view and through constant exegetic reflection on the work of a thinker of high intellectual standing repeatedly and publicly renews and demonstrates its inner unity. Here, on the contrary, we have to do with a large number of small minds who at first sight seem very different and whose inner cohesion and common trend are fully apparent only to a historian. The emanations of Social Darwinist thought are obscure and diffuse.

Under such circumstances it is not profitable to ask "Who took what from whom?" and try to demonstrate dependencies and connections on the basis of direct borrowings and influences. It will be best to start by estimating the potential field of influence of Social Darwinism. One might begin with an inquiry into the number, social position, and organization of its exponents, and above all into the extent of their audience. This last might be estimated by the distribution of figures for Social Darwinist books and their reception by the press, the circulation figures of periodicals carrying this material, and the distribution of articles by Social Darwinist authors published elsewhere.

First one should explore these sectors of political publishing in which one might expect to find a special affinity to Social Darwinist ideas. Then the positive findings should be tested for their relation to the ideological context of the time, and on this basis it should be determined to what extent they influenced men's actions and attitudes. Independently of this, it should be determined, on the basis of the speeches and writings of leading party politicians or statesmen, whether and to what extent Social Darwinist conceptions have entered into the horizon of persons in responsible positions.

Unfortunately the tools for such an undertaking are lacking. For example, little biographical material on the bourgeois "rightist opposition"—the gathering place for nationalistic activists under the empire and the sphere which is of chief interest to us here—has thus far become available. This applies still more to the authors and groups whose dissatisfaction with the heritage of the nineteenth century found expression in criticism of civilization and reform movements of all sorts. Along with investigations of this kind, a chronological table of the sales figures for publications which either ran into large editions or otherwise attracted attention would be helpful, as would a lexicographical work giving the circulation figures, editorial board, distribution area, type of readers, special aims, etc. of the more important periodicals (and, if possible, newspapers as well).

In a word, any attempt to explore the phenomenon of Social Darwinism points up the necessity of expanding the traditional history of ideas into a social history of ideas.[14] The urgency of this need is not confined to our special problem; it concerns problems confronting historical research in general, at least in the period extending from the late nineteenth century to the present day. For, to cite Meinecke's image, the history of ideas is like the ascension of a peak in "an ideal mountain range." In striving to show how "the essence of events is reflected" in leading minds,[15] it leaves concrete history far behind. Nevertheless it has made a significant contribution to the elucidation of concrete history because in the modern era down to the middle of the nineteenth century the social structure and the workings of tradition were such that inferences of general historical relevance can be made from the works of the great political thinkers and interpreters of history from Machiavelli to Hegel, and even up to Ranke and Treitschke.

This has been less true since the old European social forms and mechanisms of domination were broken down by the dynamic of technological, industrial, and social change. Since then the historical process has undergone a transformation—deplored by Huizinga—that obliges the historian to deal more than before with collective phenomena and statistics.[16] The traditional dividing line between a relatively small group of recognized cultural and political protagonists and the great masses of the population who *undergo* history has been blurred, and this in turn has changed the relationships between ideas and actions, spirit and politics. It is becoming less and less possible to interpret history on the strength of a few unifying categories. Instead we encounter an inflation of competing outlooks which relativize one another. As the number of those who contribute to the formation of the political will increases, their intellectual level drops and with it their ability to make productive use of ideas. Specialized education and semi-education become dominant; appeals to the emotions and passions, the suggestive force of the demagogic will and of irrational mythical images crowd out rational arguments and form the integrating nuclei of conglomerates of ideas which invoke cultural traditions with which they often have little more in common than borrowed catchwords. Thus the factor of transformation is favored over against the factor of continuity, while ideal values and aims become far more than before a manipulable raw material in the hands of mere technicians of demagogy.

But even under these circumstances a relation still subsists between political behavior and the way in which each historic situation is interpreted. A situation is never a sum of facts; it is a horizon seen in contours imprinted by the prevailing culture. To this extent the behavior of the most pragmatic politician or the most primitive demagogue, and of their blindest supporters as well, is indirectly culture-determined and can consequently be elucidated on the basis of cultural forms. But the operation is more difficult than it was before. Our selection of phenomena to investigate must be determined not by intellectual rank but by demonstrable effect; since we shall be dealing with phenomena of low intellectual density and rationality, we must avoid overly literal definitions and interpretations of positions and attitudes if connections are to be made visible between a multiplicity of coexisting and overlapping trends. In other words: Anyone inquiring into the influence of ideas on actions in this

sphere of history, or seeking a reflection if not the very
essence of events in ideas, must come down from the high
mountains, forgo magnificent panoramas, and in the
manner indicated above investigate the plain where these
small minds dwell. Then alone will it become possible to
understand the "crude naturalism and biologism" whose
significance for political thinking was pointed out by
Treitschke and more recently by Meinecke.[17]

This brings us back to the question of the influence
that can be attributed to Social Darwinism. First it should
be noted that the Social Darwinist authors of the second
wave never received remotely as much public attention as
those exponents of "philosophical" Darwinism who attacked the Christian doctrines of Creation and Incarnation. Many such attacks were made during the sixties and
seventies in the Western cultural sphere.[18] It was in Germany, however, that they assumed the most spectacular
forms. Here, even before Darwin, Bible criticism and
materialism had fostered skepticism toward Christian rev-
elation. At the time of the *Kulturkampf* the arguments
provided by Darwin's theory were exploited all the more
ruthlessly by vulgar liberalistic thinkers. It was thus that
Ernst Haeckel became one of the best-known and most
controversial figures of his day. His polemics and those of
his companions in arms[19] were held to be so dangerous
that in the early eighties, for fear of the poison of Darwinist monism, the teaching of biology was forbidden in the
upper classes of the secondary schools, first in Prussia and
then in the rest of Germany—a prohibition which, with
some exceptions, remained in force for three decades. Another striking indication of the importance of a Darwinism twisted into a philosophy is the enormous success of
Haeckel's *Welträtsel*.[20] Appearing in 1900 and soon translated into twenty languages, the book sold more than
300,000 copies in Germany alone by 1914 and 100,000
more in the next decade.

These two examples indicate the two social spheres in

which we shall have to investigate the influence of Social Darwinist thinking. Haeckel had at first attracted the attention of *Kulturkampf* liberals belonging to the upper bourgeoisie. But by the turn of the century the educated bourgeoisie had ceased to be greatly impressed either by the crude monistic materialism that now assumed a particularly crass form in his writing or by his bitter attacks on the clergy. Haeckel had meanwhile been outdistanced by the progress of science and his philosophy had reduced itself to the absurd. To the intellectual world he was no more than a voice from the grave. But where ignorance of science, semi-education, and a tendency to criticize the established authorities coincided—in sections of the working class, among the declassed petty bourgeoisie, and in the young of all classes—this half-baked book made a profound impression. This is indicated by canvasses made at the time, by statements to be found in autobiographies, and by the more than 10,000 letters received by the author. With this book Social Darwinist thinking reached the social groups from which the radical elements of the nationalist movement would later issue, and the socialist workers as well.

This influence, to be sure, cannot be defined with precision. Essentially Haeckel's following was an antimovement; that is, the readers of his book were attracted less by what the book advocated (a nature religion on a pseudo-Darwinist foundation) than by what it attacked and how. An attempt in 1907 to enlist the like-minded in a monist association under Haeckel's patronage brought meager results. All this indicates that philosophical Darwinism as such was not an independent basis for orientation, but merely one factor in a more comprehensive vulgar enlightenment whose adherents were committed to a scientific interpretation of the world, the belief in progress and views ranging from anticlerical to anti-Christian.

It is even more difficult to define the specific influence of bio-organic social theories. It was in any event much smaller in Germany than in England and particularly the United States, to which Social Darwinist conceptions had spread chiefly through the work of Herbert Spencer and where they were well received thanks to a climate of extreme political and economic laissez-faire liberalism. In Germany Spencer's positivist evolutionism appealed chiefly to the Marxists, because it attached to a far greater extent than the Darwinian theory to the thesis that functionally acquired characteristics were hereditary and consequently laid special stress on the formative power of the social environment. Still, as "the most radical exponent of individualism" among the sociologists of his day, Spencer was only partially acceptable to the Marxists.[21]

He met with little response among the more state-minded members of the German liberal bourgeoisie, especially as his crude naturalism was rejected by the great majority. His chief importance in Germany was to have prepared the way for Darwin—after all, he had developed the basic principles of his evolutionist thinking before Darwin. He had been made known to a broad public chiefly by the works of Ludwig Büchner (1824–1899), who before Haeckel was the most widely read exponent of scientific materialism.[22] But even in Büchner the influence of Darwin and Haeckel overshadowed that of Spencer from the sixties on.

There was no lack of independent German attempts to construct sociological theories on the basis of Darwinist biology, but they were either ephemeral[23] or owed their influence to concepts deriving less from Social Darwinism than from the philosophical tradition of German idealism.[24]

Whereas the Social Darwinism of the first, evolutionist phase reached bourgeois and socialist circles alike, the second, selectionist phase was rejected by the Socialist camp. Its interpretation of the social process as an unrestricted struggle of forces fighting blindly for their right to live ran counter to Marxist ideology, as did the rejection, by the racial anthropologists and racial hygienists alike, of the environment theory and of egalitarian principles. At the same time the Social Darwinist audience within the bourgeois camp shifted to the extreme political right. But even here the most radical forms of the second phase of Social Darwinism, especially its consciously antihumanitarian and anti-Christian ethics, met with little response because they were too sharply opposed to the spirit of Wilhelminian Germany.[25] They had few active proponents. We need mention only two extremely active publicists, Friedrich von Hellwald (1842–1892), who in addition to numerous articles published a gloomily fatalistic *Kulturgeschichte in ihrer natürlichen Entwicklung* [Cultural History in its Natural Development] which ran into four editions from 1874 to 1890,[26] and Alexander Tille (1866–1912), who attracted attention in the nineties by his radical critique of Christian humanitarian ethics.[27]

The most essential contribution of Darwinism to the political thinking at the turn of the century has rightly been held to be the brutality emanating from the idea of the struggle for existence. Social Darwinist authors were among the most vociferous advocates of ruthlessly imperialist policies. These authors were more influential in the Anglo-Saxon countries[28] than in Germany, where only a few obscure writers based their arguments for imperialism directly on Social Darwinism.[29] In Germany, however, an extremely militant body of publicists proclaimed that the struggle for existence was both necessary and salutory in the lives of nations, and were still doing so at the turn of the century when in the Anglo-Saxon countries the tide of imperialist passion had ebbed and such voices had quickly died down. But these nationalist writers, among whom Theodor von Bernhardi was the best known, were not Social Darwinists. They borrowed more or less disconnected catchwords from Social Darwinism, but did not consistently apply the Darwinian theory to the interpretation of the politicosocial process.

Such political writers found it possible to conciliate the progressive naturalization of political concepts, which found its expression in a willingness to adopt certain Darwinisms, with a sense of pursuing high ethical aims. In retrospect, of course, it is only too obvious that this attitude was a façade. Thus it seems reasonable to suppose that sections of the bourgeoisie gradually became blinded to the immoralizing effect of a brutal struggle-for-existence ideology such as that subsequently advocated by Hitler. Hitler's vulgar Darwinistic monism also indicates that radical Social Darwinist ideas must have been massively propagated on a socially lower level. The middle links are probably to be sought in Austria, where the seemingly unbridgeable antagonisms between nationalities and the bitter struggles for national liberation made the older Social Darwinism seem more plausible than in prewar Germany. Also the shock of the defeat of 1866, felt to be a triumph of brute force and unscrupulousness over justice, operated in the same direction. For it is men who feel that they have been unjustly defeated who become most keenly aware that political and social life are essentially a struggle.

These motives were demonstrably determinant in Hellwald, a former Austrian officer; the same applies to the beginnings of sociology in Austria, which are associated with the names of Ludwig Gumplowicz (1838–1909) and Gustav Ratzenhofer (1842–1904).[30] Here again the idea of struggle occupied a central position and Darwinism exerted a powerful influence. It also influenced certain political leaders, as can be seen from the memoirs of Conrad von Hötzendorf. Such examples permit us to infer that works such as Hellwald's and of even more popular purveyors of Social Darwinism gained wider influence in Austria than in Germany. The matter has not yet been systematically investigated.[31]

The younger Social Darwinism also found its first expressions outside of Germany. The most internationally known and at the same time the most radical exponent of the anthropological trend was the Frenchman Georges Vacher de Lapouge, whose chief works appeared in the nineties.[32] However, he remained an isolated case in his own country.

The ideas of the racial hygiene school were first put forward by Francis Galton, a cousin of Darwin, who as early as the sixties stressed the hereditary character of intelligence, believed he had discovered that gifted persons tended to have fewer children than others, and from such observations developed a new branch of applied science which he later called eugenics.[33] Its purpose was to develop means of improving the innate qualities of individuals for the greater good of the community, while respecting the values of the liberal social order. Most of his successors continued in this ethically inoffensive direction. Only a few English authors put forward more radical demands.[34]

The first German exponents of a scientifically grounded (at least in its own opinion) social biology also aimed to avoid conflict with the imperatives of humanitarianism. But gradually humanitarian considerations were crowded out by concern for the future of their own people—fostered at first by the nationalistic power politics of the early twentieth century and later, after the military and political catastrophe of the First World War, by a desire to help a defeated and weakened Germany to rise again.

The German school took its orientation neither from Lapouge nor from Galton, but started out independently. It came in, as it were, with the new century: on January 1, 1900, the head of the firm of Krupp offered an unusually high prize for the best essay on the question: "What does the theory of descendance teach us in regard to the internal political development and legislation of states?" The papers submitted showed a conspicuous sociological trend which, as the concluding résumé declared, confronted the state with novel tasks.

Ideas of this kind had been in the air for ten years but now the appearance of two new periodicals gave them shape and form. The racial anthropologists rallied round the *Politisch-Anthropologische Revue,* which was founded in 1902,[35] while from 1904 on the program of the racial hygienists was put forward in *Archiv für Rassen- und Gesellschaftsbiologie.*[36] In the prewar period each of these publications had an average circulation of 1,200; then the former went quickly downhill, suspending publication in 1922, while the *Archiv* increased its circulation in the twenties and still more after 1933, and continued to appear until 1941.

The racial anthropologists had no common program or organizational cohesion. Yet, though few in number, they were untiring publicists. On the whole their scientific qualifications were more than questionable, but a few of them enjoyed a certain reputation, as for example—to cite the most prominent—Otto Ammon (1842–1915), engineer, journalist, and anthropologist, who received the degree of *doctor honoris causa* from the University of Freiburg for his anthropological-statistical work on the population of Baden, and Ludwig Woltmann (1871–1907), physician, philosopher, and ethnologist, who gained a considerable reputation with his attempts to show by iconographical methods that the leading lights of European culture were of Germanic blood.

The racial anthropologists found their main audience among the nationalist right-wing opposition, which began in the nineties to organize outside the political parties. Their arguments were welcomed by those who were trying to build up national consciousness on the basis of the

racial idea. Characteristic of this trend was the founding
of a Gobineau society in 1902. Its sponsors included the
Pan-German League, the Deutschbund [German Federa-
tion], the Ostmarkverein [East March Association], the
German School Association, the Association of German
Students, the German-National Association of Commercial Employees, and a number of sectarian nationalist
groups. This list indicates the principal area accessible to
racial-anthropological ideas, but not their degree of influence. For though membership in organizations can mean
a good deal, it usually means very little. For present purposes it is probably rather significant in the case of the
Deutschbund and the Pan-German League, because their
leaders made a serious effort to forge racial theory into a
political weapon. After the First World War, when the
publications of the racial anthropologists had become obsolete and their magazine failed, their efforts were continued in a rather less crude form and with far greater
success by the racial writings of Hans F. K. Günther,
whose *Rassenkunde des deutschen Volkes*[37] sold over
50,000 copies by 1932. The high esteem in which Günther
was held even then by the National Socialists is shown by
the fact that in 1930 Wilhelm Frick, then minister of the
interior of Thuringia, obtained a chair for him at the
University of Jena over the opposition of the faculty and
Senate.

In 1905 the racial hygienists provided themselves with
an organizational base, the Society for Racial Hygiene,[38]
with a clearly formulated program. The society never attained a large membership, but included a relatively high
percentage of academicians from whose influence and social prestige it benefitted. Before the war, however, racial
hygiene had no very broad audience; only the Deutschbund, a highly active group but with no more than a few
hundred members, featured the demands of the racial hygienists in its program. But after the war, which had so
forcefully demonstrated the importance of "human mate-

rial" and created in Germany a favorable climate for the idea of a biological renewal, public interest in questions of population policy and eugenics increased. Well-known periodicals such as *Süddeutsche Monatshefte* opened their pages to racial hygiene. An attempt was also made to attract the interest of educated nonspecialists: in addition to *Archiv* a new, less specialized periodical, *Eugenics*, was founded;[39] new local groups were formed,[40] and lecturers became more active. Of course all this amounted to very little in the light of the keenly felt necessity of showing a nation of seventy millions new ways. Only on the extreme right wing of the political front, where racism and anti-Semitism, hence the dogma of biological inequality, was a central ideological factor, were the demands of the racial hygienists taken up, though agitators made little use of them. Thus until 1932 racial hygiene played only a modest, marginal role.

With the National Socialist seizure of power it suddenly gained in importance, and with it to an even greater degree, "racial science." [41] The younger Social Darwinism provided the vague "racial" and sociobiological ideas of the National Socialists with a supposedly scientific justification and a certain clarity of formulation indispensable for purposes of indoctrination. Moreover, Social Darwinism offered a theoretical basis for practical sociobiological measures. In this sense the spadework of the younger Social Darwinists helped to make possible the sociobiological practice of the Third Reich. It confirmed the National Socialists in their certainty that biologicoracial quality was the highest criterion for the worth and historical rank of individuals and nations and that by systematically employing scientific and technical methods they would be able to control and modify this quality. Thus the younger Social Darwinism exerted a historical influence less by its direct appeal to the masses than by its formulations of plans and methods for the reorganization of society on a biologistic foundation.

The development is generally known: starting out with legal measures to prevent the transmission of hereditary ills, which, though the voluntary principle was already abandoned, were by and large confined to a limited number of scientifically definable pathological conditions, it led to the mass extermination of so-called "unworthy life" —and later to plans and experimental preparation for the sterilization of whole peoples, whose realization was prevented only by the collapse of the Third Reich. Even more sinister was the development leading from the theoretical postulate that the Jews were an alien body endangering the people to social discrimination against them and finally to their physical extermination.

Nevertheless it would be a crude oversimplification to derive this descent into barbarism directly from Social Darwinist impulses. To be sure, Social Darwinist elements played a significant role in Hitler's ideas. But the virulent form they ultimately assumed cannot be blamed entirely on Social Darwinist efforts. A number of internal and external factors were here at work, not the least important of which were certain very personal qualities of the dictator and the opportunity for unrestricted coercion offered during the Second World War. These factors explain in part why it was now possible to sweep aside the previously existing barriers to race hatred which had hitherto stood in the way of a crude biologistic "national health" program. But how such ideas of national health and racial valuation arose cannot be adequately understood unless Social Darwinism is taken into consideration. Though the acts of barbarism performed in the interest of national health cannot be termed the necessary consequences of Social Darwinism, it is fair to say that Social Darwinism provided the ideological and practical conditions without which such actions would not have been possible.

This brings us to the question: To what degree were the proponents of Socialist Darwinist thinking responsible for the crimes committed in the Third Reich in the name of biologism and racism? Let us concede that they did not will these crimes. Nevertheless, we should be falling short of the truth were we to regard them as mere victims of a historical process for which they, with their ethical attitude and political aims, were to no significant degree responsible.

In view of their aims as here set forth it cannot come as a surprise that the racial hygienists—not to mention the proponents of "racial science"—wished the National Socialists to take power. True, they criticized the crude radicalism of the National Socialists, but this meant little beside their feeling of fundamental agreement. The younger Social Darwinism and the folkish movement stemmed from very similar ideological positions. They were united in their rejection of industrial society and democracy and in their admiration for a social order based on a class elite; in their condemnation of mechanistic, materialistic civilization in favor of an "organic" culture; in their critique of liberal individualism, to which they opposed a sense of community rooted in a racial and national bond. In short: they concurred in their resentment-charged protest against the processes of restratification that had been set in motion by the political and industrial revolutions of the modern era. They also shared the conviction that the future of the German people could be secured only on the basis of natural inequality, that is, in the last analysis, by a new social order hinging on socio-biological and racial criteria—and that such a social order could be brought about only by a resolute statesman wielding enormous power.

Thus it is hardly to be wondered at that as early as 1931 the *Archiv für Rassen- und Gesellschaftsbiologie* declared Hitler to be the only political figure of any weight to have recognized the signs of the times. All misgivings (and these, it must be stressed, were by no means lacking) were submerged by the hope of at last seeing racial hygiene applied on a large scale. Consequently Hitler's assurance that in questions decisive for the future being or nonbeing of the German people he would not be deterred by petty, typically bourgeois scruples, that he would not, for example, confine the sterilization of inferior persons to extreme cases, was taken as a promise rather than a warning.[42] Even after 1933 satisfaction at the desired turn of events was the dominant note in the utterances of the racial hygienists, which culminated in the following profession of faith:

> The significance of racial hygiene in Germany has for the first time been made evident to all enlightened Germans by the work of Adolf Hitler, and it is thanks to him that the dream we have cherished for more than thirty years of seeing racial hygiene converted into action has become reality.[43]

True, the racial hygienists expected Hitler to adhere to the advice of the recognized specialists, that is, themselves. And they personally were inclined to carry out their intentions by humane methods. But their attitude was also influenced by the maxim, rooted in their own special science, that a desirable end (namely, the success of social biology) justified even inhuman means. Thus they became after 1933 apologists for measures whose inhuman cruelty they privately deplored. Typical of this is the statement in which one of the leading figures of the German Society for Racial Hygiene, the respected anthropologist Eugen Fischer, commented in 1934 on measures of this sort taken by Hitler:

> Many highly estimable and valuable human beings who are quite willing to adjust themselves [to the new order] have been struck hard and cruelly. Is any sacrifice too great when a whole people is to be saved? Did the war not cost precisely this people infinitely more of its precious hereditary lines? Folk renewal, the conscious culti-

vation of the race, is raising a people from the abyss to which the so-called culture of the past decades has brought it.[44]

In a word: the folkish idea grounded in racial biology proved stronger than humanitarian reservations or concern for individual human rights.

Such attitudes prevailed far beyond the confines of the younger Social Darwinism. Thus we may say that Social Darwinism was indeed historically significant as a *pars pro toto*. When in the perspective of the history of ideas we look back over the early thirties, we cannot but be struck by the failure of those members of the educated bourgeoisie who opened the way to Hitler more by toleration than by activism to react more strongly against the crude biologism of National Socialist ideology.

The elucidation of this complex is of greater historical relevance than the search for the men who provided Hitler with his ideas. For to the man of today Hitler remains an alien phenomenon, a singular caricature of human potentialities, in whom he is not likely to recognize himself. The same is not true of Hitler's contemporary, the estimable well-intentioned citizen who incurred grave historical responsibility by neglecting to do the right thing at the right time. That is a situation with which every man can identify himself. To confront it as a historical example is to learn for the future. In the present case, to be sure, this involves special difficulties. For the investigation of the state of consciousness and political ideas of the German bourgeoisie of the Wilhelminian and Weimar periods is barely in its beginnings and must moreover deal with extraordinary complexities. Many forces of diverse origin are at work. We can determine certain central trends, but the relations between them are confusingly intricate. The contours are blurred, the phenomena merge.

In this situation the younger Social Darwinism provides a valuable guiding thread precisely because we are able to isolate it. Its representatives can be followed continuously from the turn of the century on; and moreover they were obliged to concentrate and to formulate their ideas clearly because it was through scientific solutions that they hoped to bridge the gap between the social reality of their day and the social development to which they aspired. True, their "scientific solutions" do not hold water. But what they had to say is more clearly formulated and hence easier to understand than any other statements of comparable relevance.

We may attribute such relevance to the younger Social Darwinism because behind its strictly sociobiological aims—but related to them—impulses are discernible which were at work in circles of the German bourgeoisie extending far beyond Social Darwinism. Though these circles may have looked on racial hygiene as something far removed from them and on racial science as the concern of others, they nevertheless shared with the racial hygientists and racial scientists the ideological positions which, as we have shown, led the younger Darwinists to look upon the rise of National Socialism as a promising development. How then could they have been expected to take up arms resolutely against the dogma of the natural inequality of men and races? Under these circumstances even those who did not hold the racist and anti-Semitic ideas of the National Socialists and were personally opposed to all violation of human dignity were no longer able to take a reasoned stand against biologism or to realize that a decision in favor of the National Socialist state amounted to a vote against humanity. The younger Social Darwinism was symptomatic of the gradual growth of such blindness to values, and in Social Darwinism this process can be observed in its most central and fateful aspect: the effacing of those limits which respect for the personal dignity of the individual had hitherto imposed on the demands of the social organism.

The younger Social Darwinism not only reflected

Hans-Günter Zmarzlik

but at the same time radicalized this trend; it was not only an expression of far-reaching currents, but also the motive force behind them, and this was also true of the older forms of Social Darwinism, first in the liberalistic, then in the imperialist era. If amid the situation-conditioned transformations of Social Darwinist thinking we look for a constant that may enable us to view it as a whole and to determine its specific share in the overall development, we may say that Social Darwinism posits a causal or final relationship between the human individual and natural (or more precisely, scientifically interpreted) development. His personal worth is derived first from his biological origin and then from his biological efficiency. The inviolable and indivisible dignity of man is degraded to the level of a variable, measurable against the standard of what is desirable for the health of the people and subject to regulation by correction and planning. Thus almost imperceptibly the individual becomes human material, and the road is opened to state policies that ultimately equate the right to live with biological utility.

Thus an analysis of Social Darwinism reveals a process of declining standards, accompanied by a tendency to sacrifice the individual to the species, to devaluate the humanitarian idea of equality from the standpoint of a "natural" inequality, to subordinate ethical norms to biological needs. The rise of the Darwinist social diagnosis and therapy goes hand in hand with the decline of the human rights that safeguard the domain of the individual against arbitrary encroachments. Undoubtedly this development was not in the intentions of most Social Darwinists. It nevertheless stands out clearly in retrospect. The study of Social Darwinism reveals a segment of a degenerative process that has become more and more pronounced in the last hundred years—the decline of ethics as a social determinant.

This places our subject in a timely context. Here it

touches on a problem that is not confined to the prehistory and history of the Third Reich. For there is evidence enough in every field of social life—from everyday occurrences to international affairs—that this process has gone still further.

True, Social Darwinism no longer plays a part in it. Not only because it was discredited by Hitler's crimes, but also because the empirical and epistemological progress of biology have deprived the Social Darwinist conceptions of their last semblance of credibility. The more recent findings make it impossible to view biological development as progressive and unilinear; they oblige us to draw a fundamental distinction between biological and psychological evolution. Another of their consequences is that the principle of selection, important as it still is, has receded into more complex contexts and taken its place beside other such factors as mutation, inheritance, and the formation of distinctive species in determining the evolutionary process. Further, the enormous deepening of our knowledge of genetics over the last few decades has conclusively demonstrated the fallacy of regarding the inherited constitution of man as a socially decisive factor, let alone of explaining the rise and fall of nations on the basis of genetics. And finally, in view of the enormous complexity that the biological process has today assumed for the scientific observer, and of the correspondingly refined methods employed by biologists, including the mathematization of data, modern biology has ceased to offer concrete, visual models that can be adduced for the popular interpretation of the social process.

Thus Social Darwinism is a historical phenomenon in the full sense of the word. But at the same time it provides an access to the enduring question of the relation of modern biology to society, social ethics, and humanity. What is meant by this can be shown by the example of the efforts of the racial hygienists. They took as their point of departure empirically demonstrable hereditary injuries which can arise under the conditions of modern civilization, thus accepting a challenge which scientists could not ignore once they had gained awareness of it. In practice, however, they tried to accomplish too much with too little knowledge, because they were misled by extrascientific motives and aims. In consequence they contributed to a triumph of inhumanity. Still, if we disregard the element of demonstrable scientific error and political blindness in their work, there still remains a problematical core, namely the question: How can insights and methods developed within a specialized discipline, which necessarily derives its orientation from natural science, be applied to social questions without producing dangerous effects? Of course society cannot dispense with biological health, but it is regulated by norms that cannot but be impaired by the systematic application of biological principles. For the norms which have thus far determined the self-understanding and social conduct of our cultural sphere are oriented by "superreal" values deriving from the tradition of two and a half millennia. They have been rendered questionable by the findings of an empirical biology which in the last hundred years, the age of Darwin, have penetrated so deep into the structural and functional principles of living nature as to provide hitherto undreamed-of possibilities of acting upon the human physis and psyche and hence of manipulating social life. This conflict is the lasting problematic core of the ephemeral, situation-conditioned errors of the Social Darwinists.

In our own times it has further increased in importance. With every advance of knowledge man's power to intervene in social and biological processes in accordance with his plans and desires increases. Spurred on by the power conflicts between states, pressed by numerous problems in an age of headlong political, economic, and technological revolutions, but also needlessly seduced by the possibility of controlling individual destinies even where it involves manipulation of the reproductive process, man is availing himself of the means that science offers. And with every step in this direction not only the functioning of the social mechanisms but man himself becomes more dependent on the achievements of science, so that he tends more and more to seek the solution of all problems in scientific, pragmatic calculation.

The Darwinian theory was a revolutionary breakthrough in this direction. Like all progress in the natural and social sciences, it brought with it an enormous increase in man's knowledge of the material conditions of social life and hence in his freedom of action. But the use that the Social Darwinists made of this increased knowledge indicates its potential threat to a humane social order.

This insight points the way to special tasks. Since the sciences cannot stop providing society with more and more far-reaching instruments of power, it becomes more than ever incumbent upon them to provide better conditions for the proper use of such power. History makes a contribution to this task when it systematically investigates the interdependences between scientific development and the politicosocial process of the nineteenth and twentieth century and studies the decline of the traditional "superreal" values in favor of pragmatic, positivist, or even naturalistic maxims of conduct.[45] By creating awareness of this process through descriptive analysis, it can reasonably hope not only to elucidate the past, but also to lay bare constitutive factors and latent possibilities of the present, contributing to a realistic (in the deepest sense of the word) and hence productive answer to the most urgent problems of our day.

NOTES

1. The term first appears in German in an article by the sociologist S. R. Steinmetz in *Zeitschrift für Sozialwissenschaft*, Vol. IX, 1906, pp. 423 ff. The first critical survey pointing out the possible dangerous consequences of Social Darwinist thinking to appear in Germany is provided by the sociologist O. Hertwig in his book, *Zur Abwehr des ethischen, des sozialen, des politischen Darwinismus,* 1918.

2. The most penetrating account to date is that of Hedwig Conrad-Martius, *Utopien der Menschenzüchtung. Der Sozialdarwinismus und seine Folgen,* 1955. Her theses are rejected by Fritz Lenz, "Die soziologische Bedeutung der Selektion," in G. Heberer and F. Schwanitz, eds., *Hundert Jahre Evolutionsforschung. Das wissenschaftliche Vermächtnis Charles Darwins,* 1960, pp. 385 ff. Cf. also Georg Lukács, *Die Zerstörung der Vernunft,* 1954, pp. 537 ff; Karl Saller, *Die Rassenlehre des Nationalsozialismus in Wissenschaft und Propaganda,* 1961.

3. Cf. Lenz, *loc. cit.,* p. 369.

4. Cf. Sir William C. Dampier, *Geschichte der Naturwissenschaft in ihrer Beziehung zu Philosophie und Weltanschauung,* 1952; Stephen F. Mason, *Geschichte der Naturwissenschaft in der Entwicklung ihrer Denkweisen.*

5. Quoted from Julian Huxley, "Darwin und der Gedanke der Evolution," in Heberer and Schwanitz, *op. cit.,* p. 3.

6. The German translation of "struggle for life" by *Kampf ums Dasein,* current from the very first, is an intensification of Darwin's meaning. Darwin's " 'struggle' means competitive rivalry and not *Kampf* [fight, war, battle]. He distinguishes sharply between 'struggle' and 'war' (or 'fight'), and employs the latter terms only once: in connection with sexual selection, when two males fight over a female." W. Ludwig, "Die Selektionstheorie," in *Die Evolution der Organismen. Ergebnisse und Problems der Abstammunglehre,* ed. G. Heberer, 2nd ed., 1959, Vol. II, p. 666.

7. Cf. F. Wieacker, "Rudolph von Ihering (1812–1892)," in Wieacker, *Gründer und Bewahrer. Rechtslehrer der neueren deutschen Privatrechtsgeschichte,* 1959, pp. 197 ff.; quotation, p. 207.

8. R. Goldscheid, in *Das Jahr 1913. Das Gesamtbild der Kulturentwicklung,* ed. D. Sarason, 1913, p. 425.

9. The words of Max von Gruber, the Munich hygienist, quoted in *ibid.,* p. 367.

10. Cf. E. Mühlmann, *Geschichte der Anthropologie,* 1948, pp. 92 ff.

11. This aim is stated by Ludwig Woltmann, a leading prewar proponent of the racial anthropology school, in his chief work, *Politische Anthropologie. Eine Untersuchung über den Einfluss der Descendenztheorie auf die Lehre von der politischen Entwicklung der Völker,* 1903, p. 1.

12. On the potentialities and limits of scientific social anthropology, cf. Ilse Schwidetzky, *Grundzüge der Völkerbiologie,* 1950, and *Das Menschenbild der Biologie. Ergebnisse und Probleme der naturwissenschaftlichen Anthropologie,* 1959.

13. E. Baur, E. Fischer, F. Lenz, *Grundriss der menschlichen Erblichkeitslehre und Rassenhygiene,* 4th ed., 1932, Vol. II, p. 419.

14. Cf. also Alvar Ellegard, "Public Opinion and the Press: Reactions to Darwinism," *Journal of the History of Ideas,* Vol. 19, 1958, pp. 379 ff.

15. F. Meinecke, *Die Idee der Staatsräson in der neueren Geschichte,* ed. and with an introduction by W. Hofer, 1957, p. 24.

16. Cf. W. Conze, *Die Strukturgeschichte des technisch-industriellen Zeitalters als Aufgabe für Forschung und Unterricht,* 1957.

17. Meinecke, *op. cit.,* p. 480.

18. An instructive survey is provided by H. Hermelink, *Das Christentum in der Menschheitsgeschichte von der französischen Revolution bis zur Gegenwart,* Vol. III, *Nationalismus und Sozialismus,* 1955, pp. 215 ff., 445 ff.

19. Among Haeckel's immediate disciples the most successful popularizer was Ernst Krause, editor in chief of *Kosmos. Zeitschrift für einheitliche Weltanschauung auf Grund der Entwicklunglehre,* a monthly founded in 1877, and also (under the pseudonym Carus Sterne) author of a Darwinist cosmology, *Werden und Vergehen. Eine Entwicklungs-Geschichte des Naturganzen in gemeinverständlicher Fassung,* 1876; 6th ed., 1905. Ludwig Büchner took a similar direction, though his work was begun before Darwin and he is more independent: *Kraft und Stoff,* 1955; 21st ed., 1904. Another highly influential work was David Friedrich Strauss, *Der alte und der neue Glaube. Ein Bekenntnis,* 1872; 11th ed., 1882, a disavowal of the Christian religion based on Darwin.

20. E. Haeckel, *Die Welträtsel. Gemeinverständliche Studien über monistische Philosophie,* Bonn, 1899.

21. Cf. L. von Wiese, *Soziologie, Geschichte und Hauptprobleme,* 4th ed., 1950, p. 62.

22. Cf. note 19 above.

23. E.g., by Paul von Lilienfeld (1829–1903), the most consistent advocate of a Darwinist theory of society. Principal work: *Gedanken über die Sozialwissenschaft der Zukunft,* Parts 1–5, Mitau, 1873–1881.

24. E.g., Albert Schäffle (1831–1903), who made a significant contribution to the development of sociology in Germany. Principal work: *Bau und Leben des Sozialen Körpers,* 4 vols., Tübingen,

472 Hans-Günter Zmarzlik

1875–1878, Schäffle was guided to a very considerable extent by bio-organic ideas, but basically, to cite L. von Wiese, he was "closer to Hegel and Schelling than to Darwin, Spencer, or Haeckel."

25. Nietzsche is a special case. He was often been regarded quite mistakenly as a Social Darwinist because of a superficial resemblance between his radical critique of the Christian humanitarian tradition and certain Social Darwinist theses. Nietzsche was of course influenced by the Darwinian theory, though he probably knew it only at second hand and in a strongly Lamarckian coloration, as has been demonstrated by Charles Andler in *Nietzsche, sa vie et pensée*, 5 vols., Paris, 1920–1930. The influence of Darwinism on Nietzsche's philosophy as a whole has never been seriously investigated. Only on the basis of such an investigation will it be possible to engage in a meaningful discussion of Nietzsche's Social Darwinism.

26. F. von Hellwald, *Culturgeschichte in ihrer natürlichen Entwicklung von den ältesten Zeiten bis zur Gegenwart*, 2 vols., 1874.

27. Cf. the anonymously published book, *Volksdienst. Von einem Sozialaristokraten*, Berlin and Leipzig, 1893, and especially, A. Tille, *Von Darwin bis Nietzsche. Ein Buch Entwicklungsethik*, 1895.

28. In regard to England, cf. William L. Langer, *The Diplomacy of Imperialism, 1890–1902*, 2 vols., 1935, pp. 85 ff; to the United States, Richard Hofstadter, *op. cit.*, 2nd ed., 1955, pp. 170 ff. On the relative significance of Social Darwinist elements in the European context of the late nineteenth century, cf. Carlton J. H. Hayes, *A Generation of Materialism 1871–1900*, 1941, *passim*.

29. E.g., Claus Wagner, *Der Krieg als schaffendes Weltprinzip*, 1906, a book occasionally cited by Pan-German authors.

30. The most important works of these two authors in this connection: L. Gumplowicz, *Rasse und Staat. Eine Untersuchung über das Gesetz der Staatenbildung*, 1875, and *Der Rassenkampf*, 1883; G. Ratzenhofer, *Wesen und Zweck der Politik also Theil der Soziologie und Grundlage der Staatswissenschaften*, 3 vols., 1893.

31. A beginning of such an investigation in Wilfried Daim, *Der Mann, der Hitler die Ideen gab. Von den religiösen Verirrungen eines Sektierers zum Rassenwahn des Diktators*, 1958. The writings of Lanz von Liebenfels, the Austrian racial fanatic and religious enthusiast, exploited by Daim, often came close to Social Darwinist ideas. Unfortunately this book is confined almost exclusively to the person of Lanz and does not fulfill the promise of its title.

32. Main works: *Les Sélections sociales*, 1893; *L'Aryen, son rôle social*, 1899.

33. Principal works: *Hereditary Genius. An Inquiry into Its Law and Consequences*, 1869; *Inquiries into Human Faculty and Its Development*, 1883.

34. As for example in John B. Haycraft, *Darwinism and Race Progress*, 1895, 2nd ed., 1900; Charles H. Harvey, *The Biology of British Politics*, 1904.

35. Full title: *Politisch-Anthropologische Revue. Monatsschrift für das soziale und geistige Leben der Völker.* Founder and editor (until 1907), Ludwig Woltmann.

36. Full title: *Archiv für Rassen- und Gesellschaftsbiologie einschliesslich Rassen- und Gesellschafts-Hygiene. Zeitschrift für die Erforschung des wesens von Rasse und Gesellschaft und ihres gegenseitigen Verhältnis, für die biologischen Bedingungen ihrer Erhaltung und Entwicklung sowie für die grundlegenden Probleme der Entwicklungslehre.* The founder and editor (until 1937) was Alfred Ploetz (1860–1940), who after practicing medicine for ten years devoted himself exclusively to racial hygiene. Ploetz coined the term *Rassenhygiene* [racial hygiene] and explained it in his book *Die Tüchtigkeit unserer Rasse und der Schutz der Schwachen. Ein Versuch über Rassenhygiene und ihr Verhältnis zu den humanen Ideen, besonders zum Sozialismus,* 1895. The more prominent of the contributors to *Archiv* included the following academic scientists, who were also for a time coeditors: the zoologist Ludwig Plate, the psychiatrist Ernst Rüdin, the racial hygienist Fritz Lenz. A special position is occupied by Wilhelm Schallmayer (1857–1919), who as early as 1891 had pointed to the "physical degeneration threatening civilized man" and in the prewar period had written the most complete work on questions of racial hygiene. Strongly opposed to the racism and nationalism of the sociobiological trends, he stood aloof from the main group of racial hygienists around Ploetz.

37. *Rassenkunde des deutschen Volkes,* 1922; 14th ed., 1933; *Kleine Rassenkunde des deutschen Volkes,* 1925; 3rd ed. 1933.

38. From 1911 on it bore the name of Deutsche Gesellschaft für Rassenhygiene. In 1914 it had roughly 350 members with local groups in Berlin, Munich, Freiburg, and Stuttgart.

39. *Eugenik, Erblehre, Erbpflege. In Verbindung mit E. Fischer, F. Lenz, H. Muckermann, E. Rüdin, O. von Verschuer,* ed. A. Ostermann. Sales for 1933: 4,200 (figures unavailable for previous years).

40. From 1924 to 1930 twelve additional local groups were founded in Germany and four in Austria. The membership increased to roughly 1,300. Cf. E. Fischer, "Aus der Gesichte der Deutschen Gesellschaft für Rassenhygiene," in AfRGB, Vol. 24, 1930, pp. 1 ff.

41. The Gesellschaft für Rassenhygiene numbered 68 local groups in 1936; its official organ *Volk and Rasse* had a circulation of 13,300 in 1939; in 1936 Ploetz obtained the title of professor; in 1938 Ernst Rüdin, who had been its director since 1933, was awarded the Goethe medal for art and science; in 1936 doctorates in racial hygiene were offered at all universities where the subject was taught (Berlin, Munich, Leipzig, Königsberg, Frankfurt a.M.). At the same time information on racial hygiene was intensively disseminated by government and party bureaus, through newspapers, periodicals, schools, and indoctrination courses. At the end of 1934 the Thuring-

ian Bureau for Racial Matters alone had given two-week courses on racial hygiene, population policy, and the "breeding of families" [*züchterische Familienkunde*] to some 9,000 members of specified occupation groups (physicians, jurists, mayors, policemen, political leaders, etc). On the subject of racial science suffice it to note that H. F. K. Günther was called to the University of Berlin, that in 1935 he was awarded the newly established NSDAP Prize for Science, and that by 1945 the sales of his books totaled almost half a million.

42. Cf. F. Lenz, "Die Stellung des Nazionalsozialismus zur Rassenhygiene," in AfRGB, Vol. 25, 1931, pp. 300 ff.

43. E. Rüdin, "Aufgaben und Ziele der deutschen Gesellschaft für Rassenhygiene," in AfRGB, Vol. 28, 1934, p. 228.

44. E. Fischer, "Erbe," in *Mein Heimatland*, Vol. 21, 1934, p. 150.

45. An impressive example of the fruitfulness of this undertaking is provided by F. Wieacker, *Privatrechsgeschichte der Neuzeit unter besonderer Berücksichtingung der deutschen Entwicklung*, 1952.

Index

Security Service (Sicherheits-
dienst, SD), 236, 256–8
Seeckt, Hans von, 18 *n.*
Seldte, Franz, 29
Semler, Rudolf, 300, 307–11
Severing, Carl, 28–9 *n.*, 51–2, 56,
58, 60–1, 178
Sicherheitsdienst (SD, Security
Service), 236, 256–8
Slavic peoples, 367–8, 372
Social Darwinism, 435–74; Darwin's evolution theory, 437–
441; Hitler's belief in, 435–
436, 456, 461, 463–4; Na-
tional Socialist use of, 460–
467; racial hygiene and,
444–8, 458–66; of Social
Democrats, 96
Social Democratic Party (SPD),
4, 51–105, 111, 181; in
Brüning's government, 8,
53; Communist Party and,
67–9, 99; disintegration of,
77–8; dissolution of, 74, 87;
in elections, 52, (1933), 74–
76; Erfurt Congress (1891),
73 *n.;* executive committee
(*Parteivorstand*), 56 *n.*, 83,
86–7; failure reasons for,
52–4, 61–3, 94–101; illegal
activities, 64, 77, 87–94, 98–
99; Independent, 51; Na-
tional Socialist repression of,
74–6, 83–7; and Papen's
Prussian *coup d'état*, 53, 56;
party council (*Parteiausschuss*), 65 *n.;* in Prague,
83–7, 98; in Reichstag, 74,
83–6; in Reichstag fire, accused, 167, 169, 171; re-
sistance to National Socialists, 54–67, 69–79, 94–101;
trade unions and, 55–7, 65–
66, 79–83; in Weimar Coalition, 3
Social Democratic Youth Organization, 77, 88–92

Socialist Front, 87–8, 92, 98–
100
Socialist Workers' Party (So-
zialistische Arbeiterpartei,
SAP), 91
Society for Racial Hygiene
(Deutsche Gesellschaft für
Rassenhygiene), 459
Sommerfeldt, Martin, 132, 140,
141, 153, 165, 174, 177
Sonthofen, Hitler's speech, 372
Soviet Union, *see* Russia
Sozialistische Arbeiter-Jugend
(SAJ, Young Socialist Work-
ers), 77, 88
Spain, German relations with,
368, 370
SPD, *see* Social Democratic
Party
Speer, Albert, 301 *n.*, 314, 315,
317
Spencer, Herbert, 440, 454
Spiegel, Der, 133, 134
SS, *see* Schutzstaffeln
Staff Guard (Stabswache), 254–
257, 268
Stahlhelm, 29, 33, 46, 74, 121,
122, 239
Stalingrad, 299, 306, 307, 309,
315, 319–20, 323–5
Stampfer, Friedrich, 51, 55, 56,
64, 67–9, 76, 83, 84
Stassen, artist, 420
State Party, 31
Statthaltereien (provincial gov-
ernorships), 121
Steinacher, Hans, 352–3
Stennes, Walter, putsch, 256 *n.*
Stephan, Werner, 311, 316
Storbeck, Mimi, 151 *n.*
storm troopers, *see* Sturmab-
teilungen (SA)
Stosstrup Hitler (Hitler Shock
Troop), 254, 255
Strasser, Gregor, 46 *n.*, 231–2,
234; in purge (1934), 243
Strasser, Otto, 405
Strauss, Richard, 411, 417